D0130876

Jancis Robinson's Wine Course

JANCIS ROBINSON'S WINE COURSE

ABBEVILLE PRESS PUBLISHERS

NEW YORK LONDON PARIS

First published in the United States of America
in 1996 by Abbeville Press
488 Madison Avenue
New York, N.Y 10022

First published in Great Britain
in 1995 by BBC Books
an imprint of BBC Worldwide Publishing
BBC Worldwide Ltd
Woodlands
80 Wood Lane
London W12 OTT

Copyright © 1995 Jancis Robinson

All rights reserved under international copyright
conventions. No part of this book may be reproduced
or utilized in any form or by any means, electronic or
mechanical, including photocopying, recording, or by
any information storage and retrieval system, without
permission in writing from the publisher. Inquiries should
be addressed to Abbeville Publishing Group. The text of
this book was set in Goudy

First edition
2 4 6 8 10 9 7 5 3 1
ISBN 0-7892-0256-5
Designed by Judith Robertson
Cartography by Eugene Fleury
Illustrations by Neil Tully
and Alicia Durdos
Picture research by Nadine Bazar

Printed and bound in Great Britain by
Butler & Tanner Ltd, Frome

CAPTIONS

BACK JACKET & PAGE 2 Verdicchio dei Castelli de Jesi vineyards in the Marche, Central Italy.

PAGE 3 Italian grapes being dried for Vin Santo, Tuscany's sweet wine speciality.

PAGE 6 Top: Fermentation tanks at Bulgaria's Sliven winery.

Bottom: Liquid gold from California, made from botrytized Semillon grapes.

PAGE 7 The basics of winemaking are taught in a nursery school in Umbria, Central Italy.

PAGES 10–11 Tasting Chardonnays in the Hunter Valley, New South Wales, Australia.

PAGES 58–9 Bottles of pale pink sparkling Saumur are upended to lose the all-important yeast deposit.

PAGES 94–5 Cabernet Sauvignon grapes at the Ornellaia estate in Tuscany.

PAGES 154–5 Spring mustard, a vineyard cover crop, flowering in Carneros in California.

For Julia and Rose
may they never lack confidence

This book owes its existence to the tenacity of Suzanne Webber, its visual appeal to the eye of Judith Robertson, and its attention to detail to the good humour of Nicky Copeland. Others who have played an important part in this enterprise include Jerry Alexander, Nadine Bazar, Vicky Bishop, Bill Blatch, Jo Brompton, Tony Bulley, Steve Burns, Bob Campbell, Denis Charlois, Simon Clark, David Darlow, Pat Dudley, Jonathan Earp, Robin Eastwood, Dereck Foster, Jean and Noelle François, D. Garfield Davies, Chris Gill, Laura Harper, Tan Harrington, Norbert Heine, Dr Tony Jordan, Claudia Josephs, Geoffrey Kelly, Julia Kennedy, Catherine Manac'h, Stephen Metzler, Jasper Morris, Fiona Morrison, Hazel Murphy, Richard Neill, Jeremy Parkes, Frank Phillips, Stuart Pigott, Sue Pike, Edwin Pritchard, Belle and Barney Rhodes, Jacqui Rubin, Hubert Sandhofer, Daniel Thomases, Ernie Vincze, Geoff Walls, Chris Weller, Joanna Wiese, and many others further along the production line.

Rowan Jenkins has made superb sense of the Vintage Guide on pages 306–9. Richard Mayson saved me from making two or three serious slips in the sections on Portugal, while Victor de la Serna was extremely helpful with the Spanish section. Masters of Wine Neil Tully and Angela Muir have been quite exceptionally helpful in their respective provision of tailor-made illustrations and photographs. Gareth Lawrence checked the maps with admirable diligence. Barry Lynch kindly provided the initial impetus, and an excuse for the seminal lunch.

But the people to whom I owe most of all are my ever more astounding
family, particularly William and, of course, Nick.

CONTENTS

2 HOW WINE IS MADE 59

3 WINE GRAPE VARIETIES 95

4 THE WORLD OF WINE 155

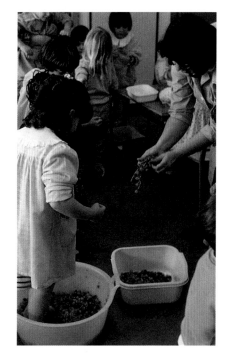

INTRODUCTION

The point of wine is to give pleasure, as much of it to as many people as possible. Anyone who suggests otherwise – that wine appreciation is a difficult business which only a very special élite are worthy and capable of, for example – should be treated with scorn. In my experience, anyone who claims to be a wine expert invariably has little to offer except prejudices.

Wine is emphatically not a serious subject. Wine is one of life's perks, an indulgence, a mood-lifter, a social mixer. It's just that understanding a bit more about it brings the confidence to relax and enjoy it.

Although wine is clearly much more than mere lubrication, to appreciate it, all you need is an interest and a sense of smell. This book explains that by taking you from the glass in your hand, back along the supply line, making sense of tasting, serving, choosing and buying wine (Getting the Most Out of Wine pages 11–57), to How Wine is Made (pages 59–93) before embarking on two important and parallel guides to help make sense out of the thousands of wines available: Wine Grape Varieties on pages 95–153 and The World of Wine on pages 155–305.

From the outside, the world of wine looks horribly complicated. Wine's great attribute, its variety, is also one of its drawbacks. Wine lists in restaurants and rows of bottles on a shelf can seem like an impenetrable jungle of proper names in foreign languages.

But help is at hand. Learning about wine has become a great deal easier over the last few years as more and more wine producers are putting the names of the main grapes from which their wines are made on labels, either the main label or an explanatory one on the back of the bottle. Classicists deplore this trend, arguing that wine should be an expression of place

---

A FEW INSIDER TIPS TO SET YOU ON YOUR WAY:

Wine amateurs may say...	**But professional winos say...**
Opener	Corkscrew
Crate (of wine)	Case (= 12 bottles)
Drink (active verb)	Taste
Champagne (for all fizzy wine)	Sparkling wine (for all fizzy wine except that made in the Champagne region in north east France)

Wine amateurs may think:	**But professional winos know:**
Sediment in a bottle is a bad sign	It's a sign of a producer who worships quality above cosmetics
Claret is any old red	Claret is a word used in Britain exclusively for red bordeaux
Zinfandel is white	Zinfandel's a red grape that no one wanted so someone cleverly began to make a very commercial off dry white out of it in California in the 1980s

rather than grape variety and that only wines labelled geographically with no mention of grape varieties are 'real' wines.

With respect, as they say, I think this is rubbish. Of course the perfect wine is an expression of the exact slope of the vineyard, its latitude, altitude, soil texture (though not, as is commonly thought, soil composition) and so on, but that's the second stage in wine appreciation (and how many wines demonstrate their provenance so clearly that any experienced blind taster can immediately locate the village in which they were made?). The first stage, the main factor shaping the characteristics of most wines in commercial circulation, is the grape variety or varieties used. And the pathways through that supposedly impenetrable jungle are to a large extent the result of recognizing the relationships between, say, different Chardonnays from around the world – all of which in any case also carry some geographical clues that help us make up a picture of the world of wine and its influences on grape varieties so that eventually we reach the second stage by accumulating an impression of, for example, California's Carneros or Meursault in Burgundy.

So the great thing is that to learn about wine today, you don't need to learn hundreds of different foreign place-names. All you need to begin with are about seven names, those of the main grape varieties from which a sizeable proportion of wines you are likely to come across are made: Chardonnay, Sauvignon Blanc and poor, undervalued Riesling for whites and Cabernet Sauvignon, Merlot, Pinot Noir and Syrah (or Shiraz) for reds.

Wine Grape Varieties provides a detailed guide to these seven varieties as well as a great deal of information about hundreds more varieties, those that will be mentioned more and more on labels over the next few years as producers increasingly experiment, and become more conscious of consumers' needs in their labelling. Here and throughout the book I have tried to explain the most important thing – how wines are likely to taste.

The World of Wine takes you on a detailed tour of those corners of the globe where wine is produced, highlighting what makes them different and, of course, which grape varieties are grown there, and explaining not just how things are but giving the real explanation (not necessarily the same as the public relations pitch) of why they are that way.

As a subject for study, wine happens to come with an amazing amount of baggage, which we can choose to revel in or ignore. Its history stretches back past the Bronze Age, to at least 5500 years ago. Its geography encompasses all of the world's temperate zones (and quite a few of the tropical ones too). The wine business is conducted in some of the most beautiful corners of the world, and its personalities are some of the most colourful in any field of commercial activity. Wine is rich in religious symbolism, and has the unusual attribute of being able to last and evolve for centuries, providing a direct, tastable link with past generations. Yet today, wine production is a scientifically sophisticated business that is unusually open about what in many other businesses would be its secrets.

This book, which has been a seriously exciting project for me, aims to give you an insider's view of the world of wine. As I became involved in planning and then began writing, I realized not just how rapidly the world of wine has changed in the last decade or so, but how much less ignorant (I would certainly not say more knowledgeable) I am now – partly thanks to spending the last five years editing *The Oxford Companion to Wine* – and how much more insider information and advice I want to communicate. My hope is that in some small way this book will help its readers to get even more pleasure out of wine.

1

GETTING THE MOST OUT OF WINE

THE TRUE SENSE OF TASTE

As far as I'm concerned, the enjoyment of wine has to begin with the glass in your hand. Swotting up on wine geography and vintage ratings is an optional extra and comes a very long way down the line from working out how every single drop of wine can give as much pleasure as possible.

I often wonder what proportion of all the wine that is consumed in the world today actually manages to deliver all the messages it is capable of, and how much is just thrown down the gullet without a thought or even a sniff. It is very difficult to overestimate the sensitivity of the nose as a tasting instrument, and if I could give just one piece of advice to any newcomer to wine, it would be: *don't forget your sense of smell.*

You have only to think of how food, even quite strongly flavoured food, tastes dull when you have a nose blocked by a head cold to realize what an important role the sense of smell plays in what we call taste. Tasting something involves persuading it to release molecules which stimulate special nerve cells in the mouth or the much more discriminating ones in the nose. In fact we can sense flavour only as an aroma because our flavour-sensitive nerve cells are concentrated in a small, postage-stamp-sized area at the top of the nose

We each have an olfactory area (A) at the top of our noses where millions of nerve cells react to volatile molecules bearing flavour messages to the brain. These messages are merged and sorted into patterns which may be recognized and identified by the brain. Vapour also reaches the olfactory area from the back of the mouth up the retro-nasal passage (B).

called the olfactory area, which transmits specific messages to the brain, and the only way of getting molecules up there is as a vapour given off by a liquid. (This is why hot food always seems to be so much more smelly than cold food – the vapour that it gives off transports flavour-packed molecules up the nose.)

To be able to experience the flavour of a liquid such as wine to the full, therefore, molecules should be encouraged to escape the wine's surface by swirling the wine around before the taster takes a deliberate sniff. Doing this before each mouthful of wine may feel rather pretentious at first, but makes simple good sense. If wine has anything to offer other than the alcohol you can find in vodka or beer, it is the extraordinary range of flavours available not just in a single bottle, but in individual glasses of wine as they change under the influence of oxygen. Since man and nature went to so much trouble to put them there, it really does make sense to smell a wine every time before you taste it. This ensures not only that you get maximum value out of every wine you buy, but also slows down the consumption rate – which is useful for both body and bank balance.

At this point many wine drinkers may be puzzled. They will reckon they already have a

12

pretty good grasp of wine flavours, without ever having consciously sniffed (or 'nosed', as professional wine-tasting parlance has it) a glass in their lives. This is partly because wine naturally vaporizes quite easily, and some wines such as those made from Sauvignon Blanc and Riesling grapes are inherently quite aromatic so their molecules need very little encouragement to float up the nose of the drinker. It is also, however, because of the retro-nasal passage (see B on the diagram opposite) which allows some flavour molecules to reach the olfactory area directly from the back of the mouth, without any conscious effort.

This is how most foods are 'tasted'. Food is chewed in the mouth, transforming it into a liquid from which flavour molecules ecape up the retro-nasal passage to reach the olfactory area – although many food professionals take just as much trouble to smell different ingredients and dishes before consuming them as wine tasters do.

But what of all those nerve cells in the mouth? These also have an important, but quite different role to play in the business of tasting, and are what we call taste buds – about 10 000 of them distributed all over the tongue and, to a much lesser extent, the inside of the mouth, with a few at the back of the throat. Rather than distinguishing between thousands of different flavours the way that the olfactory nerve cells can, taste buds are sensitive to nothing more sophisticated than the basic 'tastes': sourness or acidity, sweetness, bitterness, and saltiness (although very few wines taste salty). We all vary enormously in the distribution and concentration of our taste buds and as a result there is a certain amount of disagreement about exactly how they function but, in very general terms, the taste buds around the tip of the tongue are most likely to be sensitive to sweetness; those on the upper edges of the tongue may well tingle most obviously at sourness; the flat back of the tongue is usually most sensitive to bitterness; and the front edges are most often particularly susceptible to saltiness.

Wine contains three more components that can also have an effect on the inside of the mouth. Tannin (see page 73) is a red wine preservative that comes from the grape skins, pips and (sometimes) stems, and has the same effect (tanning, as in leather) on the inside of the cheeks as it does when encountered in very well-stewed tea. Some tannins can also be bitter to taste. Alcohol (see page 72), quite apart from giving an impression of sweetness, has its own, often delightful, effect on our nervous system, but wines that are particularly high in alcohol can leave a 'hot' sensation on the palate after they have been swallowed. And many wines contain a perceptible amount of gassy carbon dioxide (see page 72), which has a physical effect that can vary from a gentle prickle in the mouth to an uncomfortably overwhelming froth.

HUMAN VARIATION

Almost anyone can be a wine taster; all it takes is a will and a nose. We vary from person to person not just in terms of the compounds we're particularly sensitive to, and the strength of those sensitivities, but also in our physical make-up. A small minority, sometimes called anosmics, have a poor, defective or damaged sense of smell – either from birth, or as the result of hormonal upsets, head injury, radiation therapy or, most commonly, advancing years. Smell and taste nerve cells may be the only cells in the nervous system that are replaced when they become old or damaged, but the human sense of smell still tends to be most accurate between the ages of 30 (when we have sufficient understanding and experience to interpret what our nerve cells tell us) and 60 (when the messages tend to start to become fainter). Different animals have different smelling and tasting abilities; whereas the human has quite a small part of the brain devoted to interpreting messages from the nose area, a dogfish has a very large one.
Dogfish would make great wine tasters.

13

HOW TO TASTE WINE

All you need is a glass (see pages 26–7) and a moment's attention. A lot of unnecessary fuss is made about extraneous smells (taking that argument to its logical conclusion we'd never serve food with wine) and about the condition of the palate. The handful of seriously distracting foods is considered on page 34, but a mouthful of water or neutral food such as bread is enough to neutralize the palate after all but the fiercest chilli. A more serious enemy to wine is toothpaste; many's the glass of champagne that has been wasted because of toothbrushing immediately before drinking it. Non-minty mouthwashes can freshen the palate without immobilizing it.

Step 1 Looking at a wine is the least important (and least pleasurable) part of wine tasting – although it can be immensely useful to someone trying to guess the identity of a mystery wine.

Tilting the glass away from you, preferably against a white background, exposes the different shades of colour (the more the better), especially at the rim where the age of a wine tends to show. The browner a wine the older it usually is. Red wines tend to go from deep purple to pale tawny, while whites go from pale greenish yellow to deep gold (see photographs on page 43). The best wines usually have a luscious sheen to them, while commercial, heavily treated ones can look dull and monochrome.

Some wine professionals hold the glass by the base, but using the stem is much easier and keeps wine equally unaffected by body heat.

Step 2 The importance of smelling the wine is outlined on pages 12–13. Since a wine's flavour molecules are given off only on the liquid's surface, they can be seriously encouraged by maximizing the wine's surface area, by swirling the wine round in a glass, ideally one with a stem so that a graceful movement which has no effect on the wine's temperature can be achieved, and preferably no more than half-full so that no wine is spilt. The ideal wine glass goes in towards the rim so that swirled wine tends to stay in the glass and so does the heady vapour above it. Just one short sniff while you concentrate is enough.

Notice whether the smell is clean and attractive (if not, either reject the wine as on page 54, or deliberately avoid smelling it!); how intense the smell is; and what the smell reminds you of. Grapes contain thousands of compounds, many of which are also found in other familiar substances. Furthermore, the processes of fermentation and maturation can add their own layers of flavour as different compounds react with each other. It is not surprising, therefore, that words are poor describers of something as subtle, subjective and private as smell perceptions. The best we can do to describe the smell, or flavour, of a wine is list those things of which it reminds us (see page 17), but there may be many thousands of other substances in wine which have no direct counterpart elsewhere, or which are too obscure to have their own name. Flavour compounds – the monoterpenes found in florally aromatic grapes and the grassy methoxypyrazine found in

Sauvignon Blanc and Cabernet Sauvignon, for example – are being energetically researched by the wine industry and may even eventually be created artificially and added to cheaper wines.

Step 3 Take a mouthful of wine and try to ensure that all of the palate, or at least all of the tongue, is exposed to the liquid, the better to gauge the dimensions that can be sensed in the mouth. Notice how sweet, sour/acid, bitter, tannic/astringent, alcoholic and gassy the wine is, as explained on pages 12–13. Try to gauge the **body** of the wine (see page 16) i.e. how unlike water it is. It also helps draw vapour up the retro-nasal passage if you take a little air into the mouth at the same time (which is the reason why all professional wine tasters sound so disgusting). Try also to note a wine's overall impact on the inside of the mouth. Some people use the term 'mouth feel' for sensations of varying intensity

which may be rasping, gripping or satin smooth. Then comes the great divide between tasting for work or play: workers (who may taste 100 wines a day) spit, while players swallow.

Step 4 Now is the moment to assess the wine as a whole. Were the dimensions of sweetness, acidity, alcohol and the possible elements of bitterness, tannin and gassiness in **balance**, or was one of them obtrusive? In young red wines, for example, tannin often dominates, while young whites are often very acid. This lack of balance would be a fault in an older wine. Was the sweetness counterbalanced by acidity or did it taste sickly? The other great indicator of quality is **length** – how long did the impact of the wine last after you swallowed it? A mediocre wine may leave no trace on the palate or in the olfactory area at all, but a fine wine can still continue to reverberate for 30 seconds or more after it has been swallowed.

SOME TASTING EXERCISES

• *Put a clothes-peg or diving clip on your nose, and see whether you can tell black coffee from black tea. Blindfold as well, you probably couldn't tell milk chocolate from cheddar cheese. All of this demonstrates just how important the nose is in identifying flavour.*

• *To work out how your palate reacts to* **acidity**, *smell and then taste lemon juice or vinegar. It takes only a smell to make the sides of my tongue start to crinkle up, but different tasters react differently.*

• *To identify tannin in wine, rinse a mouthful of cold black tea round your palate and notice which*

parts of your mouth react most dramatically. The insides of my cheeks pucker up. (Notice how you can't smell tannin, or sugar, however.)

• *To get some idea of body as it relates to wine, notice the difference in palate impact between a light bodied Mosel (German wine in a tall green bottle) with an alcohol content of less than 10 per cent and a full bodied Chardonnay or white Rhône wine with an alcohol content of more than 13 per cent. Notice in particular how unlike water the latter is, and how it may leave a hot, sweet sensation on the palate (alcohol often tastes sweet).*

TASTING TERMS

The following list includes terms used, often with a delightful lack of precision, in connection with both the **dimensions** of wine and tasting itself. 'B' for 'Bad' indicates critical descriptive terms, 'G' for 'Good' is used in praise. See the aroma wheel opposite for terms used to describe actual **flavours**. See pages 72–3 for any technical terms missing from here.

Acetaldehyde, compound formed when alcohol is exposed to air. Marginally present in all wines but ideally noticeable only in flor sherries (see page 234).

Acetic, VOLATILE acid. Often found in cool-fermented whites, but a fault when excessive.

After-taste, strictly the flavour(s) left after the wine is swallowed. See FINISH.

Aroma describes a simple, often fruity smell or flavour present in young wine. See BOUQUET.

Astringent, critical term usually used for relatively TANNIC white wines. (B)

Balanced, a wine in which all dimensions – acidity, sweetness, tannins, alcohol – make a harmonious whole. (G)

Blind tasting, an attempt to identify and/or assess wines without knowing their identity. Bottles, not humans, are masked.

Body, important characteristic of a wine determined chiefly by its alcoholic strength (see pages 36–7) but also by its EXTRACT. The more body a wine has the less like water it tastes.

Bottle age, the mellowing effect of years spent inside a bottle.

Bouquet, the complex and multi-layered smells or flavours which develop as a result of ageing. See AROMA.

Chewy, some but not obtrusive tannins.

Closed, not very smelly, assumed because of its stage of maturity.

Concentrated, good EXTRACT and/or intense flavour(s). (G)

Corked, wine that has been spoilt and smells off-puttingly mouldy because the cork is tainted. See page 18. (very B)

Crisp, perceptible acidity. (G)

Dried out, old wine in which the initial FRUIT has faded diminishing flavour and EXTRACT. (B)

Dumb, not smelly.

Esters, compounds formed by acids and alcohols either during fermentation or ageing, often intensely aromatic (nail polish remover smells strongly **esterified**).

Extract, an important dimension, the sum of a wine's solids, includes phenolics (see page 73), sugars, minerals and GLYCEROL; i.e. what would be left after boiling.

Finish, the sensory impact of a wine after it has been swallowed (or spat). Wines can be said to have a LONG or SHORT finish.

Firm, tannins perceptible. (G)

Flabby, too low in acid. (B)

Flavour, is really AROMA.

Forward, having aged more rapidly than expected.

Fresh, attractively acid. (G)

Fruit is the youthful combination of flavour (AROMA) and BODY coming from the grapes rather than winemaking or ageing.

Fruity is used either to describe wines with good FRUIT or, often in white wine marketing speak, as a euphemism for slightly sweet.

Full, or **Full bodied,** wine with considerable BODY.

Glycerol, colourless, natural, sweet-tasting substance which can add to the impression of BODY.

Green, too acid. (B)

Hard, too TANNIC. (B)

Hollow, lacking FRUIT. (B)

Horizontal tasting, comparative tasting of different but related representatives of the same year.

Hot, too alcoholic. (B)

Lean, lacking FRUIT but not acid. (B)

Legs, see TEARS.

Length, persistence of the tasting experience in olfactory area and mouth after swallowing. Such a wine may be called **long**. (G)

Lift(ed), wine with perceptible but not excessive VOLATILITY.

Light, or **Light bodied,** with relatively little BODY.

Mature, probably aged to its full potential. (G)

Mellow, sometimes used for reds as a euphemism for sweet.

Middle palate, jargon for the over-all impact of a wine in the mouth, as in 'There's not much FRUIT on the middle palate'.

Mouth feel, the physical impact of a wine on the mouth, its texture. Tannins and BODY surely play a role here.

Nose, used as both noun and verb, as in 'It's a bit DUMB on the nose' and 'Have you **nosed** this one?'

Oxidized, harmfully exposed to oxygen. See page 73. (B)

Powerful, high level of alcohol or EXTRACT. (G in this competitive day and age.)

Rich, with some apparent sweetness; curiously, much more complimentary than 'sweet'. (G)

Round, good BODY and not too much tannin. (G)

Short, opposite of LONG. (B)

Soft, not much tannin.

Spritz(ig), slightly gassy.

Supple, not too TANNIC. (G)

Tannic, aggressive tannins (see page 73). All young red wines destined for ageing are expected to have some tannins, but these should ideally be counterbalanced by FRUIT. (B)

Tart, very acid. (B)

Tears, the colourless streams left on the inside of a glass after a relatively alcoholic wine has been swirled. They have nothing to do with GLYCEROL.

Vertical tasting, a comparative tasting of different vintages from the same provenance.

Volatile, a wine with such a high level of volatile, not particularly stable, acids that it smells almost vinegary. (B)

AROMA WHEEL

Everyone has their own battery of 'tastes like' terms for flavour (i.e. aroma) terms. The following is my own personal adaptation of a ground-breaking graphic which was devised by Professor Ann C. Noble and her colleagues at the University of California at Davis in an attempt to instil some rigour into the use of tasting terms. It may help develop your own tasting vocabulary.

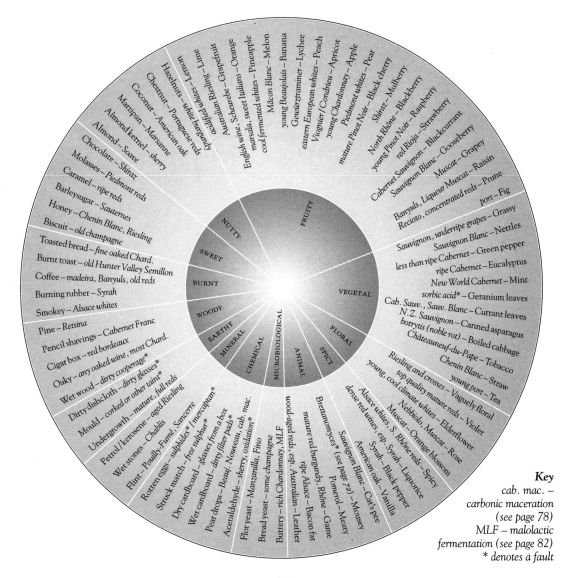

Key
cab. mac. –
carbonic maceration
(see page 78)
MLF – malolactic
fermentation (see page 82)
* denotes a fault

BECOMING A WINE TASTER

I believe that anyone with a sense of smell and an interest in wine can become a wine taster, and that it takes hardly any time at all. I am bolstered in this belief by years of listening to professionals trying to describe the same wines and doing it with completely different and even contradictory words. In practice, applying words to wine is a complete free-for-all.

No one other than you can ever know exactly how a wine strikes your senses. When it comes to wine tasting there are no absolutes. And so the opinion of the novice is every bit as valuable as that of the expert. The only difference is that the expert has been allowed to gain self-confidence, so we propound our theories rather more loudly than most newcomers.

In fact I often find that novice tasters are much better at coming up with the perfect word to describe a wine flavour than us professionals who used up our tasting vocabulary years ago. (Débutants can even be better at blind tasting than professionals, partly because they have tasted fewer confusing exceptions to the rule, and also because less is expected of them.)

Wine tasting is the definitive subjective sport. Once you have consciously tasted a few wines, you can build on that experience by starting to notice the common characteristics of the wines you like. Putting that together with the profiles of different grape varieties (in most cases the dominant factor in shaping how a wine tastes) in Section 3 and the chart on page 53 should help you pick out the sorts of wine that happen to appeal to your palate.

A FEW CLUES FROM TASTING

See the aroma wheel on page 17 for clues from specific flavours.

General
• Colourless streams after swirling – high alcohol and therefore very rich grapes which means either a hot climate or else an exceptionally hot summer in a cooler region).
• Slight fizz – could be a New World wine that is naturally slightly low in acidity and has been pepped up by retaining a bit of carbon dioxide in solution. If a supposedly still wine is visibly foaming at the edge this could be a second fermentation in bottle – a fault.

Reds
• Deep colour – warm summer, Cabernet, Syrah/Shiraz, Nebbiolo, or long maceration.
• Pale – cool climate, Beaujolais, Pinot Noir.
• Purple – young.
• Brick rim – old.

Whites
• Light body – cool climate or very high yields, German if aromatic to boot.
• Full body, pale colour – barrel fermentation?
• Brownish tinge – old, oxidized or barrel matured after protective winemaking.

And if the wine smells plain horrid…
• Wines that have been affected by a tainted cork smell off-puttingly mouldy and are described as **corked**. The longer the wine is exposed to the air, the stronger the smell gets, and the wine usually tastes rather nasty and unfruity too. The only thing worth doing with a corked wine is to return it to the supplier, who should provide a substitute. Cork moulds develop because cork processing plants, most of them in Portugal, are still relatively unsophisticated. The incidence of cork taint seems to have been increasing (perhaps partly because consumers are increasingly knowledgeable) and is currently put at between one bottle in 12 and one in 40. This wide disparity is because, as with all compounds, we vary in our sensitivity to corkiness. In a sense, those of us with a high corkiness threshold are the lucky ones.

SCORING WINE

Professional wine judges often give wines points out of 100, 20 or 10 because they are expected to come up with a ranking of how a group of wines showed on a given day. It might amuse you to keep written notes like (or probably neater than) the ones shown here and to append scores to them. For my own interest I certainly try to make a record of the state of maturity of each wine I taste, using arrows in different directions for their likely future.

Many wine critics and wine publications publish wine scores, which can be useful summaries of how the particular bottles seemed to that particular taster on the day of the tasting. Wine changes so unpredictably, however (and different casks and even bottles vary), and wine preferences are so subjective, that it is important not to be mesmerized by the apparent precision of these ratings. Find a wine critic whose taste you share and follow his or her recommendations, but not slavishly, please. And always remember that wine critics tend to taste scores of wine at a time, so the flashy ones get the highest scores. The saddest thing

I ever heard was when my most intelligent, wine-loving friend reported, crestfallen, about a wine tasted the previous evening, 'I really enjoyed it, but I looked it up in Parker [the powerful American wine critic] and he only gave it an 83.'

THE MECHANICS OF SERVING WINE

I am almost certainly biased, but I think there are few social acts as hospitable, relaxing and inclusive as offering someone a glass of wine. Pouring wine into a couple of glasses is so much less of a performance than anything involving 'How much tonic/water do you like? Ice? Lemon?' And a modest glass of wine (which nowadays costs far less than most bottles of beer) can transform the simplest food into an occasion (quite apart from making the food taste better). But these, I happily admit, are the rantings of a confirmed wine addict.

If the occasion is an informal one, I see no shame or disrespect in pouring from an already opened bottle. See page 25 for reasons why the wine might actually taste better, and for advice on keeping opened bottles of wine.

More formal entertaining does call for a certain amount of planning, however. About the most disconcerting way of greeting your guests is with 'Just hang on a minute; I have to pop out and get something to drink.' Imagine substituting the word 'eat' at the end of this sentence... See pages 32–3 for specific suggestions about wine styles and quantities.

The thoughtful host is just that, working out how many bottles of any wine to be served may be needed and, most importantly, getting them ready in advance. If by any chance you're serving a wine with a sediment such as vintage or crusted port and most fine red wine more than about five years old, these bottles need to be stood upright for at least a day and preferably several to let the deposit fall to the bottom. (It is a good sign incidentally, if a wine has a sediment. It means that the winemaker didn't filter it too heavily, and left it with enough tiny particles to age and bond together to make a more interesting wine.) For most wines, however, the most important aspect to plan is the crucial question of serving temperature (see page 28).

Sparkling wines and light white wines can, conveniently, be put in the refrigerator the morning before the evening you plan to serve them. Full bodied whites (see page 36) are usually better off given only an hour or two's chilling before your guests arrive. Most red wines will get to approximately the right temperature if left all day in the room in which they'll eventually be served – although lighter bodied styles (see page 37) may need half an hour's chilling before serving, or could be kept in cellar conditions (see pages 42–4) until just before serving. I tend to move bottles round the house according to their style. The top of the tumble drier (when it's switched off) is usefully cooler than our dining area, but one of these days a bottle of red burgundy will be spun off it into messy smithereens.

Big parties tend to put impossible stresses on most domestic refrigerators. I find the Great British winter can be a fine outdoor alternative to chilling bottles mechanically. A bucket, basin or even bath full of ice and water (a much more effective cooling agent than ice cubes alone, which inevitably touch only a fraction of a bottle's surface) is a viable solution, no matter what the outdoor temperature.

If you need to chill bottles in a hurry, an ice (and water) bucket is a most effective method. Microwaves can be used to warm bottles fast, but err on the side of caution when setting the timing. And remember that a glassful of too-cool wine can be warmed quite fast by being cupped in the human hand.

See pages 24–5 for advice on when to open bottles and decanting. One little question, however: should one wipe clean bottles which have painstakingly acquired cellar dust? Most hygienically minded people would answer with an unequivocal yes. I think they should know, however, that in the United States it is possible to buy artificial dust to spray on wine bottles.

OPENING THE BOTTLE

THE IDEAL STOPPER?

The world's wine producers spend a lot of time asking themselves and each other how to persuade more people to drink wine (fewer than one in every three Americans, for example, does so with any regularity). And yet they continue to sell one of the very few products left in the world which cannot even be opened, let alone consumed, without a special bit of equipment, great patience and dexterity, and acceptance of a considerable failure rate. The continuing use of cork, a cylinder of tree bark, to stopper wine bottles is in many ways extraordinary – especially since a growing body of scientific research suggests that a crown cap or possibly screwcap would do the job just as well (provided bottle tops are redesigned to accommodate them). But what is even more extraordinary is that producers dare not switch to easier, more reliable stoppers because all research suggests that consumers are wedded to corks and corkscrews as part of the wine-drinking experience. Plastic corks are therefore encroaching.

I too love the 'pop' sound of a cork being pulled (and, especially, the popping of a champagne cork, which, restaurateurs report, can have an instant effect on other diners), and I love the idea that cork is an ecologically sound material. But I feel even more passionately about how difficult some corks are to extract (especially from Italy's narrow bottle-necks), how they can eventually crumble and fatally let in air, and how frequently they are affected by cork taint and result in completely spoilt 'corked' wines (see page 18).

Cork is a unique material in that it is light, elastic, inert (i.e. does not normally react with the wine), and shouldn't let liquids out or air, wine's enemy, in. Once it is lodged in a bottle-neck and absorbs wine it should offer an airtight seal. Crystals on the bottom of a cork are not sinister, just harmless tartrates deposited by wine's naturally high level of

(Continued on page 24)

1 *The cheapest and least elastic corks are short and made from cork agglomerate, little cork chips stuck together, reminiscent of soles and notice-boards.*

2 *The flashiest, most expensive corks can be up to 6 cm long. Fewer natural marks mean better quality.*

3 *Some top producers such as those at Château Mouton-Rothschild have deliberately reduced the length of their corks to stop them absorbing too much wine and lowering the level in the bottle, which can age the wine prematurely.*

4 *A champagne cork before it is hammered into a bottle. It is too wide to be punched out of a single thickness of bark so it is made up of rings of agglomerate with a disc of natural cork on the bottom, in contact with the wine.*

5 *The same cork (as **4**) after many months in a bottle-neck.*

6 *The crown cap is used for the first stage of sparkling wine maturation, and has been shown to keep any wine in good condition for decades.*

7 *The screwcap – effective and reliable but spurned.*

CORKSCREWS

1 Regular corkscrew with a perfect hollow, pointed helix.

2 Butterfly, twin levered model (usually all metal). This model requires less strength because of its twin levers but has a potentially problematic solid helix.

3 This wooden model employs an inner screw and therefore needs less effort than some, but has the disadvantage of concealing where the action is.

4 Screwpull broke new ground in corkscrew design by introducing Teflon coating of the screw and adapting advanced engineering to minimize the human effort in cork extraction. This Lever model, however, is Screwpull's most magical offering by far, screwing corks out of the bottle and off the screw with two easy movements. Its cost, about the same as two bottles of expensive bordeaux, makes it a viable proposition only for the rich or seriously wine-demented, however.

5 This twin-pronged (for insertion either side of a cork) model, called a 'Butler's friend' for its ability to remove corks without marking them and thereby facilitating their reinsertion, is particularly popular with American wine drinkers. It depends on wrist-twisting but may end up pushing in particularly loose corks.

6 The 'waiter's friend' incorporates a penknife for cutting foils and allows corks to be levered out against the rim of the bottle. It also requires considerable dexterity and strength, however, and might not be such a friend to the average waitress.

7 The Screwpull foil cutter costs about as much as a bottle of Muscadet and, once it has been used, becomes an essential wine serving tool. Clasp the foil over the bottle-neck between its two prongs, give it a quarter turn and its four tiny circular blades should neatly trim off the top of the foil, leaving a decent margin below the rim (see page 24 for more details).

WINE PARAPHERNALIA

1 Ice buckets, either glass or metal, are much heavier and potentially messier than a vacuum bottle holder. The trick is to fill them as full as possible with a mixture of ice and water, not just ice, so that every bit of the bottle is in contact with a cooling agent.

2 Just one of many designs of bottle holder whose job is to keep a wine at the temperature it was when inserted. It works on much the same principle as a vacuum flask, is easy to clean and can be just as useful for keeping red wines from heating up in very high temperatures as for keeping white wines chilled.

3 and **4** Decanters tend to come in single-(**4**) or double-bottled (magnum) size. Antique ones can be unearthed from junk shops for relatively little money, especially since you don't strictly need a stopper for a decanter used only for serving. Spirits and madeira can be kept in a (stoppered) decanter virtually for ever, but port and even sherry tends to deteriorate after a week or so. And most table wines deteriorate after just 24 hours – although some tannic monsters may improve.

5 The Vacuvin works by pumping out air from an opened bottle and trying to create a vacuum therein. It is better than nothing but is not very effective over more than a day or two.

6 This sparkling wine stopper will keep the bubbles in an opened bottle in the fridge for several days.

tartaric acid (see page 73). Some mould on the top of a cork is not necessarily a bad thing either, as it is probably the result of the cellar rather than the wine (I still remember the glory of a Château d'Yquem 1945 from under a cork that was so mouldy it was visibly moving). If a cork is very damp at both ends, it may have allowed some wine out and, more dangerously, some air in. If you notice that a bottle is leaking, or a cork fits so loosely in a bottle-neck that it can be moved, extract the cork and replace it with a tighter one as soon as possible, after checking that the wine has not been oxidized (see page 73) by taking a small sample.

THE MECHANICS OF OPENING

Before wrestling with the cork, the wine drinker encounters another illogical barrier to wine enjoyment, the often impenetrable foil or capsule that covers the cork. An increasing number of wine bottles are allowed on to the market without this addition, once useful for protecting against cork weevils but now largely cosmetic, except for bottles kept in a wine rack where foils can be useful for identification. Although the practice was outlawed in 1993, lead was often used for foils, potentially leaving harmful deposits on the rim of the bottle (which is why it is sensible to get into the habit of wiping the rim of every wine bottle once the cork has been pulled). For the same reason professionals try to cut the foil in a straight line round the bottle-neck a few millimetres below the rim so that wine doesn't come into contact with the foil when it is poured. (The wine won't taste any different if you rip the entire foil off, as is sometimes inevitable, but it deprives you of one of the wine's distinguishing marks.) A sharp knife and a steady hand can achieve a neatly cut foil, but a specially designed foil cutter such as the one shown on page 22 does it with much less effort. A foil cutter is no good, however, for those few bottle-necks still dipped in wax which, in my experience, has to be painstakingly chipped off with a sharp knife and a chisel.

Once the foil has been removed, you have to hope that a corkscrew such as one of the best of those illustrated on page 22 will do the rest. Aim the screw down the centre of the cork. Ideally it should be a hollow, sharply pointed helix rather than a solid cone which can all too easily pierce a hole straight through the cork. It can help to stand the bottle on a flat surface, holding it steady, while inserting the screw, and to jam it between your knees while pulling. As with modern business, leverage is all.

If the cork crumbles under the impact of the corkscrew but won't come out, try inserting a corkscrew with a long narrow screw at an angle and/or into a different part of the cork. If that doesn't work, as with any intractable cork, you could try inserting the two prongs of a butler's friend type corkscrew down either side of the cork and pulling it out, or you may have to simply push the cork into the bottle using, for example, the handle of a wooden spoon (a little more wood contact won't harm the wine). Because the remains of the cork tend to float and block the bottle-neck (provided the wine is not some terribly fragile ancient liquid whose precious bouquet may be lost after a few minutes' exposure to air) it is worth continuing to push them down with your stick-like instrument while pouring the wine into a jug. You can then pour the wine, through a funnel lined with a clean coffee filter or muslin if necessary, into a clean bottle or decanter. I cannot tell you how useful I find a plastic funnel and muslins.

Another possible ploy which requires some cunning is to warm the bottle-neck without actually warming the cork. A cloth soaked in boiling water can be held round the bottle-neck using an oven glove.

If none of these ploys works, and it is feasible, take the bottle back to where you bought it and complain. (This is just one of the reasons why it can be a good idea to keep more wine in the house than you expect to consume.)

Plastic cylinders dyed and mottled to look like corks are used increasingly to avoid the problem of cork taint while offering some of the 'cork experience'. I can't stand them. They have none of the ecological soundness of real cork. They look silly. The ones I have come across are far too inelastic to re-stopper an opened bottle. And, worst of all, they involve all the effort of trying to pull a fat cork out of a narrow bottle-neck.

LEFTOVERS

Too much air, or at least oxygen, turns wine into vinegar eventually, which is why it makes sense to store leftover wine in a *stoppered* bottle with as little head space as possible, i.e. in a bottle whose capacity is as close as possible to the volume of wine left over (clean half- and quarter-bottles can be very useful). All sorts of complex reactions (accelerated by heat) take place when wine is exposed to air, as happens when a wine is poured or sits in a glass, which is why a wine can taste quite different 10, 20 or 30 minutes after being poured.

BREATHING

Many wine drinkers deliberately open bottles an hour or so before pouring them because they like the wine to 'breathe'. Wine scientists point out that the surface area of wine in a bottle-neck is so small relative to its volume that very little is likely to be achieved by this except, in some rare cases, the dissipation of any 'bottle sickness' (see pages 39–41).

In that opening a bottle an hour or two ahead of time is unlikely to do any harm to all

OPENING A BOTTLE OF SPARKLING WINE

An eye doctor in the champagne town of Épernay treats up to 20 people a year who have been injured by wayward corks. The pressure in a bottle of sparkling wine is about three times that in the tyre of a double-decker bus, so champagne corks must be eased out of the bottle-neck with enormous care. Untwist the wire muzzle and keep a thumb over the top of the cork. Point the bottle away from you and away from anyone else or any precious object, at an angle to increase the surface area of the wine and decrease the pressure in the bottle-neck. Twist the bottle off the cork rather than vice versa (to avoid breaking the cork), all the while holding the cork into the bottle-neck with the thumb so that it is eased out producing 'the gentle sigh of a satisfied woman', as cricket commentator and wine writer John Arlott would have it. Pour the wine gently into each glass, possibly taking a lesson from pub staff by holding the glass at an angle to control the foam.

but the most fragile wine relics, however, there are practical reasons for getting this job out of the way before, for example, your guests arrive.

TO DECANT OR NOT

There are also strong practical reasons for separating a wine with sediment (see page 20) from that sediment, which can taste bitter and physically gets in the way of enjoyment. This traditionally involves standing the bottle upright for a day or two beforehand and pouring the wine into another clean glass container (glass is inert and if clear allows you to enjoy the colour of a wine, which can be a great pleasure) with a strong light source behind the bottom of the bottle-neck so that you can stop pouring when the sediment is about to slip into the neck. That light source could be a candle or any strong light such as a desklight or a table lamp without the shade.

I often decant full bodied white wines which may have no sediment at all, simply because they look so gorgeously golden in a decanter. See page 23 for some classic decanter shapes, but a glass jug or clean bottle would do just as well.

Scientists say we should decant at the last possible moment so that no part of the wine's reaction with air be lost to us. As a host I confess I am prepared to sacrifice completeness for convenience with all but the most fragile old wines, say those over 25 years old, depending on their body and the style of the vintage.

GLASSES

Wine is drunk out of glasses rather than teacups or silver goblets because glass is inert, relatively thin and allows full appreciation of a wine's appearance. The perfect wine glass has a stem and a bowl that goes in towards the rim (see page 14). It is also made of clear glass so that the wine's colour, an important element in assessing and enjoying wine to the full, can be appreciated. Wine nuts also like to commune with their wine as physically closely as possible, which means that thin crystal is highly valued whereas patterned and cut glass are not.

There is no real need for glasses of different sizes except that we tend to need smaller servings of sweet wines and fortified wines. It has always seemed unfair to me that white wines are conventionally served in smaller glasses than red wines.

1 Tumblers may be used in earthy and aspiringly earthy Italian restaurants, but the thickness of the glass and the difficulty of swirling the wine makes them pleasure-killers for wine enthusiasts.

2 The 'Paris goblet' is one of the cheapest wine glasses available (four can be bought for the price of a bottle of the cheapest wine). It fulfils the criteria of having a stem and going in towards the rim, and is better than narrower 'tulip' shapes, but the glass is too thick to provide intimate or luxurious contact with the wine.

3 The ISO glass carefully designed in the 1970s by the International Standards Organization, advised by a panel of professional wine tasters, does the job extremely well without winning any prizes for glamour. Machine-made versions are available and each one costs no more than the cheapest bottle of wine.

4 and **5** Classic wine glass shapes on an attractively spindly stem. Eastern Europe, and the Czech Republic in particular, have a long history of providing good-value glassware.

6 The classic 'copita' used for serving sherry by those who really understand it – the people who make it. Like any wine, sherry is best appreciated in a glass only half to two-thirds full.

CARING FOR GLASSWARE

Glasses should be stored upright somewhere free from dust and strong smells. Aesthetically, glassware needs to be clean, and has the annoying habit of being extremely breakable and showing every speck and dribble. The important thing as far as the wine is concerned is that the glass smells of nothing – not washing up liquid (which can stop the formation of bubbles in fizzy wine), and certainly not dirty glass cloths.

Many smart wine glasses, including the Riedel range, are happy in a domestic dishwasher and benefit from the high temperatures there. Water has to be soft, however, and there is no need for detergent. Hand washing glasses achieves best results if glasses are washed in very hot water, rinsed in cold, and polished with linen tea towels reserved for the purpose – I'm told. In an ideal world we would all have unlimited supplies of new, fine crystal glasses.

1, 2 and 3 No one has done more work on wine glass design than Austrian Georg Riedel. Working on the principle that how the liquid hits the tongue affects how it will taste, he has evolved slightly different glass designs for dozens of wine types which include, for example, young as opposed to mature red bordeaux, both non-vintage and vintage champagne, and a glass for each of vintage port, tawny port, Chianti Classico and Brunello di Montalcino. To indulge freely in the Riedel way of life you would clearly need to build a special glass storage wing on to your house. The Gourmet glass (1) is his least expensive all-purpose model; the Chardonnay machine-made Vinum (2) is perhaps more elegant for the dinner table. Glasses in the beautiful,

similarly shaped but hand-blown Sommelier range (3) cost so much that I would not dare wash one.

4 The only non-standard glass shape you might think of investing in is a tall, thin glass for sparkling wines (often called a flûte), which allows minimal gas escape, lets you watch each bubble's journey and is a suitably glamorous shape in itself. Some champagne producers prefer a glass that has more of a bowl so that you have a better chance of smelling the wine's bouquet.

5 The old-fashioned coupe, supposedly modelled on the shape of Marie-Antoinette's breast, is easy to spill and encourages the precious carbon dioxide to escape as fast as possible.

TEMPERATURE – THE CRUCIAL ELEMENT

It is impossible to overestimate the effect of serving temperatures on how a wine will taste. Serving a wine at the most flattering temperature may seem absurdly high-falutin and precious as an activity, but it really can transform ink into velvet. Conversely, getting the temperature wrong turns zest into flab. (Unlike the wine itself, it need not cost anything either...)

The principles are delightfully simple:
1 The cooler the wine the less it will smell.
2 The warmer the wine the more it will smell.
3 Low temperatures will emphasize acidity and tannin.
4 High temperatures will minimize them.

The result of rule 1 is that if you find yourself with a wine that tastes (i.e. smells) truly horrid, but you have to serve or drink it, then chill it to pieces. (If it's a full bodied red such as those listed on the bottom half of page 37 it could be difficult to pull this off – you'll just have to boil off the flavour and serve it, with added spice and sugar, as mulled wine. See page 56.)

Rule 1 also means that the more naturally aromatic a wine is (Riesling, Sauvignon Blanc, Cabernet Franc, Gamay for example), the cooler you can afford to serve it – a useful observation if you need the refreshment of a cool drink. Sparkling wines also suit low temperatures, which slow down the release of carbon dioxide.

Rule 2 means that full bodied wines (whites too), those which appear towards the bottom of the charts on page 36–7 and whose flavour molecules struggle to escape to deliver messages to the olfactory area, can be served much warmer than lighter wines. The limit to this rule is reached above 20°C (68°F) when some compounds may be literally boiled off.

Rule 3 means that you can make a flabby wine taste infinitely better by chilling it a little. Thus, all but the most perfectly balanced sweet wine benefits from being chilled, as do many red burgundies and soft red wines such as Beaujolais, which could do with a bit of artificially encouraged structure.

Rule 4 is particularly useful because it means that young red wines, and those listed on the right hand side of page 37, which would seem almost hideously tough when served slightly cool, can be immeasurably improved by serving them on the warm side.

The chart gives a rough guide as to suitable serving temperatures. See also pages 36–7 for guidance on which wines are light/full bodied, which sweet or dry, and likely tannin levels.

WINE STYLE	IDEAL SERVING TEMPERATURE, °C (°F)	PRACTICAL ADVICE: REFRIGERATOR FOR (HRS)
Light, sweet whites	5–10 (41–50)	4+
Sparkling whites	6–10 (43–50)	4
Light (aromatic), dry whites	8–12 (46–54)	2
Sparkling reds	10–12 (50–54)	1.5
Medium bodied, dry whites	10–12 (50–54)	1.5
Full, sweet whites	8–12 (46–54)	2
Light reds	10–12 (50–54)	1.5
Full, dry whites	12–16 (54–61)	1
Medium reds	14–17 (57–63)	–
Full or tannic reds	15–18 (59–64)	–

NB Throughout, rosés behave as slightly fuller bodied equivalent whites.

SERVING THE RIGHT BOTTLE

For me, choosing the right wine to serve on a particular occasion is almost as thrilling as drinking the wine itself, perverse as that may seem. It gives me real pleasure to feel that the bottle, or bottles, have been just right for the circumstances, the people, the time, and any food that's served with the wine. Slowly, as I have learnt more about wine, I have learnt a little more about this aspect of wine appreciation, which is by no means a modern phenomenon. In the first century BC the Latin poet Horace wrote extensively about the art of matching wine to guest and occasion. And it is an art.

It is by no means the single most important thing about wine. It is hardly catastrophic to serve a wine that jars with your main course, or your guests' tastes or expectations, but a few simple considerations can ensure that you maximize your own and your friends' enjoyment, and that the money you spend on wine is spent most effectively.

It is usually a waste, and entirely inappropriate, for example, to think that the more you spend on wine, the more it will please. Typically, the most expensive bottles in a wine shop are tough little babies in terms of their evolution: mute, scrunched-up bundles of ingredients that have many years' bottle maturation ahead of them before they will begin to prove, in mellow middle age, why they were worth paying through the nose for. (See pages 39–41 for more about this magical process.)

And there is a place and a time for everything – even the fanciest bottle of wine. I shall never forget that the first time I ever tasted the fabulous Château Cheval Blanc 1947 was at an outdoor lunch in a sunny Suffolk garden where the breeze playfully wafted into the hot, blue sky every nuance of its subtle bouquet. A well-chilled, flavourful dry rosé would probably have been just the thing for this outdoor lunch, and yet it would probably taste extremely dreary at an urban dinner party in midwinter.

Other examples of the right bottles in the wrong place (for a wide variety of reasons) include: Mosel Riesling with hearty stews; New Zealand Sauvignon served to any but the most cosmopolitan native of Sancerre; heavy Chardonnay at lunchtime; tough, tannic young reds served to wine débutants; Châteauneuf-du-Pape drunk in midsummer in Châteauneuf-du-Pape (or indeed most full bodied, alcoholic reds in the heat of the summer that is responsible for that alcohol).

HOW TO CHOOSE

It is worth trying to match a wine's
quality level
style
flavour
geographical origins
to:

people – take account of an individual's likes, dislikes, prejudices, and capacities for alcohol.

occasion – whether it's the most casual encounter or a formal celebration may influence the most appropriate price level.

weather – the ambient temperature and humidity level can have an enormous effect on what sorts of wine taste best. In hot weather we crave cool drinks, which means choosing wines that taste good when chilled. On muggy days it can be difficult to persuade the flavour molecules out of the glass, so choose an aromatic wine.

time of day – may be a significant factor as far as alcohol intake is concerned.

place – inside or outside? Is more than one wine appropriate, or feasible?

food – see pages 34–7 for full details of the extent to which food and wine matching matters; and see pages 32–3 for ideas on wines to be served without food as an aperitif and those that come into their own after a meal.

29

BRINGING A BOTTLE

Some people think that because of their age or status, it is somehow not 'done' to bring a bottle of wine, whereas others would never dream of crossing a friend's threshold without a bottle of wine in hand. I can't see why anyone would resent the gift of a bottle thoughtfully chosen; although anyone who expects every guest to bring a bottle and gets upset if they don't, is probably wise to spell this out in advance.

One of the touchier questions of modern etiquette is whether you have to open a bottle that someone brings, or can you keep it and savour it on another occasion? I would say that if someone brings a bottle of white or sparkling wine ready-chilled or, as has frequently happened to me, a red wine already decanted, then this should be taken as a pretty strong hint that its donor expects the wine to be drunk there and then. If, however, your guest arrives and puts a bottle on one side without comment, then you are not duty-bound to open it – although the perfect host would probably unwrap it at some point, express thanks, and ask whether the guest would like to taste it ('taste' being such a useful euphemism for 'drink').

Two useful rules are never to take a bottle that you would not be happy to drink yourself, and, if you really want to drink it, hand it over personally and explain how keen you are to 'taste' it.

Bottles to blush about
• Branded wines e.g. Piat d'Or, Mateus or Lancers Rosé, Blue Nun or any Liebfraumilch.
• Any really inexpensive table wine.
• Wines in funny, asymmetrical bottles.

More respectable than people think
• Supermarket own-label wines: although few look good enough to present to design gurus, some taste quite good enough for the rest of us.
• Mineral water: perhaps it's just my friends, but some hosts are much better at providing booze than the water needed to stop the dehydration effect.

Smart bottles
• Champagne: almost always appreciated. Bollinger and Louis Roederer (or Krug if you can afford it) are gold chip presents; Deutz, Gosset, Alfred Gratien, Charles Heidsieck, Laurent Perrier, Moët & Chandon, Bruno Paillard, Perrier-Jouët, Pol Roger, Pommery, Renaudin, Ruinart, Taittinger, de Venoge and Veuve Clicquot are all reliable; Billecart-Salmon Rosé would show that you really know your stuff; as would a bottle from one of the best growers such as Château de Boursault, Gimonnet or Vilmart. Vintage-dated is a treat.
• Obscure wines: either a small, unknown producer of a well-known wine such as Beaujolais or California Chardonnay, or something new (a weird new grape variety or curiosity from Latin America or the Far East), or something not in general commercial distribution (such as Château Latour's basic Pauillac, effectively its 'third wine', for example). A good independent wine merchant can be invaluable here, or a bottle brought back from abroad.
• Sweet wines: good Sauternes, Vouvray, Monbazillac, Jurançon and Late Harvest Riesling are all stylishly unusual, and usually appreciated even in half-bottles.
• Olive oil: estate bottled oils are what wine pros take to each other's houses.

The ultimate bottle party, the annual Paulée de Meursault, a marathon lunch held in the village of Meursault on the day after the annual Hospices de Beaune auction. Guests from all over the world converge on particularly good bottles brought by Burgundy's wine producers.

ENTERTAINING WITH WINE

QUANTITIES

A tricky one, this. Individuals' capacity for alcohol varies enormously, as you have doubtless observed yourself. No one could possibly accuse a host who provided his or her guests with the equivalent of a bottle of wine a head over the course of an evening of meanness. And yet there are some occasions, a weekday lunch, for example, at which it would be extremely sophisticated to provide one stunning bottle (of champagne or white burgundy perhaps) for six people, allowing them each one generous glassful of luxury but minimizing the dangerous snooze factor of a bibulous lunch.

As a general rule, an average of between half and a bottle a head consumed over several hours at a table makes for a very jolly occasion. If there are many drivers in the party then the lower limit would be more sensible.

Wine served without a meal is potentially much more potent, especially before lunch when most bodies contain little food to buffer alcohol's effect. A quarter of a bottle a head, or two small glasses, could well be enough if there is a significant proportion of abstainers in the group, although for a long daytime reception such as a wedding it would be safer to allow up to half a bottle a head (and as much as a bottle for an all-evening event).

Like many hosts, I frequently overlook the non-alcoholic drinks in my concern to serve just the right wine(s). Try to serve as much water as wine at the table, and to provide a reasonably sophisticated non-alcoholic alternative at parties such as fizzy mineral water with fresh orange juice or a drop of elderflower syrup, or spiced tomato juice cocktails before lunch.

Serving something to eat cuts down quite dramatically on the intoxication rate of an alcoholic aperitif. Eating olives out of doors (the only time I encourage my children to throw stones) can seem just right, though they can seem distractingly mediterranean and strongly flavoured for a northern wine like champagne.

Radishes, celery, pistachio nuts and quail's eggs are less intrusive, but most of these involve some potentially inconvenient debris (although halves of quail's egg on a dollop of mayonnaise on toasted rounds of French bread are easy to eat and look glamorous). Little cheesy biscuits such as the Dutch Roka brand complement most wines, as do Italian breadsticks or *grissini*, even with prosciutto wound round them.

SOME SPECIFIC SUGGESTIONS

Pre-meal drinks party

Wine (plus a non-alcoholic alternative) is much easier to serve than lots of different mixed drinks. People with carpets tend to prefer to serve white wine, and it is true that most reds are too full bodied and tannic to be at their best without food. Sparkling wine seems special and (in some cases *but*) goes to the head quicker; a good champagne can be the greatest treat of all, but perfectly well-made, more economical alternatives can be found from Saumur, Limoux, Alsace, California, Australia, New Zealand and even England (a cool, or cooled, climate is vital). Still white wines that fit the bill of being light enough but not too acid to drink without food include many not-too-expensive examples from Alsace; Kabinett and Spätlese wines from Germany (Mosel especially); light Chardonnay and Sauvignon Blanc such as a Vin de Pays d'Oc, Chablis and unoaked examples from the southern hemisphere; well-made Pinot Blanc/Bianco and Pinot Gris/Grigio which manage to combine the softness of Pinot with an appetizing tang.

All-evening informal party

The wines listed above could certainly be served all evening, but after a while your guests may start to crave something more substantial. Red wines that can happily be sipped at with no substantial food to break their fall on the palate tend to be light bodied and low in tannin (those in the top left hand quarter of page 37). Beaujolais and other Gamays; red Loire and other Cabernet Franc wines; simpler Merlots; young

Pinot Noir (except for most red burgundy); the new generation of juicy young reds from Spain and Portugal; Dolcetto; light Zinfandel; many eastern European reds; and of course practically any rosé can fit the bill here. And if you really are fonder of your carpets than of humouring your guests, you could always switch to a fuller bodied, oaked white such as a Chardonnay or Semillon when you start to serve the food.

Extended lunch party

A similar range of wines as for an evening party could be served here, but in smaller quantities perhaps. Warmer weather may require the addition of some examples from the following.

Outdoor wines

It is usually a waste to serve too fine a wine out of doors, especially in hot weather when the bouquet is lost all too easily to the sun and breeze. Barbecued food, however, calls for its own brand of earthy, robust flavours and, perhaps not too surprisingly, hot climate wines come into their own here, including wines from Australia, the southern Rhône, dry rosés and reds from Provence, practically anything produced on the shores of the Mediterranean, even retsina from Greece.

Before a meal

Any of the wines suggested for a pre-meal drinks party make fine aperitifs, as drinks designed to stimulate the appetite are called. The classic aperitif is dry sherry, probably too strong and too misunderstood for general consumption, but one of the wine world's great, undervalued treasures. In warm weather a freshly opened bottle of Fino or Manzanilla can give even more concentrated pleasure than a fine white wine (and is the perfect foil for green olives and salted almonds), while a dry, nutty Amontillado is the perfect antidote to cold weather and an incipient cold. Sercial Madeira can also be beguilingly tingly. The most classical unfortified wines to serve as aperitifs are champagne, Mosel and lighter Alsace wines.

Dinner party

I usually serve an aperitif (see above), one or two (related) first course wines, usually two and sometimes even three different main course wines (moving from lighter to fuller bodied and from young to old), one of which may continue with the cheese, and sometimes a strong, sweet wine at the end. The whites might be two Californian Chardonnays or white burgundies from different producers, the reds could follow a geographical, varietal or even vintage theme. But then I want to show off, and this is wildly in excess of what is necessary or even sensible, which is probably an aperitif, a white and a red (to cater for those who just can't handle one or other colour). All I would say in my defence is that you learn so much more when comparing similar wines than when drinking them in isolation. Also see Wine and Food on page 34.

After a meal

To my mind and palate, sweet wines taste much more delicious drunk on their own (or with cheese) than they do with most sweet food. Any reasonably sweet wine can be delicious after a meal, and those with a fair degree of acidity such as Germans, Austrians, Loire or Jurançon can refresh as well. This is also the time to serve sweet fortified wines (port, sherry, madeira, marsala, malaga, Liqueur Muscat, southern French and indeed all rich Muscats, and so on) as well as wine in its strongest, i.e. distilled, form: cognac, armagnac and other brandies. The spirit that finds most favour with wine fanatics other than brandy is Chartreuse which, like wine but unlike any other spirit, has an uncanny way of developing in the bottle.

Daytime drinking

I may be a killjoy, but low alcohol (see page 72) seems the crucial element when sipping between meals. Mosel comes into its own here, as does Italy's panoply of lightly fizzing Moscato, the wrongly reviled Asti included. Buying an example other than the cheapest is the key to enjoyable grapey froth instead of a headache.

WINE AND FOOD

With its relatively low alcoholic strength, appetizing acidity and lack of sickly artificial flavours, wine is the perfect accompaniment to food. Am I kidding myself that a well-chosen wine makes food taste better? Surely not...

The most important rule about food and wine matching is that there are no rules. You can drink any wine at all with any food – even red wine with fish! – and the world will continue to revolve. Anyone who thinks worse of you for serving the 'wrong' wine is stuffy, prejudiced and probably ill-informed.

There are, however, some very simple guide-lines for getting the most out of particular foods and bottles.

• The single most important aspect of a wine for food matching is not colour but body (which corresponds closely with alcoholic strength).

• The second most important aspect is tannins for reds and sweetness for whites.

See the charts on pages 36–7 for help in assessing these vital statistics.

• Try to match a wine's body to the power of the strongest ingredient in the food (some examples are given between the white and red wine charts but the list is very far from exhaustive). Serve delicate-flavoured foods such as simple white fish or poached chicken with lighter bodied wines (on the top half of pages 36 and 37) and stronger, more robust foods such as grilled tuna with spiced lentils or osso buco with full bodied wines (on the bottom half). It should be clear from the charts that many white wines will do jobs which are conventionally regarded as red wine jobs, and vice versa.

• A tannic wine such as those on the far right of the chart on page 37 can taste softer when served with chewy foods, notably unsauced red meat. (Sauces are often more powerful than what they are saucing and are usually a better guide to the ideal wine accompaniment.)

• All wines taste horribly acid if served with sweet food, unless they are sweeter than the food itself – which seriously limits the choice of wines to be served with most sweet courses to those on the very far right of the white wine chart on page 36 and the asterisked reds on page 37. It also makes wine purists wary of sweet relishes such as chutneys, jellies and fruit sauces. (But sweetish wines can go surprisingly well with savoury food – a Vouvray demi-sec can taste gorgeous with a savoury creamy sauce, for example – while sweet wines can go well with cheeses on the sweet and salt principle, as in melon and prosciutto.)

• Very acid foods such as citrus fruits and vinegar can do funny things to seriously fine, perfectly balanced wine, but can flatter a slightly acid wine (from a particularly cool climate or year) by making it taste less sour.

• Similarly, freshly ground black pepper might distort our impression of a complex, venerable wine but acts as a sensitizing agent on most palates and flatters young, light wines (in the top half of the chart) by making them taste fuller and richer.

DIFFICULT FOODS FOR WINE

There are very few foods that destroy wine, but very hot spices tend to stun the taste buds so that you could still smell a wine but would find it impossible to experience its dimensions because the sensory equipment in the palate is ablaze.

Globe artichokes and, to a lesser extent, asparagus can make wine taste oddly metallic, and most chocolate is so sweet and mouth-coating that it tends to annihilate all but the sweetest, strongest wines.

And don't forget how wine styles can be manipulated by care with serving temperatures (see page 28).

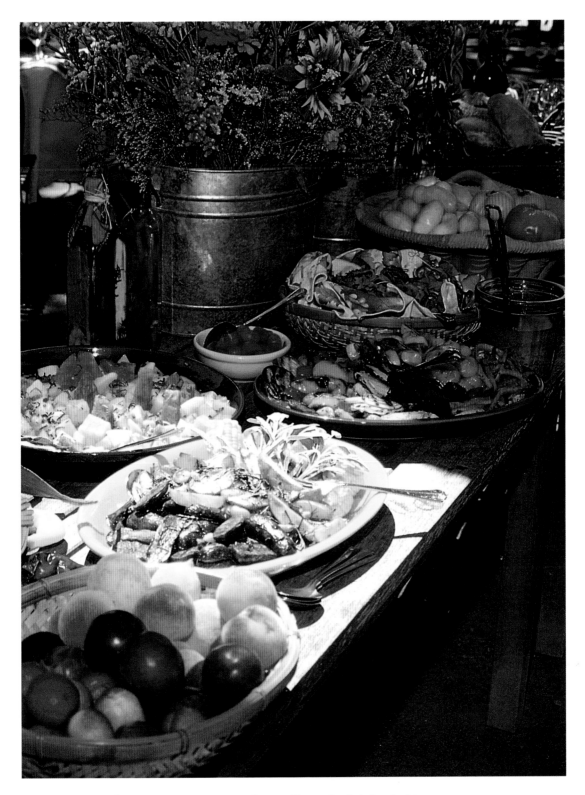

*The increasing importance of vegetables and salads has had its own sunny
influence on food and wine matching. Their direct flavours can seem better suited to New World
wines than the dusty complexity of many an Old World classic.*

CHARTING WINE AND FOOD

To match food and wine, try to assess the power of the food by its similarity in terms of impact on the palate to the foods listed, in increasing powerfulness, between the white and red wine charts. Then choose a wine type at about the same height on the page, but remember the guide-lines about sweetness (page 36) and tannin (page 37) offered on page 34, which mean that special conditions may apply to wines on the far right hand side of each page

% Alc	BONE DRY	DRY	MED. DRY	MED. SWEET	VERY SWEET	WHITE
8	Mosel trocken	Mosel Kabinett		Moscato Spumante		
			Mosel Spätlese			(all foods
		English wine		Moscato d'Asti		usually
			Mosel Auslese			best with
			Liebfraumilch / QbA			dry wines)
9	Gros Plant			Mosel BA/TBA		
	Colombard	Swiss wine				
	Rhine trocken	Rhine Kabinett	Mateus Rosé	Asti		
		vin de table	Rhine Spätlese			
	Ugni Blanc / Trebbiano					
10			**Riesling**			
	Muscadet	S. African Chenin Blanc		Rhine Auslese		oysters
	Vinho Verde	Vin de Pays		Rosé d'Anjou		unadorned white fish
			Cal. Chenin Blanc		Rhine BA/TBA	
		Soave				
11	Pinots Grigio & Bianco					
	Rhine Spätlese trocken	Loire Chenin Blanc				fish tartare
	Aligoté	Vouvray	Vouvray demi sec	Vouvray moelleux		spring rolls
	Sancerre / Pouilly-Fumé	European whites				prawns
	Albariño	Alsace Riesling				
12	**Sauvignon Blanc**					salmon
		Entre-Deux-Mers / AC Bordeaux / Bergerac				goats cheese
	Chablis Champagne					
	Vino de mesa			Jurançon moelleux		risotto
		Vernaccia	**Grüner Veltliner**			fish cakes
	Chardonnay	Graves				savoury soufflés
		Frascati	S. Aus. Riesling			garlic mashed potatoes
	Washington & Chile whites			Blush wines		
	Semillon Viognier			White Zinfandel		lemon grass
	Bourgogne Mâcon	S. African Chardonnay		Ste-Croix-du-Mont		
	Cal. Sauvignon Blanc	Pinot Blanc				
				Monbazillac		battered fish
						sweet breads
	Pouilly-Fuissé	dry Muscat				
13	Provence rosé Portuguese & Spanish whites					tapenade
	Village Burgundy					
	Côtes-du-Rhône					
	Premier Cru Burgundy			Loupiac		crab
		Aus. & Cal. Chardonnay		Alsace Vendange Tardive		red mullet
	Retsina					tuna / ham
	Pinot Gris d'Alsace			Alsace SGN		curry sauce
	Châteauneuf-du-Pape		**Gewürztraminer**			
	Aus. Semillon					chops
				Barsac		roast meat
13.5	Grand Cru Burgundy	Hermitage	Tavel rosé	Tokay 5 puttonyos		
		Mediterranean whites		Sauternes		
15	Manzanilla		Vin Santo			olives
17	Fino			S. French Muscats		chorizo
	Dry Amontillado	Sercial		Marsala		nuts
			Amontillado			
	Dry Oloroso					
			Bual Oloroso		Malaga	
				Pale Cream		
				Malmsey	Cream Sherry	
18				Moscatel	PX	

and asterisked reds (which are sweet). Of course there is wide variation between different examples of the same wine type. Warmer climates and years produce fuller bodied wines and vice versa. Tannin levels drop dramatically with age (see pages 39–41) and can vary according to the year's weather and wine-making techniques. Variation is particularly marked between different regions' renditions of a single grape variety, although I have marked an average spot for varietal (see page 48) examples of the main ones in bold.

RED	SOFT	MEDIUM TANNINS	HARD	TOUGH AS OLD BOOTS	%Alc
	Sangria*				9
	vin de table				
baked / scrambled eggs	Nouveau				
	German reds	Alsace reds			
	Gamay	Lambrusco* cheap Italian reds			10
		vino de mesa			
		AC Beaujolais			
poached chicken		Bardolino			
plain pasta		cru Beaujolais			
		vin de pays Valpolicella			
	Eastern European reds				11
cold cuts / charcuterie		AC Bourgogne			
carpaccio	red Loire	**Cabernet Franc**	Portuguese reds		
			AC Bordeaux		
			Sangiovese		
	Pinot Noir	**Barbera**			
roast chicken		village Burgundy	Chianti Classico		12
pizza		**Merlot**			
bresaola		Navarre Languedoc ACs	**Cabernet Sauvignon**		
turkey and trimmings	**Dolcetto**	Premier Cru Burgundy Cahors **Syrah**			
			Madiran		
duck	Oregon Pinot Noir	Côtes-du-Rhône Provence			
roast lamb		Chile & Washington reds	Médoc		
aïoli	Cal. Pinot Noir	Rioja St-Émilion	Graves		
sauce bolognese			Cal. Cabernet Sauvignon		
lamb shanks		Grand Cru Burgundy Pomerol			
		Pinotage Aus. Cabernet Sauvignon Supertuscans			
lentils			Ribera del Duero		
roast beef		Côte-Rôtie			
teriyaki		**Zinfandel**	Douro red		13
steak			Hermitage		
boeuf bourguignonne		Mediterranean reds **Nebbiolo**			
venison			Vino Nobile di Montepulciano		
game					
osso buco		Shiraz			
		Southern Italian reds Brunello di Montalcino			
sausages		Châteauneuf-du-Pape			
jugged hare			Barbaresco		
		traditional Argentine			
			Barolo		14
		North African reds			
			Amarone		16
		Banyuls*			
strong cheese	ruby port*	Recioto*			18
	tawny port*				
			vintage port*		20

This chart is my personal adaptation of a graphic cleverly devised by Michael Broadbent MW in his classic handbook *Wine Tasting*.

Key

BA/TBA – *Beerenauslese/Trockenbeerenauslese*
QbA – *Qualitätswein bestimmter Anbaugebiet*
PX – *Pedro Ximénez*
Cal. – *California   Aus. – Australian*
AC – *Appellation Contrôlée, i.e. generic version*
SGN – *Sélection de Grains Nobles*
* *indicates sweet red*
Grape varieties are in bold

WINE AND HEALTH

Wine contains alcohol, which is just one of the many reasons I like it so much. A glass of wine can lift the spirits and make the world seem a very much more attractive place. But alcohol has the power to change our behaviour, and in particular to make us less careful, which is why I try never to drink without thinking of the consequences. I try to limit my wine drinking to times, places and circumstances in which the effects of alcohol are minimized or easy to cope with – with food, in the evening, relaxing either at home or somewhere I won't have to drive from, for example.

Wine's alcohol content is also my most serious occupational hazard. Conventionally the palate is thought to be most suited to professional wine tasting in the morning, so many is the day on which I've tasted 80 wines before lunchtime. Like all professional wine tasters I carefully spit out every mouthful, but some alcohol always enters the system, either as dribbles of liquid or as vapour, so it takes enormous control and determination to feel stone cold sober after a wine tasting (which may be one of the reasons why everyone in the wine trade seems so frightfully nice).

In the days before proper sanitation, wine was regarded as a much healthier drink than water, because the alcohol and particular acid it contains kill off almost all bacteria that are harmful to man. Wine was regularly prescribed by doctors well into the twentieth century but for many decades we wine drinkers have received less encouraging messages.

Drinking too much alcohol can lead to alcohol dependency, accidents, liver damage and dementia. Connections have been made between heavy drinking and cancer of the mouth, strokes, raised blood pressure, increased infertility. A host of other unwelcome conditions have also been reported, which for much of the 1980s cast a shadow over even light social drinking. And in the United States women have been persuaded that any alcohol consumption during pregnancy 'may lead to birth defects', a message printed on every bottle of wine in commercial circulation.

The more recent news that there may be some positive health benefits from light to moderate drinking is therefore particularly welcome. Any sensible person can imagine how alcohol can relieve stress, but it has taken some rigorous research to demonstrate that drinking one or two glasses of red wine a day may help to reduce the risk of heart disease, the most common killer in Western society. It seems that the phenolics (see page 73) that distinguish red wine from white reduce the amount of cholesterol deposited in the arteries, making heart attacks less likely.

In the late 1980s British medical authorities issued 'safe limits' for average drinkers of 14 'units' of alcohol a week for women and 21 for men (women's body tissue being more prone to alcohol-related damage). A 'unit' of alcohol is one-ninth of an average bottle of wine whose alcoholic strength is 12 per cent (see pages 36–7). To some of us these limits seem very conservative. I drink between a third and half of a bottle of wine most evenings and am consoled by the fact that safe limits are based on people's own reporting of how much they drink. When you gross up any representative survey of how much Britons say they drink, you find it is almost exactly half as much as HM Customs *know* they consume.

Which neatly brings us to hangovers. Self-inflicted injury is by far the worst sort. Drinking at least as much water as wine can help enormously, as does a good painkiller, particularly one that contains ibuprofen, after really serious celebrations.

See also page 57 for information on wines for special medical conditions.

WHETHER TO STORE WINE

It is difficult to devote 20 years of your life to commenting on wine without developing some bees in your bonnet. One of my most treasured bees concerns wine and time, and the way that so many wine producers and retailers leave their customers completely in the dark about how long to keep individual bottles, especially that minority of bottles that actually needs keeping.

Most wine made today should be drunk as young as possible, while its youthful fruit can be enjoyed. But the myth that all wine improves with age lingers on and the reality is that *far more wine is drunk too late than too early.*

Wine, like any fresh food, changes with time. But whereas most consumables deteriorate from the moment we buy them, wine is one of the very few things we buy regularly that has the capacity to change for the better. Perhaps the top 10 per cent of all reds and five per cent of all whites (and those are generous estimates) will be more pleasurable and more interesting to drink when they are five years old than at one year old. The top one per cent of all wine made has the ability to improve for a decade or two or, in some cases, even more. The great majority of all wine, however, will actually start to lose the fruitiness that gives it youthful appeal within six months of being bottled. But how is the poor old consumer to identify which bottles to store lovingly and which to consume as fast as he or she possibly can?

The supermarkets, to give them credit, have responded quite well to this problem in recent years. Many back labels on their own bottlings give specific advice on when to open them (typically 'within six months to a year of purchase'). But it can be extremely difficult to get reliable advice on when to open finer wines. How many people realize, for example, that the most expensive bottles of red wine in a store are probably those least likely to give pleasure that evening – because they are the ones with a long life expectancy which have been stacked full of mouth-puckering, inky tannin and are generally commercially available only in their youth?

The most obvious candidates for long-term ageing in bottle are the reds on the right hand side of page 37, botrytized sweet wines (see pages 87–9), Loire wines made from the Chenin Blanc grape (see pages 182–4), most wines made from the Riesling grape (see pages 120–21), and grand cru white burgundy (see pages 166–9).

Much is made of a wine's need to 'settle down' after a journey and certainly any wine

Just one corner of Baroness Philippine de Rothschild's cellar under Château Mouton-Rothschild – only a dream for most of us.

with a sediment (i.e. no wine younger than five years old) will need to be stood upright for a day or two simply to allow the deposit to fall. But it is difficult to see what would be particularly traumatic for a bottle about its journey from shelf to household. The most traumatic operation a wine is ever likely to be subjected to is bottling, and many commercial bottling lines shake up the wine so much, and expose it to so much oxygen, that it can take some weeks afterwards to recover from 'bottle sickness', before all its ingredients have fully reacted with the oxygen that has dissolved in the wine. More sophisticated bottling lines treat wine more gently by using inert gas. Some wines, particularly slightly sweet, very cheap ones, may be pasteurized before bottling so that they are incapable of any change in bottle. But how is the consumer to know how long ago a wine was bottled and in what way? The best advice I can give is to relax. Unless a wine has sediment, or is extremely expensive, it can usually be opened as soon as you like.

WHAT HAPPENS WHEN WINE AGES

The more fruit, acid and phenolics (see page 73) that go into a bottle of wine at the beginning, the more complex interactions there can be between all these compounds and the more rewarding it can be to age that bottle. This means that the less water there is in the grape

DOES WINE 'TRAVEL'?

Many people who bring wine back from foreign parts are disappointed with the results and blame this on wine's supposed inability to travel. It is difficult to see what is different for a bottle of wine about a ride in a private vehicle or as hand luggage as opposed to one on the back of a container truck (the most common commercial means of transport for wine).

What this difference in perceptions illustrates is not some particular shortcoming in the wine, but the general fact that wine tasting is extremely subjective, and we tend to be in a much more receptive, forgiving mood when travelling abroad than in our own homes. Wine can and indeed does travel all the time. The only serious hazards it can be exposed to are excessive heat and sharp temperature swings which can literally boil off some of the flavour (see pages 28 and 42–3). Wines that have not been heavily filtered are particularly vulnerable to sharp swings in temperature and are often deliberately shipped only in cooler weather.

(and therefore the thicker the grape variety's skins, the drier the growing season, the less irrigation used, and the lower the yields), the more likely it is that the resulting wine will repay cellaring. Tannins and colouring matter known as anthocyans are the most obvious types of phenolics and they are what preserves red wine as these interactions occur. These and other compounds continue to interact, forming bigger and bigger complex compounds which, after a few years, are too big to remain in solution and are precipitated as sediment. So as good quality, concentrated red wine ages it becomes paler and softer to taste, while gaining considerably in the range of flavours it presents (which by now constitute a bouquet [see page 16] rather than simple aromas). Any red wine with visible sediment is likely to be relatively mature.

Even less is known about how white wine ages, although acidity is thought to be the preservative white counterpart to tannin. Undoubtedly, the longest-lived white wines are those with good extract (see page 16) but good acidity too. The fact that white wines have far fewer phenolics explains why fewer of them can last as long in bottle (although botrytis, the 'noble rot' described on pages 87–9, can preserve sweet white wines for decades). Very few rosé wines improve with age, presumably because they tend to have less acidity than white wines and far fewer phenolics than reds.

For more information see page 42.

WINES TO DRINK AS YOUNG AS POSSIBLE

It follows from the previous section that the majority of wines, made to be easy to appreciate in youth, are not worth giving 'bottle age', the jargon for what happens when wine is kept for years in sealed bottles. The economics of producing a wine selling for less than about £5 or $7 a bottle mean that there is unlikely to be a sufficient concentration of ageable ingredients in that bottle. All of the following should usually be drunk within a year of bottling, and ideally sooner when their youthful fruit is most obvious.

Table wine (Europe)

Jug wine (US)

Wine in boxes or cans

Most inexpensive varietals (with the possible exceptions of some Cabernet Sauvignon)

Most vins de pays

Nouveau/primeur/novello wines

Branded wines (with the exception of better vintages of branded red bordeaux)

Germany's QbA wines

Rosé and blush wines

Asti and Moscato Spumante

Vermouth, basic port, most sherry, all spirits, sweet Muscats

The most common examples of the white wines in the top left hand corner of the chart on page 36 and those down the left hand side of the red wine chart on page 37.

WINES THAT REPAY KEEPING

In very general terms, the more expensive a bottle, the more it will repay bottle ageing. One simple clue to how long to keep a bottle is (yet again) the principal grape variety from which it was made. Below are some rough guide-lines with an approximate number of years in bottle in brackets (although there is considerable variation between wine regions and different vintage conditions). Remember that storage conditions can affect the rate at which wine ages. See page 42.

Red wines

Aglianico of Taurasi (4–15)

Baga of Barraida (4–8)

Cabernet Sauvignon (4–20)

Kadarka of Hungary (3–7)

Melnik of Bulgaria (3–7)

Merlot (2–10)

Nebbiolo (4–20)

Pinot Noir (2–8)

Plavac Mali of Croatia (4–8)

Raboso of Piave (4–8)

Sangiovese (2–8)

Saperavi of Russia (3–10)

Syrah/Shiraz (4–16)

Tannat of Madiran (4–12)

Tempranillo of Spain (2–8)

Xynomavro of Greece (4–10)

Zinfandel (2–6)

White wines

Botrytized wines (5–25)

Chardonnay (2–6)

Furmint of Hungary (3–25)

Hunter Valley Semillon (6–15)

Loire Chenin Blanc (4–30)

Petit Manseng of Jurançon (3–10)

Riesling (2–30)

WHEN WINES ARE BEST

CLASSED GROWTH BORDEAUX

NEW WORLD CHARDONNAY

NEW WORLD CABERNET

PREMIER CRU RED BURGUNDY

GOOD QUALITY RIESLING

CHEAP WHITE

CHEAP RED

high · quality · dead

0 · 2 · 4 · 6 · 8 · 10 · 12

years in bottle

How to Store Wine

Ideal storage conditions

Once it is firmly stoppered in a bottle, wine should be protected from its greatest enemy, the oxygen in the air (see page 73). If, however, the cork dries out and eventually shrinks so that it no longer acts as an airtight seal, it may start to allow oxygen into the wine, which will spoil it. For this reason, wine bottles have traditionally been stored on their sides, so that the wine keeps the cork thoroughly damp and swollen to fill the bottle-neck.

There is a revolutionary new school of thought, however, which suggests that it may be

better for wine to store bottles at an angle, which ensures that both wine and the air bubble are in contact with the cork. This will keep the cork damp but allow any expansion and contraction of the air bubble due to temperature variation to result in air, and not wine, passing through the cork. When bottles are stored horizontally the distance of the air bubble from the cork means that when higher temperatures cause it to expand, wine may be forced out between the cork and bottle-neck (the sugary deposits round the neck of many sweet wines are cited as evidence for this). Then when the temperature drops, the air bubble contracts to form a vacuum and oxygen may be drawn into the bottle. That amount of oxygen may reach harmful levels if temperatures fluctuate dramatically.

For the moment, almost all wine racks in commercial circulation are blithely ignorant of this new theory, however, so if you want to store wine in a place in which the temperature can vary by more than 10°C (18°F) it might be wise to put a wedge underneath the front of the rack so as to tilt the whole thing at the (newly) approved angle.

For the reasons outlined previously, **temperature fluctuation** is the most serious hazard for wine storage, although the cooler wine is kept, the slower, and very possibly more interestingly, it will develop. The warmer it is stored, the faster it will mature (because heat inevitably speeds up all reactions and vice versa).

A London basement in which the most common problem of all – a central heating boiler in the most suitable wine storage space – has been completely solved, by boxing in the boiler with foam-insulated, silvered panels like the one propped up on the right (used to block out sunlight in high summer).

Red wines become browner (and less blue) with time but they lose colour and become paler as tannins and colouring agents, or anthocyans, are precipitated as sediment. The one-year-old fine red bordeaux on the left will taste tough and inky, while many of the tannins have fallen out of its 12-year-old counterpart on the right, leaving a mellow, much more interesting liquid.

The left hand white wine is one year old, while that on the right has had 20 years to deepen and turn browner, as various components oxidize.

The actual **temperature** at which wine is stored is also important. Care should be taken that it never falls below −4°C (25°F), the temperature at which the lightest wines freeze, which can fatally force corks out of bottle-necks. On the other hand, there is a temperature, about 25°C (77°F), above which a wine's more volatile compounds may be boiled off forever. In very general terms the ideal wine storage temperature is probably between 10 and 15°C (40–59°F), but no great harm will come to wine stored between 15 and 20°C (59–68°F) – so long as the temperature does not fluctuate dramatically. Maximum and minimum thermometers can be very useful for monitoring potential places to store wine.

Wine dislikes **light** as well as heat. Strong light can adversely affect the taste of wine, particularly sparkling wine, and particularly if the bottles are made from clear or pale glass. (This is why wine is sold increasingly in almost black bottles, and why champagne is often wrapped in tissue paper or a special light-proof cellophane.)

Humidity is also quite important. If wine is stored in too dry an atmosphere for several years, the corks can dry out and stop being an effective seal. Damp storage places are good for the condition of the wine but can rapidly damage labels. (The Japanese will apparently pay a premium for old wine with perfect labels, whereas some British wine connoisseurs are wary of this combination.)

Lack of **vibration** is useful for wines with a sediment, although this widespread belief is based more on hunch than hard evidence, and an absence of strong **smells** is absolutely vital (no old cans of paint or garden chemicals). In practice, **security** has to be weighed against **ease of retrieval**, with the relative importance of these two factors dependent on things like your income and willpower.

THE IDEAL CELLAR

It follows from all of the above that the ideal place for wine storage is a nice, dark, roomy, slightly dank cellar with a single discreet entrance to which only you have the key. It is lined with wine racks but has masses of room to walk around and to stack wine in its original cases, as well as a little tasting corner and a large desk for keeping cellar records up to date. For most of us, alas, this cellar belongs in the realm of fantasy.

THE REALITIES OF STORING WINE AT HOME

Most modern dwellings have a shortage of storage space of any kind, let alone somewhere cool, dark, quiet, slightly damp and roomy enough for a cache of bottles. Garden sheds and all but the most protected outbuildings are unsuitable in the British climate because of the danger of the temperature's dropping below –4°C (25°F). The main problem with most possible indoor places, on the other hand, is that they are too warm. Central heating boilers tend to be put wherever there is spare storage space, which rules out storing wine there – unless the boiler can be insulated, as in the photograph on page 42. Insulation of this sort is generally the key to establishing some decent permanent territory for a large wine collection, whether of a basement, an attic, or a slice of a room which becomes a walk-in wine cellar. Many people will be unwilling to make this much commitment, however, and are really looking for somewhere to store a dozen or two bottles. They could be kept in an attic, basement or corner of a spare room under an insulation blanket, or even in an old fireplace or possibly under the stairs. It is useful if possible to keep a bowlful of water on the ground near the wine to keep the humidity level up.

Bottles can be stored in wooden wine cases, or those made from the strongest cardboard, so long as the corks are kept damp. A proper wine rack will last longer and can be made to any shape required. Double depth models are useful.

The worst place to store wine (a fact unbeknown to most kitchen designers) is by a cooker or on top of a fridge where there are frequent blasts of hot air.

If you are serious about wine there are several relatively expensive 'artificial cellars' you could buy. It is quite possible to buy a large, humidity-controlled cabinet like a refrigerator which keeps reds and whites at desirable temperatures in different parts of it, but such things can usually store only a few dozen bottles. It is also possible to buy a spiral cellar which can be sunk into a specially excavated hole under ground level, but the installation can be very messy.

TRUSTING YOUR WINE TO SOMEONE ELSE

Much the easiest option in some ways, particularly if you have a large quantity of young wine, is to have it stored by professionals, either under the auspices of the merchant(s) you bought it from or directly with one of the specialists in wine warehousing. This will cost a few pounds per year per 'case' (the standard box containing a dozen bottles) and should ensure that the wine is stored in ideal conditions, but it rules out the spontaneity of picking bottles at random from your wine collection.

GETTING SERIOUS ABOUT COLLECTING WINE

Wine sometimes gets to otherwise sane people. They are smitten with the desire to exchange large sums of money for a collection of bottles that will mature over their lifetime. They scramble for smart or rare wines offered *en primeur*, as futures, paying for it (from a respectable merchant, please) long before it's delivered. They may also fill gaps in their collections by buying older wines at auction, notably from Christie's or Sotheby's. It is a mistake to buy wine solely as an investment. Wine prices go down as well as up. But, like all forms of collecting, it can bring a great deal of pleasure (and costs much less than collecting, say, works of art). Reasonably good record-keeping is needed to ensure that wines don't languish past their drink-by dates. And some wine collectors need to be reminded every so often that *wine is for drinking!*

CLUES FROM THE PACKAGE

A wine shop is a terrifying place, with rows and rows of virtually identical packages labelled in a dizzying range of languages with hundreds of unfamiliar proper names. However is the poor consumer to pick up the clues available? Happily, the proportion of wine stores staffed by people who know one end of a bottle from the other is slowly increasing. (See pages 310–11 for some specific recommendations.) Self-service stores are also getting better at putting useful information on back labels and on the shelves themselves, but it can be difficult to get answers to the most basic questions of all, which is what I try to provide below.

BOTTLE SHAPES AND COLOUR

The bottle is the standard wine container because, supposedly, its capacity, usually 75 cl (27 fl oz), is about one lungful of air, an important consideration when all bottles were individually blown. Straight-sided bottles developed to make storage easier, and the diameter of the bottleneck may well have evolved because this is roughly the thickness of the strips of bark peeled off cork trees every nine years or so to provide suitable stoppers for bottles (see page 21).

There are two basic red wine bottle shapes, the narrow, high-shouldered 'bordeaux bottle' and the wider, sloping-shouldered 'burgundy bottle' (see photographs overleaf). In very general terms wines sold in bordeaux bottles are either from the greater Bordeaux area (south west France) or are made in the image of red bordeaux, whether from Cabernet and Merlot grapes, or simply sharing red bordeaux's characteristics of being relatively tannic (i.e. slightly tough and possibly worth ageing) and not very full bodied (such as most reds from the Languedoc, Central Italy and Portugal). Red wines in burgundy bottles are typically from greater Burgundy (including Beaujolais and Mâcon), or

from the Rhône valley, or are made from Pinot Noir grapes, or are meant to taste softer and perhaps more full bodied than average. Rioja producers, for example, quite often produce wines in these two different styles, bottled in the two different shapes.

Red bordeaux producers (and those making other long-lived wines such as Barolo, Barbaresco and vintage port) have been putting their wines into darker and darker glass because of the threat of damage by strong light (see page 42) to these wines designed for the long term. Burgundy has traditionally been put into pale green glass, possibly acknowledging that red burgundy does not usually need to be kept as long as red bordeaux.

There are three different basic white wine shapes: the bordeaux and burgundy shapes plus a taller, slimmer shape, which is used for more aromatic wines such as those from Germany and Alsace, and from Riesling and Riesling-like grapes generally. Green glass is used for Mosel, Alsace and lighter bodied wines, while brown glass often signifies a heavier wine or one from Germany's Rhine regions.

The bordeaux shape is used for white bordeaux, in clear glass for most sweet wines and green glass for dry wines (although clear glass is used for some dry wines too). It is also used for a wide range of sweet wines and dry wines from the Bordeaux grapes Sauvignon Blanc and Semillon and for a wide variety of lightish dry whites. The high alcoholic strength and extract of sweet wines means that most can withstand the exposure to light they get from clear glass quite well, but a producer has usually to be confident of a fast turnover to put a light dry white into clear glass.

The standard white burgundy bottle is made of pale greenish-yellow (*feuille morte* or 'dead leaf') glass and is widely used for all sorts of white wines, especially those which, like white burgundy, are dry, full bodied and, often, aged in oak. This includes not just a wide range of Chardonnays but also many a Sauvignon, Semillon, and – so popular is this wine style – almost any white grape variety you can imagine.

In very general terms, therefore, *the wider the bottle, the more body it is likely to have.*

Top quality bottles are made from thick glass and often have large indentations in the base called 'punts'. Most champagne bottles (which are made of particularly heavy glass to withstand the pressure inside) have these and they enable you to pour even this bottle with one hand, the thumb anchored in the punt. A producer can save a significant amount per case by packaging wine in thin glass stoppered with a short, agglomerate cork.

Different regions and even different producers have developed their own special bottles. These can often add slightly to the cost of the wine and, especially in the case of those strange deformed assymetrical ones, add nothing whatever to its quality.

BOTTLE SIZES

You are usually charged a premium for any bottle size other than the standard one, partly because the bottling technology costs more. Half-bottles are extremely useful but wine producers hate the special bottling lines they

demand and wine scientists argue that the relatively high ratio of air to wine in a half-bottle accelerates the ageing process, sometimes to the detriment of the wine. (This problem can be even more acute for quarter-bottles.) Bottles containing 50 cl are becoming increasingly popular with health-conscious consumers.

Purists argue that magnums, containing 1.5 l or the equivalent of two standard bottles, provide the perfect size for stately wine maturation, but you are usually asked to pay a little extra for this, unless the wine is particularly cheap and cheerful. Larger sizes still are available, particularly for red bordeaux, but need buyers with a very long-term view. Larger sizes of champagne are a better idea for exhibitionists than wine lovers (see page 86).

CONTAINERS OTHER THAN BOTTLES

Today wine is sold in boxes, cartons, cans, pouches, plastic bottles and all manner of materials other than glass. Few of the materials used are as inert as glass and none has so far proved itself suitable for keeping wine for more than a few months. Wine boxes can be extremely useful for big parties and for those who want to keep on drawing off quantities smaller than a bottle at a time over a week or two, but the wine can deteriorate quite rapidly once the seal has been broken.

THE BACK LABEL

The role of the back label is conventionally to give the consumer additional information not accommodated on the front label. As con-

Typical bottles for (from left to right) white bordeaux, Semillon, Sauvignon Blanc; red bordeaux, Cabernet Sauvignon, Merlot; white burgundy, Chardonnay; red burgundy, Rhône, Loire, Pinot Noir; Rhine wines (Mosels are green glass), Rieslings; half bottle of champagne.

These two pairs of wines show just how powerful packaging is. On the left, a red bordeaux and burgundy bottled and labelled following their respective regional conventions. On the right, how the same wines would look if the bordeaux were dressed up like a burgundy and vice versa. It would take very careful study to work out that, for instance, the bottle on the far right is not bordeaux.

sumers have become more knowledgeable, the proportion of genuinely informative back labels, often giving useful production details, has risen substantially. The standard back label typically used to claim that the wine was 'made from the finest grapes, grown on the best sites, picked at the optimum moment and vinified with the greatest care'. If the wine was white it would invariably be suggested that it was drunk with fish and white meats, while red meats and cheese were routinely suggested for red wines.

THE FRONT LABEL

This is by far the most important clue to how a wine is likely to taste, although there is annoyingly little uniformity about naming wines.

The label is also effectively the wine's travel permit, which means that it has to give certain information. (Artistically minded producers sometimes put this mandatory information on something clearly meant to be a back label but pretend to officialdom that this back label is in fact the principal label rather than the technically illegal creation on the other side of the bottle. See Cloudy Bay labels on page 50.)

WHAT'S THE WINE CALLED?

It can be extremely difficult to work out which of the many rows of type on the label is actually meant to be the crucial name of the wine, although technically it should be the letters in the biggest type.

Some wines, and almost all of those made in the less traditional wine-producing countries, are named after the grape variety (or varieties) from which they are made. These are the so-called **varietal** wines called after the grape varieties detailed in Section Three (Chardonnay, Cabernet Sauvignon, etc.). This sort of naming gives the consumer a very clear idea of the sort of flavours and style he or she is likely to encounter in the bottle, which is probably why varietal labelling has become so popular.

The other, and more sophisticated, way of naming wine, that embraced by France and many other European countries, is to name it **geographically**, after the region where it was produced (such as Chablis, Bordeaux, Valpolicella, Rioja, etc.). It is much more difficult than most wine retailers realize, however, for newcomers to remember whether it's Chablis or Chardonnay that is the grape and which of them is the place.

There are thousands of wine place-names but probably no more than a score of important grape varieties. (This is just one of the reasons why I believe that knowing one's way round the major grape varieties [see Section Three] is such a useful starting-point to learning about wine.)

Branded wines tend to be named with a heavily promoted invented name such as Blue Nun or Mateus Rosé.

QUALITY DESIGNATIONS – OFTEN USEFUL

If a wine is labelled geographically, the label usually carries not just the name of the region but also the name of one of the carefully regulated quality designations listed in the table below. Division One comprises, in theory at least, the crack corps of that country's wines, whereas Division Two is the middle ranks. Division Three is included for completeness. In fact wines which qualify for these lowly titles are not usually allowed to claim any geographical provenance; they simply belong to Europe's soft underbelly of, often surplus, wine production.

The quality designations listed under Division One lay down very strict regulations about the exact land included, permitted grape varieties, yields, minimum ripeness levels and vine-growing and winemaking techniques allowed. Many New World producers are thrilled that they do not have these constraints and can plant anything they like where they like, but an increasing number of them are seeing the virtues of developing awareness of their own region (which cannot be duplicated elsewhere) and geographical labelling is generally on the increase, often supplementing varietal labelling (as in, for example, Sonoma Valley Chardonnay, Coonawarra Cabernet Sauvignon and Casablanca Sauvignon Blanc).

OFFICIAL CATEGORIES OF WINE			
COUNTRY	DIVISION ONE	DIVISION TWO	DIVISION THREE
FRANCE (see page 157)	Appellation Contrôlée[a] (AC or AOC)	Vin de Pays	Vin de Table
ITALY (see page 207)	DOCG (likeDOC but 'Garantita' too)	Denominazione di Origine Controllata (DOC)	Vino da Tavola[b]
GERMANY (see page 245)	Qualitätswein mit Prädikat (QmP)	Qualitätswein bestimmter Anbaugebiete (QbA)	Deutscher Tafelwein
SPAIN (see page 224)	Denominacíon de Origen (DO)	Vino de la Tierra	Vino de Mesa

a There is also a small category called Vin Délimité de Qualité Supérieure (VDQS) which is basically an Appellation Contrôlée-in-waiting.

b The Italian system is predictably anarchic with some of the country's finest wines qualifying only as a Vino da Tavola because they do not conform to the DOC regulations.

WHO MADE IT?

The name of the producer, or at least the bottler, should be on every wine label. In most cases this is the single most important bit of information. There can be a world of difference between a lacklustre bottler's Chablis blended to meet a price and one from a seriously quality-conscious individual with a reputation to lose. It is at this point that wine knowledge becomes complicated, but see Section Four for hundreds of names of recommended producers.

ALCOHOLIC STRENGTH

This is one of the most useful vital statistics about a wine which should be on the label of almost all wines in commercial circulation. A guide to the approximate alcoholic strength (expressed as a percentage of pure alcohol by volume) of the main types of wine is given on pages 36–7. Generally speaking, less alcoholic wines come from the coolest climates and vice versa, sunshine being converted directly into sugar in grapes, most of which is fermented into alcohol (see page 74). Although one might think that the drinker would hardly notice the difference between a 12 per cent wine and a 13 per cent one, I find that a higher alcohol wine can really catch me out the morning after, whereas most German wine is so light it can be gulped with abandon.

OTHER INFORMATION

Almost all wines in Divisions One and Two should be vintage dated. See pages 306–9 for details of specific **vintages** in specific regions. Division Three wines are not usually allowed to specify a year but are almost invariably made from the produce of the most recent vintage or, in crossover periods, a blend of the two most recent. Table wine is held in store, often lightly refrigerated, until an order is received.

Most labels should give some **bottling information**, ideally stating the wine was bottled by its producer (Estate Bottled, Gutsabfüllung, or Mis en Bouteille à...etc). This may refer simply to a mobile bottling line which visits the property and in some cases professional contract bottlers may do a better job. I am always slightly wary of wines bottled a long way from their source as it can expose the wine to more risk from temperature variation and oxygen. It can also save considerably on its cost, however, as in some of the wines shipped in bulk from Australia (where bottling costs are exceptionally high) to use up spare bottling capacity closer to their eventual consumers.

Many more precise, geographically specific clues to quality may appear on wine labels: expressions such as premier cru, cru classé, vieilles vignes, Villages, Classico, Kabinett, etc. See Section Four for more details.

WORDS FOR SWEETNESS LEVELS				
	FRENCH	ITALIAN	GERMAN	SPANISH
BONE DRY	brut	–	–	–
DRY	sec	secco	trocken	seco
MEDIUM DRY	demi-sec	abboccato	halbtrocken	semi-seco
MEDIUM SWEET	doux	amabile	mild	–
SWEET	moelleux	dolce	lieblich	dulce
VERY SWEET	liquoreux	–	süss	–
WORDS FOR FIZZINESS				
GENTLY SPARKLING	perlant	frizzante	spritzig	–
FULLY SPARKLING	mousseux	spumante	Sekt	espumoso

DECIPHERING THE LABEL

VARIETAL WINES

A pair of varietal labels from the southern hemisphere. Cloudy Bay's 'front label' is purely cosmetic, although it shows all the information vital to the consumer. (Its design is based on a photograph taken by the winemaker.) The narrower label on the back of the bottle has all the information vital to the regulators, however, and is therefore officially the main label.

3 *Name of (ambitious, up and coming) producer*

4 *Vintage (a good one for Chilean whites)*

1 *Grape variety*

5 *Wine region, still forging an identity for Chardonnay*

8 *Alcoholic strength*

FOUNDED IN 1850
CARMEN
RESERVE
1994
CHARDONNAY
MAIPO VALLEY
PRODUCED AND BOTTLED BY
CARMEN VINEYARDS LTDA.
PRODUCT OF CHILE
ALC 13.3 % BY VOL   750 ML

6 *Special bottling – although some producers use the word Reserve so loosely that in many other cases it is no guarantee of superior quality*

7 *Bottling information (actually this wine is bottled by the sister company Santa Rita just a few hundred yards away)*

2 *Country of origin*

CLOUDY BAY

SAUVIGNON BLANC 1994

CLOUDY BAY ®

MARLBOROUGH
SAUVIGNON BLANC 1994

The Cloudy Bay vineyards are situated in the lee of the Richmond Ranges in Marlborough county, at the northern tip of the South Island. With stony, free draining soils, a temperate climate and abundant sunshine, the region produces wines of unique character. Vinified with techniques that retain the distinct aromas and flavours of the variety, this is an intensely aromatic and balanced wine with appealing fruit and crisp acidity.

PRODUCED AND BOTTLED BY
CLOUDY BAY VINEYARDS LTD.,
JACKSONS ROAD, BLENHEIM.
PRESERVATIVE 220 ADDED.
PRODUCE OF NEW ZEALAND
750 ml   ALC/VOL   13.5%

4 *Name of (world-famous) producer*

3 *Wine region – already famous for Sauvignon Blanc*

5 *Vintage (a small one for NZ. Buy, buy, buy!!)*

1 *Grape variety*

6 *Bottling information: wines bottled on the winery's own bottling line*

2 *Country of origin*

7 *Alcoholic strength*

Explanations are numbered in the order I would examine the label. Grape type is usually the most important aspect of a varietal wine followed by country of origin and then producer and any more specific geographical information in an order determined by the maturity of the wine-producing country and the extent to which its wine regions have managed to establish a meaningful identity. Vintage and any other information are usually of less vital importance than in the most marginal wine regions.

GEOGRAPHICALLY NAMED WINES

A fine white and red from complex Burgundy. Note the two forms of showing the name of the controlled appellation. Also, how the Meur- sault is obviously a 'domaine bottled' wine, produced and bottled at the same small wine *domaine*, while the Chambolle-Musigny, per- haps a blend from different producers, is bottled by a large merchant, or négociant.

5 Bottling information (bottled at the cellar)

6 Alcoholic strength

2 Quality designation or appellation (Charmes is a Premier Cru vineyard within the village of Meursault)

4 Vintage – extremely important in Burgundy, excellent for white burgundy (see pages 307)

3 Name of (irreproachable) producer

1 Country of origin

3 Name of producer, an extremely reputable négociant who also owns vineyards (whose produce would be described on the label as mis en bouteille à la propriété or au domaine)

4 Bottling information for a wine made from bought-in grapes (or wine)

2 Quality designation of appellation (this 'village burgundy' can contain wine made anywhere within the village of Chambolle-Musigny)

1 Country of origin

Explanations are numbered in the order I would examine the label. If a wine is French, then the name of the appellation is paramount, and should give a fine clue as to the likely taste of the wine. The name of the producer is almost as important, though – especially in Burgundy, and in Bordeaux where the producer is usually Château Something. Vintage is generally much more important in northern Europe than elsewhere and Drouhin puts its vintages on neck labels.

HOW TO BUY THE RIGHT BOTTLE

How, faced with the array of bottles in a wine store, do you pick the right one off the shelf? Here are a few random but specific suggestions.

• Decide on a price bracket and stick to it, but it can be worth spending at the top of the bracket. Bear in mind that in Britain, where excise duty alone is about £1 a bottle, the price of the wine inside a bottle selling at £2.99 is roughly 60p, whereas there is about £1.50 worth of wine in a bottle selling at £4.99 and more than £4 worth in a bottle priced at £9.99.

• Take special offers very seriously. In the competitive market-place of today, heavily scrutinized by a bevy of wine critics, these bargains are almost certainly there to lure you into the shop rather than to offload rubbish.

• If possible, pick a bottle that has been lying on its side, and has not obviously been kept in a place where the temperature may have varied considerably. Avoid bottles which have been standing upright in strong light (although the better stores have a policy of constantly changing the one representative bottle with another from a horizontal lot).

Be wary of bottles which have 'wept' around the cork or have a relatively low fill level as both of these are signs of temperature variation (see page 42).

• Try to grasp the names at least, and ideally the characteristics, of the major grape varieties (see Section Three).

• If, once you have become relatively familiar with the most common wine names, you spot a bottle with an unrecognizable pedigree, give it a try. It is probably there only because someone passionately believes in its inherent quality; wine buyers generally err on the side of caution.

• On the subject of familiar names, the well-known international wine brands such as Mateus Rosé, Blue Nun, Black Tower, Jacob's Creek, Gallo and Mouton Cadet can offer a reliable minimum quality level in a strange place with a very limited selection but are usually relatively expensive (all that advertising has to be paid for).

• Be wary of wines designed for early consumption (see pages 39–41) that are more than two years old.

• Bear in mind that wines (especially reds) that are extremely expensive and carry vintage dates less than three or four years old are almost certainly years from being fun to drink.

• Try to remember to make a note of any wine that you particularly like so that you can use the chart opposite as a way to discover new wines with a similar style.

SOME PARTICULARLY CONFUSING NAMES:

Pouilly-Fuissé (pronounced 'Pwee-Fwee-say') is the most concentrated white wine of the Mâconnais between Beaujolais and Burgundy proper and is a broad, full bodied wine made from Chardonnay grapes. Pouilly-Fumé, on the other hand, is very like Sancerre, a piercingly aromatic Loire relatively light, tart, dry white made from Sauvignon Blanc grapes.

Muscadet is a bone dry, somewhat neutral white from the mouth of the Loire while Muscat is the name of a particularly fruity grape variety usually made into very sweet, strong wines, also sold under the name Moscato and Moscatel.

Semillon is a grape variety which makes full bodied white wines, notably in Bordeaux and Australia. St-Émilion, on the other hand, is the name of a pretty town in the Bordeaux region, and the deep-coloured, plummy red wines made around it.

SOME RELATIVELY UNDERPRICED WINES

The market changes all the time according to the weather (e.g. crop reduction caused by frost damage), fashion and supply, but the following wines were better bargains than most at the time of writing.

Whites

Modern Spanish Vino de Mesa
The best Corbières, Minervois and Coteaux du Languedoc, from individual estates
Chilean Sauvignon and Chardonnay
Hungarian varietals
South African Colombard and Chenin
Vins de Pays des Côtes de Gascogne
Better AC Bordeaux and Entre-Deux-Mers
Alsace Pinot Blanc
Menetou Salon, Quincy and Reuilly
Mature fine German wines
Australian traditional method sparkling wines

Reds

The best Corbières, Minervois and Coteaux du Languedoc, from individual estates
Chilean Cabernet, Merlot and some Pinot Noir
Hungarian varietals
Montepulciano d'Abruzzo
Valdepeñas
Ribatejo
Alentejo
AC Bordeaux
Premières Côtes de Bordeaux
Oak-aged Piedmont Barbera

HOW TO TRY A NEW WINE

Here are some possible routes from some of the most popular wines to less familiar names offering better value and/or a slight variation on the taste.

Whites

Chardonnay

LIGHT, CRISP	FULL, OAKY
Chablis	Semillon Chardonnay
Pinot Blanc	Semillon
Chardonnay, Vin de Pays d'Oc	Bordeaux blanc (oaked)
Limoux	Graves
New Zealand Chardonnay	White Châteauneuf-du-Pape
Sauvignon Blanc	Fino sherry or Manzanilla
Jurançon Sec	

Sancerre/Pouilly-Fumé

New Zealand Sauvignon Blanc
Chilean Sauvignon
Fumé Blanc from anywhere
Slovenian whites
Friuli whites
Riesling!

Liebfraumilch

German Spätlese
Riesling Kabinett
Alsace Riesling
any Alsace white
any Gewürztraminer or Traminer
any Pinot Gris
Argentine Torrontes
Albariño/Alvarinho
Viognier
Condrieu

Reds

Cabernet Sauvignon

LIGHT, AROMATIC	CRISP, CRUNCHY	OAKY, TANNIC	MELLOW, ROUND
Cabernet Franc	Teroldego	Syrah	Merlot
Anjou-Villages	Tempranillo	Hermitage	Bordeaux
Bourgueil	Sangiovese	Nebbiolo	St-Émilion
Chinon	Chianti Classico	Barbaresco	Pomerol
Cru Beaujolais	Brunello	Barolo	New World Pinot
Old World Pinot Noir	Supertuscans	Douro reds	
Burgundy			
Overdraft			

CHOOSING WINE IN A RESTAURANT

Thanks to the advent of self-service in wine retailing, about the only time we have to make a public statement about wine and our wine preferences is when ordering in a restaurant, pub or bar. In fact for most consumers this is probably the only time that they have actually to pronounce wine names, and it is certainly the time that they pay most for the pleasure of drinking wine.

HOW MUCH TO PAY

It is standard practice in restaurants with high overheads to calculate prices on the wine list by doubling, trebling and sometimes even quadrupling the basic wholesale prices. It is naive to expect a restaurateur to sell wine at exactly the same price as a wine retailer. He or she has all sorts of extra bills to pay, not to mention the cost of building up a cellar. But you can ensure that the premium you pay for drinking wine in a restaurant is kept to a minimum: wherever a straight percentage mark-up is applied it is pure folly to go for one of the seriously grand wines and *it makes sound financial sense to order one of the cheapest bottles on the wine list.*

A benevolent minority of restaurateurs add something closer to a standard cash mark-up to all bottles, no matter what the price, in order to encourage customers to buy something special to go with what one hopes is a superior standard of cooking. Unfortunately, however, you need to know quite a lot about wine and wine prices to take advantage of this sensible approach.

SOME SAFE CHOICES

The following have been chosen because they are relatively inexpensive, go with a wide range of foods, and poorly made examples are relatively rare. See also previous page.

Whites
• South African Sauvignon Blanc (cheap but can be thin).
• Alsace whites, especially please-all Pinot Blanc.
• Many Chardonnays, especially St-Véran and other Mâconnais whites and good bottlings from California and Australia.

Reds
• Corbières, Minervois and Coteaux de Languedoc with a Château or Domaine name.
• Beaujolais-Villages or cru Beaujolais (i.e. Morgon, Moulin-à-Vent, Juliénas, Chénas, Regnié, Brouilly, Côte-de-Brouilly, Fleurie, St-Amour and Chiroubles).
• Estate bottled Côtes-du-Rhône and Gigondas Bourgueil, Chinon, Anjou-Villages.
• Zinfandel (restaurateurs don't usually list the dross).

THE GREAT TASTING RITUAL

The joke about this often embarrassing restaurant practice is that few of those who offer or taste the initial sample from the bottle ordered have a clue why they are doing it. The great wine-tasting ritual has its origins in a time when the wine was much less reliably stable and healthy than it has become.

The customer is meant to be checking the temperature and that the wine is not out of condition (corked, oxidized, refermenting, hazy). To check this, all you need do is look to see that the wine is clear and still (unless it is meant to be sparkling) and then smell it to ensure it smells clean and not musty or mouldy. *This tasting has nothing to do with whether you like the wine or not.* You can send the wine back only if it has one of the faults listed above, in which case the restaurateur can return it to the supplier and get a refund or replacement. Because I am paranoid about seeming a fussy wine bore, I probably err on the side of caution, but I have sent wine back only three or four times in 20 years of tasting wine and dining out, by saying 'I think this wine is corked/oxidized/refermenting/hazy'. The wine should be presented, by the way, to whoever ordered it. It is then up to them to suggest someone else tastes it if they'd rather. Despite the ceremony of some wine waiters, or 'sommeliers', sniffing the cork is no reliable guide to the condition of the wine.

Wine with bits of cork floating in it, by the way is not 'corked'. These are harmless cork fragments which may be the result of an inefficient corkscrew. They should simply be scooped out with a spoon (although many waiters have the annoying habit of whisking away the entire glass – of wine you have paid for – and pouring a new one).

A wine that complements your mood and meal certainly need not be the most expensive.

WINE BY THE GLASS

This is a fantastically good idea, imaginatively executed by most American restaurants and completely ruined in most British pubs. Now that wine is such a democratic drink (and usually well made), and it is so easy to preserve wine leftovers (see pages 23–5), there is no excuse for serving out-of-condition filth by the glass.

SOME COMMONLY MISPRONOUNCED NAMES		
	CORRECT	INCORRECT
Riesling	Reece-ling	Rize-ling
Moët	Mow-it	Mo-way
Montrachet	Mon-rashay	Mont-rashay

SOME SPECIAL WINES

REDUCED ALCOHOL WINES

Some wines are naturally low in alcohol, either because they are produced somewhere far from the equator such as the Mosel valley with limited amounts of sunshine to produce fermentable sugar in the grapes or because, like Asti, the fermentation is deliberately stopped half-way through to produce a sweet, low alcohol wine.

As we have become more aware of our alcohol intake, however, all sorts of semi-industrial low-alcohol and no-alcohol wine-like products have been concocted. Most of them taste decidedly unlike wine. The Lambrusco producers willing to offer a Lambrusco Light (and White, and Pink) are not exactly among the noble Italian region's most respected. The dealcoholized Ariel range from California and Loxton products from the Australian wine giant Southcorp are more convincing than most, but they do strike me as quintessentially substitute products, just like nut cutlets. Why fashion something without ingredient X in the mould of those things that contain X? A really good soft drink (see page 32) or a spritzer (see below) usually gives me more pleasure.

COMMERCIAL WINE MIXES AND COOLERS

Commercial bottled blends of fruit juices and wine sell in relatively vast quantities. The development of artificial essences of peach, apricot, raspberry and so on have helped this trade enormously. When it comes down to it, some of the best are duplications of the most successful fresh mixes of wine and fruit juice – orange juice and sparkling wine (Buck's Fizz) and peach juice and sparkling wine (Bellini). The commercial brands can taste a bit artificial, however, and are invariably very sweet.

WINE MIXES TO MAKE AT HOME

Buck's Fizz, a blend of dry sparkling white wine with one to two times as much fresh orange juice, makes a great Sunday morning refresher. It's useful for a short party but a bit wearing after two glasses (and fresh juice can make washing up the glasses tricky). A **Bellini** is a Venetian version in which peach juice is substituted for orange juice. It is best made with jars of Italian peach juice which is incredibly thick. To allow the bubbles to escape with more abandon, dilute the juice with some water. The Irish mix Guinness stout with dry fizz to produce the powerful **Black Velvet**. Drink with caution.

Perhaps the simplest mix, and the most refreshing aperitif in hot weather, is a **Spritzer**, made up of roughly equal parts of white wine and sparkling water.

Another way of livening up a glass of dull or neutral dry white is to add enough blackcurrant cordial or the alcoholic version from Burgundy, crème de cassis (about half a teaspoonful), to make a pale pink, fruity **Kir** or **vin blanc cassis**. Served with sparkling wine it becomes a **Kir Royale**, with red wine a **Cardinale**. You can substitute other strong fruit cordials.

Any red wine, even the cheapest and nastiest, can provide a base for the spicy, warming brew known as **Glühwein** or **mulled wine**. Gently heat three to five bottles of red wine with an orange studded with cloves, a cinnamon stick and white sugar, and possibly a little lemon juice. The alcohol is boiled off unless you are careful about how the mixture is heated. Once warmed, it is best left on a low heat as the first duty of mulled wine is to be hot.

LOW-CALORIE WINE?

Wine is not slimming. The two components which contribute to its calorific value are alcohol and sugar, so the most fattening wines are those in the bottom right hand corner of page 36 and the asterisked examples in the lower half of page 37. The least calorific are those in the top left hand corner of page 36 and those along the top of page 37. It is by no means the case that white wine is less fattening than red, nor that dry wines are necessarily low in calories (all the wines in the bottom half of page 37 are relatively high in calories).

WINES FOR SPECIAL MEDICAL CONDITIONS

Diabetics should take care to choose bone dry wines, which means any wine down the left hand side of page 36 and any red wine except the ones asterisked on page 37. Wines sold specifically as Diabetic are usually low in both sugar and alcohol.

Many people find that their bodies react badly to either white or red wines. Since red wines contain a much wider range of components than white, the second of these reactions is easier to understand and some think it may reflect red wine's histamine content. Perhaps the white wines which have caused an allergic reaction are rather higher than most in sulphur (see page 73) and some asthmatics react particularly badly to this common food preservative.

Much more research is needed in this area, but the wine trade is generally composed of people who react extremely well to wine and there has therefore been little enthusiasm for this research.

Some wine drinkers report that they feel much better after drinking organic wines (see page 65) rather than those produced using agrochemicals.

Since some finings (see page 73) contain animal products (egg whites, fish bladders and casein from milk), some wine producers deliberately use other finings so that they can offer their produce as vegan wines. It should be noted, however, that finings are not designed to remain in the finished wine.

NOUVEAU, NOVELLO AND ALL THAT

The Beaujolais producers had such enormous success with their Beaujolais Nouveau released in November that a flood of similar infant wine has flowed onto the market. These wines are generally light in body and alcohol and are fermented and stabilized at top speed so that they can be sold just a few weeks after the harvest. Very good for the cash flow. The Gamay grape of Beaujolais does lend itself to this somewhat brutal treatment and versions from the Loire valley, notably Gamay de Touraine, have been quite successful. The craze spread downriver to the Muscadet region for a white version. Some of these French wines are labelled Primeur rather than Nouveau. Italy has its own riposte in various wines labelled Novello, while the New World has also tried its hand. None of these wines is desperately exciting, and they rarely improve in bottle, but they don't decline quite as rapidly as some authorities would have us believe. I have drunk a five-year-old Beaujolais Nouveau and lived.

COOKING WITH WINE

There is a school of thought that any wine used in cooking should be top quality and/or of the same region as the dish. I find this hard to accept, particularly as so little research has been done on exactly what happens to wine when you cook with it. I am sure that if the wine in the dish (as in steeped strawberries, for example) is never heated, then it is worth choosing one that tastes as delicious as you can afford. If you want to reduce a sauce using wine, however, I would have thought you wanted one with as much body as possible – and that the wine's components may go through so many transformations that the initial flavour could not possibly be preserved. More research, please! Meanwhile, in our household we will continue to see cooking as a particularly satisfying way of using up wine leftovers.

2
HOW WINE IS MADE

THE IMPORTANCE OF PLACE

There is a saying in the restaurant business that the three factors which determine whether an establishment will be a success are location, location and location. In wine production place is not quite that important. The vineyard's location is just one of four main factors determining how a wine tastes. The others, in roughly decreasing order of how powerfully they can shape a wine's character, are the vine variety or varieties used (see pages 100–153), how the wine is made (see pages 74–93), and how the vines are grown (see pages 64–71). The most obvious reason why a vineyard's location is important is because it determines its weather and climate, but it has many other, more subtle but potentially crucial effects on the wine produced from it (see pages 62–3).

WEATHER AND CLIMATE

The weather that makes up the climate of a wine region, the so-called **macroclimate**, defines whether grape-growing is an activity that is (a) feasible and (b) commercially sensible. So long as there is enough warmth to ripen grapes every year, and winters are cool enough to give vines a restorative winter break, vine-growing can be a profitable agricultural activity.

The map opposite, showing the distribution of the world's wine regions, indicates how vine-growing, or viticulture, is essentially confined to two temperate bands around the globe, with local exceptional conditions resulting in a bit of manipulation here and there. Many of Mexico's best vineyards, for example, are so high that their altitude compensates for their relatively low latitude. England's vineyards, on the other hand, may be further from the equator than any others but warm ocean currents help to moderate the climate, so that vines need no special protection in winter, unlike many of their counterparts in Canada and Russia.

Dangerously cold winters apart, the main problem for vine-growers in cool climates is that in some years the grapes may not reach full ripeness, so that the sugar content of the juice needs additional help to ferment into the sort of alcohol levels we expect from wine (see chaptalization, page 72). Unreliable weather during the vine flowering in late spring can also cause havoc to vine-growing economics by severely affecting the number of flowers that are fertilized and therefore the number of grapes produced (see page 69).

Regions with high rainfall, however hot or cold they are, bring their own problems to vine-growing: fungal diseases such as various rots and mildews which flourish in damp conditions and usually demand frequent and expensive spraying to keep them at bay. Vine pests are becoming increasingly tolerant to many of these chemical preparations however, and every growing season sees more and more converts to some form of organic viticulture (see page 65).

Many very dry climates are quite capable of producing reasonably good wine, provided enough water is available for irrigation. Many of the vineyards of Chile and, especially, Argentina depend for their existence on irrigation channels dug, often a century ago, to direct the melting snows of the Andes into the land beneath them. Irrigation is not necessarily an evil thing designed to produce huge crops of dilute wine, although because it can be (and because northern Europe has quite enough water from the sky without recourse to ditches, sprinklers, or drip systems) the practice is regarded with deep suspicion by European lawmakers. In much of the New World, irrigation is an economic necessity. Without it a very substantial proportion of the vineyards of, for example, the United States and Australia simply could not exist as wine production centres. Almost all new vineyards in climates with an average minimum annual rainfall of less than about 500 mm (20 in), or 700 mm (28 in) in hotter climates, are automatically designed to incorporate irrigation systems. Many of these systems are sophisticated enough to apply doses of water carefully determined by precise measurements of the amount of water in the soil at various times during the growing season.

Because in general terms the flavour elements in a grape need as long as possible to develop, and so the longer it takes for grapes to ripen the better, it is difficult to produce good quality wine too close to the equator. Problems also occur in such areas partly because tropical rains can result in galloping fungal disease (a problem in Japan and parts of China), and partly because where there is no winter the vine keeps on producing not-particularly-ripe fruit. In Brazil and Kenya, for example, vines may produce two or three crops a year, in 'seasons' artificially manipulated by careful timing of pruning and irrigation.

In some of the world's warmer wine regions some really determined vine-growers may also combat nature by using chemicals which encourage buds to burst or persuade the vine to stop growing.

Specific hazards of weather (as opposed to more general climate disadvantages) are described on pages 68–71, the vineyard year.

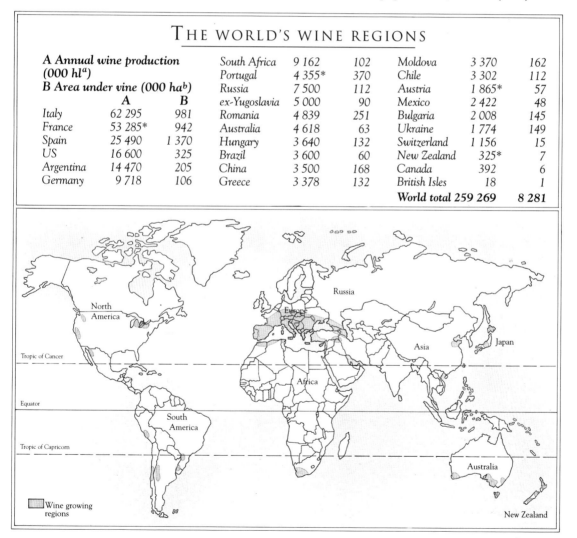

THE WORLD'S WINE REGIONS

A Annual wine production (000 hl[a])
B Area under vine (000 ha[b])

	A	B		A	B		A	B
Italy	62 295	981	South Africa	9 162	102	Moldova	3 370	162
France	53 285*	942	Portugal	4 355*	370	Chile	3 302	112
Spain	25 490	1 370	Russia	7 500	112	Austria	1 865*	57
US	16 600	325	ex-Yugoslavia	5 000	90	Mexico	2 422	48
Argentina	14 470	205	Romania	4 839	251	Bulgaria	2 008	145
Germany	9 718	106	Australia	4 618	63	Ukraine	1 774	149
			Hungary	3 640	132	Switzerland	1 156	15
			Brazil	3 600	60	New Zealand	325*	7
			China	3 500	168	Canada	392	6
			Greece	3 378	132	British Isles	18	1
						World total	**259 269**	**8 281**

Wine growing regions

[a] hectolitres (100 litres) – approx. 133 bottles   [b] hectares (2.5 acres)
Totals for the most significant wine-producing countries according to the Office International du Vin's figures for 1993, when the countries marked * suffered a particularly small grape harvest.

DOES THE ANSWER LIE IN THE SOIL?

While the macroclimate of a wine region may govern whether it is capable of producing ripe wine grapes at all, the subtle characteristics of a much smaller area – a particular vineyard, or even part of a vineyard – may determine the sort of wine that can be produced from that area. These characteristics include the climate of that smaller area, its **mesoclimate** (for long called its 'microclimate', but see page 66 for more up-to-date usage); its soil; the lie of the land, or its topography; and the effects each of these three elements have on each other. Any gardener, or even garden observer such as myself, can see at a glance (on a frosty morning, for example) how each part of the garden is heavily influenced by all these characteristics.

The French, typically, have one elegant word for this long list of natural characteristics: **terroir**. Indeed they have based their entire wine industry on the premise that a wine's characteristics are uniquely determined by the terroir, the natural environment, of the place in which the grapes were grown (see pages 48–9 and 157 for a description of the famous appellation contrôlée system). One has only to look at the complicated, hierarchical patchwork of different vineyards and appellations in Burgundy's Côte d'Or (see pages 166–8) to see how fundamental is this principle in grading and pricing fine burgundy. The produce of one vineyard separated only by a narrow track from another, lowlier one may fetch three or four times as much. To the outsider this seems like hocus pocus, and the argument would certainly be a lot more convincing if all wine experts could immediately identify which vineyard a wine comes from when blind tasting. But there is no denying that an individual producer's wine from a humble Bourgogne Blanc vineyard is always discernibly less concentrated than his or her smart Premier Cru white burgundy, which

itself rarely develops the grandeur of a Grand Cru. (One producer's Bourgogne Blanc may be better than another's Grand Cru, but that is another story.)

Because in very well-established wine regions such as Bordeaux and Burgundy it was possible to map wine quality, and therefore to rank individual vineyards, for long it was thought that it was the individual chemical composition of the soil of each vineyard that uniquely determined the sort and quality of wine it could produce. Much human effort over the years has gone into studying the individual geology of specific sites and there was a time when it seemed impossible to be a real wine expert without detailed knowledge of Quaternary deposits and Bathonian oolitic limestone. No one could have been more delighted than me to discover that more recent research suggests the chemical composition of a vineyard's soil, subsoil and underlying rock is very much less important than their physical characteristics, the most important factors that contribute to wine quality being that the soil is not too fertile, and is well drained but can store water within reach of vine roots so that the vine always has a steady but not excessive supply of water. The gravels of the Médoc, the clays of Pomerol, the marly limestone of the best Côte d'Or vineyards all fit these conditions and put the natural energy provided by sunlight into ripening fruit rather than producing too many leaves. Too much water means too much foliage at the expense of fruit.

Man can manipulate terroir by irrigation, or by persuading vines to grow in particular shapes (see page 64), but in the classical Old World wine regions terroir has been very much left to dictate what sort of wine is produced from a given site. Since sites for New World vineyards tend to be chosen because of pragmatic reasons (the grower happens to own the land, for example, or the plot happens to be for sale), then the argument that terroir is all-important becomes far less attractive. Some French in particular have also left wine producers in the New World with the vague but implicit notion that because terroir is a French word, and because only the French have fully mapped their vineyards, only French

Just a glance at these vineyards demonstrates how their precise angle and altitude affects, for example, how much sunshine they receive, how sheltered they are from the wind, and how much soil erosion is likely.

vineyards have terroir! All spots on the globe have their own terroir of course, and there is no reason to suppose that the French, or indeed Europeans, have any kind of monopoly on suitable terroirs for fine wine production – it's just that the New World is a few hundred years behind most Europeans in finding them (and its vine-growers are more accustomed to manipulating them).

63

GROWING VINES

Only a few, ground-breaking vine-growers have a choice about the location of their vineyard, but they all have many **viticultural** choices about exactly how to grow the vines they plant there. For many Old World vine-growers, those choices are never consciously made; they probably live in an area which has evolved a way of growing vines that is perfectly adapted to their local conditions, their terroir (see page 62). On the poor, pebbly soils of the Médoc in Bordeaux, for example, vines are densely planted in low, neat, hedges in vineyards that are as carefully drained as finances allow. (The first thing the Mentzelopoulos family did when they acquired Château Margaux in 1978 was to dig miles of drainage ditches to avoid their precious first growth vines' ever being waterlogged and becoming lazy about ripening fruit.)

Any tourist travelling around the wine regions of the world will notice some very obvious differences between how vineyards look, but because so many of the world's vine-growers simply do what their neighbours do or predecessors did, they are not always able to describe *why* their vineyards look as they do with the vines trained in a variety of ways.

The average Spanish peasant, for example, would probably be amazed by the difference in **vine density** between his vineyards and those of northern France – about 1400 and 10 000 vines per hectare respectively (560 and 4050 per acre). A tiny area of the relatively infertile soils of wet northern France can support one vine and good quality fruit, whereas a vine planted on the arid plains of La Mancha needs to draw on a large area of soil moisture to survive at all.

Vine density is also a function of **row spacing**, which can vary considerably. Old World vineyards tend to have just enough space between rows of vines for people or horses to move easily, and the advent of mechanization

has simply meant that vineyard machinery is designed to straddle the relatively low, neat vine rows. Many New World vineyards were designed to be worked by tractor right from the start and rows can be as much as 3 m (9 ft) apart, needing much less investment in young plants, but with what look like wastefully wide margins to allow machines to turn at either end.

There are many different theories about **row orientation**, whether vine rows should go north–south or east–west to maximize exposure to the sun and/or protect vines from the wind, and whether they should follow contours or go directly uphill. Following contours minimizes soil erosion, particularly when special terraces are built, and makes the vineyard much easier for humans and machines to work. In places where vine rows go directly uphill and down dale, such as the Mosel and Côte-Rôtie, individual vines may be trained on stakes instead of along restrictive wires so that the vineyard workers don't have to combine mountaineering with vineyard maintenance and picking.

One particularly obvious viticultural divide is between old-fashioned, relatively arid vineyards in which vines grow unsupported like wild bushes, and vines that are deliberately trained on stakes or along wires to control the leafiness, or **vigour**, of the vine. This helps prevent the spread of vine diseases and can also force the vine into the particular shapes deemed suitable for various combinations of vine variety, terroir and mesoclimate. In fertile soils a vine's natural tendency is to produce a luxuriant growth of leaves, or **canopy**, that can thoroughly distract from the process of yielding grapes, and can even hide the grapes from the sunlight that is so vital to ripening them. Excess irrigation and high rainfall exacerbate this pro-vegetation, anti-fruit situation. **Canopy management** is all about sculpting the vine into the most efficient grape factory. The precise climate of the leafy

ORGANIC AND OTHER VINES

One of the major reasons why average yields (usually measured in volume of wine per unit of land) have increased dramatically since the 1960s is the widespread use of chemicals, both as fertilizers and sprays, to combat the spread of rot and other fungal diseases of the vine (see page 96). Crops which were once decimated by a humid spell during ripening could be saved by a spraying or three, or sometimes as many as 10 or 12.

As in so many other forms of agriculture, and horticulture, an increasing number of growers have begun to wonder whether the sustained use of agrochemicals is such a good idea. Some of them are motivated by concern for the environment and possible pollution from chemical residues; some want to minimize the risk of any residues in the wine; some are inspired by the obvious deterioration in the quality of the soil after years of repeated applications of the same chemicals; while others, more hard-nosed perhaps, are simply exasperated by vine pests' increasing tolerance to the conventional preparations.

Whatever the reasons, there is a perceptible shift in viticultural philosophy world-wide towards more 'natural' methods of growing vines. 'Organic viticulture' encompasses a wide range of such practices.

Like most evangelical organizations, those governing organic viticulture tend to be locked in conflict with each other, but the basic principles are that no synthetic chemicals should be added to the vineyard, that the health of the soil is of paramount importance (compost, manure and bugs are highly valued), and that **cover crops**, other crops between the vines, even weeds, can substantially improve the quality and all-important texture of the soil. Growing grasses, barley or vetch between rows can, for example, make a real difference as to whether a tractor can make progress in a vineyard during the wet winter and spring seasons, or whether it risks being completely mired. These crops can also reduce vine vigour (the leafiness of the vines) by providing competition for the soil's nutrients and water and, sometimes, can distract predatory insects, which is particularly important if insecticides are not used.

The most extreme philosophy is the Steiner-inspired system called **biodynamism** or **biodynamics** whereby the soil is nurtured, often by minute, homeopathic doses of such substances as ground nettles and camomile, according to the phases of the moon. It sounds crazy, but the demonstrable health of the vines and wines produced by such adherents as Lalou Bize-Leroy of Burgundy, Michel Chapoutier of the Rhône, Nicolas Joly of Savennières and Didier Dageneau of Pouilly-Fumé, even in vintages that were disastrous for other, more conventional vine-growers, suggests that this may be a very successful recipe for those pursuing quality above all else.

It should be said, however, that it is much easier to practise organic viticulture in a dry climate than in a damp one where fungal diseases are a perennial threat.

A rigorous system of winemaking which might be described as organic is much less common than using vaguely organic methods to grow vines. Only tiny amounts of sulphur dioxide are used and minimal fining and filtration are allowed, so the wines can be relatively unstable. As in the vineyard, there is a perceptible trend thoughout the world to use fewer and fewer additives and to reduce the level of sulphur additions to a practicable minimum. Some of the official organic organizations, however, have rules apparently dictated more by fanaticism than wine quality.

Can the experienced taster distinguish an 'organic wine' from a conventional one? The many indifferent organic wines made by less-than-inspirational winemakers do their best to cloud the issue, but it can be revealing to compare the 'organic' offerings from a single producer such as Robert Mondavi of California or Penfolds of Australia with the rest of their range. There does seem to be an intensity and sometimes even wildness of flavour, perhaps partly because yields are lower when organic methods are applied.

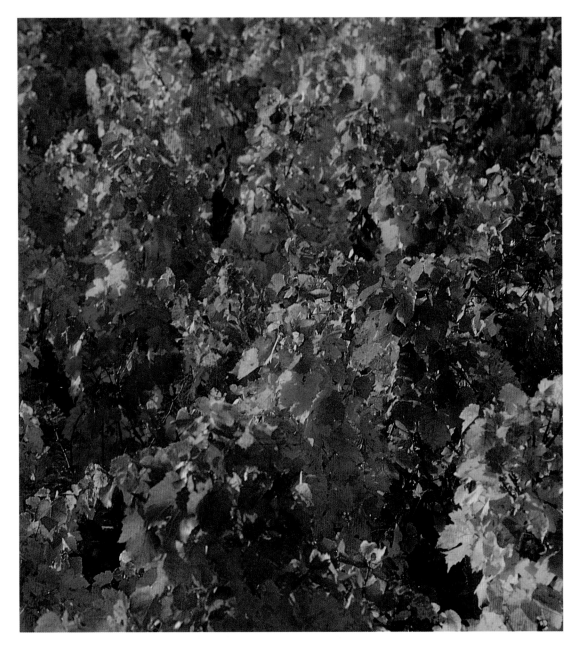

part of a vine is known by professionals as the **canopy microclimate.**

Some wine tourists are intrigued by the variation in colour of leaves between different patches of vines. A patch of summertime yellow in the middle of mainly green-leaved vines is usually caused by an iron deficiency in the vine. As grapes ripen the natural differences in leaf colour between

This Beaujolais vineyard looks mouth-wateringly beautiful, but the variation in colour may be a sign that some of the vines are suffering from viral diseases.

different vine varieties are accentuated, but many of the reds and oranges that make vineyards so beautiful in autumn are the result of vine virus diseases, some of which can inconveniently delay the ripening process. Leafroll virus is the most common example. Growers now try to plant vines which nurserymen guarantee as virus-free, but this is still a serious problem in many areas.

THE WINE PLANT AND ITS FRUIT

For all its heady symbolism and the beauty of its foliage, the vine is basically a fruit tree, which happens to produce a fruit, the grape, whose juice is particularly good when fermented. Any sweet liquid can be fermented into an alcoholic one (see page 74), whether it be a starchy mash into beer, pear juice into perry, or apple juice into cider. Grape juice is special, however. It has a naturally high sugar content, and so can be fermented into a relatively alcoholic liquid. But it is also unusually high in a particular acid, tartaric acid (in fact the cooking additive cream of tartar is made from the scrapings off the inside of old wine vats). This acid can fight off the sort of bacteria that attack most other foods and drink far better than, for example, the dominant acids in milk, citric fruit and apples (lactic, citric and malic acid respectively). Consequently fermented grape juice can last and, even better, evolve for much longer than most ferments. And the fact that there are thousands of distinct varieties of vine, and therefore grape, means that the flavours of wine, real grape wine, can be far more varied and rewarding than the fermented juice of other fruits.

The professional vine-grower's annual job is to ripen a commercially viable quantity of grapes in which the grape sugars, produced from sunlight and water by the photosynthesis that makes all plants grow, are balanced by a suitable level of acidity. The major component in grape juice is water, up to 85 per cent. The proportion of other components such as sugars and acids,

however, varies considerably according to how ripe the grape is and how heavily it is pressed, as the illustration suggests. As the sugars in the grape increase so do all the exciting flavour elements and astringent preservatives such as pigments and tannins, which are to be found in highest concentrations just under the skin in Zone C. Some bitter tannins are also to be found in Zone A just round the pips. The least astringent juice is therefore that in Zone B, which also happens to be the first juice to be pressed from a mass of crushed grapes, known as the **free-run juice.** This is highly valued for making many delicate white wines which would be spoilt by being astringent.

Although a vine's yield is strongly influenced by both pruning and annual weather conditions, the quality and quantity of grapes produced by a vine also vary considerably according to its age. Most vines produce a crop of commercially interesting size only in their third year and reach a plateau of productivity between the ages of about six and 20 years. After this, quantity starts to decline but, as a direct result, quality often increases, which is why so many labels boast of *vieilles vignes*, or old vines (although 'old' can mean anything, from under 10 to 100 years). Many producers uproot vines in their twenties because they produce too little (or because they want to plant a more attractive variety or clone).

See pages 100–153 in Section Three for full details of the vine family and hundreds of different grape varieties.

Cross-section through a grape.

Labels: Stalk, Skin, Zone A, Zone B, Zone C

THE VINEYARD YEAR

One of the greatest miracles of nature, it has always seemed to me, is the annual transformation of the barren, black-stumped midwinter vineyard into the luxuriant, juicy, green jungle that is a field of vines in high summer. Here's how it is done, and what humans need to do to shape the quality of wine produced as a result.

I have deliberately not mentioned specific months as these vary according to the hemisphere of course. In very general terms the grape harvest takes place in September and October in the northern hemisphere and from February to April in the southern hemisphere.

WINTER

Dormancy is the key word here – both in the vineyard and in the winery. The vine enjoys a prolonged period of inactivity after the rigours of carrying and ripening a crop and the canopy to support it. In extremely cool climates, however, frozen grapes may be picked for Eiswein/Ice wine (see page 89), sometimes as late as January in Germany.

In wine regions with particularly cold winters, such as Canada and Russia, vines may be routinely banked up so that they survive hard winter frosts.

Pruning is the most important, indeed the only, almost universal vineyard job to be done during the winter, although there is no rule about its precise timing. Pruning is extremely important, particularly in cooler climates where the amount of warmth and sunlight available to ripen grapes is more limited, because it is the chief way a vine-grower can impose his policy on **yield**, the quantity of wine produced, usually measured in Europe as hectolitres of wine per hectare of vineyard and in the US as tons of grapes per acre. (Although the conversion of weight of grapes to volume of wine depends on the characteristics of the grapes, what sort of wine is made and how hard the grapes are pressed, 1 ton/acre is equivalent to about 17.5 hl/ha.) Yields can vary from less than 20 hl/ha (1.1 ton/acre) in the case of extremely old, harshly pruned and non-irrigated grapes grown in a dry season to 200 hl/ha (11 ton/acre) from generously pruned and heavily irrigated vines. The association between low yields and high-quality wine is accepted so unquestioningly in Europe that maximum yields are laid down for each sort of wine by most European wine regulations (see page 48). Some New World producers, however, are unconvinced that a small quantity necessarily means high quality, arguing that many of Bordeaux's finest wines were produced in some of the highest-yielding vintages. In some circumstances climatic conditions can have a greater effect on quality than yield alone.

With a few careful snips of the secateurs (often in icy winds) the vine-grower can deter-

FLYING WINEMAKERS

Because September's a quiet month for Australian (and New Zealand) winemakers, hundreds of them migrate each year to make wine in the northern hemisphere. This trend started in the early 1980s and has now spawned a phenomenon known as 'flying winemakers' whereby an increasing proportion of wine is made by itinerants. The most famous of these are Jacques Lurton and Hugh Ryman, each of whom runs teams of international winemakers from a base in Bordeaux. Although the result has been a dramatic increase in technically well-made wines, flying winemakers are not as good as they think at extracting regional character. Let us hope the locals will learn, absorb, but not slavishly copy.

mine both the number of bunches each vine is likely to produce (by leaving only a certain number of buds on the vine) and the shape of the vine during the growing season. Pruning is a much more skilled job than, say, picking grapes and can therefore be one of the more expensive vineyard operations, but it is in the throes of being mechanized.

Some vine-growers in warmer climates, notably in Australia, have been experimenting with **minimal pruning**, a much more casual method, leaving vines unpruned so that they look like giant thorn bushes. As with wild vines, the fruit grows on the outside where the light can help ripen it. The argument is that the vine will itself find the correct balance between grapes and leaves, but in cooler regions it would be difficult to ripen all the bunches produced by an unpruned vine.

Cuttings for new plantings are usually taken in winter before the sap rises.

SPRING

Apparently miraculously, tiny green shoots emerge from the buds left on the vine after winter pruning at some point in early spring depending on the weather, the variety of vine, when it was pruned, and the amount of energy it managed to store during the previous growing season. This is the most important time for the growth of shoots, leaves and, beginning slightly later, roots.

Frost danger is the chief preoccupation of most vine-growers in early to mid-spring when vines, particularly varieties which bud early such as Chardonnay, are most vulnerable.

Heaters, wind machines and sprinkler systems can all help to protect tender young vine growth (and the subsequent crop, the commercial *raison d'être* of vine-growing). Heaters help to raise temperatures at vine height above the –1°C (30°F) which is cold enough to cause damage. Wind machines act like a giant mixer of the cold, dense air at ground level with the warmer air above. Sprinklers (which in some

areas may double as irrigation systems) protect young vine leaves and shoots by coating them in ice, and warm the soil to boot. Vines are damaged only at temperatures below –5°C (23°F), but the ice coating keeps them at 0°C (32°F), so long as they are sprayed as soon as the temperature reaches zero.

The single most important event in the springtime vineyard, however, is **flowering**, a one- to two-week period anything from six to 12 weeks after the first buds appeared, during which the potential size of the crop is pre-ordained. Tiny vine flowers appear from each bud and, depending on the weather, a proportion of them are fertilized to become berries, or baby grapes. Strong winds can blow off these delicate little plant fragments, which reduces the size of the potential crop, as does cold, wet weather, which discourages healthy growth and causes many individual baby stems to shrivel, a crop-diminishing phenomenon called **coulure**. Certain varieties such as Grenache and some clones of Merlot are especially prone to coulure.

The weather during the flowering period has an effect not just on the size of the current year's crop but also on the following year's, since this year's miniature buds on the vine will become next year's shoots.

SUMMER

During the summer it is essentially nature rather than man that does the work, although humidity may encourage vine diseases, which most growers combat with assiduous spraying.

In years when the vines are very heavily loaded with grapes, as a result of a particularly successful flowering for example, some producers may practise **crop thinning**, also known as summer pruning, *vendange verte* or *éclaircissage*. This highly skilled process involves cutting off individual bunches by hand so that the available energy will ripen the remaining bunches more successfully.

The canopy, the green parts of the vine, grows rapidly in early summer and will continue to do so unless it is trimmed or there is shortage of water and the vines are subjected to **water stress**, a little of which may be good.

The berries or grapes meanwhile grow from hard, green little pellets to large, juicy fruits in which the acidity continues to diminish while the sugar increases. The most obviously decisive stage in this continuous process is called, in English as well as French, **veraison**, when the grapes begin to soften and change colour, those on the outside of the bunch first. Immediately after veraison, six to seven weeks after the completion of flowering, the grape ripening process goes into top gear, especially in warm, sunny, dry weather. If the water stress is too severe, however, the **ripening** process comes to a halt.

At about the same time as veraison, the shoots start to turn from green and springy to brown and hard. The vine is starting to store energy for the winter and the following year.

AUTUMN

All of the above operations have been directed towards the great event of the vine-growing and winemaking year, the **harvest**. The vine-grower's most crucial decision is when to pick and depends on whether the vine is an early, mid or late ripening variety; the health and characteristics of the grapes; the weather forecast; and what sort of wine is being made. Early ripening varieties (such as Chardonnay and Pinot

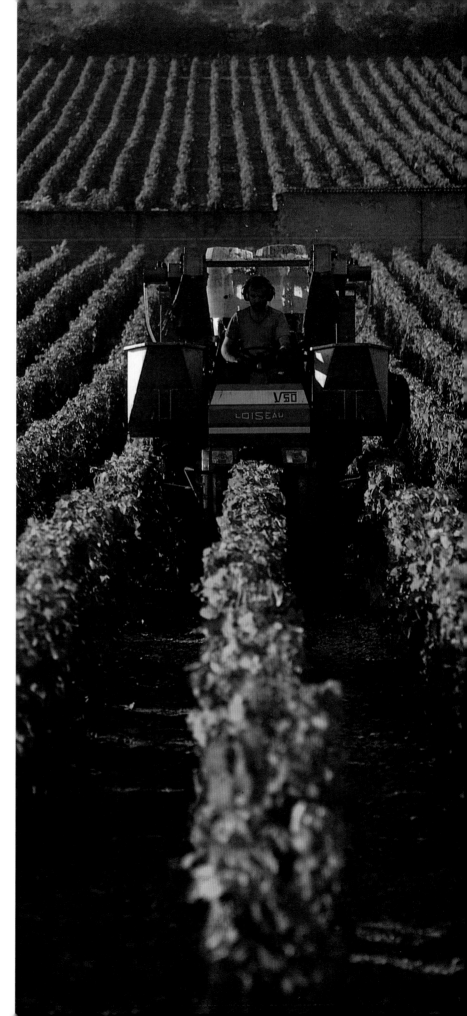

Grapes may be picked skilfully, expensively and picturesquely by hand, or automatically, economically and fast by machine.

As labour costs and bureaucracy increase, the machine (which does not require a three-course lunch) is winning, although hand picking is the rule for many top European estates.

Noir) that are destined for sparkling wine may be picked several weeks ahead of late ripening varieties such as Cabernet Sauvignon, whose deep colour and tannins are highly desirable, and even months ahead of some grapes destined for late harvest sweet wines.

As the grapes ripen they are analysed with increasing frequency to check levels of the acidity that keeps wine refreshing and the sugar that can be fermented into alcohol. In hot climates the aim is to keep the former as high as possible while having grapes that have accumulated enough flavour, while in cool climates, especially after a poor summer, the main aim can often be simply to reach a legal or self-imposed minimum sugar level before autumn rains set in or rot spreads.

As autumn progresses the leaves turn colour and fall off, notably after the first frost of the season.

A BLUFFER'S GUIDE TO WINEMAKING JARGON

Acidity is what gives wine, and most other drinks, its tang. Lemons have lots of it; potatoes very little. A wine's acidity comes from the **acids** (mainly MALIC and TARTARIC) in grape juice, which diminish as grapes ripen. A hot summer may reduce acids to such an extent that some have to be added from a sack. This is called **acidification**.

Alcohol is the potent mood-changer that differentiates wine from grape juice. A wine's **alcoholic strength** is its concentration of alcohol (see page 49).

Anthocyans, PHENOLICS which most strongly influence a red wine's colour, which is directly affected by its PH.

Ascorbic acid, or Vitamin C, is often added to MUST during winemaking since it prevents OXIDATION, usually together with SULPHUR DIOXIDE to keep white wines fresh.

Barrel, the winemaker's most fashionable tool. See pages 91–3 for more information about **barrel fermentation, barrel maturation**, etc.

Bâtonnage, French for LEES STIRRING.

Baumé, measure of sugar concentration in grape juice (and therefore grape ripeness) or MUST common in Australia.

Botrytis, fungus affecting grapes benevolently (as in the 'noble rot' responsible for great sweet wines, see page 88) or simply spoiling them with 'grey rot' or mould, depending on conditions.

Brettanomyces, wine fault so fashionable in the US that it is sometimes just called Brett. Wines affected by this spoilage YEAST smell off-puttingly mousey.

Brix, measure of sugar concentration common in the US. See BAUMÉ.

Cap, layer of skins floating on red wine in the fermentation vat.

Carbon dioxide is the harmless gas given off during fermentation that is responsible for the bubbles in all fizzy drinks, including wine.

Carbonic maceration, special way of making fruity, early maturing red wines, most notably Beaujolais, by fermenting them in a sealed vat filled with CARBON DIOXIDE. See page 78.

Chaptalization, common cool climate winemaking procedure which compensates for underripe grapes by adding sugar to the fermentation vat to produce a more alcoholic wine.

Clarification, umbrella term for processes designed to ensure wine is crystal clear, including FINING, FILTRATION and refrigeration.

Concentration, new technique for concentrating flavour (and ACID and TANNIN) in less ripe vintages.

Élevage, French term with no direct English equivalent for the wine-maturing processes involved between fermentation and bottling.

Enology, US spelling of OENOLOGY.

Ethyl alcohol, or **ethanol**, is the sort of ALCOHOL found in alcoholic drinks such as wine.

Fermentation, see pages 74–5.

Filtration, controversial CLARIFICATION process of pumping wine through various different sorts of filter to remove suspended solids. It can also strip out flavour.

Fining, CLARIFICATION technique involving adding a **fining agent** (such as egg whites or bentonite) which attracts solids to fall out of suspension (see page 83).

Flavour compounds, complex, still underexplored maze of compounds, many of them PHENOLICS, responsible for wine flavour.

Free-run is the juice or wine which flows without PRESSING.

Inert gas, one such as nitrogen which does not react with wine. May fill the head space of a container to prevent OXIDATION.

Lees are the solids left at the bottom of a fermentation vat after fermentation. Relatively neutral-tasting white wines are often deliberately given prolonged **lees contact** and even **lees stirring** to generate more flavour and make them more stable.

Malic acid, the sharp, appley acid most notable in grapes from cool years.

Malolactic fermentation (MLF or 'le malo'), increasingly common second fermentation in which harsh MALIC ACID is converted to softer, lactic (milky) acid softening the resulting wine.

Mercaptans, wine fault popular with Australian tasters. A skunky smell results from YEAST reacting with the LEES. It can be cured by careful RACKING.

Must, useful word for the pulpy mass at any stage between grape juice and wine.

Oak, see pages 91–3.

Oechsle, measure of sugar concentration common in Germany. See BAUMÉ.

Oenology is the science of winemaking, practised by a (usually qualified) **oenologist**.

Organic winemaking, avoidance of chemical additives and, often, of certain fining agents. See page 65.

Oxidation, potentially serious calamity that can strike grapes, grape juice and wine if they are over-exposed to OXYGEN, making them go brown (like a cut apple) and taste flat. Wines suffering from oxidation, often from a less-than-airtight stopper, are **oxidized.**

Oxygen, both good and bad fairy in the winemaking process. A small amount during barrel maturation deepens colour, smooths flavour and makes the wine more stable. But too much oxygen causes OXIDATION and may eventually turn the wine to vinegar. Winemaking may be deliberately **oxidative** or PROTECTIVE.

pH, one of the wine bore's buzz words. pH is a measure of the concentration of ACIDITY in a liquid but higher readings mean lower acid. Water, for example, has a pH of 7, while most wines have a pH of between 3 and 4, with very acidic wines having a pH of less than 3. pH and colour are also closely related: the lower the pH, the brighter the red wine.

Phenolics, varied group of compounds found mainly in skins, stems and seeds in the case of grapes. They include ANTHOCYANS, TANNINS and some FLAVOUR COMPOUNDS. Precipitated, they form an important part of wine's sediment and play a considerable role in wine ageing. Red wines are much higher in phenolics than white, which is why red wine is better at protecting against heart disease.

Pressing, important winemaking operation involving pressing the juice (white wines) or astringent **press wine** out of the skins. The quality of the resulting juice depends on how hard the grapes are pressed (as explained on page 67).

Protective winemaking involves protecting the grapes, juice, MUST

and wine from OXYGEN, typically by using sealed containers, low temperatures, SULPHUR DIOXIDE and sometimes ASCORBIC ACID.

Punching down, winemaking process whereby the CAP of skins is physically immersed in the MUST so that more PHENOLICS are leeched into the resulting wine.

Pumping over the juice, alternative to PUNCHING DOWN.

Racking is the operation of transferring wine from one container (typically a barrel) to another, leaving behind the LEES. It can usefully expose the wine to oxygen and avoid REDUCTION.

Reducing conditions are those which favour **reduction,** or losing OXYGEN, the opposite of OXIDATION. In excess, where a (usually red) wine is starved of oxygen, they can result in off-putting MERCAPTAN or SULPHIDE smells.

Residual sugar (RS), the amount of unfermented SUGAR left in a wine after fermentation is complete, usually measured in grams per litre (g/l) or per cent. A residual sugar level of less than 2 g/l (0.2 per cent) is imperceptible to most palates. Although ACIDITY counterbalances residual sugar, most wines with 25 g/l (2.5 per cent) residual sugar taste distinctly sweet.

Skin contact, deliberate policy of trying to extract from the grape skins as many FLAVOUR COMPOUNDS, and ANTHOCYANS into red juice, as possible.

Sorbic acid, additive widely used in the food and drink industries to stun YEASTS and moulds. Sometimes used for inexpensive sweet wines, it smells of crushed geranium leaves, excessively to some particularly sensitive humans.

Stabilization, umbrella term for all the winemaking operations (e.g. FILTRATION, chilling to precipitate TARTRATES, adding ASCORBIC ACID) designed to stop wines developing a fault in bottle such as a haze, cloud or fizz, no matter what the storage

conditions. It is practised most brutally on everyday wines.

Sulphides, off-smells reminiscent of bad eggs which can taint heavily REDUCED wine. Hydrogen sulphide (H_2S) is most common.

Sulphur dioxide, the most common and most useful winemaking additive used since Roman times, mainly as a preservative, disinfectant and to ward off OXIDATION. Its use has been declining as consumers have become less tolerant of the freshly-struck match smell associated with sulphur. Some asthmatics react badly to high doses of sulphur, which has led to some countries requiring the legend 'contains **sulfites/sulphites'** on wine labels. A tiny but increasing proportion of wines are made using no sulphur at all but they tend to be fragile. Sulphur reacts readily with many other wine ingredients to form **bound sulphur;** it is only **free sulphur** which can be detected, although individual sensitivities vary considerably.

Sugar is built up in the pulp as grapes ripen, and is transformed into ALCOHOL during fermentation.

Sur lie, French for a wine treated to LEES CONTACT.

Tannins, preservative PHENOLICS found mainly in red wine and derived chiefly from dark grape skins as well as seeds and stems. Tannin management is one of the red winemaker's most important jobs. See pages 16–17, 40 and 79.

Tartaric acid, the most common and distinctive wine ACID (see page 67) and a particularly good preservative. A lot of the acid is precipitated as crusty deposits called **tartrates,** usually seen as harmless white crystals in white wine, and dyed deep red in red wines.

Topping up, the regular filling of barrels to avoid oxidation.

Whole bunch pressing and fermentation. See page 78.

Yeast, see page 74.

THE WINEMAKING PROCESS

It is a healthy sign that more and more wine-makers are admitting that 'Wine is made in the vineyard not the cellar'. Some of them are even getting their boots dirty nowadays. But presumably modern winemaking man has been skulking in the winery all this time because, as we have seen on pages 60–71, he has so much less power over nature in the vineyard.

Turning grapes into some sort of wine is a rela-tively easy process (it's only making a wine that tastes thrilling and will last for-ever that is difficult). Ripe grapes contain sugar which can, under the influence of minute organisms called yeasts, be converted into alcohol and carbon dioxide gas. (Much the same thing happens when jam starts to ferment: it starts to bubble and taste headier and less sweet.)

Those who share my enthusiasm for neat expla-nations in the form of equa-tions may find comfort in the following:

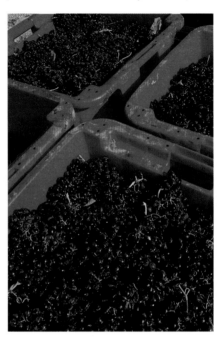

Trucked grapes may get crushed and start to ferment, so increasingly they are transported in shallow plastic boxes.

$$C_6H_{12}O_6 \rightarrow 2C_2H_5OH + 2CO_2$$
sugar   alcohol   carbon dioxide

Those who hated chemistry should ignore this bit, and those wary of such scientific precision are quite right. This is a gross simplification of the horrifyingly complex sequence of opera-tions that is alcoholic fermentation. All sorts of other things happen, but a detailed grasp of them does little to enhance our enjoyment of the resulting liquid.

To set the fermentation process in motion, all that is needed is to put the sugar present inside ripe grapes in contact with the millions of invisible yeasts that are present in the atmos-phere of any wine region by splitting the skins, which means crushing the grapes. This explains why wine (unlike spirits) could be made so many thousands of years ago – no special skill or equip-ment was needed other than a container in which to keep the resulting alco-holic liquid. But if wine is exposed to air it will turn, sooner or later, into vinegar (as anyone clearing up the morning after a particularly good dinner will know). In fact the very word vinegar derives from *vin aigre*, which is French for sour wine. Until the development of stoppered containers such as amphorae, the ancients knew wine almost exclu-sively as a nouveau (see page 57) or a weak liquid that was heavily disguised with herbs, honey, lead or even sea water.

Modern consumers are more demanding, however, and modern wine-makers like to be in control, so winemaking today is a much less hazardous process.

The following are some of the more impor-tant decisions modern winemakers have to make and how they influence the resulting wine – although all co-operative wineries and many wine producers, especially in the New World, have their work cut out to control some of the first operations described below since they buy in, rather than grow, most of their grapes.

Winemakers' decisions appear in roughly the order in which they have to make them, although that order depends on the very first decision of all. Consult the bluffer's guide on pages 72–3 for a fast track to understanding the technical terms, and the diagram on pages 76–7 for the basic steps in winemaking.

WHAT SORT OF WINE TO MAKE

Grape colour and quality determine to a certain extent what sort of wine can be made. Red wines can be made only from dark-skinned grapes as all grape juice is the same dull grey and will be tinted red only if anthocyans can be leeched out of the skins into the must. This means that red wines have to be made from skins as well as pulp. Grape skins, though, are high in other phenolics which make them astringent. This may be a good quality in a tannic young red wine but is unattractive in a light white. Juice alone is also much easier to work with than a mixture of skins and juice, so the juice is separated from the skins before white wine fermentation. The principal difference between red and white winemaking is whether the grapes are pressed before or after fermentation.

Dark-skinned grapes are needed to make Léoville-Barton this colour – the warmer the summer the deeper the pigment.

White wines can be made from dark-skinned grapes (many sparkling white wines are) provided the juice is separated from the skins carefully and early enough. See pages 84–6 for details of sparkling winemaking. Rosés, or pink wines, are made just like white wines, except that the juice is lightly tinted from short contact with dark skins before fermentation. Very ripe grapes can be used to make sweet wines (see pages 87–8) or fortified wines.

WHEN TO PICK

Until very recently grapes were picked by numbers: as soon as sugars reached an acceptable level in cool climates, and in warmer regions just before acids fell dangerously low (and pH rose dangerously high). Today more and more wine producers understand that numbers alone may not be sufficient indicators of real, sometimes called 'physiological', ripeness. Visible ripening of the grapes' skin and stem (including the ease with which a grape can be pulled off it) is one of the indicators that quality-conscious producers now use to decide the optimum picking time. They are especially interested in fully ripe, or sometimes even overripe phenolics, particularly for red wines, because the tannins will be much riper and the wines more welcoming. Some growers even deliberately pick a mixture of slightly underripe, ripe and slightly overripe grapes to give a wine complexity, notably with slightly anodyne grape varieties such as Semillon or Sauvignon Blanc.

HOW TO PICK – MAN OR MACHINE

Hand picking may be the only option in some places – either particularly steep or inconveniently designed vineyards for example – and for certain sorts of wines such as sweet wines which involve selection on the vine or those made using whole bunches (including stems), such as some burgundies and sparkling wines. Vineyard labour is generally becoming scarcer and more expensive, however, and only the very top estates and domaines of France can afford to boast that they will never, ever use mechanical harvesters. Machines can harvest much more

Unoaked white winemaking options

10 mins–3 hrs

2–3 weeks

Destemmer/ crusher

(Optional) cooler

Settling

Draining

Press

R.D.V. Filter

Fermentation (Temperature-controlled)

High-quality red winemaking options

(Sealed)

Crusher/ destemmer

Fermentation vessels

(Open topped)

2–14 days

Drainer

Press

Malolactic fermentation

1–2 weeks

cheaply and quickly than humans, but they do give the vines a terrible shake every year, are unable to discriminate between healthy and unhealthy grapes, tend to harvest not a few leaves and vine fragments too, and like mud even less than humans. Machine harvesters are particularly useful in hot climates where they can be used at night to deliver grapes at naturally low temperatures, which can save refrigeration costs and the use of sulphur dioxide in some cases.

HOW (AND WHETHER) TO TRANSPORT GRAPES TO THE WINERY

The longer grapes sit around between the vine and the winery, the more likely they are to be crushed by their own weight, to oxidize and to lose their fresh, fruity flavours (which matters particularly for light white wines). Adding sulphur dioxide can help but the early 1990s saw two important developments in grape harvesting: using shallower and shallower containers for transport to the winery and a perceptible move towards building crushing (and destemming) centres immediately beside vineyards so that what is transported in the midday sun is not fragile, freshly-picked grapes but carefully treated and protected pulp or juice. Heat speeds up all reactions, so picking in the cool of the night can also help.

WHETHER TO SORT

A multitude of Bordeaux and Burgundy producers installed sorting tables, or *tables de tri(age)*,

for the rain-sodden vintages of the early 1990s when there was wide variation in the health and quality of the grapes coming into the winery. A slowly moving belt between trailer and crusher allows sorters to discard any rotten or unripe grapes as well as 'MOG' (material other than grapes).

WHETHER TO CHILL GRAPES OR MUST

Chilling helps to preserve fresh, primary aromas and inhibits yeast, harmful bacteria and oxidation, allowing winemakers in hot climates to delay fermentation until the must is in a fit state for this complex process. Some producers store juice at low temperatures for months before fermentation in order to cut down the amount of fermentation capacity and winemaker attention needed at the busiest time of year. *In warmer wine regions and for white winemaking in all but the chilliest extremities of the wine world, refrigeration is an important winemaking tool. Cooling grapes, must or wine preserves the fruity primary aromas and gives winemakers breathing space.*

PROTECTIVE OR OXIDATIVE JUICE HANDLING?

Many winemakers actively protect grapes and juice against oxidation by using sulphur dioxide and/or tank presses which are completely enclosed (see picture opposite). This effort is particularly important for white grapes because as soon as they are crushed the juice starts to brown as a result of reactions between oxygen and phenolics in the juice. Some producers, however, deliberately expose white juice to oxygen in order to exclude these 'heavy' phenolics from the resulting wine, and with them the risk of browning the wine prematurely in bottle.

The equipment above, at Undurraga in Chile, is just part of what's needed to keep temperatures low enough to make fresh fruity wines.
Below is a typical destemmer. Stems are separated from grapes in the perforated rotating cylinder.

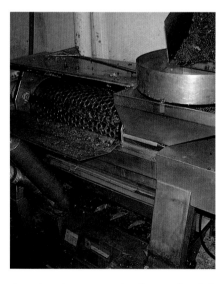

sugar in contact with the yeast, and most are automatically destemmed (increasingly before rather than after crushing) to eliminate the harsh flavours and astringent characters that stems can impart.

The main exceptions to this are wines such as most Beaujolais, and the Languedoc-Roussillon's Carignan, which are fermented using some form of carbonic maceration. This bathes whole berries in carbon dioxide and depends on a particularly fruity sort of yeast-free fermentation taking place inside each berry (although the grapes at the bottom of the vat are crushed anyway of course and tend to ferment in the normal way). The resulting wines are bright red, soft and have a distinctive smell of pear drops.

Other wines made using whole bunches of grapes include some ambitious still white wines (especially botrytized sweet wines) and most top quality sparkling wines which are very gently pressed using the stems as conduits for the resulting juice.

A number of top quality red wine producers, notably in Burgundy, pour whole bunches into their fermentation vats (which must be open to allow the cap to be broken up). If the grapes (and therefore stems) are anything less than very ripe, however, or are a highly tannic variety such as Cabernet Sauvignon, the inclusion of stems can result in unpleasantly tough wines.

WHETHER TO DESTEM AND CRUSH

Practically all grapes are deliberately fed into a crusher before fermentation in order to put the

DURATION OF SKIN CONTACT

The incidence and timing of this pre-pressing operation is different for red and white wines (see diagram on pages 76–7). Red wines are red precisely because of skin contact before, during and sometimes after fermentation. In cooler regions wine-makers tend to try to extract every last ounce of colour and phenolics from the floating cap of skins by maximizing the contact between them and the juice. They typically manage this either by pumping juice over the cap, by punching it down once or twice a day or submerging it beneath some form of perforated headboard. Many European producers also deliberately leave the new wine in the fermentation vat for a week or two after fermentation has finished in order to extract more colour, tannins and flavour from the skins. This is particularly effective since alcohol is a good solvent. In warmer regions, however, where grapes tend to be too deeply coloured, the result of such a policy can be a bitterly tannic wine and some producers even separate the juice from the skins before fermentation is over, finishing it off in small barrels (see pages 90–3).

For white wines, skin contact has to work its magic before fermentation, but the exact nature of this magic is much less clear-cut. A few hours' skin contact for relatively bland varieties such as Sauvignon Blanc and Semillon can add extra flavour but in this case the grapes must be perfectly healthy and protected from oxidation.

Rosé is the result of applying the technique described above to dark-skinned grapes.

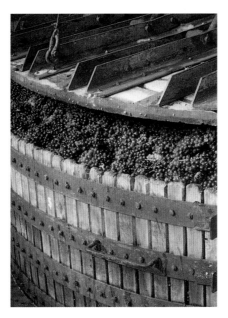

Two of the many sorts of press: a modern tank press (above) completely protected from the air, and an old-fashioned basket press (below), treasured by many traditionalists.

PRESSING THE GRAPES OR PULP

Juice is pressed out of white grapes after the free-run juice has been run off but before fermentation. In red winemaking the job is to extract as much usable wine as possible from the solids left in the fermentation vat after the free-run wine has been run off. The gentler the pressure, the less coarse the wine or juice, which is why presses are designed to be ever gentler.

The typical modern horizontal press consists of an inflatable airbag inside a perforated rotating cylinder through which juice falls to a tray below (see diagrams on pages 76–7). If the whole thing is enclosed from the harmful effects of oxygen it is called a tank press.

Alternative highly regarded presses include the vertical 'basket press', of which variants are used in Champagne and Sauternes, and for some full bodied red wines. Whereas most horizontal presses can be worked (if not cleaned) mechanically, the basket press uses up both time and manpower, but similarly squeezes juice gently through slats into a tray below.

Inexpensive wines are frequently made using much harsher continuous presses which don't need expensive human supervision of individual batches.

An important decision in winemaking is what to do with the press juice or wine. Almost all top quality white wines are made exclusively from free-run juice. The best of what's left in the press may be recovered using a rotary drum vacuum (R.D.V.) filter. The character of each vintage may determine how much red press wine is included in the final blend. A very dry year may produce very tannic wines which would not be flattered by adding the even more tannic press wine. Different labels provide homes for the rejects.

AMBIENT OR CULTURED YEASTS?

This, with filtration, is one of the hottest issues in winemaking. Traditional winemakers in traditional regions simply rely on the local, varied population of yeasts in the air which have built up over the years and seem perfectly trained to do the job in hand. Modernists are perturbed by this practice, which can sometimes mean waiting a few days for fermentation to start, increases the danger of the harmful effects of 'wild yeasts' which may not be as well disciplined as wine yeasts, and may occasionally result in a 'stuck' fermentation. The debate began because winemakers in new wine regions had to import their own, single strains of specially cultured yeasts (themselves originally selected from ambient yeasts) which tend to be much more predictable. Some producers in newer wine regions have experimented successfully with ambient yeasts, showing that it does not take too long to build up a useful local wine yeast population. They argue that ambient yeasts may result in wines with a wider range of flavours than a single strain of cultured yeast, but the genetic complexity of the yeast world has acted as a brake on conclusive research.

WHAT SORT OF CONTAINER
FOR FERMENTATION?

Size, shape, material and design of a container can all have a tastable effect on any wine fer-

mented in it, and certainly have enormous practical ramifications for the winemaker. The larger the fermentation vat the more difficult it can be to control the vast amounts of heat generated by the fermentation process, and the more likely it can be that certain flavour compounds are 'boiled off', unless careful refrigeration is used. Whereas white wine can be made in a very tall, relatively narrow, space-saving tank, makers of red wine generally prefer wider vessels which maximize the area of the cap, putting as much liquid as possible in contact with the skins so as to extract lots of colour and flavour. And if they want to punch down the cap regularly, either with special long-handled tools, or, even better, feet, the vessel will have to have an open top, or at least a board over the top that can be lifted off. Pumping over also requires an opening at the top, and submerged caps require specially designed tanks with movable headboards.

White, rosé and many red wines are made in fermentation vats with closed tops to avoid oxidation, although they must have some valve to allow the carbon dioxide given off during fermentation to escape. A winery during vintage is heady with the smell of carbon dioxide, grape solids and, increasingly, alcohol. Because carbon dioxide reduces the available amount of oxygen, it can be very dangerous to spend too long in an enclosed space in which must is fermenting; cellar work can occasionally be fatal.

Although some fermentation vats are made of stone, ceramic, concrete, and various forms of plastic, by far the most common material selected by modern winemakers is stainless steel. It is easy to clean and can easily be fitted with temperature control devices such as refrigerated jackets and special coils.

European traditionalists may well favour wooden vats, however (closed for whites and open for reds), as wood's capacity to retain heat can be useful for extracting colour. White wines fermented in large, old wooden vats include many top Alsace, Loire, German and Austrian wines, while white burgundy and ambitious dry white wines the world over are fermented in small, new oak barrels. (See pages 91–3 for more details.)

WHICH ADDITIONS TO MAKE

As explained on page 73, a little sulphur dioxide is added to the raw ingredients of almost all wines, especially those made from slightly rotten grapes, but perfectly healthy, ripe grapes may need no further additions.

Cool summers may result in underripe grapes whose natural sugars would ferment into a liquid that the winemaker, or local regulation, reckons is not quite alcoholic enough. Chaptalization is therefore regularly practised throughout northern Europe, in Canada, in the wineries of China and Japan, and in the far south of New Zealand and Chile. It is banned (i.e. formally deemed unnecessary) in South Africa and Australia but some very southerly producers on the Cape coast and Tasmania would dearly love dispensation to chaptalize, particularly in less successful vintages. In Europe winemakers are rarely allowed to add more than 2 per cent to the final alcoholic strength of the wine as a result of chaptalization (although English winemakers regularly need more). In Bordeaux and Burgundy chaptalization is almost routine in some cellars, however, as these regions often lack sufficient sun to ripen the grapes enough to provide the sort of alcohol levels the producers like. This seems crazy in an age when alcohol and additives are popularly regarded as demons, but many oenologists argue that the extra alcohol is needed to 'support' the flavour.

The routine addition in warmer wine regions, on the other hand, is acid, most commonly in the form of added tartaric acid. Winemakers would rather harvest grapes a little late but with all the additional flavour compounds that develop late in the ripening process and then compensate for the reduced natural acidity level.

In official recognition of a succession of hot summers in the 1980s, many Europeans are now allowed to acidify too, although acidifying and chaptalizing the same vat is officially deemed too much of a good thing. After particularly cold summers, in northern Germany for example, seriously underripe grapes may need to be deacidified (commonly by adding chalk or a similar soother) as well as chaptalized.

DOES THE FERMENTATION NEED A KICKSTART?

Fermentations that are slow to start because of underripe or unhealthy grapes can be encouraged by adding special nitrogen-based yeast nutrients. Many New World winemakers routinely add nutrients to make the fermentation efficient and predictable (when Australian-trained flying winemakers introduced this trick to eastern Europe in the early 1990s they were regarded as wizards by the locals). If air temperatures are particularly low, the fermentation vat may have to be heated to begin with.

A WARM OR COOL FERMENT?

Once underway, fermentation generates huge quantities of heat and one of the main refinements of modern winemaking has been to install methods of cooling fermentation vats so that the winemaker can control the temperature of the must throughout fermentation. This means that not only is the danger of boiling off flavour compounds avoided, but also the winemakers gain potential control over the extraction of all sorts of soluble elements, particularly different tannins and other phenolics, since they all dissolve at different temperatures. Many modern wineries have sophisticated control panels which can monitor and control the temperature of each vat with the flick of a switch. Low-tech enterprises may still employ the early twentieth-century Bordeaux technique of using ice blocks.

The winemaker can dictate the flavours and character of a wine by controlling the fermentation temperature. Whites, which depend more on primary fruit aromas and have no need to encourage extraction, are almost invariably fermented cooler than most reds. Those fermented at the low end of the normal New

World white wine fermentation temperature range of 12–17°C (54–63°F) tend to smell of tropical fruits (particularly pineapple) and their own varietal flavour. This suits highly aromatic varieties but Europeans tend to ferment Chardonnay in the 18–20°C (64–8°F) range or even warmer so that they can benefit from some of the more complex aromas associated with warmer fermentations. Reds, being less delicate, withstand higher fermentation temperatures and in cooler regions may need them to encourage the extraction of colour, flavour and tannin. (Red wines fermented cool are generally higher in these primary fruit aromas and can often taste skinnier than their more complex counterparts that are fermented at higher temperatures.)

Again, Europeans tend to be less wary of high fermentation temperatures, allowing some vats to reach 30°C (85°F) or even more – although to go much higher risks stunning the yeast into total inactivity and the fermentation may be fatally stuck.

Shiny stainless steel tanks are so much easier to clean than the barrels involved in the traditional Burgundian method of lees stirring, or bâtonnage, now practised all over the world.

MALOLACTIC FERMENTATION?

Virtually all red wines and an increasing proportion of whites undergo this second, 'softening' fermentation which, under the influence of heat and some special, 'lactic' bacteria, takes place some time after the main alcoholic one. As well as making a wine more stable, this process helps to make it taste softer, fuller and more complex, but can add a rather obvious buttery flavour if overdone. The winemaker can encourage the 'malo' by keeping the new wine at relatively high temperatures and/or by deliberately introducing lactic bacteria. This method is expressly avoided, however, in simple, warm-climate white wines in which every ounce of acid is needed to keep them lively.

LEES CONTACT AND STIRRING?

Red wines usually sit on the lees – the deposit left after fermentation – as a matter of course if the winemaker believes in a post-fermentation steeping period.

For white wines, leaving new wine in contact with the lees involves a conscious decision. Some winemakers, particularly those fermenting white burgundy and its Chardonnay counterparts in small barrels, deliberately stir up the lees every week or so to stop sulphides and mercaptans developing and to encourage extra layers of flavour from the lees themselves. Stirring lees also has the effect of minimizing the wine's absorption of harsh tannins and flavour from the wood and tends to result in pale wine with a smooth texture.

MATURATION CONTAINER AND DURATION

The major decision here is oak or not (see pages 91–3 for more details). Basically, the longer the producer can afford to leave the new wine to settle, the fewer clarifying treatments detailed below are needed. Time (and oak) is a great alternative to additives.

Nouveaux may be 'matured' for no more than the few weeks needed to clarify and stabilize the liquid (see below), while some full bodied reds may be kept in cask for years before being bottled (especially in Spain, Italy and Argentina). In very general terms, most high-acid white wines and commercial wines of any hue are matured in inert containers and bottled during the spring following the vintage, while serious red wines are usually bottled during the second spring or summer after fermentation.

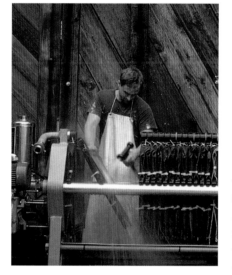

HOW MUCH AIR?

Oxygen can easily harm delicate white wines but full bodied red wines can benefit from a little exposure to air, particularly because it encourages many of the reactions involved in barrel maturation (see pages 91–3) and avoids reduction and the formation of sulphides and mercaptans. Because of this, many producers have a deliberate policy of regular racking from one barrel to another, which can introduce an ideal amount of oxygen.

The purist's nightmare, a sheet filter (above). If the sheets are not clean, the wine may taste of wet cardboard. If there are too many of them, the wine may be tasteless. The wine writer's nightmare, a bottling line (below).

MAKING THE WINE LIMPID AND STABLE

Most wine drinkers, or at least wine retailers, prefer wines that are crystal clear and clear of crystals, even harmless ones such as tartrates. To this end commercial wines are routinely chilled (cold stabilization) before bottling to precipitate all these crystals and are rigorously filtered in order to remove any organisms that might cause nasty smells, hazes, cloudiness or an embarrassingly fizzy fermentation in bottle. Slower but cheaper and in some cases less brutal than using filters are various forms of fining. Beaten egg whites are regularly used as a fining agent in individual barrels at top estates in Europe, while sacks of bentonite, a useful American clay, are commonly added to tanks of wine (and juice) around the world. Fining agents do not remain in the wine; they merely serve to attract the larger solids – those that might subsequently discolour white wines or make red wines taste bitter – to fall to the bottom of the container so that clear wine can be racked off.

Wines that are designed for early consumption, particularly white wines which are more fragile, may well have preservatives added to them. The most common are ascorbic acid and sometimes sorbic acid for sweet wines, added together with sulphur dioxide to stop relatively delicate wines from oxidizing or refermenting in bottle. Time, settling and racking can, however, be an alternative to all this. Wines which have not been harshly filtered must be treated gently and kept cool so that no unwelcome reactions, refermentations or bacteria develop.

HOW SPARKLING WINES ARE MADE

This account should really be called 'how wines are made to sparkle', for the fundamental principle of making a sparkling wine is somehow to dissolve carbon dioxide in a given base wine and bottle it so that when the bottle is opened, the gas escapes in the form of bubbles.

CARBONATION, OR THE BICYCLE PUMP METHOD

The crudest way of doing this is to borrow a technique from the fizzy drinks industry and simply pump carbon dioxide into a tankful of wine and bottle it under pressure so that the gas cannot escape. Only the very cheapest, most basic sparkling wine will have been subjected to this process, however, which results in a dramatic, but short-lived explosion of large bubbles.

THE CHAMPAGNE OR TRADITIONAL METHOD

The most painstaking way of making a wine sparkle, and one which can give it a persistent stream of tiny bubbles which may still be fizzing slightly even the next morning in an open bottle, is the method used in Champagne. It may variously be described as the traditional or classic method, *méthode traditionnelle, méthode classique, metodo tradizionale/classico,* or in South Africa Méthode Cap Classique. Wines made this way may even be described on the label as 'fermented in this bottle', which is the essence of the technique.

But any serious maker of sparkling wine would agree that his job starts long before this curious bottle-as-fermentation-vat stage. The real key to making a fine sparkling wine lies in the particular character and qualities of the grapes used to make the still base wines. These base wines should emphatically not taste delicious in their still state. Fine sparkling wine demands relatively neutral, acid, light wines because the classic method of sparkling winemaking changes them so substantially, adding not just carbon dioxide, but alcohol and many layers of additional flavour.

Chardonnay, Pinot Noir and Pinot Meunier are the classic grape varieties for champagne and are widely used for top quality sparkling wine elsewhere, with local variations such as Pinot Blanc in California and Italy. The dark-skinned grapes especially have to be pressed with particular care and speed so that a minimum of pigments, and none of the harsh tannins, taint the juice.

This grey juice is then fermented in the normal way, with wines from different varieties and vineyards kept separate, so that over the winter the young wines can be tasted and assessed and, ideally, a perfectly matched blend of them, or **cuvée**, can be assembled. One of the major differences between blenders in Champagne and the New World has been that the former tend to have much more experience of how different components in a blend react with each other and with time, although the gap is narrowing.

By spring the base wines have been blended and are then bottled, in the extra-strong, semi-opaque bottles in which the wine will eventually be sold, along with a carefully measured dose of sugar and yeast. The point of this is to achieve a second fermentation in bottle which, like any fermentation, will give off just the right amount of carbon dioxide (see page 74). This gas is then trapped inside the bottle until it escapes as bubbles in the glass of the eventual consumer. This second fermentation also raises the alcohol content, typically from about 11 to 12.5 per cent, and, crucially, leaves a sediment of dead yeast lees.

Lees contact is increasingly used to make still wines (see page 82), but this sparkling winemaking technique is the only one which depends on the slow but myriad reactions between the dead yeast cells and the wine in a completely sealed container. Bottles are laid on their sides, ideally in dark, cool conditions with a constant temperature, and simply left to their own devices (sparkling wines are particularly sensitive to light). The longer this process is allowed to continue, the more complex the flavours to compensate for the naturally high acidity and neutrality of a young sparkling wine. Unfortunately, however, keeping thousands, and sometimes millions, of bottles on their sides for years at a time is extremely expensive, so truly fine sparkling wine is necessarily a luxury item. Those who have studied the ageing of sparkling wines in bottle claim that they need at least 18 months on the sediment to achieve any perceptible development.

Once the sparkling wine producer decides he or she can no longer stand the financial strain of maturing a particular lot of wine, the sediment has to be removed – not because it makes the wine taste nasty, but simply because consumers expect their wines to be crystal clear. The traditional way has been to literally shake the sediment off the belly of the bottle and into the bottle-neck by gradually moving the bottle from a horizontal to upended vertical position, simultaneously giving the sediment a quick, loosening shake. This process is called *remuage* in French, **riddling** in English.

The bottles are then moved, still upside down with the sediment just above the crown cap with which ageing champagne bottles are stoppered, to a bath of extremely cold brine which freezes the bottle-neck and its contents, allowing the sediment to escape as a frozen pellet when the bottle is sharply returned right way up and unstoppered. This process is called **disgorgement**, or *dégorgement*.

Before the proper champagne cork (a curious amalgam much wider than the usual wine cork) can be driven in, the bottle has to be topped up, usually with some more wine of the same sort blended with a predetermined amount of sugar known as the **dosage**. The driest sparkling wines are usually labelled Brut and contain an amount of sugar that would make most still wines taste distinctly sweetish, but the naturally high acidity of most sparkling wines means that the dosage is usually imperceptible (although many very cheap champagnes are betrayed by the amount of sugar added to compensate for their toe-curling acidity). Sec or Dry, Demi-Sec or Medium Dry, and Rich betray increasingly high dosages.

The cumbersome *remuage* operation, although concerned far more with cosmetics than inherent wine quality, has come to play a large part in what is viewed as the mystique of champagne and similar sparkling wines. It is very labour intensive, however, and during the 1970s when labour costs rose rapidly, the Spaniards developed an automated substitute, pictured overleaf.

There are even newer alternatives too, such as yeasts encapsulated in tiny alginate beads which look like shot, inside which the dead yeast cells are trapped, enabling the sediment simply to be poured out of the bottle before disgorgement. A special cartridge that can be inserted into the bottle-neck has also been developed and, like the beads, results in wines very similar to those made by the traditional method. Neither technique finds favour with traditionalists, however, nor with those concerned about unemployment.

THE MOST COMMON METHOD – IN TANK

This process, developed by an enterprising Bordeaux wine merchant early this century to transform his region's white wine surplus into something more commercially attractive, involves provoking the second fermentation in giant tanks rather than in bottle, so that the wine can simply be settled and the clear wine pumped off the lees to be bottled under pres-

The girasol, gyropalette in French, is a large metal cube-shaped crate into which bottles are packed parallel to each other and riddled by computer (which needs no sleep or weekends off). This results in bottle-necks like the ones below, and dramatic clunks and clicks at unexpected intervals in many of the more automated sparkling-wine cellars, including quite a number in Champagne.

sure. It takes months rather than years, and is very much less labour intensive, but the resulting wine has none of the interest and character generated by extended contact between maturing wine and the lees in a container as small as a bottle. That said, few grape varieties other than the Pinots and Chardonnay seem particularly well suited to the champagne method, and the tank method is a much more suitable process for grape varieties such as the Muscat used to produce Italy's light, fruity spumante (see page 89). The tank method is also known variously as the Charmat, Carstens, and cuve close process.

OTHER METHODS

Variations on the two principal methods outlined above have also been devised. The **transfer** method, for example, involves the rather cumbersome process of conducting the second fermentation in bottle and then either sucking out the deposit or emptying the contents of the bottles into a large tank, filtering it, and then rebottling the result under pressure.

Transversage is an occasional twist on the champagne method whereby, immediately following disgorgement, the contents of bottles of sparkling wine made by the champagne method are emptied into a pressure tank to which the dosage is added before the wine is bottled, typically in another (often small) size of bottle, under pressure. This is how many half-bottles, all airline 'splits' or quarter-bottles, and virtually all giant bottles of champagne are filled. For this reason champagne usually tastes best from a regular bottle or magnum.

HOW SWEET WINES ARE MADE

Why do strong men and women waste so much time and effort making top quality sweet wines? Because they taste so uniquely other-worldly, that's why. And why is it a waste of time and effort? Because so few consumers appreciate great sweet wines, the wine world's most hard-won treasures.

The extraordinary Botrytis cinerea fungus, or noble rot, which literally and systematically desiccates ripe grapes, increasing their sugar content and complexity – if the weather co-operates. If it attacks grapes that are less than fully ripe or if the weather is too wet, the grapes simply putrefy on the vine.

This is probably because so much bad quality sweet wine has been launched on the poor consumer. The more residual sugar a wine has, the greater the danger of some yeast acting on this sugar and starting a fermentation in bottle, giving off gas which will disturb both the wine and the consumer and may even break the bottle. Winemakers have therefore tended to add vast quantities of sulphur dioxide to ward off any possible yeast activity. This, together with the fact that in the days of 'Spanish Sauterne' (*sic*) far too many sweet wines lacked enough acidity to balance the residual sugar, must have put thousands if not millions of potential consumers off all sweet wines. Today, winemakers add much more conservative doses of sulphur, and tend to be much better at balancing sweetness with its natural antidote, acidity. A great sweet wine is so well balanced that it is quite possible to drink it throughout a meal, with all sorts of savoury dishes. I know because I've done it, with drools of pleasure.

BOTRYTIZED WINES

The *Botrytis cinerea* fungus can work magic on ripe grapes, making the skins thinner, encouraging evaporation of water and thereby concentration of the sugar and acidity, and adding all sorts of extra, still mysterious ingredients into the bargain that add extraordinary flavour and longevity. It will do this, however, only to grapes that are ripe and healthy, and only if the weather co-operates by alternating misty, moist mornings to encourage the fungus with warm, sunny afternoons to dry out the grapes and stop the mould spreading too rapidly. If the fungus attacks unripe grapes, or those whose skins have been broken (by hail for example), or if the weather is rainy or humid, then the fungus is an unremitting curse rather than a blessing and copious sprayings may be needed to combat rampant rot spreading through the vineyard, spoiling colour and flavour, especially in reds.

'Good botrytis' is called noble rot in English, pourriture noble in French, Edelfäule in German and muffa in Italian. Bad botrytis is called grey rot (or sometimes just rot). Sweet wines made from grapes affected by good botrytis are often called botrytized.

Making botrytized wines is particularly difficult because the juice is extremely viscous (and in very short supply, given the concentration effect of the fungus). The grapes have to be picked by hand, sometimes involving many forays through the vineyard to pick only grapes at the optimum point of (apparent) decay.

Botrytized wines, which have a distinctive sort of cabbagey smell in youth and seem almost immortal, include château-bottled Sauternes in suitable vintages, lesser sweet white bordeaux appellations and Monbazillac in exceptional vintages for Bordeaux sweet whites (see page 306), Loire wines labelled Moelleux in vintages such as 1989 and 1990, Alsace wines labelled Sélection de Grains Nobles, Germany's Trockenbeerenauslese and Beerenauslese rarities, Austria's much less rare counterparts (notably from Burgenland), Hungary's sweetest forms of Tokay, a few Italian specialities labelled Muffato, and a host of speciality bottlings from all over the world, among which botrytized Chardonnay and Sauvignon Blanc seem to work surprisingly well. Some producers, notably in California and some in Australia, pick grapes and then spray them with botrytis spores in the winery, replicating the ideal weather conditions artificially. The resulting wines often taste similar although it is too early to say whether they age as well.

LATE PICKED SWEETNESS

Some sweet wines are sweet simply because they are made with ultra-ripe grapes, unaffected by botrytis but sometimes almost raisined on the vine. Jurançon is made like this every year, as are cheaper Sauternes and other sweet whites from south west France, or grander ones in less successful vintages. Germany's Spätlese and Auslese wines also depend on this sort of natural ripeness for their sugar content.

SWEET WINES MADE FROM DRIED GRAPES

Another way of concentrating a grape's natural sweetness is to dry, or raisin, the grape, encouraging its moisture content to evaporate, typically by spreading whole bunches on trays, well aerated to avoid the danger of mould (or outside in the hot sunshine in very dry climates). This classical practice is most obviously – though by no means exclusively – continued in north east Italy where sweet wines made this way are often described as Recioto (dry ones as Amarone). France also makes some *vin de paille* from grapes dried traditionally on straw (a rare speciality of Hermitage).

EISWEIN AND ICE WINE

These fashionable wines are, for obvious reasons, the speciality of wine regions as cold as northern Germany and Canada. Ripe, healthy grapes are picked when actually frozen on the vine. When such grapes are pressed, water is eliminated in the form of crystals left in the press and the natural sugar content (and acidity) is thereby concentrated. An increasing proportion of grapes are devoted to making such wines, rather than botrytized wines, in suitable parts of the world, since low temperatures are usually more reliable than the coincidence of botrytis fungus with suitable weather conditions, and yet Eiswein and proper Ice wine (made as a result of natural rather than artificial freezing) sells for almost as high a price.

ADDING EXTRA ALCOHOL

One way of making a wine that is both sweet and stable is to add alcohol to it, to make a mixture in which yeast would be completely incapable. This is the classic recipe for sweet fortified wines. Port, madeira, malaga and marsala, indeed all of the world's sweet fortified wines are sweet and strong because fermentation is stopped half-way by the addition of enough spirit to stun the yeasts. The only exception to this is sweet sherry, which is sweetened by adding specially concentrated grape syrup. See pages 240–42 for full details of how port and madeira are made.

The technique is also applied to grape juice that has hardly started to ferment to make France's *vins doux naturels* such as Muscat de Beaumes-de-Venise and other Languedoc-Roussillon Muscats, and red and tawny Rasteau (in the southern Rhône) and Banyuls as well as Maury and Rivesaltes in Roussillon. These sweet, alcoholic, but slightly raw mixtures of alcohol and part-fermented grape juice may then be carefully matured, either in wood or glass, in varying degrees of heat and humidity.

France also produces a range of sweet, grape-based drinks made by adding neutral grape spirit to grape juice before it has even started to ferment. Pineau des Charentes is the most important of these, made in Cognac.

EVERYDAY SWEET WINES

Some commercial sweet white wines, notably in Bordeaux and the Loire, are still made by leaving high levels of sugar in the wine and then adding lots of sulphur, but much more common (and more attractive to taste) is to ferment all the grape sugar into alcohol to produce a dry wine and then to add sweetness in the form of unfermented grape juice, sometimes concentrated. The sweet mixture (which is of course a little less alcoholic than the original wine) is then heavily filtered to remove any possible yeasts and bottled carefully to produce a stable liquid that should be drunk as young as possible. This, for example, is how most commercial German wines (Liebfraumilch *et al.*) are made.

Then there is the north Italian way of making a wine that is both sweet and fizzy: stopping the fermentation part-way through so that the wine is low in alcohol, high in sugar and still contains some carbon dioxide given off by the fermentation. This results in wines such as Asti and Moscato Spumante.

Trees grow so slowly in the Tronçais forest in France's Allier département that its oak (shown here during the all-important years of outdoor seasoning and being shaped into barrels) is tight-grained and highly sought-after.

OAK – INGREDIENT X

There is no doubt whatsoever that the second most important plant in the late twentieth-century world of wine, after the vine, is the oak tree. Winemakers everywhere are seeking to add cachet, dimension and value to their products by making or ageing them in oak barrels. And whereas they may haggle with their customers over pennies when it comes to the price of the wine they sell, these same producers seem willing to pay the earth in order to acquire what is widely seen as the magic winemaking ingredient, a top quality barrel. French oak carries the highest reputation and price tag and, while France's wine producers have seen their exports shrink over the last decade, the country's coopers (*tonneliers* in French) have enjoyed unparalleled prosperity, exporting barrels to wine producers all over the globe.

At one time wooden barrels were used to transport and store practically every commodity. Today the cooperage industry is kept alive only by demand from wine and dark spirits producers. Much less than 10 per cent of all the wine produced in the world today is aged in small barrels, but these wines attract a disproportionate amount of attention because they are some of the world's most exciting.

WHY OAK?

Wood can have two possible sorts of effect on a wine held in it: it can impart flavour, colour and tannins from the wood itself; and it has the physical property of allowing the wine much more contact with air than an inert material such as stainless steel or lined cement. But different woods vary enormously in their suitability for wine containers. Chestnut, pine, redwood, acacia and various other woods have all been used for larger wine vats, but oak is ideal for small barrels because it is hard, strong, watertight yet supple, and its characteristics seem to have an affinity, however ill-understood, with those of wine. Fully understanding the complicated interactions between flavours and physical properties of different sorts of oak and wine will keep researchers busy well into the next millennium. What is known, however, is that most of the oak's flavour is leeched into the first wine put into a barrel, and that ageing wine in a small oak barrel encourages it to become clear and stable in the most natural way.

WHAT WOODEN CONTAINERS ARE USED FOR

Many older wineries are equipped with large wooden storage and/or fermentation tanks which are so old that they can no longer

FAR LEFT Barrel remnants (top) are sometimes inserted, in a perforated container, in an old barrrel while the toasted oak chips (bottom) are suspended in the fermentation vat in a sort of teabag. LEFT Much finer oak chips (the bottom ones have been toasted and therefore have more flavour) are either suspended in a teabag or used as a flavoured fining agent.

impart anything directly to the wine (see below) but, so long as they have been kept scrupulously clean, they can still be useful for settling and clarifying wine.

Modern wineries actively choose to invest in wood for one of two purposes in most cases: either large fermentation vessels of any age, often open-topped, in which wood's physical properties can be useful (but stainless steel is much easier to cool and clean); or small, new barrels expected to impart the wood's own flavour as well as its physical characteristics to wine deliberately matured in them for many months (barrel maturation) and often, especially in the case of full bodied white wines, fermented in them too (barrel fermentation).

OAK-RELATED FACTORS WHICH AFFECT HOW WINE TASTES

WHERE THE OAK COMES FROM

Perhaps partly as a result of a particularly well-publicized research program (sic) at California's Robert Mondavi Winery in the late 1970s, winemakers tend to be punctilious in their choice of oak provenance. Many is the New World winery visitor who seeks or receives exact information on the percentage split between Vosges, Allier and Tronçais barrels in a particular blend. Some of those who have wandered through forests and timber yards are a little more wary of oak labelling.

Like the wine-producing vine family (see page 96), the wine-maturing oak family is most readily divided into its European and American members. The United States is the biggest commercial grower of oak (a business sustained by the regulation that requires bourbon to be matured in a new American oak barrel). American oak is in general more powerfully flavoured than European oak, often with a slightly sweet vanilla-like note, and is so dense that it remains watertight even after sawing. Its more obvious flavours mean that it has been used mainly for powerfully flavoured red wines, notably in the Americas, Spain (which for historical reasons has a tradition of importing American barrels) and Australia, but carefully seasoned American oak can be used to quite subtle effect on other wines such as warm climate Chardonnays too.

France is by far the most important source of European oak, and its forests, which cover a quarter of the country, have been carefully managed for at least three centuries – an important consideration in a business where the ideal product should be at least 80 and ideally 100 years old. Coopers usually distinguish between 'tight-grained' oaks (the result of slow growth in close planted, dense forests) and more porous, more tannic, 'wide-grained' oaks, typically Limousin oak grown in western France, which are of more interest for brandy than for wine maturation. France's most revered oaks for winemaking come from central France (Allier and Nièvre/ Nevers in the upper Loire) or from the hills west of Alsace as pale Vosges wood. Tronçais and Bertranges are specific forests within the respective *départements*, France's 'counties', of Allier and Nièvre.

Before the Russian revolution Baltic oaks were the most highly prized and trade in eastern European oaks is once more increasing, even though many forests have been poorly maintained. Slovenian oak is widely used in Italy.

HOW THE WOOD WAS SEASONED

Barrels are made from staves cut from long planks of wood left outside in a suitably unpolluted environment for two or more years so that the harsher elements are leeched out naturally. Drying in a special steam kiln is a way of artificially accelerating this process. It is increasingly obvious that the duration and quality of this 'seasoning' plays just as important a role as the provenance of the oak. One ancient tree typically provides fewer than two small wine barrels.

HOW THE BARREL IS MADE

Staves are fashioned as gently as possible from these planks and bent over small fires, secured by hoops and hammered into a barrel shape.

The extent to which these fires are allowed to 'toast' or char the wood has become an important dimension in buying and selling barrels (again, partly because of the focus of the Mondavi experiments). Barrels given only a light toast are more likely to impart substantial oak flavour and tannins than one with a medium toast, although heavily toasted barrels, popular in Burgundy, can impart their own charred flavour to a wine matured in them.

SIZE OF CONTAINER

The larger the barrel the lower the ratio of surface area to volume and the less impact the wood is likely to have on the wine in either physical or flavour sense. However, barrels holding less than 190 l (50 gal) can overwhelm a wine with oak flavour and tannins, especially if they are new (see below). The most widely used barrels hold either 225 l (59 gal) like the Bordeaux barrique or 228 l (60 gal) like the Burgundian pièce, but hogsheads of 300 l (79 gal) are also used quite widely in the New World.

AGE OF CONTAINER

The newer a barrel the more oak flavour and tannin it has to be leeched into the wine. For this reason, brand new barrels are prized by most wine producers (except Piedmont traditionalists and those who make sherry, which is best matured in an old example of the traditional 600 l [158 gal] American oak 'butt'). In practice a new barrel is used once or possibly twice for a top-of-the-range wine, before being used once or twice for a medium-quality wine. After that it has almost no flavour to impart and will be used on lesser wines merely for its physical properties of helping to clarify the wine.

PERIOD IN CONTAINER

One crucial factor in determining how a wine will taste is whether it is fermented in a new oak barrel. A small but increasing proportion of fine white wines are fermented in barrel, which leads naturally to the enriching process of lees contact (see page 82). The natural variation in temperature of such a small container can add complexity and the buffering effect of the lees can result in delicate, pale wines that have an extra-silky texture. (White wines put into small barrels after fermentation often turn brown in the bottle because they still contain heavy phenolics.)

Some red wines, particularly in warmer climates where grapes are deeply coloured enough without extended maceration on the skins after fermentation, are drawn off the skins and put into small barrels part-way through fermentation. Barrel fermentation of reds is particularly popular in Australia, where it can result in wines with a charred, 'sweet' aroma reminiscent of tomato ketchup and, combined with frequent rackings, can accelerate ageing.

The length of time a wine is matured in oak will strongly influence how it tastes. Even if it is only in the first few months that much oak flavour is imparted from a new barrel (and that depends on the toast and the extent to which any lees are stirred), the longer a wine stays in the lightly aerated atmosphere of a barrel, the more phenolic compounds will be precipitated and the faster it will age (see pages 39–41). This ageing process is accelerated by each racking because of exposure to oxygen.

A CHEAP ALTERNATIVE – OAK CHIPS

The most common alternative to an expensive oak barrel is to add a sackful of small oak chips or shavings to the fermentation tank and rely on some oak flavour being leeched out by the heat and alcohol generated by fermentation. There will be none of wood's physical advantages, however, and the oak flavour may be shorter lived than in a barrel-aged wine. The labels on such wines may refer to 'oak ageing', 'oak influence' or 'oak maturation' but the B-word (barrel) should be obvious by omission.

Chips are not necessarily a bad thing; they provide consumers with the sort of flavours they seek for a fraction of the cost of a real oak barrel, but they cannot provide the physical properties of barrel fermentation and maturation.

3
WINE GRAPE VARIETIES

THE VINE FAMILY

The grapevine, the world's most important fruit crop, is a natural creeper, a distant relative of Virginia creeper in fact, as can be seen by inspecting closely this colourful plant that clings to many houses. All sorts of vine grow wild wherever plants thrive. Botanists call the family to which the vine belongs *Vitis* and have identified about 60 different species within it. The Far East has its own native vine species such as the *Vitis amurensis* of Mongolia, which has particularly good resistance to extreme cold. Europe and the Middle East has just one native vine species, the one from which almost all of the world's famous wines are made, called *Vitis vinifera*, often called simply **vinifera**. (The word does not exist in classical Latin but was dreamt up by a botanist to convey 'wine-grape bearing'.) Within each species, hundreds, often thousands, of different varieties have been identified. Cabernet Sauvignon and Chardonnay are two of the most famous varieties of vinifera.

As the early European colonists discovered to their initial delight (see page 264), North America has the greatest diversity of vine species, most of which look quite different from vinifera, having much flatter leaves and thinner shoots. Some of the most famous are called *Vitis labrusca*, *Vitis riparia* and *Vitis rupestris* and, in the south eastern states, *Vitis rotundifolia*, which has particularly round leaves with less marked indentations than most other vines. Wine made from many of these American vines, particularly *Vitis labrusca*, tastes quite different from wine made from vinifera vines. It has a strong smell reminiscent of musk or very strong artificial wild strawberry flavour which wine tasters often call 'foxy'. It can be quite attractive to palates brought up on such wine, but comes as a shock to those used to the flavours of 'European' varieties, by now widely disseminated all over the wine-producing world, including North and South America, Africa and Australasia.

The early American settlers, seeking familiar flavours in their wine, imported European vine cuttings and were puzzled as to why they refused to flourish in the new colonies. The explanation did not emerge for more than 200 years, at the end of the nineteenth century.

In the mid-nineteenth century the vineyards of France in general and Bordeaux in particular were ravaged by a fungal disease called *oïdium*, or **powdery mildew**. Eventually spraying vines with a preparation of copper sulphate (called Bordeaux mixture) was found to ward off this debilitating disease, but no sooner had the vines recovered from this, in the 1860s, than they started to suffer from another much less explicable condition, apparently slowly dying before horrified growers' eyes. This phenomenon spread throughout France and eventually to almost all parts of the wine-producing world. After decades of despair, trials and research, it was found to be the work of a tiny louse, called **phylloxera**, which loves nothing more than a nice juicy vinifera vine root. It munches its way through root after root, literally killing the plants above. The only vines which in the long term have demonstrated apparent immunity to phylloxera are certain native American species and vines growing in very dry and/or very sandy conditions.

It is now clear that the dreaded louse and the fungus responsible for powdery mildew (and that which causes another vine disease, **downy mildew**, which arrived in France soon after the first effects of phylloxera were noted, just to complicate an already traumatic situation) are native to North America. Most native American vines have therefore developed a good resistance to them, but when in the mid-nineteenth century Europeans began to travel and bring back across the Atlantic botanical specimens kept alive in special glass cases, the effects on the European vine were devastating, for they brought phylloxera, to which European vines had no resistance whatsoever, with them too.

Phylloxera literally threatened the entire world's wine industry and a long-term solution had to be found. Eventually, after all sorts of experimentation with chemicals and flooding, it was found that phylloxera could be combated by **grafting** vinifera vines on to American **rootstocks**, so that the part of the plant vulnerable to phylloxera became resistant to it. Since the late nineteenth century nurserymen have worked hard at breeding rootstocks designed for particular environments and goals. Today about 85 per cent of the world's wine-producing vines are European vinifera varieties grafted on to rootstocks containing a high proportion of American genes in order to minimize the risk of phylloxera damage. There are some particularly isolated, or very dry or very sandy wine regions where growers are prepared to take the risk of planting ungrafted vines. Chile, for example, has never suffered phylloxera damage. The vineyards of the French Camargue and Colares in Portugal are almost all seaside sand. South Australia (but not neighbouring Victoria) is unaffected by phylloxera and, so far, growers in New Zealand, Greece, the Pacific Northwest and England have been prepared to trade off the cost savings of planting ungrafted vines against the very obvious presence of phylloxera.

The most obvious effects of phylloxera in the 1990s are to be seen in Northern California where the great majority of vines were vinifera grafted on to a rootstock called AXR 1, a hybrid of the vinifera vine Aramon (see page 130) and a member of the *Vitis rupestris* species. (Crosses of members of different species are called **hybrids**, while those of members of the same species, such as Müller-Thurgau, for example, are called **crossings**.) California growers were encouraged to choose AXR 1 as their rootstock because it was usefully productive. Its acknowledged low resistance to phylloxera was thought to be unimportant; phylloxera had not affected Northern California since the late nineteenth century, when it had almost wiped out the local

wine industry. But as the 1980s came to an end it was clear that thousands of acres of vineyard had been fatally invaded by phylloxera. A dramatically comprehensive replanting programme, designed to match popular varieties to suitable sites and to establish modern vine-training systems, will cost billions of dollars but should result in a much more robust wine industry – although there is widespread disagreement about which rootstocks are most suitable replacements for AXR 1. (Everyone, however, is agreed that high resistance to phylloxera is the most important criterion.)

For decades after phylloxera first devastated European vines, discussions raged about whether the wine produced 'pre-phylloxera' was better than the produce of vines grafted on to American rootstocks. Since so much was in flux at that time, we shall never know. Certainly I would never claim to be able to taste the difference between the produce of grafted and ungrafted vines.

It is interesting to note, however, that the most intelligent vine-growing consultants in Chile now realize that there are disadvantages to their famously ungrafted vines. Because there has never been a phylloxera epidemic (probably because the soils here are so dry), no one has any experience of vine rootstocks and there are strict quarantines, as elsewhere, on bringing in plant material. This means that it will be several years before it is legally possible to plant rootstocks on a commercial scale in Chile – and yet the right rootstock can be an extremely useful tool to a vine-grower who is plagued by over-vigorous (leafy) vines and soil pests called **nematodes**, as many Chileans are. Rootstocks are not necessarily a bad thing!

In the early twentieth century, in the wake of phylloxera and the two mildews, when quantity rather than quality was the abiding preoccupation of wine producers everywhere, vine breeders concentrated on developing an array of hybrids designed to resist all these scourges and produce lots of wine. The first generation of these so-called hybrid 'direct producers' (i.e.

ungrafted vines) was bred from American vines. Concord, Catawba and Isabella are examples of **American hybrids** still grown today in North America and humid climates such as that of Japan.

Wines made from such vines found little favour with Europeans, however, which led to a new generation of hybrids, the so-called **French hybrids**, bred from a mixture of American and European vines. These were extremely useful for a France in transition, because of their good disease resistance and lack of foxy flavour, but as the agrochemical industry obliged with preparations specially designed to fight mildew and rot, these French hybrids have gradually been replaced with vinifera vines in almost all wine regions. Baco, Chambourcin and Seyval Blanc are examples of French hybrids grown today in Gascony, New South Wales and England respectively, and none of them has the remotest hint of foxy flavour.

Vine-breeders more recently have worked on increasing yields and in Germany, where ripeness is revered, building up grape sugar fast. Germany's vineyards have accordingly been invaded by a new generation of crossings such as Ortega, Optima, Kerner and Ehrenfelser.

The French way of doing things has been to develop particular **clones** of the important varieties with particular abilities, the most popular of which is often prolific yield. Burgundy's vineyards suffered considerably in the 1970s and early 1980s as too many growers chose Pinot Noir clones designed with quantity and/or rot resistance in mind rather than wine quality.

Different varieties of vine produce discernibly different grapes, which in turn produce discernibly different wines. The science of describing and identifying different vine varieties is called **ampelography**. Some varieties are more prone to mutation than others – Pinot and Grenache, for example, both mutate easily and

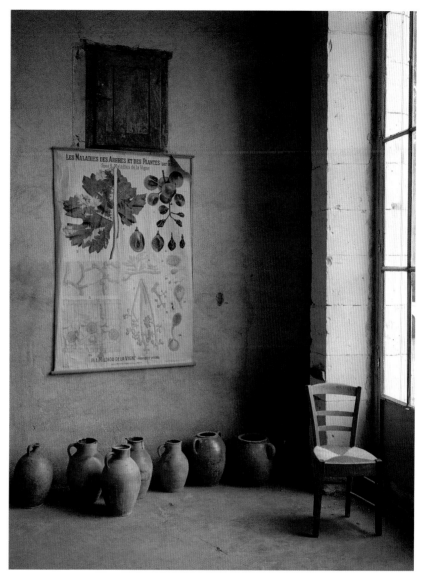

Northern California vines are burnt to rid the state of any traces of the phylloxera louse that still remain (left), while an ancient poster in Chinon in the Loire Valley (right) reminds today's vine-growers of the dangers of mildew in a damp climate such as France's.

can therefore be found with all sorts of different colours of grape skin, from dark purple through red-pink and violet to gold and green. Red and pink wine need some pigment and therefore must be made from dark-skinned grapes, but white wine can be made from grapes of any colour. Many varieties called 'grey' (Pinot Gris, for example) have pink-skinned berries but naturally produce deep-coloured white wines. If dark-skinned berries are pressed very gently on the other hand, as Pinot Noir grapes are in Champagne, they will yield pale juice and white wine. The only grapes incapable of producing white wine are those very unusual ones whose flesh is not the usual grey-green common to 99 per cent of all wine grapes harvested but is actually tinted red. Such varieties are called Teinturiers in French, Tintoreras in Spanish – literally 'dyers'.

The wine grape varieties that follow are those the enthusiastic wine drinker is most likely to come across and are divided into pale-skinned (White Wine Varieties) and dark-skinned (Red Wine Varieties). There are thousands more, however, with particular concentrations in Portugal, Galicia, Greece and Central Europe. It would be very sad if we lost this diversity to Chardonnay- and Cabernet-mania.

WHITE WINE VARIETIES

Airén, the grape of the vast La Mancha region in central Spain and therefore the world's most planted wine grape, which produces crisp, fairly neutral wine, much of it being distilled into brandy.

Albalonga, German crossing chiefly planted in Rheinhessen.

Albana, Emilia-Romagna vine related to GRECO DI TUFO, making deep-coloured wines.

Albariño, the perfumed, elegant aristocrat of Rias Baixas in north west Spain. Sometimes VIOGNIER-like.

Albillo, Spanish variety producing quite neutral but full bodied wine, mainly in Ribeiro but also used to perfume Ribera del Duero reds.

Aligoté, Burgundy's second white grape, making tartish wine for early consumption, best from Bouzeron. Also grown in Bulgaria, Romania and Russia.

Altesse, another name for Savoie's ROUSSETTE.

Alva, see ROUPEIRO.

Alvarinho, ALBARIÑO in Portugal's Vinho Verde region where it is also prized.

Amigne, Valais rarity making rich, heady wines.

Ansonica, Tuscan name for INZOLIA.

Arbois, minor Loire variety making soft wines in Touraine.

Arinto, Portuguese grape making high-acid, sometimes lemony wine in Bucelas, Ribatejo, Vinho Verde amongst others.

Arneis, floral-scented Piedmont speciality rescued from extinction. Has been fashionable. Drink young.

Arrufiac, Arrufiat, grainy traditional Gascon ingredient in Pacherenc du Vic-Bilh.

Arvine, Petite Arvine, AMIGNE's cousin.

Assyrtiko, from the Greek island of Santorini but valued increasingly widely on mainland Greece for its acidity, apple and lemon flavours, and ability to express terroir.

Auxerrois, slightly fuller, less acid version of PINOT BLANC, widely planted in Alsace and blended with it (although the blend is almost invariably called Pinot Blanc on the label). Treasured in Luxembourg for its low acid.

Avesso makes full bodied, scented wine in Vinho Verde. May be JAEN.

Azal, Vinho Verde grape with usually high acids.

Bacchus, conveniently early ripening German crossing that can bring grape sugars but little else to a blend. Some curranty varietals from Franken and England.

Baco Blanc, Baco 22A, French hybrid named after its creator in 1898. Good at being grafted but on the way out of Armagnac, once its stronghold. See also BACO NOIR.

Baiyu, Chinese name for RKATSITELI.

Baroque, full, nutty mainstay of Tursan from south west France.

Bergeron, local name for ROUSSANNE in the Savoie appellation of Chignin.

Bical, Bairrada's crisp speciality, which is useful for sparkling wines.

Blanc Fumé, SAUVIGNON BLANC in Pouilly-sur-Loire.

Boal, great rich varietal of Madeira, Anglicized to Bual.

Bombino Bianco, a widely planted vine in Apulia as well as further north up Italy's Adriatic coast. Extremely prolific but Valentini's 'Trebbiano d'Abruzzo' demonstrates what can be achieved.

Borrado das Moscas, BICAL in Dão (Portugal).

Bourboulenc, potentially fine Languedoc variety at its best in La Clape, where it can smell attractively of iodine.

Bouvier, lesser central European table grape, a crossing of Chardonnay and Zöldsilváni vines planted in Austria, Hungary and, as Ranina, in Slovenia.

Burger, once very important in California, now down to a minor role in the Central Valley.

Carignan Blanc, a white mutation of the widely planted CARIGNAN found particularly in Roussillon in France.

Catarratto, Sicily's most important grape after SANGIOVESE and therefore one of the world's most planted. Its produce is not exactly flavourful and much of it ends up as grape concentrate or at the bottom of the European wine lake.

Cayetana, prolific producer for brandy de Jerez in Spain's south west.

Cerceal, Portuguese grape responsible for the driest, most elegant form of madeira, Sercial (see page 241). This late ripening vine, also grown on the mainland, provides grapes that are eye-tinglingly high in acidity and wines that can last for decades.

Cereza, basic pink-skinned Argentine.

Chardonnay, the most famous vine variety of all. So powerful is the C-word on a wine label that, like Cabernet Sauvignon, Chardonnay has virtually no synonyms – although in Styria in southern Austria some winemakers persist with the tradition of calling it Morillon.

In the 1980s something extremely important to the history of wine happened: 'Chardonnay' became a name more familiar to the world's wine buyers than any of the geographically named wines this vine variety had for centuries produced, such as Chablis, Montrachet or Corton-Charlemagne.

When the emerging New World wine industries introduced varietal labelling, calling wines by the name of their principal grape variety, it was Chardonnay that made the most friends. Wine drinkers find it flatteringly easy to enjoy, with its broad, exuberant charms, relatively high alcohol and low acidity, and lack of powerful scent. Vine-growers find it easy to grow productively and profitably (it can yield well, ripen usefully early, although buds rather too early for frost-free comfort in cool climates). And winemakers revel in the range of different winemaking techniques to which Chardonnay readily submits: not just a wide range of dry white wines with more weight than most, but delicate sparkling wines and even a few extremely successful sweet white wines made with the benefit of 'noble rot' (see page 88).

All over the world, producing Chardonnay is seen as a rite of passage in new wine regions. Almost any wine producer with ambitions to belong to the great international club of wine grown-ups has to prove that he or she can make a Chardonnay with the best of them, preferably a Chardonnay fermented and matured in new-(ish) oak barrels the Burgundian way. The fact is that most of this sort of wine is far more a product made in the cellar than in the vineyard. Or, to put it another way, skilfully made barrel-fermented Chardonnays tend to taste much the same wherever they are made. Indeed when many people say they like the taste of Chardonnay, what they often mean is that they like the taste of oak, or at least the qualities of oak maturation.

So, although in terms of total area planted, Chardonnay lags well behind such workhorse varieties as Spain's Airén, Italy's Trebbiano, and the old Soviet Union's Rkatsiteli, it is more widely distributed than any other grape variety – probably even more widely than its red wine counterpart Cabernet Sauvignon, which needs more sunshine to ripen it than Chardonnay.

However, Chardonnay mania, of which French coopers have been the major beneficiaries, is a relatively recent phenomenon. In the early 1970s it was hardly grown outside its Burgundian homeland and Champagne. It accounted for only a tiny proportion of all vines grown in California and Australia, for example, whereas by the early 1990s it had become the most planted white wine grape in both.

At times demand for Chardonnay grapes from wine producers has been so much greater than supply (Australia in the mid-1990s springs to mind) that Chardonnay has been blended with one or two other varieties. Semillon-Chardonnay ('SemChard') and Chardonnay-Colombard blends became the pragmatic solution to an industry's problem.

The Chardonnay vine is nothing if not adaptable. Commercially acceptable Chardonnay can be produced in really quite hot wine regions such as the hot interiors of California, South Africa and Australia, where clever winemaking can give it tropical fruit flavours and even some suggestion of oakiness, often using oak chips. In cooler wine regions such as Chablis, Carneros and Tasmania, on the other hand, it can produce apple-crisp tingle juice which, in less ripe years can have rapier-like acidity. The best examples can benefit from five or even more years in bottle to soften that acidity and develop rounder flavours to balance it – although less concentrated examples produced in cool years may simply taste even leaner as the bloom of youth fades. Excluding premier cru and grand cru burgundy, Chardonnay does not make wines for long ageing.

Cooler regions are also particularly good sources of lively, relatively subtle Chardonnay

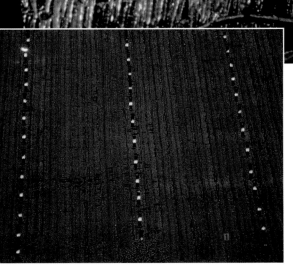

fruit for makers of sparkling wine, who value acidity and an absence of obvious flavours. Chardonnay is, for example, the second most important grape variety grown in Champagne (see page 172), and it was largely the dramatic expansion of the Champagne vineyard that propelled Chardonnay into first place among France's white grape varieties in the 1980s. Chardonnay can bring a floral or even steely

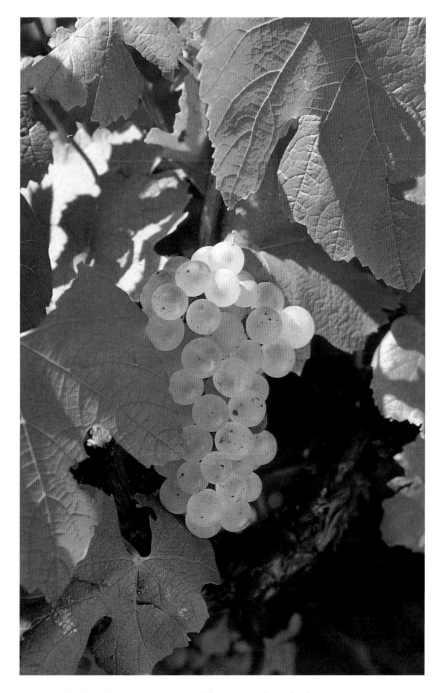

Chardonnay's tendency to bud early means that in very northerly wine regions such as Chablis (left), frost is a perennial hazard against which fires have to be lit in the vineyard. The Chardonnay grapes grown in New South Wales, Australia (right) have no such threats to their existence. Overripeness is the problem here.

character to a sparkling wine in its youth, which can age into toastiness after years in bottle.

The wines of Chablis, one of the coolest wine regions in France, have a very particular flavour. It reminds me of wet stones, with some suggestion of very green fruit, but without the strong aroma and lean build of a Sauvignon Blanc. Traditional, top quality examples designed for a long life can even taste slightly

musty in middle age, as though those wet stones had sprouted some moss. And then after about eight years in bottle they can develop much more complicated, often deliciously honey-like, flavours.

In more temperate climates Chardonnay can yield some of the finest dry white wine in the world. The heartland of Burgundy, the Côte d'Or, is effectively the nerve centre of this style of wine: savoury and dense, the grape a transparent medium through which different vineyards (and winemakers) can communicate their own individual styles, often only after many years in bottle. Most of the wines are made with extensive use of small oak barrels, and many of them are simply too 'closed' (low in aroma and flavour) and dour to enjoy before their third birthday, depending on the vintage. Hazelnuts, liquorice, butter and spice are just a few of the many aromas that can be found in the heady perfume that can develop in these markedly full bodied wines. Montrachet, Puligny-Montrachet, Chassagne-Montrachet, Meursault and Corton-Charlemagne are some of the most famous names. Typical Meursault tends to be butter-golden and a little heavier and earlier maturing than a typical wine from 'The Montrachets' (as the villages would doubtless be called in Britain), which has more lean, pure, nuanced character capable of developing for up to a decade in bottle, while Corton-Charlemagne can be nutty, almost almond-flavoured. But 'typical' burgundy hardly exists. Wines here are made with exasperatingly varied levels of skill, so that one winemaker's Bourgogne Blanc, the most basic appellation, may be better than another's Montrachet, even though it costs a fraction of the price.

The Mâconnais tends to produce a more New World style of Chardonnay: plump, open, user-friendly wines that can taste of melon, or apples warmed by the sun. Most of these wines, particularly Mâcon Blanc and St-Véran, are designed to be drunk within two or three years of the vintage, although the most ambitious producers in the region, notably in Pouilly-Fuissé, are making wines with Côte d'Or pretensions, but usually without Côte d'Or prices. Chardonnay grown between the Mâconnais and the Côte d'Or in the Côte Chalonnaise tends to taste somewhere between the two styles.

These are France's traditional Chardonnay vine strongholds, but the variety's influence has been spreading within France as elsewhere. Wine producers in the Loire valley have embraced this fashionable grape so enthusiastically that the laws explicitly ban more than 20 per cent of the variety in blends for sparkling Saumur and the dry whites of Anjou and Touraine in order to preserve the Loire's own traditional character. Some producers of Muscadet have also been experimenting with oaked Chardonnays. And several of France's more cosmopolitan producers in distinctly non-Chardonnay territory have quietly planted a row or two for their own interest.

Within the appellation system Chardonnay has invaded Limoux with the blessing of the authorities, to add finesse to the local sparkling Crémant de Limoux as well as producing rather fine, lemony barrel-fermented still wine.

Increasing amounts of Chardonnay are also grown on the lower, flatter vineyards of the Languedoc to produce Vin de Pays, usually Vin de Pays d'Oc. As one would expect in an area known as France's New World, the quality of these wines varies according to the position of the vineyard(s) (for many of them are blends) and the quality and style of the winemaking. Price offers a fairly good guide. The cheapest Languedoc Chardonnay is simply a relatively full bodied dry white wine, while the very best, usually given full oak treatment in the winery, can offer some of the class of Burgundy.

Thanks to an extraordinary 1980s boom in plantings, Chardonnay has become synonymous with white wine in California (see page 268) and is responsible for a remarkably homogeneous ocean of off-dry, golden, quite alcoholic, easy-to-drink liquid. While the most commercial examples are usually deliberately slightly sweetened to give them wide appeal, the key to serious quality in a California Chardonnay is climate. Wherever coastal fogs reliably slow down the ripening process, extending the growing season of this early ripening variety, and yields are kept in check, then California can produce some very fine wines indeed, with considerable Burgundian savour to them, but without the Old World surliness in youth. Carneros, Santa Maria, and much of Sonoma, particularly Alexander Valley, have all produced some fine Chardonnay made very much in the mould of a good Meursault.

The variety is also grown almost everywhere in North America where it has even half a chance of thriving, including the cool wine areas of Canada and New York state (where Long Island has proved successful) as well as Washington and Oregon, which may respectively be better suited to Riesling and Pinot Gris.

Australia's strong suit is the reliable quality and varied character of her middle-range Chardonnays (see page 285). They have been hugely successful commercially with their obvious, simple fruitiness, perked up with (usually added) acid and, often, oak chips. Lindemans Bin 65 is now an international brand and quality has been staggeringly high, considering the volumes of it that gush forth from the company's vast plant at Karadoc in Australia's irrigated interior. More concentrated examples of this exuberant, user-friendly style are also produced, typically from warmish regions where yields are more restrained. Cowra in New South Wales, for example, has long been a source of golden Chardonnays that somehow taste as molten and lustrous as they look. Mudgee too has produced some fine Chardonnay from a rare clone of the variety that locals believe was imported in the nineteenth century, decades before Chardonnay mania hit Australia in the early 1980s.

Cooler areas of Australia can produce more subtle Chardonnay, more reminiscent of Côte d'Or wine in structure if not flavour. Tasmania makes the leanest examples, some so lean they are snapped up by Australia's bubbling sparkling wine industry. The Adelaide Hills, Yarra Valley and the southern vineyards of Western Australia have all proved themselves capable of making top quality Chardonnays, whose higher acidity levels can preserve them for several years in bottle (whereas most commercial Australian Chardonnay should be drunk as young as possible and ideally before its second birthday).

Australian producers may envy the high acid levels that their counterparts in New Zealand can hardly avoid, while New Zealanders would probably be happier with more reliable ripeness (see page 296). Despite New Zealand's reputation for Sauvignon Blanc, the country consistently produces more Chardonnay. Winemaking standards have been varied but those prepared to restrain yields and oak influence can produce subtle, sometimes exciting wines. Gisborne Chardonnay has long had its followers but there have been dramatic examples from wineries all over the North and South Islands.

Experimentation with the world's favourite grape variety in South Africa was severely hampered in the 1980s by the fact that the original official planting stock was seriously inferior, but quality is improving rapidly, even if a Cape style is yet to emerge. Blending with other varieties, Sauvignon Blanc and even Riesling, is common.

The vineyards of South America have also been invaded by Chardonnay only relatively recently. The vine has shown a certain amount of promise in Chile, where the produce of cool Casablanca can blend well with riper Maipo fruit. Argentina has, for the moment, only a tiny proportion of its extensive vineyards planted to Chardonnay, but almost exact reproductions of California Chardonnay have been produced under the Catena label and Peñaflor, the largest producer, is busy catching up with the 'international' style by establishing cooler vineyards such as those at Tupungato.

In the Old World, Spain has relatively limited plantings of Chardonnay, for the variety tends to ripen too fast in many regions, and its affinity with the prevailing American oak has been less obvious (although Australians and Californians have provided some excellent examples). Portugal has some experimental plantings and may fare better, although its own array of native vine varieties is surely reason enough to resist the international invader.

Italy made some of the earliest varietal Chardonnays and pretty vapid they were too, but it is now possible to find some stunningly ambitious wines made with great care. Chardonnay has long been grown in the north east of the country and can be found, often in simpler, unoaked varietal versions in Friuli, Trentino and Alto Adige, although much of the fruit is siphoned off for the spumante industry.

Since the break-up of the Soviet bloc British wine consumers have been treated to an ocean of eastern European wines labelled Chardonnay, but relatively few have so far demonstrated much varietal character and the first wave of oak-aged examples were often oily and heavy. Keeping yields down to a level at which interesting flavours develop has been a serious problem but doubtless by the turn of the century Bulgaria, Hungary, Moldova, Romania and Slovenia will all be producing Chardonnays of truly international standard (Slovenia is already starting to).

Austria and Switzerland have proved they belong to the international fine winemaking club by producing some very fine, concentrated barrel-fermented Chardonnays. The variety is also responsible for some delicious botrytized sweet wines in Austria's Burgenland, sometimes blended with Welschriesling for additional acidity and aroma.

Other excellent sweet wines made from nobly rotten Chardonnay grapes have come from the Mâconnais in France, Romania, New

Zealand and Coonawarra in Australia, proving yet another of Chardonnay's attributes.

Chasan, increasingly common crossing of CHARDONNAY and LISTAN. Useful Languedoc varietals.

Chasselas, table grape that is especially widely planted in Switzerland, where it is known as Fendant and Dorin, and is also an important if neutral ingredient in some of the light whites of Savoie. In Alsace it tends to play a subordinate role in cheaper blends and in Germany it is known as Gutedel. In its time it has also been

LEFT *Chasselas may not be a noble grape but it is widely grown in rural France such as here in Quercy.* RIGHT *In Bonnezeaux, Chenin Blanc grapes begin to submit to the dramatically ennobling process of botrytis mould (or noble rot) which, if the conditions are favourable, will leave the grapes looking like bundles of ash.* *See page 87.*

cultivated throughout central Europe and even in New Zealand.

Chenin Blanc, surely the most chameleon-like of vine varieties. Most wine drinkers encounter Chenin Blanc on the labels of very cheap, sometimes slightly sweetened, everyday varietals from California (usually Central Valley) or South Africa where, sometimes known as Steen, it is the most planted vine. In these relatively hot wine-producing environments, Chenin Blanc's ability to hang on to its natural grape acidity is highly prized, and stops these inexpensive, usually rather bland wines tasting flabby.

In its homeland in the middle Loire (see pages 182–4), Chenin Blanc is also marked by its high acid, which is not necessarily a virtue in cooler years, but gives dry and medium dry (Sec and Demi Sec) white wines from here a much longer life than most. Damp straw, flowers, something vaguely honeyed and (sometimes) the acrid sting of sulphur are the usual distinguishing features.

Chenin Blanc comes into its own, however, in exceptional Loire vintages when seriously high sugars develop in the grapes, particularly when they are concentrated by noble rot (see page 88). A Vouvray or Montlouis labelled Moelleux or Liquoreux, Bonnezeaux, Quarts de Chaume and the best Coteaux du Layon and Coteaux de l'Aubance can be an absolute marvel of honey, lime and toast which can continue to improve in bottle for decades.

An increasing number of producers in South Africa, New Zealand and California are taking Chenin Blanc seriously for it can also make attractively assertive, full bodied dry wines if the site is right and yields are restricted. It is widely distributed and its reliable acid level is valued as an ingredient in sparkling wines such as Blanquette de Limoux and those of South America, notably Argentina.

Chevrier, occasional name for SEMILLON.

Clairette, widely distributed southern French variety producing full, often flabby whites which can oxidize easily. It is a common ingredient in many southern French whites, but generally needs UGNI BLANC and/or TERRET to make a wine with enough freshness to please modern palates. Clairette du Languedoc has its own somewhat historic appellation. Clairette de Die, the curious sparkling wine in the far eastern Rhône Valley, depends heavily on MUSCAT for flavour. Clairette is also widely planted in South Africa, where it is generally used for blending. Clairette is also, confusingly, used as a synonym for other varieties, including Ugni Blanc and BOURBOULENC.

Clare Riesling, South Australian name for CROUCHEN.

Clevner, see KLEVNER.

Códega, Douro name for ROUPEIRO.

Columbar or **Colombard,** widely planted Cognac vine producing neutral, relatively crisp wine, particularly in California where, as vast tracts of French Colombard in the Central Valley, it was for some time the state's single most planted wine grape. It can make fruity, crisp, inexpensive white wine to be drunk straight off the bottling line from California, South Africa, Côtes de Gascogne and the Charentes in France. The vine is on the wane in France's damp south west, however, because it suffers from mildew.

Completer, strangely feral east Swiss speciality.

Cortese, speciality of south east Piedmont in general and Gavi in particular. Crisp and, with luck, fruity.

Criolla Grande is Argentina's most common vine (in both senses) and makes huge quantities of deep-coloured white or light pink wine which is rarely exported except as a very minor constituent in a blend.

Crouchen, vine which was difficult to grow in its native south west France but which has surfaced in Clare, South Australia and South Africa where it is known respectively as Clare Riesling and Cape/Paarl/South African Riesling. Its wine can, like real Riesling, develop well in bottle and, within South Africa itself, it may be labelled simply Riesling.

Debina, a sprightly grape used to make the lightly sparkling white wines of Zitsa in Epirus, north west Greece.

Dimiat, Bulgaria's most planted native white vine, which makes vaguely perfumed everyday whites.

Dinka, very ordinary but widely planted white grape variety in Hungary and over the border in ex-Yugoslavia.

Doradillo, productive, undistinguished vine still grown in South Australia's Riverland.

Dorin, CHASSELAS in Vaud, Switzerland.

Drupeggio, the white-berried form of CANAIOLO that adds interest to Orvieto.

Ehrenfelser, one of Germany's better Riesling-based crossings, found mainly in Pfalz and Rheinhessen. Fussier about site than KERNER.

Elbling, an historic German vine that is still planted in the Mosel valley where it produces extremely tart, lean wine which is sometimes made into Sekt.

Emerald Riesling, bumptious and quite floral California crossing of MUSCADELLE × RIESLING, which is designed for hot climates such as in South Africa.

Encruzado, useful ingredient in Dão.

Erbaluce, north Piedmont speciality which can make sweet golden wines round Caluso.

Ermitage, see HERMITAGE.

Esgana and **Esgana Cão,** mainland Portuguese names for CERCEAL.

Ezerjo, Hungarian rarity associated with a sweet style from Mór.

Faber or **Faberrebe,** early ripening Weissburgunder (PINOT BLANC) × MÜLLER-THURGAU crossing which can reach high ripeness levels while retaining acid, but is better at blending than ageing.

Favorita, pear-flavoured varietal from Piedmont whose wines can age better than ARNEIS.

Fendant, CHASSELAS in the Valais (Switzerland).

Fernão Pires, widely planted Portuguese grape whose wines can smell rank to outsiders but which have good assertive build. Popular in Ribatejo and, as Maria Gomes, in Bairrada. Some is grown in South Africa.

Feteasca, Fetiaska, Feteaska, scented Romanian speciality also found in Hungary as Leányka. Its wines tend to be full and peachy and rarely bone dry. **Fetească Albă,** with GRASA, spawned the widely planted 1930s crossing **Fetească Regală,** known in Hungary as Királeányka.

Fiano, ancient vine of Campania in Italy. Strong wines.

Fie, middle Loire speciality which is related to SAUVIGNON BLANC.

Flora, rare but quite elegant GEWÜRZTRAMINER × SEMILLON crossing bred in California.

Folle Blanche, once important brandy grape making tart wine in south west France.

Franken Riesling, SYLVANER.

Freisamer, Freiburger, German SILVANER × PINOT GRIS crossing still grown in Baden and eastern Switzerland, where it makes some full, sweet wines.

French Colombard, see COLOMBARD.

Frontignac, Frontignan, synonyms for MUSCAT BLANC À PETITS GRAINS.

Frühroter Veltliner, Früher Roter Veltliner, early ripening red-skinned, flabbier version of GRÜNER VELTLINER.

Fumé Blanc, developed as a more glamorous name for SAUVIGNON BLANC by Robert Mondavi of California in the 1970s, it is now used all over the world, typically but by no means reliably to denote an oak-aged style of Sauvignon.

Furmint, famous in Hungary's sweet Tokaji (see page 257). Grapes succumb well to noble rot, producing fiery, heady wine with good acid and ageing potential.

Garganega, Veneto vine capable of making fine, lemon and almond-scented wines, notably but not exclusively from low-yielding vines in Soave, also Gambellara, Bianco di Custoza and so on.

Garnacha Blanca, Spanish name for GRENACHE BLANC.

Gewürztraminer, important vine grown all over the world to produce deep-coloured (from its pink skins), full bodied whites with the characteristic and distinctive smell of lychees, veering towards bacon fat in very ripe examples. For many wine drinkers this (or SAUVIGNON BLANC) is the first varietal they learn to identify. It invariably ripens to a very high alcohol level and can lose acidity dangerously. Malolactic fermentation (see page 72) is therefore almost invariably avoided. Although there is probably a great deal of confusion, especially in newer wine regions, strictly speaking Gewürztraminer is the aromatic or *musqué* version of TRAMINER, and certainly the Italians distinguish between Traminer and Traminer Aromatico.

Alsace is Gewürztraminer's stronghold and here it can produce late harvest wines more reliably than any of the other three noble grape varieties. Winemakers of all nationalities like to play with it, however, and fine examples can be found in Washington, Oregon, northern California, New Zealand and northern Italy. In Iberia it is grown to a limited extent in the High Penedès. If ripened too fast in a warm climate it can be oily or even bitter.

Godello, the tangy grape of Valdeorras, north west Spain.

Goldburger, Burgenland in Austria's answer to German crossings.

Gordo, See MUSCAT OF ALEXANDRIA.

Gouveio, Douro name for VERDELHO.

Grasă, Romanian speciality responsible for the once-famous sweet wines of Cotnari.

Graşevina, the name the Croatians use for WELSCHRIESLING.

Grauburgunder, German name for PINOT GRIS, when made into a dry and crisp wine, in contrast to full, rich RULÄNDER.

Gray Riesling, California producer of off-dry wine, probably TROUSSEAU Gris.

Grecanico Dorato, increasingly planted Sicilian vine.

Grechetto makes characterful, rather tangy, full bodied wines in Umbria (Italy).

Greco, like the above two varieties, presumably originally a Greek vine which makes the sturdy

The pink skins of Gewürztraminer grapes (left) result in deeply coloured golden wines. 'Gewürz' is a speciality of Alsace in general and the Schlossberg vineyard above the village of Kaysersberg in particular (right).

Greco di Tufo in Campania and the extraordinary Greco di Bianco in Calabria.

Green Hungarian, diminishing and undistinguished California variety.

Grenache Blanc, light-berried Grenache which is planted all over southern France, producing full, scented, sometimes flabby wines which can oxidize easily, although careful winemaking can make attractive wines for early drinking.

Grillo, often astringent, earthy Sicilian variety.

Grolleau Gris, minor middle Loire variety used mainly for Vin de Pays du Jardin de la France.

Gros Manseng, the lesser sort of Manseng which usually makes drier forms of Jurançon.

Grüner Veltliner, Austria's grape speciality making crisp, peppery wines with real spark.

Gutedel, German synonym for CHASSELAS.

Gutenborner, MÜLLER-THURGAU × CHASSELAS crossing, more successful in England than Germany.

Hanepoot, South African name for MUSCAT OF ALEXANDRIA, the Cape's most common Muscat.

Hárslevelü, FURMINT's traditional blending partner in Tokaji, named after the lime leaf its wines can smell of.

Hermitage, occasional synonym for MARSANNE.

Humagne, Valais rarity, even richer than AMIGNE and ARVINE.

Huxelrebe, German crossing (also popular in England) which can produce full bodied sweet wine if the yield is checked.

Inzolia, western Sicilian speciality with promising nuttiness.

Irsai Oliver, relatively recent crossing, a Hungarian table grape which can also produce rather fat, vaguely MUSCAT-like varietal wine.

Italian Riesling/Rizling, synonym for WELSCHRIESLING.

Jacquère, common Savoie vine.

Jaen, central Spanish grape grown as AVESSO in Portugal.

Johannisberg, Swiss name for SYLVANER.

Johannisberg Riesling, sometimes abbreviated to JR, a synonym for RIESLING in California.

Juhfark, very rare Hungarian vine associated with SOMLÓ.

Kéknyelü, Hungarian 'blue stalked' variety grown in the Badacsony region on Lake Balaton, producing heady, smokey wine.

Kerner, bred as recently as 1969 and one of Germany's most successful crossings, yielding wine of real RIESLING-like substance and ageing potential, yet ripening in a wider range of sites than EHRENFELSER. Can smell of blackcurrants.

Kevedinka, Kövidinka, see DINKA.

Királeányka, Hungarian name for the FETEASCA REGALA of Romania.

Kişmiş, Turkish name for SULTANA.

Klevner, occasional Alsace synonym for PINOT BLANC and local variants.

Lairén, synonym for AIRÉN.

Laski Rizling, Slovenian name for WELSCHRIESLING.

Leányka, Hungarian name for Romania's FETEASCA.

Len de l'El, Len de l'Elh, traditional vine of south west France which makes strongly flavoured but sometimes slightly flabby wine in Gaillac, usually blended with MAUZAC.

Lexia, see MUSCAT OF ALEXANDRIA.

Listan, French name for the PALOMINO of Spain's sherry vineyards.

Loureiro, fine Vinho Verde grape grown increasingly across the border in Spanish Galicia as **Loureira**. It is often found blended with TREIXADURA but sometimes it is sold as a varietal wine.

Macabeo, very common grape in northern Spain and, as **Maccabéo** or **Maccabeu**, in the Languedoc and Roussillon. It is known as Viura in Rioja, where it is very much the dominant variety for white wines. Its vaguely floral character develops at full ripeness but it is often picked earlier to retain acidity. As Macabeo it is an important ingredient in Cava.

Madeleine Angevine, table grape that produces some attractive wine in England.

Malagousia, Malagoussia, vine capable of making elegant, almost too aromatic Greek whites, saved from extinction and now at work at Domaine Carras in the north.

Malvasia, widely and sometimes loosely used name for a range of usually relatively ancient grape varieties, the most famous of which inspires the richest style of madeira (see page 241). The word is derived from the Greek port Monemvasia, through which so many rich, dessert wines passed en route for western and northern Europe in the Middle Ages. **Malvasia di Candia** (of Crete) is one important subvariety. In modern Italy there are at least 10 distinctive forms of Malvasia, planted all over the country, most notably **Malvasia Bianca di Chianti** or (Tuscan) **Malvasia Toscana,** which is commonly blended with much more TREBBIANO in a wide range of Tuscan and Central Italian whites. White Malvasia tends to be a deeply coloured, quite alcoholic wine which can oxidize easily but has an intensely nutty character, sometimes with notes of orange peel and dried fruits. Malvasia is also grown in Spain and is the richest of the Madeira grapes, its name having been Anglicized to Malmsey, and can be an interesting diversion (from the ubiquitous Chardonnay) in California.

Malvoisie, a name as confusing in France as Malvasia is in Italy. A wide range of often unrelated varieties are called Malvoisie, although most are light berried and make full bodied, aromatic white wines. Perhaps it is most commonly encountered, in the Loire, Savoie and Switzerland, as a synonym for PINOT GRIS. The Languedoc's BOURBOULENC and MACCABÉO, Roussillon's TORBATO and Corsica's VERMENTINO have all been called Malvoisie in their time, however.

Manseng, see both GROS MANSENG and PETIT MANSENG.

Maria Gomes, see FERNÃO PIRES.

Marsanne, fashionable vine thanks to its origins as most common variety in the white wines of the Northern Rhône. (ROUSSANNE is declining, mainly because it is more difficult to grow.) Its wines tend to full bodied, veering to heavy with flavours reminiscent of glue and marzipan. Marsanne is a permitted ingredient in many of the Languedoc's whites and is increasingly sold as a varietal Vin de Pays. The Australian state of Victoria has some of the world's oldest Marsanne vineyards, which produce sturdy examples, and California is also catching on.

Mauzac, or **Mauzac Blanc,** is the chief grape of Gaillac Blanc (in which it is blended with LEN DE L'EL) and sparkling Blanquette de Limoux (in which its is softened with CHENIN BLANC and CHARDONNAY). It has a particularly distinctive smell that is reminiscent of dried apple peel. Its late budding and ripening meant that it was traditionally fermented long and slowly, still bubbling in the spring. Hence its association with wines of varying levels of fizz and sweetness.

Melon, Melon de Bourgogne, the Muscadet grape, so successful in this region because it withstands cold well and is quite prolific. So popular is it in the Muscadet region that, unusually, plantings have been increasing. The wine it produces is neither very acid nor strongly flavoured, but rather a neutral base on which to embroider terroir and *sur lie* (lees contact, see page 82) characteristics. Some of California's 'Pinot Blanc' may be Melon.

Merseguera, bland Spanish variety that is grown widely in Alicante, Jumilla and Valencia.

Misket, Bulgarian crossing of DIMIAT with RIESLING, producing vaguely grapey wines.

Molette, relatively neutral Savoie grape improved by blending in ROUSSETTE.

Morillon, rare synonym for CHARDONNAY, still used in Styria.

Morio-Muskat, German SILVANER × WEISSBURGUNDER (PINOT BLANC) crossing which has not a single Muscat gene, yet manages to taste almost obscenely Muscat-like with its heady grapiness. Varietal Morio-Muskat can easily be overpowering, but the variety is widely used by German bottlers to add a 'Germanic' note to an otherwise neutral blend, notably destined to be sold as Liebfraumilch. To ripen properly, however, it needs a good site, and can rot all too easily, so the variety is giving way to BACCHUS in some areas.

Moscadello, MOSCATO speciality of Montalcino.

Moscatel, Spanish Muscat, usually MUSCAT OF ALEXANDRIA.

Moscato, Italian Muscat, usually MUSCAT BLANC À PETITS GRAINS.

Moscophilero, deep pink-skinned grape variety which can make strongly perfumed white wine on Greece's high plateau of Mantinia in the Peloponnese.

Müller-Thurgau, Dr Hermann Müller's 1882 crossing has allowed the reputation of German wine to plummet. Taken up with enthusiasm by German growers after the Second World War, the vine has the practical advantages (in the cool German climate) of ripening extremely early, before the arrival of autumn rain in most years, and (unlike Riesling and Silvaner) yielding reliably on almost any site. The grape's disadvantage is that the wine, especially if produced from high yields, has little character and can be dangerously short of acid. It is almost invariably the major ingredient in Liebfraumilch and Germany's other cheap QbA blends (see pages 244–5). The crossing was either RIESLING × Riesling or SILVANER with some Riesling genes in there too. Unfortunately, they cannot be tasted. The more recent crossings EHRENFELSER, FABER, KERNER and well-ripened SCHEUREBE can produce much racier wine and there are signs that Müller-Thurgau, Germany's most popular grape variety for much of the 1970s and 1980s, is in decline.

Strangely, the variety seems to have a much higher strike rate outside Germany (although in Austria, where it is widely planted, it rarely achieves anything like as much interest as the native GRÜNER VELTLINER). Some of Washington's Müller-Thurgau, as well as Slovenia and Luxembourg's Rivaner and New Zealand and Switzerland's rather naughtily labelled Riesling-Sylvaner, and even Rizlingszilvani in Hungary, can demonstrate aroma and crispness, and some

of the better producers of Alto Adige and Friuli (most notably Pojer & Sandri) can make really quite exciting, even sought-after, wine from it. The variety also serves as a bolster to the English wine industry.

Muscadelle, with both SEMILLON and SAUVIGNON BLANC, the third grape of Sauternes, and other sweet whites in Bordeaux and Bergerac. The variety is in decline, but there is still a lot of it in Entre-Deux-Mers and it can plump out the two more famous varieties with youthful

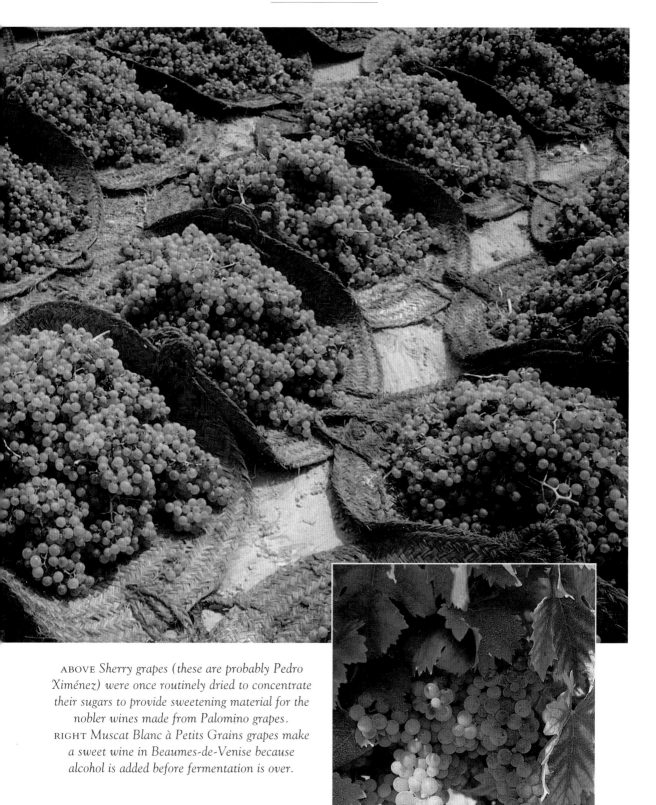

ABOVE *Sherry grapes (these are probably Pedro Ximénez) were once routinely dried to concentrate their sugars to provide sweetening material for the nobler wines made from Palomino grapes.*
RIGHT *Muscat Blanc à Petits Grains grapes make a sweet wine in Beaumes-de-Venise because alcohol is added before fermentation is over.*

fruitiness (a bit like PINOT MEUNIER in champagne blends).

It has also been identified as the variety responsible for the rich, dark fortified wines of north eastern Victoria called by Australians Liqueur Tokay.

Muscat, great and ramified family of vine varieties, unusually producing wines that actually smell and taste of grapes. Muscat vines tend to thrive in hot climates and to come in many colours of grape skin, from greenish yellow through pink to dark brown, but almost all of them produce wine that was white at least in its youth (although see the dark-skinned Black Muscat or MUSCAT HAMBURG). They have historically made rich, heady dessert wines, but are increasingly being made into dry(ish) table wines in the style of Muscat d'Alsace.

Muscat Blanc à Petits Grains, the finest, most ancient sort of Muscat vine is small berried and usually light skinned. Its berries are round rather than the oval shape of the other, almost as widely planted MUSCAT, OF ALEXANDRIA, so the variety is sometimes also known as **Muscat à Petits Grains Ronds**.

This is the vine responsible for France's most distinguished vins doux naturels, Muscat de Beaumes-de-Venise, Muscat de St-Jean-de-Minervois, Muscat de Frontignan, Muscat de Lunel, the more obscure Muscat de Mireval, and supplies the best Muscat of Roussillon. Its wines often hint at orange flowers and spice. Other names for this widely planted variety include **Muscat of Frontignan, Frontignac, Muscat Blanc, Muscat d'Alsace, Muskateller, Moscato Bianco, Moscato d'Asti, Moscato di Canelli, Moscatel de Grano Menudo, Moscatel de Frontignan, Muscatel Branco, White Muscat, Muscat Canelli** and **Muskadel** (in South Africa).

It is grown all over central and eastern Europe and is the variety responsible, for example, for the extraordinarily rich Muscats of the Crimean Massandra winery. In Russian it may be known as Tamyanka, in Romanian as Tămâioasă. This is the Muscat responsible for all of Greece's rich tradition of Muscats and, as Moscato, for north west Italy's important

spumante industry. An unusual dark-berried form known locally as **Brown Muscat** is responsible for Australia's Liqueur Muscats, although Muscat of Alexandria is by far the more common form of Muscat in Australia. Any Muscat with the words Alexandria, Gordo, Romain, Hamburg or Ottonel in its name is *not* this superior variety.

Muscat of Alexandria makes much less distinguished wine than MUSCAT BLANC À PETITS GRAINS (although Portugal's Moscatel of Setúbal and its dry counterpart João Pires can be interesting) but it can reach very high ripeness levels in hot climates and can be usefully productive. It produces more vaguely grapey wine, in which the sweetness often overpowers even its notes of geranium or, sometimes, tomcat. Marmalade rather than orange blossom is a useful shorthand. Californians use their Muscat of Alexandria for raisins, Chileans use theirs for the local spirit pisco, and the substantial harvest of 'Lexia' or 'Gordo' in Australia's irrigated wine regions alternates between the wine and raisin industries according to demand. Carefully vinified, it can provide useful blending material, particularly for medium dry blends. It is known as **Muscat Romain** in Roussillon, where it is the dominant Muscat for Muscat of Rivesaltes, **Hanepoot** in South Africa and **Zibibbo** in southern Italy. Any Spanish wine labelled simply Moscatel is likely to be made from this variety called, variously, **Moscatel de España, Moscatel Gordo (Blanco)**, and **Moscatel de Málaga**. Scholtz Hermanos of Málaga have shown that careful wood ageing can turn this Muscat into an exciting dark nectar.

Muscat Ottonel is a Muscat bred in the nineteenth century for the cooler climates of central Europe but has much less grapey flavours and substance. It makes lightish, usually dry wines and is widely grown in Alsace, but its finest incarnations may be late harvested sweet wines such as the Muscat grown round Austria's Neusiedlersee, Tămâioasă Ottonel of Romania and the Muskotaly of Hungary. The variety is sometimes known elsewhere as **Hungarian Muscat**.

Muskateller, German synonym for various MUSCATS.

Muskat-Silvaner, telling German synonym for SAUVIGNON BLANC.

Muskotaly, Muskotalyos, MUSCAT OTTONEL grown in Hungary's Tokaj region, sometimes sold as a dry varietal.

Musqué, not the name of a grape variety, but if a grape variety is described as *musqué* it usually denotes a particularly aromatic grapey version of it, as in Chardonnay Musqué.

Neuburger, popular Austrian crossing of PINOT BLANC and SYLVANER making full bodied whites.

Niagara, American hybrid making foxy wines in New York state.

Nuragus, basic Sardinian.

Olaszrizling, Hungarian name for WELSCHRIESLING.

Ondenc, declining variety in Gaillac, which is also known in Australia.

Optima, German crossing designed to notch up high must weights by ripening very early indeed. For this reason it is popular in England.

Orémus, Hungarian crossing of FURMINT and BOUVIER, occasionally sold as a dry varietal.

Ortega, another blowsy German crossing which can ripen spectacularly and is useful in cool years. Varietal examples exist but can lack acid, except in England.

Palomino, or **Palomino Fino** to distinguish it from the coarser Palomino Basto it has replaced, is the sherry grape, grown around Jerez in southern Spain. It can withstand drought well and produces a reliable crop of slightly low-acid, low-sugar grapes whose wine may oxidize easily – in short, perfect raw material for sherry. Outside sherry country, as in France where it is of declining importance, it is often known as Listan, or Listan de Jerez. It is known as **Perrum** in Portugal's Alentejo. It is grown to a limited extent in California's Central Valley and in Australia and South America, but Palomino is very widely planted in South Africa, where most of the wine is used for distilling or basic blends.

Pansa Blanca, north east Spain's XAREL-LO.

Pardillo, Pardina, undistinguished vine widely planted in western Spain.

Parellada, the finest white grape of Catalonia used, with MACABEO and XAREL-LO, for Cava and also treasured as a blending ingredient in many still dry whites of the Penedès region. Fine acidity.

Pederna, ARINTO in Vinho Verde.

Pedro, Pedro Jiménez, Pedro Ximénez, known also as 'PX', is grown in the sherry region to produce dark, sweetening wines, sometimes after drying these thin-skinned grapes (see page 115). Some varietal fortified wines of this nature are produced, presumably to the dismay of dentists everywhere. It is grown all over southern Spain, particularly in the Montilla-Moriles region, where it is more important than PALOMINO. In Australia 'Pedro' has been known to produce delicious, long-lasting botrytized sweet wines in the irrigated vineyards of Griffith, New South Wales. Argentina grows substantial quantities of **Pedro Gimenez,** which may be a distinct variety.

Perle, aromatic German crossing grown in Franken.

Petit Courbu, south west French variety often blended with the MANSENGS and/or ARRUFIAC.

Petit Manseng, smaller berried than GROS MANSENG, is responsible for the shrivelled berries needed to make top quality sweet Jurançon and Pacherenc du Vic-Bilh Moelleux in south west France. Thanks to its thick skins, Petit Manseng is low yielding and perhaps that is why the resulting wine can seem so packed with tangy, verdant flavours. Like TANNAT, the variety was taken to Uruguay by Basques in the nineteenth century. It is acquiring a cult following among the more varietally aware wine producers from Languedoc to California.

Picolit, sweet white Friuli varietal revered by Italians and extremely expensive. At its best (not stretched with the blander VERDUZZO) Picolit smells of apricots.

*The perilously steep vineyards of Urziger Würzgarten in the Mosel valley. Only Riesling is worth
the difficulty and danger of working such steep slopes, warmed by sunlight re-radiated by the local slate.*

Picpoul, Piquepoul, a many-hued traditional Languedoc variety that makes high-acid, full bodied, lemony wines of which the best known is the Coteaux du Languedoc Picpoul de Pinet made around the village of Pinet.

Pigato, ancient Ligurian with heady aromas.

Pineau de la Loire, a synonym for CHENIN BLANC.

Pinot Beurot, Burgundian name for PINOT GRIS.

Pinot Blanc, a white-berried mutation of PINOT GRIS and therefore related to PINOT NOIR. It is widely planted in Alsace, northern Italy (as **Pinot Bianco**), and in Germany and Austria (as Weissburgunder). In Alsace it provides a basic, broad-flavoured, full bodied dry white – often good value for money. It may be blended with AUXERROIS and is sometimes called Clevner or Klevner. In Italy it was worshipped as CHARDONNAY for years and continues to be made in that vaguely round-but-crisp style, as well as being used extensively for making sparkling wine. The Germans, who have few Chardonnay vines planted, tend increasingly to make dry white Weissburgunder using all the Chardonnay tricks of barrel fermentation and the like, sometimes with great success. In Austria's Burgenland, however, Weissburgunder can produce quite superb botrytized sweet wines, up to TBA levels (see page 245). The variety is also grown widely, sometimes called **Beli Pinot,** throughout central Europe and is also increasingly treasured as an alternative to Chardonnay in California. In general Pinot Blanc offers the body of Chardonnay with more smoke and less fruit and nut characters.

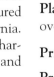

Typically blue-tinged Riesling grapes in Germany's Rheingau region.

Pinot Chardonnay, rare synonym for Chardonnay now that it has been proved it does not belong to the Pinot family.

Pinot Gris, increasingly popular member of the Pinot family, a pink-skinned version of PINOT NOIR which can make deep-coloured, full bodied, soft, gently aromatic white wines with lots of extract (see page 72), although Italians, who grow far more of it, as **Pinot Grigio,** than Pinot Bianco, have a habit of picking it before it can develop these characteristics. In Alsace it is, unlike PINOT BLANC, revered as a noble grape and can produce some commandingly rich wines from almost bone dry through Vendange Tardive to SGN levels of ripeness (see page 179). The drier of these wines are some of the finest whites to drink with rich savoury food. In the Loire and Switzerland it is known as Malvoisie and its innate smokey flavours survive.

The variety is more common in Germany than Alsace, however, where it is usually called Ruländer if it is sweet and Grauburgunder if dry. Most German Ruländer is grown in Baden and, to a lesser extent, Pfalz. In Hungary it is known as Szürkebarát and it is grown widely throughout central Europe. Admired in Luxembourg, the variety has shown real form in Oregon and is currently extremely popular with California growers, if not (yet) consumers.

Plavai, late ripening Moldovan vine planted all over central Europe.

Prinç, Moravian name for TRAMINER.

Prosecco, Friuli's sparkling varietal with varying

degrees of residual sugar, although some dry, still examples are known. The wine is made fizzy by the tank method (see pages 85–6).

PX, see PEDRO XIMÉNEZ.

Ranina, see BOUVIER.

Räuschling, ancient German variety still grown in eastern Switzerland.

Regner, Oechsle-boosting German crossing.

Reichensteiner, German crossing which usefully resists rot and ripens well. It is popular in England.

Rheinriesling, Rhine Riesling, both synonyms for RIESLING.

Ribolla, light, floral, very crisp varietal made in Friuli and, as **Rebula,** across the border in Slovenia. It is almost certainly the ROBOLA of Greece.

Rieslaner, German SILVANER X RIESLING crossing which can make lovely wines with race and curranty fruit in Franken and occasionally in Pfalz.

Riesling ('Reece-ling') must be the world's most misunderstood, and mispronounced, grape variety. Acknowledged king of German vineyards, this variety happens to share a name with so many much more ordinary grapes and wines (more commercial examples of Cape Riesling, CLARE RIESLING, EMERALD RIESLING, GRAY RIESLING, RIESLING ITALICO, LASKI RIZLING, OLASZRIZLING and WELSCHRIESLING, for example) that its image has become tarnished. And, it must be said, the Germans themselves make some pretty awful Rieslings at the bottom end of the market that have done nothing for the reputation of their greatest asset.

Wine made from Riesling is quite unlike any other. It is light in alcohol, refreshingly high in fruity acidity (quite different from the harshness of added acid – see acidification on page 72), has the ability to transmit the character of a place through its extract (see page 72) and unique aroma and, unlike CHARDONNAY, is capable of ageing for decades in bottle. Very unlike Chardonnay, but similar to top quality CHENIN BLANC, it performs best if fermented cool and bottled early without any malolactic fermentation or wood influence. Riesling is a star and, as you may discern, one of my great wine heroes.

Relative to most other internationally known varieties, Riesling ripens quite early, so when planted in a hot climate its juice can be overripe and flabby long before any interesting flavours have developed in the grapes. In a very cool climate such as that of the Mosel valley in northern Germany, on the other hand, it is regarded as a late ripening relative to the host of precocious varieties that have been specially bred for these short summers. This means that, whereas MÜLLER-THURGAU will ripen just about anywhere, Riesling stands a chance of ripening fully only on the most favoured sites, those tilted most firmly towards direct and reflected sunlight, which is where it is planted so that it stays on the vine well into autumn, developing all sorts of subtle and ageworthy characteristics. Riesling from the Mosel and its even cooler tributaries the Saar and Ruwer is one of the wine world's most distinctive, least imitable wine styles: light, crisp, racy, refreshing as a mountain stream and somehow tasting of the slate which, by reradiating warmth overnight, helps ripen so many Riesling vines. This is the wine to drink while writing or reading; it refreshes the palate and sharpens the brain (or at least that's what it feels like).

A third of all Germany's Riesling grows in the Mosel, but the Pfalz region also grows a substantial quantity, making much richer but no less entrancing wine which can often taste exotically fruity (and can reach as much as 13 per cent alcohol if fermented out to dryness). Riesling is also *the* classic grape of the Rheingau, where it perhaps best reflects – in a steely, lemony, sometimes mineral-scented way – the differences between even neighbouring vineyards. The best estates belong to the Charta group, dedicated to making great dry Rheingau Riesling – although in warm years the Rheingau can also be the source of many excellent BA and TBA sweet wines (page 245). Riesling is an extremely fine candidate for botrytized sweet wines, although this noble rot tends to blur geographical differences and result in thick, almost raisiny, deep golden wines. Württemberg is also an important grower of earthy Riesling which rarely escapes the region. Crackling Rieslings are also made in the Nahe.

Riesling is also the noblest variety of the most Germanic region of France – Alsace – where the best of its tingly-dry, steely wines such as Trimbach's Clos Ste-Hune can age for a decade or two in bottle. There is a slight talcum powder aroma about the least concentrated examples of Alsace Riesling but these are great wines to drink as aperitifs (as indeed is all but the sweetest Riesling made anywhere). The Wachau in Austria rivals Alsace and the Mosel for the purity of its Rieslings, sometimes called **Rheinriesling** or **Weisser Riesling** here, except that these wonderfully characterful, bone dry, sculpted wines tend to have a bit more body. Much of central Europe, particularly Slovenia and Slovakia, has suitable spots for ripening Riesling, whose local name usually incorporates some variant on the the word Rhine (in Croatia it is known as **Rizling Rajinski**, for example). True Riesling (as opposed to Italian Riesling) is widely dispersed in Friuli, where it is called **Riesling Renano**, although few startling examples have so far emerged from the region. Riesling is also allegedly grown widely in the old Soviet Union, but much of this may in fact be Welschriesling.

Surprisingly, in view of its relatively warm climate, Australia grows an enormous amount of **Rhine Riesling**, which is often called colloquially simply 'Rhine'. Its perfect spots are in the cooler reaches of South Australia, notably but not exclusively Clare Valley and Eden Valley (see pages 288–91 for more details). New Zealand's Rieslings are developing and some fine sweet wines are made there, just as California has a long tradition of making rich, fairly fast-maturing late harvest **Johannisberg Riesling** or **White Riesling**. Washington state can also produce some extremely delicate, toothsome off-dry Rieslings, while Canada regularly produces stunning Ice wines from this variety.

Riesling Italico is how the Italians often style WELSCHRIESLING, much to the Germans' fury, whereas Germany's Riesling is called **Riesling Renano**.

Riesling-Sylvaner, a rather misleading name for MÜLLER-THURGAU used in New Zealand.

Rivaner, the Luxembourg name for MÜLLER-THURGAU.

Rizling, a term used at the insistence of Germans for WELSCHRIESLING, so that it can be distinguished from the RIESLING that is Germany's pride and joy.

Rkatsiteli, Russia's answer to Spain's AIRÉN – although the wine can have more character. It is also grown in Bulgaria, Romania and China (where it is known as Baiyu). It keeps its acidity well and is very good at withstanding cold. It has been grown in California.

Robola, a haunting, citrus-scented white grape variety grown on the Greek island of Cephanolia. Almost certainly Italy's RIBOLLA.

Roditis, fragile, light pink-berried Greek variety often used to add acid to the softer SAVATIANO, particularly for retsina.

Rolle, ancient Provençal variety known especially in Bellet but also planted in Roussillon. The French say it is the same as Sardinia's VERMENTINO. Italians say it is Liguria's **Rollo,** which is *not* Vermentino.

Romorantin, speciality of Cheverny.

Rotgipfler, with ZIERFANDLER, a variety that is responsible for Austria's full, spicy Gumpoldskirchner.

Roupeiro, basic variety of the Portuguese Alentejo. Also known as Códega in the Douro and sometimes as Alva in Alentejo.

Roussanne, red-berried North Rhône variety which yields irregularly and is therefore less popular with growers than MARSANNE. Its wine can be very fine, however, as witness varietals such as Château Beaucastel's oak-aged version (it, but not Marsanne, is allowed into white Châteauneuf-du-Pape). It can age better than Marsanne and smells of mountain herbs. In fact it shines in Savoie as Bergeron (in Chignin) and is also grown in Italy. Improved clones are available and some growers are experimenting with it in southern France and California.

Roussette, a fine Savoie speciality that produces lively, crisp but scented wines. Roussette de Savoie has its own appellation in four communes, most notably Frangy. If followed by the name of a commune on the label the wine will be made exclusively of Roussette; if not, Chardonnay may constitute up to 50 per cent of the wine.

Ruffiac, alternative name for ARRUFIAC.

Ruländer, main German name for PINOT GRIS, usually signalling a sweeter style. Also used in Romania.

Sacy, rather ordinary white grape grown in the greater Chablis area.

St-Émilion, Cognac name for UGNI BLANC.

Sämling 88, Austrian synonym for SCHEUREBE.

Sárfehér, vine traditionally grown on Hungary's Great Plain for sparkling wines and table grapes.

Sauvignon Blanc grapes at Domaine de Chevalier (above) are responsible for one of the longest-living Sauvignon-based wines of all. Just down the road, Sémillon grapes make up the body weight of great Sauternes at Château Rayne-Vigneau.

Sauvignon Blanc, often called simply **Sauvignon** (whereas CABERNET SAUVIGNON is often called just Cabernet), extremely popular variety making crisp, dry, aromatic and extremely distinctive wines all over the world. The smell is sharp and piercing (unlike that of CHARDONNAY) and reminds different tasters variously of gooseberries, nettles, crushed blackcurrant leaves, and occasionally tomcats. With age, other aromas reminiscent of canned asparagus can develop. The smell of Sauvignon (which is most of its character) is relatively simple, so it is not surprising that it was one of the first to be explained in terms of its dominant flavour compounds, called methoxypyrazines (a name to drop at a professional wine tasting!). Sauvignon also smells and tastes remarkably similar wherever it is planted so, like GEWÜRZTRAMINER, is a very good starting-point for learning to recognize different varieties.

Sauvignon Blanc's French stronghold is the upper Loire, and the twin appellations of Sancerre and Pouilly-Fumé in particular. Superior examples of these wines are drier, denser and longer-living than most New World Sauvignon Blanc, and the best genuinely express terroir with nuances dependent on the proportion of gravel and flint (*silex*) in the soil. Sauvignon is also grown widely downstream, notably to produce oceans of Sauvignon de Touraine which can, from the best producers, be good value – as can the Sancerre-like wines of less famous Menetou-Salon, Reuilly and Quincy.

Sauvignon is even more widely planted in Bordeaux and Bergerac, although it is much less important than the fatter SEMILLON with which it is commonly blended, as elsewhere in the world nowadays, to produce both dry (particularly in Pessac-Léognan, Graves and Entre-Deux-Mers) and (in Sauternes, Monbazillac and surrounds) sweet wines. Sauvignon traditionally supplies the aroma and acidity in the whites of greater Bordeaux, and the more expensive dry wines are often aged in small oak barrels. Sauvignon and oak can be an oily mixture unless managed with a deft hand.

Elsewhere in Europe, Sauvignon is a speciality of Rueda in Spain, Styria in Austria and Collio in north east Italy. Some German speakers refer to it as Muskat-Silvaner (which mixture of characters quite accurately describes how it actually tastes).

New Zealand has been so successful with its herbaceous style of Sauvignon Blanc, heady with the tropical fruit smells of a cool, prolonged fermentation, that winemakers throughout the New World, and especially in Chile, South Africa and the Languedoc, are now emulating it. In some vintages fruit is deliberately picked underripe, ripe and overripe to bring different characteristics to the final blend. Marlborough at the north end of the South Island is New Zealand's, possibly now the world's, Sauvignon capital, while the Casablanca valley may have the potential to do the same job for Chile (being the only Chilean region to be planted substantially with Sauvignon Blanc rather than the less distinctive SAUVIGNON VERT). South Africa makes some delicious Sauvignon Blanc, perhaps partly because the vine has had so long to accustom itself to local conditions. Much of Australia, however, is too warm for the preservation of Sauvignon Blanc's characteristically 'green' (i.e. slightly underripe) aroma, but some fine examples have emerged from the Adelaide Hills.

California produces a distinct, full bodied, often oak-aged version of Sauvignon Blanc, sometimes called Fumé Blanc and the variety has also sparkled in Texas and Washington. Some Sauvignon Blanc can last for several years in bottle but very little actually improves with age, for vibrant, young fruitiness and refreshment value, rather than subtlety, are Sauvignon's strong suit.

Sauvignon Gris, a darker-berried mutation of SAUVIGNON BLANC, producing a strong, smokey perfume.

Sauvignon Vert, variety distinct from SAUVIGNON BLANC also known as **Sauvignonasse,** or TOCAI FRIULANO.

Savagnin, characteristic, small-berried vine of the Jura that is responsible most notably for the sherry-like *vin jaune* (although it can theoretically make up some of the blend of any white Jura wine). Its apogee is Château-Chalon, and Savagnin wine is renowned for its aroma and ability to age. France's most eminent ampelographer (vine specialist) maintains that TRA-MINER is Savagnin Rosé.

Savatiano, widely planted Greek vine used to add bulk to retsina, though ASSYRTIKO and RHODITIS are often added for crispness.

Scheurebe, one of Germany's most successful crossings, a SILVANER X RIESLING that was the work of Dr Georg Scheu. If the site and weather are such that the grapes ripen fully the wine can taste most appetizingly of blackcurrants or even rich grapefruit. Some Pfalz producers are prouder of their 'Scheu' than their RIESLING. Acidity levels are very good, although the wines are unlikely to age as well as Riesling. Yields are not as high as most new crossings but the right site can yield BA and TBA wines (see pages 244–5) as often as nature obliges, and Spätlese trocken examples can also be very fine. Burgenland in Austria also produces some successful late picked examples from the variety, known here as Sämling 88.

Schönburger, pink-berried German crossing involving both PINOT NOIR and MUSCAT HAMBURG, but producing mellow white wine, notably in England but also in Germany.

Schwarzriesling, or 'black Riesling', German synonym for PINOT MEUNIER.

Semillon, in France **Sémillon,** is the great white grape of sweet white bordeaux, and also widely undervalued. As well as making many of the world's greatest sweet wines, it is responsible for Bordeaux's greatest dry whites and Australia's most distinctive table wine, Hunter Valley Semillon. Semillon is Bordeaux's most planted white grape variety, although the area devoted to its traditional blending partner there, SAUVIGNON BLANC, has been increasing. Semillon is the grape primarily responsible for Sauternes, the world's longest-living white wine, and it is sanctioned in most of the dry or sweet white wine appellations of south west France. It blends well with Sauvignon (traditionally four to one in Sauternes) because it lacks positive aroma (apart from the vague citrus, lanolin and beeswax of a young wine and the burnt toast of a mature Hunter) but makes up for Sauvignon's lack of body. If Semillon is picked before it

reaches full ripeness it can almost taste like Sauvignon. Semillon's thin skins make it prone to rot, which makes it an ideal producer of botrytized sweet wines, not just in Bordeaux and Monbazillac, but also in New South Wales and occasionally California. The wine can respond well to wood ageing, as in the great dry whites of Graves and Pessac-Léognan in Bordeaux.

Semillon is planted in virtually all of the world's wine regions but for the moment little is made of it. Australia perhaps has taken the most positive line on constructing varietals out of it, but it has also been used to stretch the available quantities of the fashionable Chardonnay while new plantings come on stream, initiating a category known as SemChard. Odd varietal versions have shone in Hungary and New Zealand, and Washington state clearly has potential. Semillon is also widely planted in Chile, although little evidence has yet been exported under that name.

Sercial, an Anglicized name for the CERCEAL of Madeira.

Seyval Blanc, French hybrid which withstands cold well and is grown in Canada, New York and England (where it is the most popular vine). It can be very crisp and fruity.

Siegerrebe, a relatively low-yielding German crossing famous for its high ripeness levels but not for the quality of its wine.

Silvaner, German spelling of the variety known as Sylvaner in Alsace and Austria. It is sometimes known as **Grüner Silvaner** in Germany. Probably of central European origin, Silvaner was Germany's most planted grape variety in the first half of the twentieth century. (It took over that position from ELBLING, then passed on the crown to the thoroughly undeserving MÜLLER-THURGAU.) The vine ripens earlier than Riesling but later than Müller-Thurgau and therefore needs rather better sites. The wines it produces are high in acidity and not particularly marked by flavour or longevity, but in the right spot, such as particular sites in Franken, it is capable of producing extremely racy, excitingly sleek wines.

Silvaner is cultivated over much of central Europe, where its local name generally incorporates the letters 'silvan' and in Switzerland it can shine, known as Johannisberg or Rhin, and tasting much fatter than the ubiquitous CHASSELAS. See also SYLVANER.

Vernaccia grapes in Tuscany (above) are almost exclusively used for full bodied, characterful dry wines, whereas the Trebbiano and Malvasia grapes (opposite) are being dried to yield ultra-sweet Vin Santo, Tuscany's speciality, at the Selvapiana estate.

and California, some of its yield is often diverted into everyday white blends and the result is characterless wine produced from high-yielding vines.

Sylvaner, the Alsace and Austrian name for SIL-VANER. In Alsace Sylvaner can show the race and response to site that Riesling can, but it takes a very good vineyard and winemaker to extract much flavour from it. Most of Alsace's Sylvaner (and there is a great deal of it) is planted on the lower, less interesting vineyards of the Bas-Rhin and much of it is blended with slightly gentler wine to be sold as Edelzwicker.

Smederevka, a common vine named after the town of Smederevo south of Belgrade and planted extensively in Serbia and Vojvodina in what was Yugoslavia. It produces good acidity and is often blended. Also found in southern Hungary.

Steen, South African name for CHENIN BLANC.

Sultana, variety commonly used for dried fruit but, when the market is buoyant in Australia

Szürkebarát, Hungarian name for PINOT GRIS.

Talia, Thalia, Portuguese names for TREBBIANO/UGNI BLANC.

Tămaîioasă, a Romanian name used for various MUSCATS.

Tamyanka, a Russian name for MUSCAT BLANC À PETITS GRAINS.

Terret Gris, an ancient Languedoc variety that is widely planted and can make a full bodied yet crisp varietal. **Terret Blanc** is less common and less distinguished. They are both allowed in to the white wines of Minervois, Corbières and, to a decreasing extent, Coteaux du Languedoc.

Thompson Seedless, SULTANA in California.

Tocai, Tocai Friulano, the most planted light grape in Friuli, which can make lively, crisp, aromatic wines to be drunk young. Most authorities agree that it is identical to Sauvignonasse or SAUVIGNON VERT (the Sauvignon that dominates Chile's vineyards). Some Italians argue it is related to the FURMINT of Tokaj. Some vines are grown in Argentina, where they are called Tocai Friulano.

Tokay d'Alsace, synonym for PINOT GRIS which the Hungarians are trying to outlaw.

Torbato, a smokey-flavoured Sardinian variety that is also known, in Roussillon, as **Tourbat** (and occasionally Malvoisie du Roussillon).

Torrontés is a Galician variety that is a speciality of Ribeiro, but is much more commonly grown in Argentina, where it produces full bodied, crisp wines with a distinctive and confident aroma not unlike Muscat. It seems likely but is unproven that the vine was brought to Argentina by Galician immigrants. **Torrontés Riojano** is the most common Argentine subvariety, named after the northern province of La Rioja where, in Salta in particular, it is by far the most planted single vine variety. **Torrontés Sanjuanino** and the rarer, less aromatic **Torrontés Mendocino** are also grown. Chile has its own, similar **Torontel**.

Trajadura, Portuguese name for the aromatic Galician variety **Treixadura**.

Traminer, less aromatic progenitor of GEWÜRZTRAMINER, which is a *musqué* version of a pink-berried Traminer. It is named after the town of Tramin, or Terlano, in the Alto Adige, where a distinction is still made between Traminer and **Traminer Aromatico** (or *musqué*). Vines called variants of Traminer are planted throughout central Europe: **Tramini** in Hungary; **Traminac** in Slovenia; **Drumin, Pinat Cervena, Prinç** or **Liwora** in what was Czechoslovakia; occasionally just **Rusa** in Romania; and **Mala Dinka** in Bulgaria. It is also grown in Russia, Moldova and Ukraine, where it is sometimes used to perfume Soviet sparkling wine. Some of these vines may be the more aromatic Gewürztraminer but less than perfect winemaking has tended to obscure the aroma. Australians tend to use the term Traminer as shorthand for the rather more cumbersome Gewürztraminer.

Trebbiano, France's UGNI BLANC in its homeland, planted almost everywhere within Italy except for the far north, where it would not ripen reliably. Despite the fact that its wine is remarkably thin, tart and characterless, it is responsible for about a third of all DOC white wine production. Its many different local strains include **Trebbiano Toscano** (the most common, a possible ingredient in Chianti and chief inspiration for Galestro, the basic crisp mouthwash of the Tuscan hills), **Trebbiano Romagnolo** (making mainly vapid Trebbiano di Romagna), **Trebbiano d'Abruzzo** (of which the apparent master is Valentini, despite the fact that he uses BOMBINO BIANCO), yellow-berried **Trebbiano Giallo** and **Trebbiano di Soave**.

The variety is also planted, as Talia, in Portugal, and (where it is often called Ugni Blanc) in Bulgaria, Russia, Greece and extensively in South America. In California, too, occasional bottlings of wine made from old Trebbiano vines have shown extraordinary character and extract.

Tresallier, a rather undistinguished speciality of the Allier *département*, where St-Pourçain is produced.

Ugni Blanc, France's most planted white grape variety, widely grown as Ugni Blanc in South

America and, as TREBBIANO, ubiquitous in Italy too. As ST-ÉMILION it is the chief ingredient in Cognac and plays an important role in Armagnac too. The wine it produces is thin, light and tart. Hardly what the market wants nowadays. It is surprisingly common north of Bordeaux.

Veltliner, common name for Austria's GRÜNER VELTLINER.

Verdejo, characterfully nutty speciality of Rueda in Spain, often blended with SAUVIGNON BLANC.

Verdelho, Portuguese grape which inspires Madeira's second driest style but is most commonly found as a vibrant, lemony, full bodied table wine from Western Australia. Grapes are small, hard and acid. This is probably the Douro's GOUVEIO and possibly Italy's **Verdello.**

Verdicchio, the grape of Italy's Marche, made famous by Verdicchio dei Castelli di Jesi in an amphora-shaped bottle – although Verdicchio di Matelica can be a more concentrated wine. Many are simply crisp and vaguely citric.

Verduzzo, north east Italian speciality which can make very appetizing honeyed sweet wines, some of which qualify for the Ramandolo DOC (see page 207). Dry wines can be astringently reminiscent of dried apple skins.

Vermentino, aromatic speciality of Sardinia and, to a lesser extent, Liguria, probably the same as ROLLE. It can make some of Sardinia's liveliest whites, with a slight prickle of gas.

Vernaccia, Tuscany's most characterful white wine grape, making deeply coloured, often nutty wines, particularly around the hilltop village of San Gimignano.

Vespaiola, Veneto vine which can make tangy, golden sweet wines. Named after the wasps attracted to its sugar-rich grapes.

Vidal, French hybrid which can make delicious Ice wine in Canada.

Vilana, relatively delicate speciality of Crete.

Villard Blanc, prolific French hybrid widely planted in France in the mid-twentieth century.

Viognier, extremely fashionable variety whose home is Condrieu in the Northern Rhône but which is now being energetically planted all over southern France, in California, in Australia and wherever a cosmopolitan wine producer lurks. The vine can yield poorly in cooler climates. Its full bodied wines have a very distinctive scent of dried apricots and, almost, musk. The wine is usually best drunk young. Because of the strength of its aroma, it can withstand blending well.

Viura, Riojan name for MACABEO.

Weissburgunder, Weisserburgunder, Weisser Burgunder, German names for PINOT BLANC.

Weisser Riesling, alternative name for RIESLING.

Welschriesling, Wälschriesling, Welschrizling, just some of the many aliases under which The Other Riesling travels. This has nothing to do with the great German RIESLING, and its image was sullied for many years by poorly handled, sweetened-up liquids bearing names like Laski, Olasz and Pecs, but this central European vine can produce some good to very good wine – particularly in Austria's Burgenland, where it regularly makes superb sweet botrytized wines. It is planted widely in Friuli (Italy), Slovenia, Hungary, Romania, Albania and China. The vine ripens late to produce high-acid, gently aromatic wines.

White Riesling, occasional name for RIESLING, especially in California, where there have been Emerald, Gray and Hungarian Rieslings.

Xarel-lo, Catalonia's most characterful grape, producing wines which can smell of boiled cabbage to the uninitiated. Used widely in Cava. Known as Pansa Blanca in Alella.

Xynisteri, speciality of Cyprus.

Zalema, vine responsible for the heavier wines of Condado de Huelva in southern Spain.

Zibibbo, MUSCAT OF ALEXANDRIA in Sicily.

Zierfandler, nobler, fuller ingredient, with ROTGIPFLER, in Austria's Gumpoldskirchen. As **Cirfandli,** it is also grown in Hungary.

Zilavka, characterfully nutty variety grown mainly in Hercegovina, notably around Mostar in what was Yugoslavia.

RED WINE VARIETIES

Abouriou, minor variety in south west France.

Agiorgitiko, Nemea's St George, which can make substantial, very fruity Greek reds and some good rosé.

Aglianico, deep, dark, densely graphite-scented grape of Greek origin, most famously inspiring Taurasi of Campania and Aglianico del Vulture in Campania.

Aleatico, Italian vine, making strangely grapey sweet reds. Also planted in New South Wales.

Alfrocheiro Preto, deep-coloured Portuguese grape useful in blends.

Alicante Bouschet, often just called **Alicante** (which is also a local Languedoc name for GRENACHE), red-fleshed grape once widely used to tint southern French table wine, especially Aramon. Now found in Corsica, Tuscany, Calabria in southern Italy, Yugoslavia, Israel, North Africa, California, Portugal and Spain, where it is known as Garnacha Tintorera. Vine-breeder Henri Bouschet crossed one of his father's crossings with Grenache, or Garnacha, to produce this early ripening variety in the late nineteenth century. Makes gutsy but short wine.

Aragonez, Portuguese name for TEMPRANILLO.

Aramon, extraordinarily high-yielding, low-quality variety that dominated the plains of the Languedoc in the late nineteenth and early twentieth centuries. Replaced by CARIGNAN in the 1960s.

Aspiran, historic Languedoc vine whose light, perfumed red wine may still be blended into Minervois.

Auxerrois, Cahors name for MALBEC.

Baco Noir, Baco 1, French hybrid planted in north eastern America to produce light reds untainted by foxy flavours.

Baga, Bairrada's speciality, thick-skinned, small grapes producing some very tannic, acid wines in northern Portugal.

Barbarossa, a lively grape of Emilia-Romagna, known as **Barberoux** in Provence.

Barbera, the most common grape in north west Italy, where it is responsible for lightish, bitter cherry-flavoured wines with marked acidity. Produced at low yields and treated to barrel ageing it can make extremely exciting wines with more than a hint of NEBBIOLO's serious scent. About 15 times as much Barbera is grown in Piedmont as Nebbiolo. It is also widely grown in Lombardy, often blended with BONARDA, as well as in California and, more successfully, Argentina.

Bastardo, undistinguished grape used in the Douro valley, port country.

Black Muscat, MUSCAT HAMBURG.

Blau, Blauer, German for blue and a common prefix of red wine grape varieties.

Blauburger, Austrian crossing of PORTUGIESER and BLAUFRÄNKISCH, making ordinary light reds.

Blauburgunder, Swiss German name for PINOT NOIR.

Blauer Spätburgunder, an Austrian name for PINOT NOIR.

Blaufränkisch, central European vine, producing lively, fruity, sometimes peppery reds with sufficient substance in the best Burgenland examples (see page 253) to be worth oak ageing, or blending with CABERNET and/or PINOT NOIR. It is called Limberger in Germany, Lemberger in Washington state, Franconia in Friuli, Gamé in Bulgaria (it was once confused with Gamay), Kékfrankos in Hungary and Frankovka in Slovakia and Vojvodina.

In the Langhe hills of Piedmont, Nebbiolo will ripen only on south-facing hillsides whereas Barbera is much less fussy about vineyard site. In autumn, the result is a patchwork of varieties at different stages of maturity.

Bobal, Spanish vine, making huge quantities of deeply coloured wine (and grape concentrate) on the southern Mediterranean coast. It makes crisper, lighter wine than MONASTRELL, with which it is often grown.

Bonarda, an Italian variety or, more accurately, three different varieties by the same name. Most common is the Lombardy version, attractively juicy and the same as CROATINA.

Bordo, the name for CABERNET FRANC in north east Italy.

Bouchalès, minor variety in south west France.

Bouchet, name for CABERNET FRANC in St-Émilion and in Bordeaux's other right bank districts. It is known as **Bouchy** in Madiran.

Brachetto, north western Italian, making light, fizzy, strawberry-flavoured reds. Also known as **Braquet** in Provence, notably in Bellet.

Breton, the middle Loire name for CABERNET FRANC.

Brocol, Braucol, FER in Gaillac.

Brunello, SANGIOVESE clone developed in the Montalcino region of Tuscany.

Cabernet usually means CABERNET SAUVIGNON, although in north east Italy it can often mean CABERNET FRANC, since there is so much more of it.

Cabernet Franc, important variety famous for playing second fiddle to CABERNET SAUVIGNON, even though it has shown it can make some extremely fine wines (notably in St-Émilion and the middle Loire) in its own right. The vine looks very like Cabernet Sauvignon except that the leaves are much less indented, so it is probably an early mutation that is particularly well adapted to the Gironde right bank's cooler, damper climate where Cabernet Sauvignon can be difficult to ripen. Cabernet Franc buds and ripens earlier, which makes it more susceptible to coulure (see page 69) but it needs less heat to ripen fully. In left bank Bordeaux, on the other hand, it is seen, with Merlot, as a sort of insurance policy against a cool season. In very general terms, wine made from Cabernet Franc tends to be aromatically fruity, lighter and less tannic

than Cabernet Sauvignon and, especially in the Loire, can smell appetizingly of pencil shavings. It is often rather herbaceous and can smell like unripe Cabernet Sauvignon. Cabernet Franc is an ingredient in most of the reds of south west France, and often the sole inspiration for the fine, silky reds of the Middle Loire such as Saumur-Champigny, Bourgueil, Chinon, and Anjou-Villages.

Cabernet Franc, sometimes called **Cabernet Frank**, is widely grown in north east Italy and some of its Friuli examples are ripe enough to be thrilling. The vine is also grown over the border in Slovenia, although Cabernet Sauvignon is far more common in the rest of central Europe. See also MENCÍA.

In the New World, in most of which Cabernet Sauvignon can easily be ripened, Cabernet Franc has been widely regarded as essential for respectability to make up the holy Bordeaux trio, along with Merlot (with which it has sometimes been confused in vine nurseries). Some varietal Cabernet Francs have emerged from Australia, South Africa and California and shown just how appetizing this variety can be unblended – and how much more conveniently earlier maturing it is than Cabernet Sauvignon. Cabernet Franc may really shine in cooler regions, however, such as Long Island in New York state, parts of Washington state and New Zealand.

Cabernet Sauvignon, the world's most famous red wine grape signalled on labels all over the world. As the 'chocolate' to Chardonnay's 'vanilla', Cabernet is much more positively flavoured than Chardonnay, and ripens much later, so tends to be planted in rather warmer areas. The great distinction of the wine it produces is that it has a very powerful and recognizable aroma of blackcurrants wherever it is grown and, if matured in newish oak, can smell of cedar, cigar boxes and, sometimes, tobacco. Cabernet Sauvignon is also notable for being deep purple in youth and, although it is not especially alcoholic, it can be extremely long lived. This is because Cabernet Sauvignon's small, thick-skinned grapes have a very high ratio of solids rich in colouring matter and tannins to juice – although if the grapes are anything less than fully ripe the wine can smell of crushed green leaves, 'herbaceous', or more like CABERNET FRANC. All of this means that Cabernet can make great wine, but that it is not necessarily the best grape for wines to be drunk young, especially when it is grown in cooler climates.

While Chardonnay is a relatively recent globe trotter, Cabernet Sauvignon long ago strayed widely and successfully from its Bordeaux base. Contrary to popular belief Cabernet Sauvignon is not Bordeaux's most planted vine (see MERLOT). Because it is relatively late ripening, it needs a warmer, drier environment than most of Bordeaux can provide in order to stand a commercially interesting chance of ripening fully. In Bordeaux, therefore, it is grown in the Entre-Deux-Mers region as well as in the well-drained gravels of the Médoc and Graves where it is invariably the chief constituent, but always blended with Merlot, Cabernet Franc and sometimes with PETIT VERDOT, in the world-famous classed growths (see page 161). In the Médoc it is the main varietal component in St-Estèphes that are taut and austere in youth (although they are getting riper and more welcoming with every vintage); in the dense, mineral-scented Pauillacs; in many a lush, silky Margaux; and in the beautifully balanced yet long-lived St-Juliens. It brings crispness and long life to the wines of Graves and the suggestion of warm bricks common to several from Pessac-Léognan.

It is planted all round the greater Bordeaux region in those appellations grouped together as constituting south west France, out-tannined only by the Tannat of Madiran. Bergerac and Buzet are its chief strongholds.

Elsewhere in France there are growers who persist with it in the Loire (though Cabernet Franc is much easier to ripen), although most of the rest is in the south. In Provence it can blend beautifully with the spicier SYRAH to make ambitious, oak-aged wines for the long term. In the Languedoc it is all too often over-produced to yield rather lean, hollow Vins de Pays, although an increasing proportion of seriously fine wine is made.

Cabernet Sauvignon has been responsible for some extremely fine Italian wines, notably Supertuscans (see pages 214–17), in which it

seems happy blended with SANGIOVESE, but also bottlings from as far afield as Piedmont and Sicily. (Cabernet Sauvignon thrives in fairly hot regions as it retains its acidity well throughout its slow final ripening stage.) Bottles from north east Italy described simply as 'Cabernet', however, almost certainly contain more Cabernet Franc than Cabernet Sauvignon.

However, Cabernet Sauvignon is the dominant Cabernet planted widely and enthusiastically in central Europe. It clearly has great potential in Moldova and the Ukraine, although CABERNET SEVERNY's cold-resistance can make it more useful in Russia. Cabernet Sauvignon is extremely important to the wine industries of Bulgaria, Romania and what was Yugoslavia, and to a much lesser extent, Austria and Hungary. These Cabernets tend to be less refined than the Bordeaux prototypes, being intensely fruity, often recalling red fruits rather than black, and rarely showing any oak influence (other than occasionally that of heavy-handed oak chipping).

Cabernet is rare in Portugal and still relatively rare in Spain, although creeping internationalization of Spanish vineyards is resulting in more and more varietal examples and a dash of Cabernet in blends. In Navarre Cabernet Sauvignon has shown how well it blends with TEMPRANILLO (even though the two varieties have rather similar structures) and in Penedès has won considerable acclaim.

The variety performs well in the warmer Mediterranean regions, notably in Lebanon and Israel.

Most of South Africa's revered wines, and many of her best, are Cabernets which already show some intensely satisfying regional variations. Cape winemakers, however, have tended to make 100 per cent Cabernets, unsoftened by Merlot or leavened by Cabernet Franc, as indeed was the initial effect of varietalism in California. California in general (see page 265), and particulary Northern California, has made some great, glossy but intense Cabernets, some of them initially monstrous in their tannins (and occasionally acids) but nowadays made with great skill. Today there is growing understanding of the precise characteristics of various areas within Napa and Sonoma and how these

In the red wine hall of fame, Cabernets
reign supreme – whether Cabernet Franc,
seen in the open fermentation vats of Chinon
(top) or the darker coloured, almost blue-black
Cabernet Sauvignon grapes of California's
Napa Valley (above).
Cabernet Sauvignon has a particular affinity
with the unusual, well-drained red terra rossa soils
of Coonawarra (right) in South Australia.

are shown to best advantage. Much of the Napa Valley, other than the southern end, seems particularly well suited to Cabernet Sauvignon production and this will continue to be one of the world's most fruitful hunting grounds for lovers of Cabernet that has the ability to age. Many finer California Cabernets show a certain minty quality, others an earthiness. More and more of these wines are blends made according to the Bordeaux recipe and are often called Meritage here.

Washington's Merlot is generally more successful than its equally common Cabernet Sauvignon but there are some extremely appetizing exceptions. Cabernet may well have a future in Texas too, but has difficulty ripening in Oregon.

Cabernet cuttings were first taken to South America well over a century ago and indeed the Chilean wine industry was built on this very important variety. (In fact Chile's largest company Concha y Toro claims to be the world's most important owner of Cabernet Sauvignon vineyards.) Chilean Cabernet, most of it still ungrafted, has a very direct, fruity flavour, without the mintiness associated with parts of California and Australia.

Australia defined her perfect spot for Cabernet Sauvignon before consciously doing the same for any other variety: Coonawarra in the far south east of South Australia on a famous strip of terra rossa earth (see previous page). These wines tend to have a noticeably high level of acidity as well, often, as some notes of eucalyptus, sometimes so powerful that the wines can seem closer to cold remedies in youth. These wines can age superbly. Margaret River in Western Australia can also make great, refined Cabernet and there are other fine examples all over Victoria as well as in the Hunter Valley and elsewhere. Cabernet is extremely commonly blended with the country's much richer, fleshier SHIRAZ, and very complementary they are too.

New Zealand's Cabernet Sauvignon can be too herbaceous and acid by half but the best examples are certainly crisp and lively. In many wine regions, however, the necessarily slow evolution of Cabernet is being re-evaluated, often to the benefit of other red varieties, notably Merlot. It may well be that in a decade or two, Cabernet will be more exclusively the preserve of the world's most ambitious winemakers.

Cabernet Severny, specially bred version of CABERNET SAUVIGNON designed to withstand Russia's harsh winters by incorporating Mongolian genes.

Cadarca, Romanian KADARKA.

Calabrese, another name for NERO D'AVOLA.

Caladoc, recent southern French crossing of GRENACHE and MALBEC.

Canaiolo, decreasingly popular ingredient in the original Chianti recipe.

Cannonau, Sardinian name for GRENACHE.

Carignan, Carignane in the USA, **Carignano** in Italy, and **Cariñena** in Spain, the most important but, sadly, by no means the most distinguished vine in France. It was chosen as replacement for the ARAMON which perished in the frosts of 1956 and 1963, because it is extremely productive and buds late, so rarely suffers frost damage. It also ripens quite late, however, so can only be grown in warm to hot climates, and produces tannic, quite acid wine, too often marked by a coarse, rustic smell of hot berries. To counter these characteristics, most Carignan in the Languedoc-Roussillon, where it dominates production even of appellation contrôlée wine, is vinified using some form of carbonic maceration (see page 78). Of all the thousands of acres of vines which have been ripped out in the Midi in an effort to curb Europe's wine surplus, Carignan is by far the major casualty. Carignan tends to be on low bushes that are unsuitable for mechanical harvesting. Very old vines in really warm climates can produce deep-coloured, warm, quite rich wine and there have been some quite creditable examples from California, and good Carignano del Sulcis in southern Sardinia. Carignan's origins are Spanish and it is still grown in Costers del Segre, Penedès, Tarragona and Terra Alta. In Rioja it plays a minor part as Mazuelo.

Carmenère, rare historic Bordeaux variety found today in Chile.

Carmenet, Médoc name for CABERNET FRANC.

Carnelian, 1936 California crossing of CARIG-NAN and CABERNET SAUVIGNON with Grenache. Designed to be a hot climate Cabernet, it is grown to a limited extent in California's Central Valley and in Texas.

Castelão Frances, a versatile and characterful southern Portuguese variety known variously as Periquita, João de Santarém or Santarém, Mortágua and Trincadeira Preta. Wines are fruity, relatively fleshy, but can also be aged.

Catawba, deep pink-skinned American hybrid grown widely in New York state where it produces strongly flavoured deep pink to light reds.

Cencibel, La Mancha and Valdepeñas name for TEMPRANILLO.

Centurian, CARNELIAN's even less popular twin.

Cesanese, Latium vine.

Chambourcin, French hybrid designed to thrive in damp climates. Popular in the Muscadet region and pioneered in a particularly hot, humid part of New South Wales by Cassegrain. The dark, aromatic wine shows no trace of any non-European vine parentage.

Chancellor, productive French hybrid grown in New York state.

Charbono, unusual California speciality produced as an occasional varietal in the Napa Valley. Some authorities claim it is DOLCETTO of Piedmont.

Chenin Noir, an alternative name for PINEAU D'AUNIS.

Chiavennasca, name used in Valtellina (northern Italy) for NEBBIOLO.

Ciliegiolo, cherry-flavoured grape planted in Central Italy.

Cinsaut, Cinsault, widely planted throughout southern France and Corsica (where it is now being ripped out at a great rate). With its lighter skins and soft perfume it is particularly suitable for rosés, although low yields are needed to eke out much flavour. It has the advantage over GRENACHE of being easy to pick by machine and

there was a notable increase in plantings in the 1970s and 1980s in southern France, mainly in the Aude and Hérault *départements*. Cinsaut is used to add perfume and fruit to wines such as Minervois and Corbières. The variety withstands drought well and so has been important in North Africa, Lebanon, Israel and South Africa, where it is most famous as a parent of PINOTAGE. In southern Italy it is known as Ottavianello.

Colorino, now rare Tuscan colouring grape.

Concord, the 'foxiest' and most powerfully non-European-scented American vine planted extensively in New York state, and in Brazil.

Corvina, Corvina Veronese, the finest grape found in Valpolicella and Bardolino (see also RONDINELLA and MOLINARA), particularly good for dried grape wines such as Amarone.

Côt, Cot, alternative name for MALBEC.

Couderc Noir, French hybrid rapidly disappearing from the Languedoc, not before time.

Counoise, rare ingredient in red Châteauneuf-du-Pape. The wine can be peppery and usefully high in acid.

Criolla Chica, PAIS/MISSION in Argentina.

Croatina, a late ripening and high-yielding vine which makes juicy wines with bite. See also BONARDA.

Currant, a widely planted vine that is used almost exclusively for dried fruit, most common in Greece and Australia.

Delaware, dark pink-skinned American hybrid vine grown in New York state and, especially, Japan, where its habit of ripening early is useful. More European-flavoured than CONCORD.

Dolcetto, 'little sweet one', so named because it is naturally low in acidity. After Barbera, it is the most common red grape of Piedmont and, in youth, can be mouth-fillingly delicious. It is particularly useful to growers because it ripens much more easily than NEBBIOLO or even BARBERA, so tends to be planted on north-facing slopes. A little is grown in both North and South America.

Domina, modern German crossing useful for cooler sites but not particularly distinguished for its wine.

Dornfelder, the most successful red crossing in Germany, which makes juicy, deeply coloured red wines, especially in Pfalz and Rheinhessen. It is easier to grow and ripen than Spätburgunder (PINOT NOIR), PORTUGIESER or LIMBERGER, and can yield heavily. Understandably, it is becoming increasingly popular with German vine-growers.

Dunkelfelder, deep-coloured but otherwise undistinguished German vine.

Durif, southern French vine most famous for being possibly the same as California's PETITE SIRAH.

Early Burgundy, California vine identified as ABOURIOU.

Espadeiro, a productive vine in Galicia and Vinho Verde which makes generally rather thin wine.

Fer, Fer Servadou, wild speciality of Marcillac and encouraged elsewhere in south west France. Called Brocol in Gaillac and Pinenc in Madiran, it can add some rustic smokey flavours to the blend. It is also an important ingredient in the little-seen wines of Entraygues and Estaing, which are neighbours of Marcillac. Argentina also grows a Fer which is apparently a clone of MALBEC.

Franconia, BLAUFRÄNKISCH in Friuli.

Frankovka, see BLAUFRÄNKISCH.

Frappato, light, grapey Sicilian.

Freisa, Piedmont love-or-loathe variety making pale but quite tannic, tart wines, many of which are frothy and medium sweet.

Gaglioppo, Calabrian vine, making extremely alcoholic wines.

Gamay, the Beaujolais grape known in full as **Gamay Noir à Jus Blanc** to distinguish it from the host of red-fleshed **Gamays Teinturiers** which were once widely grown in France (and can still be found in eastern Europe). Everything about Gamay is hasty, in terms of both vine and wine, which means it can suffer frost damage but can ripen somewhere as cool as the Loire. Wines tend to be light coloured, often with a stong blue tinge and traditionally attract the vague adjectives 'fresh and fruity'. Rapid vinification using carbonic maceration (page 78), particularly to hasten Nouveau wines on to the market, can result in strong banana/peardrop/boiled candy/nail-polish remover aromas. Very

Gamay vines are cooled by autumn mists on the hills above Chiroubles in Beaujolais (left), while stereotypical Grenache grapes in Châteauneuf-du-Pape (right) are ripened by heat reflected from the large, pale stones known locally as galets.

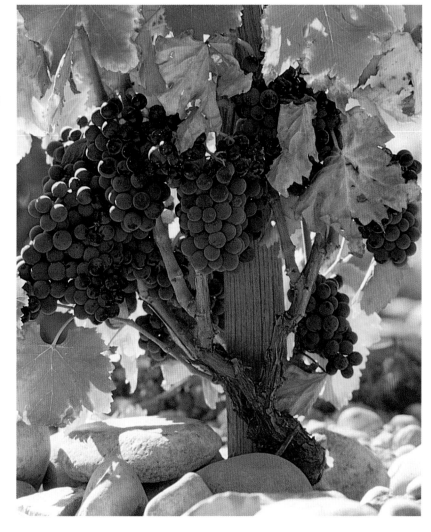

little Gamay is designed to be aged; it is the red answer to Sauvignon Blanc. It can be extremely refreshing when served chilled, thanks to low tannins and high acidity. Gamay is grown in the Mâconnais to the north of Beaujolais, in the Touraine, and in outlying areas such as Châteaumeillant, Coteaux du Lyonnais, Coteaux du Giennois, Côtes d'Auvergne, Côtes du Forez, Côte Roannaise and St-Pourçain. In the Mâconnais and Switzerland Gamay is often blended with a bit of PINOT NOIR, to produce Bourgogne Passetoutgrains and Dôle respectively. Outside France only the Swiss are particularly keen on Gamay, although it can be found in parts of central Europe. It has often been confused with BLAUFRÄNKISCH.

Gamay Beaujolais, California name for what is thought to be a clone of PINOT NOIR.

Gamé, Bulgarian name for BLAUFRÄNKISCH.

Gamza, KADARKA in Bulgaria.

Garnacha, Garnacha Tinta, GRENACHE in its Spanish homeland. **Garnacha Tintorera,** the 'dyer' version of Garnacha, is the Spanish name for ALICANTE BOUSCHET and is widely planted, notably in Almansa.

Garrut, a Catalan speciality whose relatively tough wines can taste of liquorice.

Graciano, rare but fine and perfumed Rioja grape which is difficult to grow and has largely been abandoned. It is almost certainly identical to the equally rare MORRASTEL of the Languedoc, and very possibly an obscure variety known as **Xeres** in California. Argentina grows a variety called **Graciana.**

Grand Noir, Grand Noir de la Calmette, a vine that is, fortunately, fast disappearing from the Languedoc and Cognac. High yield and red flesh.

Grenache, Grenache Noir, the world's most widely planted dark-skinned grape variety because of its popularity in Spain and southern France. In the late Middle Ages the house of Aragon apparently took it far and wide around the Mediterranean – although Sardinians (who call it Cannonau) argue it was stolen from them. This archetypal hot climate vine, which

has to be pruned very severely if it is not to produce too much bland wine, can produce slightly pale but quite alcoholic wine that can taste spicy and sweet. Like CINSAUT the grapes have relatively thin skins and musts tend to oxidize easily, but fine rosés can be made. Grenache is usually blended with other varieties higher in colour and tannin such as SYRAH and MOURVÈDRE, even in its perfect spot, Châteauneuf-du-Pape. Grenache inspires all the fine reds and rosés of the Southern Rhône, and is a permitted ingredient in most Languedoc-Roussillon AC wines. Its most distinctive produce is the vins doux naturels of Banyuls, Maury and Rivesaltes. GARNACHA TINTA is Spain's most important red grape and is grown extensively everywhere other than Andalucía. In Rioja it provides juicy ballast for the more structured Tempranillo. Priorato is Spain's finest incarnation of Garnacha Tinta (often incorporating some of the downier **Garnacha Peluda,** which is otherwise known as LLADONER PELUT).

Grenache is quantitatively very important in both California and Australia, but most of the vines are planted in hot, heavily irrigated vineyards where yields are too high to produce interesting wine. Dry-farmed, older vines are being sought out, however, as the market clamours for more and more Rhône-like wines. And in California the success of White Zinfandel spawned White Grenache. The variety is cultivated all round the Mediterranean.

Grignolino, a Piedmont speciality producing light bodied, herbal-scented aperitif wines, also grown to a very limited extent in California's Napa Valley.

Grolleau, Groslot, the middle Loire's basic, bland dark-skinned variety, used extensively with GAMAY for less distinguished pinks such as Rosé d'Anjou.

Gropello, Lombardy red.

Harriague, Uruguayan name for TANNAT.

Helfensteiner, German crossing and parent of the more exciting DORNFELDER.

Heroldrebe, another DORNFELDER parent, used for pink wine in Pfalz.

Isabella, widely planted *labrusca* vine (see page 96) grown mainly in South America, New York state and the ex-Soviet Union.

Jaen, very basic central Spanish grape. Also the name of a Dão variety in Portugal.

João de Santarém, CASTELÃO FRANCES in parts of Ribatejo.

Kadarka, Hungary's own red grape (even if its origins are Albanian) being replaced by the less rot-prone and earlier ripening KÉKFRANKOS and KÉKOPORTO. If yields are restrained it can make full, tannic wine such as supported the best Bull's Blood blends, but such wine is rare. It can also be found in Austria's Burgenland, in Vojvodina, as Cadarca in Romania and as Gamza in Bulgaria.

Kékfrankos, Kékoporto, Hungarian names for BLAUFRÄNKISCH and PORTUGIESER respectively, Kék being Hungarian for blue.

Lagrein, Trentino-Alto Adige speciality, making fullish everyday reds and rosés.

Lambrusco, very important and productive vine, making often sweet, usually fizzy red in Emilia-Romagna. About 60 subvarieties have been identified.

Lemberger, Limberger, see BLAUFRÄNKISCH.

Limnio, ancient Greek variety, making deep mineral-scented wines with good tannins.

Lladoner Pelut, Lledoner Pelut, downy-leaved, less rot-prone form of GRENACHE still grown in Languedoc-Roussillon and, as Garnacha Peluda, in north east Spain.

Magaratch Ruby, crossing of CABERNET SAUVIGNON and SAPERAVI.

Malbec, a black grape that is known as Côt in much of south west France and the Loire, Pressac in parts of Bordeaux (where it is still grown mainly in Bourg and Blaye), Auxerrois in Cahors (where it is the main grape variety) and occasionally **Malbeck** in Argentina, where it has also dominated red wine production. The vine is quite fragile in cooler climates, producing a wine that can taste rather rustically gamey, but in the best Cahors vineyards and the Luján

de Cuyo region of Mendoza in Argentina it can create deep-coloured, intensely ripe and attractively gamey wines which are well worth ageing. Because it has been so widely grown in Argentina, the local producers tend to view it as distinctly third rate, but visitors are trying to stop systematic replacement with Cabernet Sauvignon, which the whole world can supply. The vine is also grown in Chile, Australia, California and north east Italy.

Malvasia Nera, dark-skinned relative of light-berried MALVASIA, usually made as a sweet red, from Piedmont and Alto Adige to the islands of Sardinia, and Lipari off Sicily.

Mammolo, now rare, violet-scented ingredient in Chianti.

Mandelaria, grape of the Greek islands which yields dark, relatively light wines that are useful for blending.

Maréchal Foch, a very early ripening French hybrid grown in Canada, New York and the Loire at one time. The wines can show attractive strawberry fruit.

Marzemino produces a few lively wines in northern Italy.

Mataro, old-fashioned name used mainly in Australia and California for the fashionable MOURVÈDRE vine .

Mavro, is Greek for black and the name of the most common dark grape on Cyprus.

Mavrodaphne, Greek variety made into a rich, port-like varietal around Patras.

Mavrud, Balkan vine with real potential to produce intensely rich yet dry and tannic wine, which is a speciality of Assenovgrad near Plovdiv in Bulgaria.

Mazuelo, CARIGNAN in Rioja.

Melnik, an abbreviation for Bulgaria's SHIROKA MELNISHKA LOSA.

Mencía, a variety that is grown widely in north west Spain, producing light, relatively fragrant reds and thought to be a local strain of CABERNET FRANC.

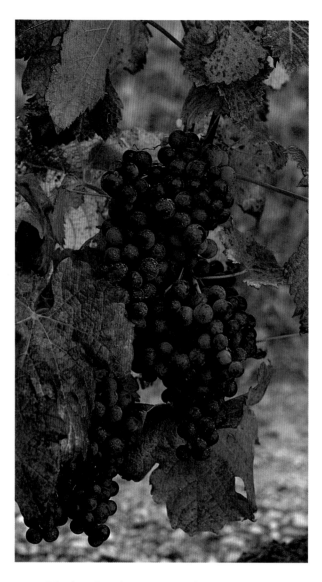

Franc) and St-Émilion (where Cabernet Franc and sometimes Cabernet Sauvignon play a more important part). Despite Merlot's reputation as the user-friendly, early maturing wine, the best of these wines can continue to develop in bottle for decades, and I have been lucky enough to taste a mid-nineteenth-century Château Ausone at the château that was as lively as the châtelaine herself.

Merlot, like the Cabernets, is widely grown throughout south west France, notably in Bergerac and in Cahors, where it is the common blending partner of MALBEC. It is also very widely planted in the Languedoc, where it can make juicy, plump Vins de Pays (being generally more successful than Cabernet Sauvignon).

Just like Merlot the wine, Merlot the vine ripens earlier than Cabernet Sauvignon, but it is less resistant to rot and, if the weather is poor during flowering, can easily suffer from coulure (see page 69). It is conventionally, but by no means exclusively, associated with damp, clay soils.

Although almost two-thirds of the world's Merlot vines are grown in France, most of the rest until recently have been grown in north east Italy, particularly in Friuli, where the variety can make plumper wines than the prevailing Cabernet. Quality varies from basic light red varietals to rich, dense barrique-aged wines, which are often blended with Cabernet and/or Sangiovese. (This observation is also true of the Merlots that are produced in Switzerland's Italian Ticino.) Romania, Bulgaria and Moldova also grow significant quantities of Merlot, which can be difficult to distinguish in terms of wine quality from their Cabernet.

Today Merlot is being planted at a lick in both North and South America. It has a proven track record in Washington state, where its

Merlot, Merlot Noir, with CABERNET FRANC, famous as a blending partner for CABERNET SAUVIGNON, but possibly more widely planted in total than either. Merlot conventionally makes lush, plummy, velvety wine that can soften Cabernet's more austere frame and, usefully, matures much faster. Very much a wine of our times, it is enjoying enormous popularity in the United States.

Merlot's homeland is Bordeaux, where it is the most planted vine variety and is the most important ingredient in most wines qualifying for the basic Bordeaux appellation. It makes its greatest wines on the right bank of the Gironde in Bordeaux, in Pomerol (where it is generally blended with minimal proportions of Cabernet charms are attractively balanced by crisp acidity and good colour. In California, its fruity charms are extremely popular when served up as a varietal wine and it is also a popular ingredient in Meritage blends. Stags Leap in Napa and Russian River in Sonoma have had particular success with the variety.

Chile has already found its own perfect spot for Merlot, the southern Maule Valley, and the best-made examples combine California gloss with even more obvious fruit. Argentina's Merlot has a less distinct identity – indeed almost all Argentine red already has inbuilt ripeness thanks to the climate, and so there is little need to augment this with a particularly ripe-tasting variety.

Although Merlot is grown as a blending partner for Cabernet in Australia and New Zealand, few varietal wines of real distinction have yet emerged, although they almost certainly will. South Africa has already shown just how gorgeous an oak-aged Merlot ripened in a relatively warm climate can be.

Meunier, see PINOT MEUNIER.

Mission, California's oldest but by no means most distinguished grape. It is rough stuff related to the PAIS of Chile and Criolla Chica of Argentina. See also MONICA.

Molinara, a variety that makes a tart contribution to Valpolicella.

Monastrell, Spain's name for MOURVÈDRE, known also as Mataro.

Mondeuse, spicy, sappy wine made from one of Savoie's most characterful varieties (see page 205). Many authorities think it is identical to Friuli's REFOSCO.

Monica, undistinguished Sardinian vine which *may* be related to MISSION.

Montepulciano, an Italian vine that will ripen only in the southern half of the country, producing good-value, full bodied and characterful wines, especially in the Abruzzi.

Morellino, SANGIOVESE in western Tuscany.

Moreto, undistinguished vine grown mainly in Portugal's Alentejo.

Moristel, speciality of Spain's Somontano. The vine is frail and the wine oxidizes easily and may be best in blends.

Morrastel, rare Languedoc variety thought to be Rioja's GRACIANO. Also used in Spain as a synonym for Monastrell (the MOURVÈDRE of France). In North Africa the name Morrastel is used for both Graciano and Mourvèdre.

Mortágua, CASTELÃO FRANCES in the west of Portugal.

Mourisco Tinto, lesser port grape.

Mourvèdre, fashionable grape variety that is most obvious in Bandol but, as Monastrell, grown so widely in south east Spain that it is Spain's second most important red grape variety, but grown more patchily throughout southern France. For years it was called Mataro and dismissed as basic blending material in California and Australia, but now is starting to appear in much more highly priced Rhône-like blends. It needs a very warm site or summer to ripen it fully and the wine produced from it is deep coloured, alcoholic and almost aggressively gamey in flavour. It may be best suited to blending, notably with the more structured SYRAH.

Outside Spain, plantings are increasing all over the world.

Müllerrebe, German for PINOT MEUNIER.

Muscardin, lively but rare Châteauneuf grape.

Muscat Hamburg, common table grape which can even be ripened in England and produces light, grapey red throughout eastern Europe. It is also important to the developing wine industries of China and Japan and is also known as Black Muscat.

Napa Gamay, dwindling California speciality thought to be VALDIGUIÉ.

Nebbiolo, Italy's noblest vine and a speciality of Piedmont. Like PINOT NOIR, fussy about both soil and site and extremely expressive of it. It is grown, only in vineyards which stand a chance of ripening this late ripening variety, all over Piedmont, but reaches its highpoint in the hills of Barolo and Barbaresco, sometimes shrouded in autumn by fog, or *nebbia*, which may have inspired its name. It is also grown successfully, as Spanna, in the north of Piedmont to produce wines such as Gattinara and Ghemme and even, just over the border in Lombardy, in Valtellina, where it is known as Chiavennasca. In the alps of Valle d'Aosta and the far north west of Piedmont, where it is called Picutener, it makes Carema.

Wine made from Nebbiolo is markedly high in both acidity and, especially, tannin – which is why the grapes need to be sufficiently ripe to supply enough fruit to counterbalance all this astringency. Wines are especially deeply coloured (although they can brown quite easily) and have a haunting smell that reminds many of tar, roses and sometimes violets. These wines are extremely serious and demand long ageing and attention. (DOLCETTO and BARBERA, however, are for glugging.)

A little Nebbiolo is grown in California and Argentina.

Negramoll, see TINTA NEGRA MOLE.

Négrette, a Frontonnais speciality, producing supple, perfumed wine for early drinking.

Negroamaro ('black and bitter' in Italian), widely planted in Italy's deep south, especially on the heel of Italy in Apulia where it can make seductively heady, ageworthy reds such as Salice Salentino, Squinzano and Copertino. Some good rosés too.

Nerello, Nerello Mascalese, important Sicilian vine, lighter than NERO D'AVOLA but can be sweet and fragrant, especially for rosés.

Nero d'Avola, one of Sicily's most serious red wine grapes, also known as Calabrese. Barrel maturation works well.

Nielluccio, Corsica's answer to SANGIOVESE. Often blended with SCIACARELLO, which is more distinctive.

Noir, French for black and often a suffix of red wine grape varieties.

Ojo de Liebre, TEMPRANILLO in Penedès.

Ormeasco, Ligurian name for DOLCETTO.

Ottavianello, probably CINSAUT in southern Italy.

Pais, Chile's commonplace grape and descended from the Spanish conquistadores. It is identical to the MISSION of California and Mexico. Grown in southern regions for very ordinary wine.

Pamid, Bulgaria's common or garden red.

Periquita, the name for CASTELÃO FRANCES in Arrábida, Palmela and parts of Ribatejo.

Perricone, soft Sicilian.

Petite Sirah makes robust, tannic, earthy wines in both California and South America. It is less noble than and probably unrelated to the true SYRAH. For some time it was thought identical to the obscure DURIF.

Petit Verdot, a late ripening ingredient in the classic bordeaux blend to which, in warm years, it can bring an agreeable peppery spice. Some Californians have been planting it for Meritage blends (see CABERNET SAUVIGNON).

Piedirosso, Campanian speciality.

Pignolo, lively, dense Friuli vine that has real potential.

Pineau d'Aunis, a light, fruity middle Loire variety declining in favour of CABERNET FRANC.

Pinenc, FER in Madiran.

Pinot Meunier, the most commonly planted grape in Champagne, where its wine adds youthful fruit to CHARDONNAY and PINOT NOIR. It is called 'miller's' vine because its leaves are dusty white underneath. As Müllerrebe it is grown in Germany's Württemberg and some varietal still wines are also made in Victoria, Australia.

Pinot Noir, the red burgundy grape capable of producing divinely scented, gorgeously fruity expressions of place but often unwilling or unable to do so. In Burgundy Pinot Noir is merely the medium through which tiny environmental differences (terroir) express themselves (see pages 166–8). Flavours found in young red burgundies include raspberries, strawberries, cherries and violets; with time these evolve into a bouquet often reminiscent of game, liquorice and autumnal undergrowth. (There is an argument that red burgundy has to be very good indeed to be worth ageing more than about five years…)

This ancient eastern French vine is very prone to mutation (hence PINOT GRIS and PINOT BLANC) and enormous variation in wine quality between different clones. Planting the wrong clone in the wrong place is one of many reasons for the wide variation in quality between different red burgundies and different varietal Pinot Noirs from elsewhere. Pinot Noir is also very sensitive to the size of crop it is expected to produce, and many vapid examples exemplify an over-demanding yield. It ripens relatively early (Chardonnay and Pinot Noir are often harvested at the same time in Burgundy) so is not suitable for very warm regions where there would be no time to develop interesting flavours before acid levels plummeted. On the other hand, many of the cooler regions in which it thrives suffer autumn rains which can rot the thin-skinned berries of this variety, resulting in pale, tainted wines. The Pinot Noir grower's lot is not an easy one.

For years the received wisdom was that it was almost impossible to make decent Pinot Noir outside Burgundy but the early 1990s have definitely disproved this – and if the new wave of New World Pinot Noir for the moment lacks any great expression of place, it in general provides considerably more pleasure per penny than the average bottle of burgundy.

RIGHT In Burgundy, Pinot
Noir has acclimatized itself
so successfully that adjoining
vineyards produce wines
with perceptibly different
characters, such as in
Gevrey-Chambertin.
BELOW Pinot Noir grapes
ripen so early that they can
even be grown in
England, as seen here
at Denbies Estate.

Oregon in the American Pacific Northwest staked its wine reputation on Pinot Noir (presumably inspired by its distinctly Burgundian wet autumns) with considerable success. More unexpectedly, California has demonstrated that it too has no shortage of spots quite cool enough (thanks to ocean fog) to keep Pinot grapes on the vine as they develop welcoming fruity flavours and some texture to boot. Notable among these are Los Carneros, the Russian River Valley in Sonoma and Santa Maria north of Santa Barbara, although Chalone and Calera wineries have proved that isolated Pinot greatness can also be found in the mountains south of San Francisco. Canada has made the odd hopeful Pinot and at the other end of the climatological spectrum even Chile has demonstrated a recent facility with this vine, in cooler corners, giving hope to Pinot Noir strugglers everywhere. Australians have identified Victoria (notably the Yarra Valley, Geelong and the Mornington Peninsula) and Tasmania as being cool enough for Pinot, and Martinborough in the south of New Zealand's North Island has also made some stunning examples. Most of South Africa is too warm for Pinot Noir, but the coolest coastal regions are being developed at this moment.

Within Europe, Pinot Noir travels under a number of aliases. In Italy it is known as **Pinot Nero** and concentrated in the north east where average quality is increasing considerably. In Germany, as **Spätburgunder**, it is the most planted red wine grape and is increasingly inspiring, often thanks to top quality oak barrels, just as it is in eastern Switzerland as Blauburgunder and from the more serious winemakers of Austria (sometimes called Blauer Spätburgunder) and Alsace. (Pinot Noir from all these places has in the past tended to be pale, sweetish and not especially inspiring.) It is planted all over central Europe, called variously **Burgundac Crni** in what was Yugoslavia, **Nagyburgundi** in Hungary (although the name is also used for BLAUFRÄNKISCH) and **Burgund Mare** in Romania, where it makes very cheap, very lush, very atypical wine.

The French grow increasing quantities of Pinot Noir outside Burgundy, however, notably in Champagne, where it has proved itself the ideal black grape for a top quality sparkling wine (for which purpose it is widely used in Italy, California and Australia), in Alsace, all over eastern France such as in Sancerre, the Jura and Savoie, and even in the higher reaches of the Languedoc around Limoux.

Plavac Mali, a Croatian speciality that makes dense, heady and tannic wines such as Postup and Dingač.

Portan, recent French crossing of GRENACHE and PORTUGAIS which ripens more reliably than Grenache. Sometimes in Vins de Pays d'Oc.

Portugieser, Blauer Portugieser, high-yielding, early ripening vine planted widely in Austria and Germany, producing rather ordinary, light wines with relatively low acid. Hungarians and Romanians know it as Kékoporto and Croatians as **Portugizac Crni,** or **Portugaljka.** A little is grown in France as **Portugais.**

Poulsard, Plousard, Jura rarity making perfumed, pale wine, usually blended with PINOT NOIR.

Pressac, MALBEC on Bordeaux's right bank.

Primitivo, most famous for being the southern Italian version of California's ZINFANDEL. Wines labelled Primitivo tend to be very alcoholic and deep coloured.

Prokupac, Serbian speciality reaching high grape sugar levels and often made into a dark rosé.

Prugnolo Gentile, SANGIOVESE in Montepulciano.

Raboso, a tough and sometimes tart, Veneto variety which can be too lean to sustain these attributes.

Ramisco, the astringent Colares vine.

Refosco, Refosco dal Peduncolo Rosso, historic, red-stemmed Friuli vine, making dense, lively wines with bite. Known as Terrano or Teran in Slovenia and Croatia. Possibly the same as MONDEUSE.

Rondinella, lesser Valpolicella grape (see CORVINA and MOLINARA).

Roriz, Tinta Roriz, common Portuguese name for TEMPRANILLO.

Rossese, a fine Ligurian vine, especially in Dolceacqua.

Rouchet, Ruchè, a scented, relatively tough Piedmont red. Rare.

Royalty, California red-fleshed French hybrid bred from TROUSSEAU.

Rubired, California red-fleshed French hybrid, bred from TINTA CÃO. Easier to grow and therefore more popular than ROYALTY. Used to add colour to less expensive blends.

Ruby Cabernet, once popular California crossing of CARIGNAN and CABERNET SAUVIGNON to combine Cabernet characteristics with Carignan productivity and tolerance of Central Valley heat. Also grown in South Africa and Australia.

Sagrantino, lively, often tough Umbrian red, a speciality of Montefalco.

St Laurent, an Austrian variety that can make lush, flattering, soft and rather PINOT NOIR-like wines. It is often blended with more internationally famous varieties and, if yields are limited, can be worth oak and bottle ageing. In Slovakia it is known as Vavrinecke.

Salvador, California red-fleshed French hybrid.

Samtrot, PINOT MEUNIER in Austria.

Sangiovese, Italy's most planted red wine vine and the underpinning of the majority of central Italian reds (notably Chianti, Brunello di Montalcino, Vino Nobile di Montepulciano – see pages 214–17 – as well as Rosso Conero and Rosso Piceno). It is known also as Brunello, Morellino and Prugnolo Gentile. There are many strains of varying quality, ranging from the lacklustre, over-produced vines responsible for the lightest Sangiovese di Romagna to the dense, long-lived Brunello. Late ripening Sangiovese makes well-structured, often high-acid wines with a certain farmyardy character, but a dense plumminess if fully ripe. Sangiovese has so far shown itself to be a much happier traveller than NEBBIOLO, turning out some quite

sumptuous (and some overpriced) examples in California – and some generally less inspiring examples in Argentina.

Santarém, the name for CASTELÃO FRANCES in parts of Ribatejo.

Saperavi, a Russian vine that produces deep-coloured wines (thanks to the pink flesh of its grapes) with good acidity. Wines respond well to ageing. **Saperavi Severny** is a hybrid designed to withstand very cold winters by incorporating Mongolian genes.

Savagnin Noir, Jura name for PINOT NOIR.

Schiava (pronounced 'Ski-arver'), Italian name for Alto Adige's common or garden variety (see page 213). The region's many German speakers also know it as Vernatsch and in Württemberg it is called TROLLINGER.

Schioppettino, speciality of Friuli whose characterful wines hint at violets and pepper.

Sciacarello, Sciaccarello (pronounced 'Shackarello'), south western Corsican speciality that can make herb-scented reds and rosés but has been overtaken by Nielluccio.

Ségalin, recent French crossing of the obscure Jurançon Noir and PORTUGAIS, capable of producing well-structured wines.

Seibel, common name for many of the French hybrids, usually numbered to distinguish them.

Severny. Most vines with Severny in their name have been specially bred in Russia to withstand cold winters.

Shiraz, Australian and South African name for SYRAH, so any wine labelled Shiraz tends to taste richer, riper and more full bodied than France's typical Syrah-based wines. Australia has recently regained her pride in Shiraz, the country's most planted wine grape variety, which can taste of baked pencils in the Hunter Valley, chocolate in Barossa Valley (arguably its spiritual home) and black pepper in cooler regions such as Macedon in Victoria. Very, very few Australian wine producers do not produce a Shiraz of some sort, and many make several qualities of Shiraz (including sparkling), as well

The Syrah grape in some of its finest
locations: (left) Shiraz grapes in a coolish
site in the state of Victoria in Australia; perhaps
the oldest Shiraz/Syrah vines in the world
(above) in Henschke's Hill of Grace
vineyard, South Australia; and terraces
of Syrah (right), trained up special stakes,
on the vertiginous slopes of Côte-Rôtie
in the Northern Rhône.

as a range of Shiraz-Cabernet *and* Cabernet-Shiraz blends. Penfolds are arguably the past masters of Shiraz production, their Grange (Hermitage) being Australia's very first serious 'collectable'. When it was first made, by the late Max Schubert after a trip to Bordeaux, it was dismissed as 'dry port tasting of crushed ants' by other Australian winemakers. In very general terms Shiraz tends to taste slightly sweet and can reach high alcohol levels. South African examples can taste rather earthy and hot.

Shiroka Melnishka Losa, means 'broad leaved vine of Melnik' in Bulgaria, close to the Greek border. This variety, oak aged, can produce spicy, powerful and ageworthy wine not unlike Châteauneuf-du-Pape, occasionally smelling of tobacco leaves. Usually sold as Melnik.

Sousão, Souzão, black grape which brings colour to port in the Douro valley and has been planted in California and Australia.

Spanna, NEBBIOLO around Gattinara.

Syrah, the great grape of the North Rhône responsible for the dense, burly, deep-coloured, long-lived wines of Hermitage and, slightly more seductively perfumed (traditionally thanks to some VIOGNIER in the blend) Côte-Rôtie. Unlike many varieties, it demonstrates a strict relationship between how severely it is pruned and how good the eventual wine is. It can also lose its aroma and acidity quickly if left past optimal ripening stage (both of which explain why so many (though by no means all) French varietal Syrah Vins de Pays are so wishy-washy). Crozes-Hermitage is probably the best-value manifestation of Syrah around at the moment, although good St-Joseph exists and Cornas rewards those prepared to wait. It can smell of black pepper or even burnt rubber.

During the 1980s Syrah was enthusiastically planted throughout southern France, where it is widely used as an ingredient in blends, notably to add structure and density to GRENACHE in Châteauneuf-du-Pape and other Southern Rhône wines, but also to spice up CABERNET SAUVIGNON in Provence. It is a much-valued ingredient in most Languedoc appellations, fast replacing Carignan even more decisively than Grenache, MOURVÈDRE and, to a lesser extent, CINSAUT. It can also make some fine wine in Italy and the sunnier spots in Switzerland's Valais.

In California it is being enthusiastically planted by the so-called Rhône Rangers, keen to demonstrate that Syrah may be even better suited to the climate of Northern California than Cabernet Sauvignon. Its influence is also increasing in Washington state. Almost all South American wines labelled Syrah are in fact the unrelated PETITE SIRAH.

In South Africa and Australia, where it is extremely important, it is known as SHIRAZ.

Taminga, Australian crossing.

Tannat, distinctive, tough variety best known as the main ingredient in Madiran but grown in other regions of south west France and, as Harriague, in Uruguay where it was taken by Basque émigrés. Wine made from it is naturally very astringent because of the thickness of the berries' skins, but Madiran's best winemakers are learning how to tame this tannic monster.

Tarrango, Australian TOURIGA NACIONAL X SULTANA crossing which ripens very late and needs a hot climate. The ultra-fruity wine is relatively light bodied and markedly low in tannin.

Tempranillo, Spain's most widely planted top quality grape variety whose name comes from *temprano,* or early, which is when it ripens (although 'early' can be well into October in Rioja). Spain's answer to CABERNET SAUVIGNON, Tempranillo is similarly high in tannins and acidity but, unusually for Spain, is not necessarily very high in alcohol.

Wines based on Tempranillo are some of Spain's longest lasting. It provides the spine for Rioja (GARNACHA providing the flesh, see page 225) and is by far the main ingredient in Ribera del Duero, where it is so common it is simply known as Tinto Fino 'the fine dark one'. In Penedès it is important as Ull de Llebre and Ojo de Liebre, and in Valdepeñas, called Cencibel, it makes rather less concentrated wines (often lightened by blending in white grapes). It is also grown in La Mancha, Costers del Segre, Utiel-Requena and increasingly in Navarre and Somontano. It is grown, as (Tinta) Roriz in northern Portugal and may well be the variety known as **Valdepeñas** in California's Central Valley. Some **Tempranilla** is grown in Argentina.

Teran, Terrano, see REFOSCO.

Teroldego, Teroldego Rotaliano, lively, tooth-smacking varietal speciality of Trentino in northern Italy, to be drunk young.

Tibouren, Provençal rarity making earthy rosés with a genuine scent of the *garrigue*, the herby scrub of southern France.

Tinta, Tinto is Spanish for red.

Tinta Amarela, productive, rot-prone northern Portuguese vine.

Tinta Barroca, sturdy port grape also planted in South Africa where varietal table wines are also made from it. Sometimes spelt **Tinta Barocca.**

Tinta Cão, fine port grape enjoying a revival in the Douro valley (see page 240).

Tinta Francisca, lightish port variety.

Tinta Negra Mole, the undistinguished but serviceable grape which steadily usurped Madeira's fine varieties in the early and mid-twentieth century. Spain's Negramoll may be identical.

Tinta Pinheira, basic Dão grape.

Tinto Fino, TEMPRANILLO in Ribera del Duero.

Touriga Francesa, perfumed, good quality port variety.

Touriga Nacional, the finest port variety grown also in the Dão region, and producing extremely concentrated, dark, tannic wines. Also grown in Australia.

Trincadeira Preta, an alternative name for CASTELÃO FRANCES.

Trollinger, German for SCHIAVA and its light, sweetish wines are a Württemberg speciality.

Trousseau, Jura vine, making robust wine but overtaken by PINOT NOIR.

Ull de Llebre, Catalan for TEMPRANILLO.

Uva di Troia, Apulian speciality.

Uva Rara, softener blended with NEBBIOLO in northern Piedmont.

Vaccarèse, rare, lightish Châteauneuf grape.

Valdiguié, prolific vine originally from south west France, now best known as NAPA GAMAY.

Vavrinecke, Czech for ST LAURENT.

Verdot, South American variety which *may* be related to PETIT VERDOT.

Vernatsch, see SCHIAVA and TROLLINGER.

Vespolina, Gattinara speciality often blended with NEBBIOLO.

Villard Noir, hybrid widely planted in France until the 1980s.

Vranac, a deep, dense speciality of Montenegro.

Wildbacher, Blauer Wildbacher, Styrian vine from which a deep, crisp, perfumed pink called Schilcher is made.

Xynomavro, 'acid black' Greek grape variety found in Naoussa. The wine ages well.

Zinfandel, California's most planted red wine grape, whose origins were for long a mystery, although DNA testing confirms the hypothesis that it is identical to the PRIMITIVO of southern Italy. The wine can be anything from a sweetened-up pale pink wine labelled White Zinfandel (an inspired 1980s solution to California's surplus of Zinfandel and shortage of white wine grapes) to a serious oak-aged, long-lived taut, spicy, dense, lively, full bodied red. Berry flavours predominate. The vine has a tendency to produce too many grapes, which themselves tend to ripen unevenly, so the vine needs careful management to yield good wine, but there are pockets of very old vines all over California, and particularly in the Sierra Foothills. So high is Zinfandel's profile in California that it is planted in many other warmer wine regions in the USA as well as in South America, South Africa and Australia, all of which have a warm enough climate for it to ripen fully.

Zweigelt, Zweigeltrebe, Blauer Zweigelt, Austria's most planted red wine grape, bred locally from BLAUFRÄNKISCH and ST LAURENT to combine the bite of the former with the body of the latter. It yields prolifically and has been planted in Germany and England.

4
THE WORLD OF WINE

FRANCE

France has an extraordinary, and in many ways extremely difficult, position in the world of wine. To many of us, France *is* wine, and a certain sort of wine, not always the easiest to appreciate but often the most rewarding. France makes more wine than any other country except Italy (see page 61), which sometimes wins the race for quantity but only sporadically comes near in terms of quality. France supplies the benchmarks by which almost all wines are judged. This perfectly temperate and varied climate and landscape can supply wines of virtually every style. Its finest red bordeaux sets a standard for the world's Cabernet Sauvignons. The millions and millions of Chardonnay vines planted around the globe owe their existence to white burgundy – just as their Pinot Noir equivalents depend on someone's memory of a great red burgundy. The produce of the Champagne region in the north east provides a model for every bottle of dry fizz, no matter where it is made. The Rhône valley supplies deep, rich reds while the Loire is better known for pinks and whites of all degrees of sweetness and fizziness. The vine dominates the Mediterranean hinterland in a swathe of vineyards across southern France which are capable of producing almost 10 per cent of the entire planet's wine output. Only Germany's wines ignore the French tradition – and look at German wine's current problems (see page 244). The French even produce their own answer to port (Banyuls) and sherry (*vin jaune*).

It has been difficult, however, for France to come to grips with the modern, fiercely competitive, tirelessly iconoclastic and innovative wine world. The problem is that the average French wine producer simply cannot understand any criticism of his (and most are male) wines. He is so imbued with the notion of terroir (see page 62), the belief that his wine can be produced only from his patch of land, in a way enshrined in the all-important AC regulations (see box opposite), and that he is really only a human instrument of the unique expression of that land, that he finds it difficult to understand the New World's unfettered winemakers who see man as the most important, controlling factor in wine production. Complacency has slowed winemaking improvements, but the great change in French wine producers since the last generation is that virtually all of them now have some formal training and understanding of why, as well as how, they do what they do. An increasing number of them now travel to other wine-producing countries as well, which must be a good thing for us all.

There is a broad difference in style between French wines and New World wines. The French feel that they don't need to woo the drinker with obviously fruity wines designed to be drunk as soon as they are bottled. Instead, they tend to make wines for the medium and long term, in the restrained style of their forebears, so that the average French wine will probably take more effort to appreciate than its New World counterpart but may well repay that effort and will almost certainly last longer.

The French themselves see wine as an important part of their heritage, but are drinking less and less of it. The generation which took a daily litre of rough red for granted is rapidly being replaced by one to whom quality is much more important than quantity. Total wine sales in France are not helped either by the fact that the French very rarely drink wine as an aperitif without food – although they have an unusual fondness for sweet drinks such as port, sauternes and Muscats before meals.

UNDERSTANDING LABELS

AC, Appellation Contrôlée, France's principal and much-imitated quality designation system, devised to protect producers from imitators and to guarantee authenticity to consumers. Well over a third of all French wine and all of its best wine is AC, sometimes called **AOC** or **Appellation d'Origine Contrôlée.** For each appellation strict regulations control the area included, which grape varieties may be planted, how they should be pruned, maximum yields, when the harvest may begin, minimum grape ripeness levels and/or alcoholic strength, and even how the wine should be made. Superior appellations typically fit inside other, less rigorous ones, e.g. Pauillac is an area within the Médoc which itself lies within the general Bordeaux appellation. Appellations are granted by, and their regulations administered by, the Paris-based INAO (Institut National des Appellations d'Origine).

cave means literally cellar or winery and is often used for a co-operative cellar, as in **Cave des Vignerons de...**

Château, French for 'castle' but in a wine context it means a registered wine-producing property whose only building may be a shed or even a corner of a co-operative winery. Most common in Bordeaux.

Clos, enclosing wall, often used in Burgundy for an enclosed vineyard.

Côte(s) de, prefix usually denoting a superior wine. Like **Coteaux** it literally means hillsides.

Cru, literally 'growth' or vineyard site. A **cru classé** is a Médoc or Graves property listed in the most famous wine classification of all. See pages 160–61 for more details.

Domaine, Burgundian name for the accumulated holdings of one grower. Thus a domaine-bottled wine is one bottled by the producer.

éleveur, one who looks after wine between fermentation and bottling.

Grand Cru is a widely used term but in Burgundy it means one of the finest vineyards.

Mis(e) en bouteille par/pour means 'bottled by/for'. France's best wines are almost invariably bottled at the château (*au château*) or domaine. Co-ops are allowed to claim 'mise en bouteille *du* château' for wines from specific vineyards.

négociant, wholesale wine merchant or bottler.

Premier Cru (1er Cru), another vague term but in Burgundy denotes superior vineyards just below Grand Cru status.

récoltant, literally 'harvester', grower.

Supérieur, infrequently used suffix denoting a slightly more alcoholic wine.

VDQS, relatively unusual quality designation for ACs-in-waiting (see page 48).

vigneron, vine-grower.

Villages, suffix usually denoting a superior wine.

Vin de Pays, superior Vin de Table (see pages 48 and 202–4).

Vin de Table, wine at its most basic.

viticulteur, vine-grower.

BORDEAUX

In a nutshell: Huge quantity of mainly long-lived, medium bodied, ultra-digestible reds (called claret by the British) with some sweet whites and extremely varied dry whites.
Main grapes: Merlot, Cabernet Sauvignon, Cabernet Franc (RED), Sémillon, Sauvignon (WHITE)

Bordeaux is France's most important weapon in the wine war. This large, south western wine region, ruled by the English for 200 years in the Middle Ages, produces more AC wine than any other. About half of all the wine produced in the sprawling Bordeaux region qualifies for its most lowly appellation, simple AC Bordeaux, whose quality varies from vapid red wine to serious, oak-aged, château-bottled liquids made by quality-conscious individuals exasperated by how little money they can get for a wine which qualifies only for the humble generic Bordeaux appellation.

The produce of most of these appellations' finest wine estates, usually called châteaux, is not only quite exceptionally good and long lasting, but also available in much larger quantities than other top wines. It is no wonder that the world has heard of Châteaux Lafite, Mouton-Rothschild, Latour, Margaux and Haut-Brion, the famous five 'first growths', in the top division of the 1855 classification (see page 161).

In many ways Bordeaux still feels like a separate kingdom from the rest of France. Financially secure, very much directed towards the Atlantic and the outside world, the region and its agriculture are dominated by neat, carefully tended vineyards, a significant number of which belong not to locals but to insurance companies, banks or absentee landlords based in Paris, Tokyo, New York and elsewhere.

MÉDOC

The Médoc, a flat spur of land on the left bank of the Gironde estuary as it widens out to meet the sea, is Bordeaux's most famous wine district, and the Cabernet Sauvignon vine's homeland. It is also home to most of Bordeaux's famous large estates, most of which have built up their international reputations for the last two centuries. (To put the scale of fine wine production here into perspective, the Médoc, with its neighbour and partner the Graves district, produces almost exactly 100 times as much as all the Grands Crus of Burgundy put together.) The four most famous parishes, or com-

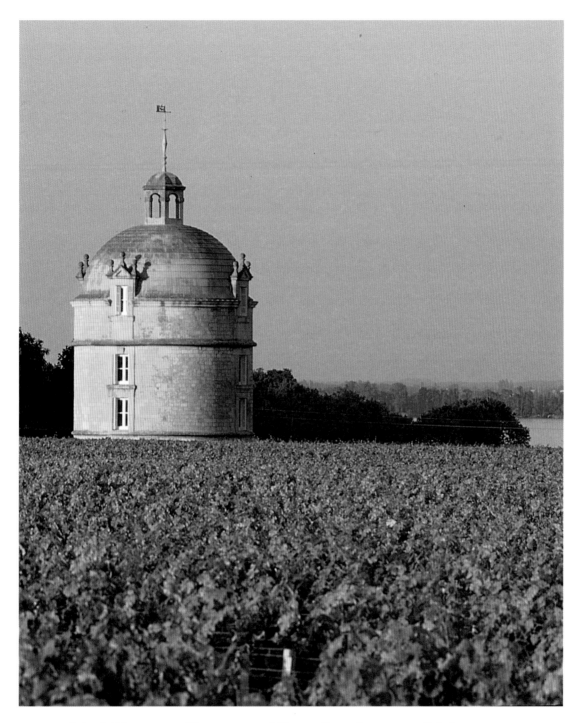

munes, of the Médoc, are, heading north from Bordeaux, **Margaux**, **St-Julien**, **Pauillac** and **St-Estèphe**.

The remnants of Château Latour's tower, which overlooks the Gironde estuary.

slightly austere respectively (see page 133 for more details). In practice, in this era of the public

In theory each of these communes produces wines of a distinctive character: silky smooth, perfectly balanced, minerals and cassis, and wine scoreboard of points and praise awarded by an international wine press, all too many producers seem to be making their wines to the

159

same, eye-catching and palate-grabbing formula, resulting in deep-coloured, full bodied, flatteringly oaky wines. Huge quantities of new oak barrels travel up the Médoc each year.

Many is the wine-minded visitor who has navigated his way through the northern suburbs of Bordeaux to worship the world's starriest wine district, only to find an undistinguished plateau sloping imperceptibly towards the grey Gironde estuary, broken only by the odd copse or huddle of houses carrying one of the names he reveres most. True, there are some magnificent railings with some impressively turreted nineteenth-century country houses behind them, but there is still little to welcome the visitor who is thirsty for wine knowledge and bottles. (And there was even less 10 years ago.)

All but the tiniest fraction of wine produced here is sold, via complicated layers of commissions and brokers, to the wholesale merchants who have been based in and around Bordeaux for centuries. Châteaux Prieuré-Lichine in Margaux and Pichon-Longueville in Pauillac are exceptional in positively welcoming visitors from the D2, the little road that snakes its way up the Médoc (although the locals thought Alexis Lichine was being horribly commercial when he first erected his signs outside Margaux welcoming tourists to the Château).

This is a district with a carefully stratified society. Only a handful of owners actually live there (Anthony Barton of Châteaux Langoa- and Léoville-Barton is an exception). Most estates are run by several ranks of manager, although at last some of the most talented winemaking managers have acquired a certain status. Every now and then the owners descend to entertain wine merchants, wine writers and influential friends and the châteaux are transformed into bustling country houses, their most important rooms being the dining-room and extremely formal salon. (It took me a long time to work out why so few of these large houses seemed to have anywhere to relax in.)

For much of the twentieth century these large wine estates made very little money, but the world economy and a succession of very successful vintages in the 1980s changed all that. During the 1980s the Médoc crawled with architects and builders renovating cellars, vineyards and, often most spectacularly, the château buildings themselves.

But the most obvious stratification was drawn up, doubtless without any realization of quite how influential it was to be, in 1855. Just before Napoleon III's Universal Exhibition in Paris, the organizers asked the Bordeaux merchants to devise a quality ranking of the top wine châteaux. What emerged was a five-division list of 61 **crus classés** which had already established their reputation, together with Château Haut-Brion, the most famous property in the Graves district. Opposite is an up-to-date version, which takes account of the fact that some estates have virtually disappeared, their land having been acquired by other proprietors. Otherwise, there has been no significant change to the classification since 1855 apart from the promotion of Château Mouton-Rothschild from second to first growth in 1973. Baron Philippe de Rothschild, one of the wine world's few marketing geniuses, responsible for the branded wine Mouton Cadet and the growth of château bottling, finally nagged the authorities into it.

Very unusually for a cosmopolitan aristocrat of his period, he had devoted much of the previous four decades to his family's wine estates in the Médoc, and the wine was well worthy of first growth status. But the heavy price premium which a first growth can command over a second (even greater than a second can command over a third and so on) suggests that there is a certain element of self-perpetuation about the 1855 classification. Properties with a higher rank can afford more drainage ditches (vital for quality in this district that was a marsh before the Dutch drained it in the sixteenth century), more new barrels, and more fastidious selection than those whose status, and therefore selling prices, are lower down the scale. Estate owners would claim that their particular land is unique, but many of them would have to admit that

BORDEAUX

The official Classification of Médoc and Graves of 1855

	Commune	Appellation		Commune	Appellation
FIRST GROWTHS (PREMIERS CRUS)					
Château Lafite-Rothschild	Pauillac	Pauillac	Château Haut-Brion [a]	Pessac	Graves
Château Margaux	Margaux	Margaux	Château Mouton-Rothschild [b]	Pauillac	Pauillac
Château Latour	Pauillac	Pauillac			
SECOND GROWTHS (DEUXIÈMES CRUS)					
Château Rausan-Ségla	Margaux	Margaux	Château Brane-Cantenac	Cantenac	Margaux
Château Rauzan-Gassies	Margaux	Margaux	Château Pichon-Longueville	Pauillac	Margaux
Château Léoville-Las-Cases*	St-Julien	St-Julien	(Baron)*		
Château Léoville-Poyferré	St-Julien	St-Julien	Château Pichon-Longueville,	Pauillac	Pauillac
Château Léoville Barton*	St-Julien	St-Julien	Comtesse de Lalande*		
Château Durfort-Vivens	Margaux	Margaux	Château Ducru-Beaucaillou	St-Julien	St-Julien
Château Gruaud-Larose*	St-Julien	St-Julien	Château Cos d'Estournel*	St-Estèphe	St-Estèphe
Château Lascombes*	Margaux	Margaux	Château Montrose	St-Estèphe	St-Estèphe
THIRD GROWTHS (TROISIÈMES CRUS)					
Château Kirwan	Cantenac	Margaux	Château Cantenac-Brown	Cantenac	Margaux
Château d'Issan	Cantenac	Margaux	Château Palmer*	Cantenac	Margaux
Château Lagrange*	St-Julien	St-Julien	Château La Lagune	Ludon	Haut-Médoc
Château Langoa-Barton	St-Julien	St-Julien	Château Desmirail	Margaux	Margaux
Château Giscours	Labarde	Margaux	Château Calon-Ségur	St-Estèphe	St-Estèphe
Château Malescot St-Exupéry	Margaux	Margaux	Château Ferrière	Margaux	Margaux
Château Boyd-Cantenac	Cantenac	Margaux	Château Marquis d'Alesme Becker	Margaux	Margaux
FOURTH GROWTHS (QUATRIÈMES CRUS)					
Château St-Pierre	St-Julien	St-Julien	Château La Tour-Carnet	St-Laurent	Haut-Médoc
Château Talbot	St-Julien	St-Julien	Château Lafon-Rochet	St-Estèphe	St-Estèphe
Château Branaire-Ducru	St-Julien	St-Julien	Château Beychevelle	St-Julien	St-Julien
Château Duhart-Milon-Rothschild	Pauillac	Pauillac	Château Prieuré-Lichine	Cantenac	Margaux
Château Pouget	Cantenac	Margaux	Château Marquis-de-Terme	Margaux	Margaux
FIFTH GROWTHS (CINQUIÈMES CRUS)					
Château Pontet-Canet	Pauillac	Pauillac	Château du Tertre	Arsac	Margaux
Château Batailley	Pauillac	Pauillac	Château Haut-Bages-Libéral	Pauillac	Pauillac
Château Haut-Batailley	Pauillac	Pauillac	Château Pédesclaux	Pauillac	Pauillac
Château Grand-Puy-Lacoste*	Pauillac	Pauillac	Château Belgrave	St-Laurent	Haut-Médoc
Château Grand-Puy-Ducasse	Pauillac	Pauillac	Château de Camensac	St-Laurent	Haut-Médoc
Château Lynch-Bages*	Pauillac	Pauillac	Château Cos-Labory	St-Estèphe	St-Estèphe
Château Lynch-Moussas	Pauillac	Pauillac	Château Clerc-Milon	Pauillac	Pauillac
Château Dauzac	Labarde	Margaux	Château Croizet-Bages	Pauillac	Pauillac
Château d'Armailhac [c]	Pauillac	Pauillac	Château Cantemerle	Macau	Haut-Médoc

[a] This wine, although a Graves (now Pessac-Leognan), was universally recognized and classified as one of the four first growths.
[b] This wine was decreed a first growth in 1973.
[c] Previously Château Mouton-Baron-Philippe, then Château Mouton-Baronne-Philippe.
* Some of the most consistently successful wines in recent years.

there has been a considerable amount of inter-château vineyard exchange since 1855.

There are also some slackers among the châteaux classified in 1855. For example, few would claim that Château Rauzan-Gassies is worthy of second growth status. On the other hand, I have asterisked some properties whose wines are usually superior to their official status.

Just below the 'classed growths', as these 60-odd châteaux are called, are the so-called 'bourgeois growths' or **crus bourgeois**, making a group of about 60 further wine estates representing some of those who try harder in the Médoc. Between them the crus classés and the crus bourgeois represent about 65 per cent of all the wine produced in the Médoc (which hardly makes any white wine at all).

GRAVES AND PESSAC-LÉOGNAN

Graves is the Médoc's mirror image on the inland side of Bordeaux and the other major 'left bank' appellation. Like the Médoc, much of it is based on grav-elly soils (hence the name of this wine region, which was famous even before the Médoc). Pessac-Léognan is an appellation created in 1987 to include all of the Graves's most famous châteaux, the greatest of which are actually in the southern suburbs of the city itself: Château Haut-Brion and, once a great rival and now under the same – American – ownership, Château La Mission-Haut-Brion just across the road. As well as making firm, dry wines with the sort of minerally, 'warm bricks' overlay often found in red Graves, these properties also pro-

Château Villemaurine (above) is one of St-Émilion's 70-odd Grands Cru Classés, while Château Ausone (right) is, with Château Cheval Blanc, one of its finest properties, making just 2200 cases a year.

duce a full bodied, oak-aged dry white wine that needs plenty of time in bottle (called Laville-Haut-Brion in the case of La Mission's white), which is typical of the Graves region too. Other properties that produce extremely good wine include Domaine de Chevalier and Châteaux Pape-Clément (since 1986), Smith-Haut-Lafitte (since 1990), de Fieuzal, La Louvière, Haut-Bailly and, for white wines, Couhins-Lurton and Clos Floridène. Less glorified properties in the Graves proper, along the left bank of the river Garonne, can provide appetizing reds and some much more interesting dry whites (which also age well) than the Bordeaux norm.

ST-ÉMILION

The Merlot vine reigns here on 'the right bank' (of the Gironde) as it does in the greater Bordeaux region, producing generally warmer, more obviously fruity wines than in Médoc and Graves, most of which mature between three and ten years earlier.

The medieval town of St-Émilion can supply the wine tourist with every-thing the Médoc lacks: pretty countryside round about, cobbled streets, a ruined but cavernous church, cloisters and literally scores of wine shops dedicated, almost too rapaciously, to sell-ing wine by the bottle to visitors. St-Émilion has its own classification system, revised every decade. Only wines described as **Grand Cru Classé** on the label are seriously superior and Châteaux Ausone and Cheval Blanc share the same ranking as a Médoc first growth; the words Grand Cru alone mean little. Other ambitious

wines include Châteaux l'Angélus, l'Arrosée, Canon, La Dominique, Figeac, Tertre-Rotebœuf and newcomer Valandraud.

POMEROL

Like St-Émilion, Pomerol is a region of small wine farms, on an even smaller scale. The most famous Pomerol of all, Château Pétrus, comprises hardly 12 ha (30 acres), and there are other properties such as Châteaux Lafleur and Le Pin whose extremely limited size helps to bolster the prices of their wines. Pomerols are velvety, rich Merlot-dominant wines which can smell almost meaty and can give an enormous amount of pleasure. Bargains from this small appellation are as rare as badly made wines, but the produce of vintages which were much more successful for Merlot than Cabernet (1987 and 1992, for example) are often relatively underpriced because the Cabernet-dominated left bank tends to make the reputation of each vintage in Bordeaux (and to a certain extent in the whole of France).

SAUTERNES AND OTHER SWEET WHITE WINES

In a sense the Bordeaux region's most distinctive (and certainly its least appreciated) wines come from its south east corner in and around Sauternes, the great sweet white bordeaux appellation. Practically every wine region in the world tries to make a fair copy of great red bordeaux, but very, very few have the particular natural conditions that favour the development of noble rot/botrytis (see page 88). Sauternes is unique in being at least theoretically able to produce reasonable quantities of long-lasting, truly noble, full bodied sweet whites.

Sauternes, including the **Barsac** appellation within it, benefits from autumnal morning mists which form where the cool Ciron flows into the warmer Garonne. Provided nature co-operates by supplying sun to burn off the mist, the botrytis fungus will concentrate fully ripe grapes and

great sweet whites can be made, if and only if estate owners are prepared to take the risk of leaving the grapes on the vine. Many of these proprietors, particularly those discouraged by the relatively modest selling prices of most sweet wines, simply pick the grapes and add sugar so that, even after fermentation, the wine is sweet, if usually over-sulphured to stop it refermenting. The most famous sweet white wine of all, Château d'Yquem (pronounced 'Ee-kem') can live for well over a century and sells for other-worldly prices but, so demanding is the production process, it is said to be difficult to make even this fabulous property pay.

Other sweet white bordeaux appellations, in roughly descending order of the quantity of wine they produce, are **Ste-Croix-du-Mont**, **Loupiac**, **Cadillac** and **Cérons**, although the appellations **Premières Côtes de Bordeaux** and **Graves Supérieures** also produce some medium sweet white.

OTHER APPELLATIONS

Perhaps the most significant development in the Bordeaux of the late 1980s and 1990s is the increasing number of seriously dedicated producers in the less glamorous appellations, **Bordeaux**, **Côtes de Blaye**, **Côtes de Bourg**, **Côtes de Castillon**, **Côtes de Francs**, **Fronsac** and **Canon Fronsac**, **Lalande de Pomerol**, **Premières Côtes de Blaye**, **Premières Côtes de Bordeaux** and the satellite appellations with St-Émilion in their name for red wines and **Bordeaux**, **Entre-Deux-Mers**, and **Blaye** for dry whites. Their wines usually fetch a mere fraction of the classed growth prices, but properties such as these offer Bordeaux's best current value: Châteaux de Belcier, Bertinerie, Bonnet, Carsin, Côte-Monpézat, l'Epéron, Fontenille, de Francs, Le Grand Verdus, Guibon, Haut Rian, Hauts Ste Marie, de Haux, Jonqueyres, du Juge, Lassime, Méaume, Monbadon, Parenchère, Puygueraud, Reynier, Reynon, de Roquefort, de Sours, Suau, Tanesse, Thieuley, La Tour de Mirambeau, Turcaud and Domaines de Cambes, de Courteillac and de la Grave.

BURGUNDY

*In a nutshell: Small, expensive, infuriating,
complicated region that can occasionally deliver
paradise in a bottle.*
*Grapes: Pinot Noir and some Gamay (RED),
Chardonnay and some Aligoté (WHITE)*

Burgundy is Bourgogne in French (the source of many a misunderstanding). Although for many people Burgundy/Bourgogne is synonymous with the heartland of this medieval kingdom, the Côte d'Or (see next page), greater Burgundy (see map on page 156) also encompasses the Côte Chalonnaise and Mâconnais to the south and the quite distinct subregions of Beaujolais even further south (stretching almost into the suburbs of Lyons) and Chablis, the white wine district a good hour's drive north west of Beaune, Burgundy's wine capital. With its gothic gables and steep, scalloped roofs, the town of Beaune is Burgundy's most obvious tourist attraction, but most wine villages still look remarkably unchanged since the Middle Ages when the Dukes of Burgundy ran the region as a rich, self-governing state.

Unlike France's other famous wine region Bordeaux, Burgundy is still a land of peasant farmers. Today, thanks to the boom in fine wine sales in the 1970s and 1980s, many of them are peasant farmers who eat in three-star restaurants and have a Mercedes in the garage, but their mentality is that of a smallholder.

There could hardly be a greater contrast in social climate between Burgundy and Bordeaux, France's two premier wine regions. While most famous Bordeaux wine estates are large and centred on a grand château inhabited only rarely by their absentee owners, Burgundy's most famous vineyards are in the hands of the men who work them. They may have a peasant's wariness of outsiders, but to people they have come to know and trust they offer the true hand of friendship – and innumerable samplings.

Land that qualifies for one of Burgundy's better appellations is so valuable that it rarely passes out of the family but is generally part of a complex inheritance system which requires all property to be shared between each child.

Until the second half of the twentieth century Burgundy's vine-growers did just that. They would sell their grapes to the region's powerful merchants, or négociants, who could then assemble reasonable quantities of wine under each appellation to be sold under the négociant's name. However, the late twentieth-century fashion for demonstrable authenticity changed all this. Demand for domaine-bottled burgundy carrying the stamp of one grower-winemaker-bottler means that the consumer has the choice of the following sorts of wine, all possibly made from the same small vineyard:

1 a négociant-bottled blend of produce from several different growers (récoltants/viticulteurs/vignerons). This can vary from the cynically dire to the extremely competent as, for example, with Drouhin, Faiveley, Jadot, Labouré-Roi and (for whites) Louis Latour.

2 a négociant-bottled wine made exclusively from the négociant's own vineyards. This is an increasingly important phenomenon. Bouchard Père et Fils and Faiveley have particularly significant vineyard holdings of their own.

3 a domaine-bottled wine made by a vine-grower who also happens to be a good wine-maker.

4 a domaine-bottled wine made by a vine-grower who isn't terribly good at making wine.

The chart shows the relative quality of each category:

CÔTE D'OR

Côte d'Or is usually translated as 'golden slope', an association all too readily made in view of the high prices charged for its wines. But in fact the name of Burgundy's glamorous heartland is an abbreviation of Côte d'Orient or 'eastern slope'. The best vineyards here lie along a narrow band of marl and limestone facing south east to maximize their exposure to the sun. Lower-lying vineyards with more clay drain less well and tend to produce less exciting wine.

The Côte d'Or is divided into the Côte de Beaune in the south, where all great white burgundy and a great deal of very fine red burgundy is made, and the smaller Côte de Nuits (named after Nuits-St-Georges) in the north, which produces Burgundy's most concentrated and longest-living reds. Over the years the villages of the Côte d'Or have tended to append the name of their most famous vineyard to the village name, so that Nuits became Nuits-St-Georges, Aloxe became Aloxe-Corton and both Puligny and Chassagne grabbed the world-famous suffix Montrachet.

There are four levels of appellation among the Côte d'Or's total of more than 60 (some producing only a few thousand bottles a year). The most basic are the **regional** ACs, the most common of which are Bourgogne (often supplementarily labelled Pinot Noir or Chardonnay in a nod to New World practice); Bourgogne Aligoté, a leaner dry white made from Burgundy's second white grape; and its red counterpart Bourgogne Passe-tout-grains in which Pinot's purity is customarily smudged by blending with the Gamay grape of Beaujolais. Wines that are labelled AC Bourgogne can come from less exalted vineyards all over greater Burgundy and should be an easy, approachable expression of Burgundian Pinot Noir and Chardonnay. Too often, however, they are made in the same way as much grander wines (whose concentration can stand long skin contact in the case of reds and high sulphur additions in the case of whites) and their message is the opposite of come-hither.

A distinct notch above these wines are **village** wines (such as those labelled simply Volnay or Meursault), carrying as their appellation the name of

At harvest time the Côte d'Or villages such as Puligny-Montrachet throb with the sound of vineyard tractors.

the commune in which they were made (see map on page 166). They can provide some of Burgundy's most delicious drinking for the first three or four years after a soft vintage but should not usually be kept for much longer than this.

Each village's sites with the potential to make distinctly superior wine (almost invariably those with particularly favourable exposure and good drainage) were classified as **premiers crus** in the last century (Burgundy's answer to the Bordeaux 1855 classification) so that wines made from them inevitably carry a price premium which is sometimes, but not invariably, justified.

The 30 best of these are acknowledged **grands crus** and, in the right hands, make quite sumptuously concentrated wines which can benefit from many years' ageing in bottle. The reds can exhibit Pinot Noir's extraordinary range of textures as well as flavours, while the whites are the most savoury, full bodied dry whites in the world – a world away from the simplistic appeal of a mass market, varietally labelled Chardonnay. But a high proportion of the wines are disappointments, either because of the weather or poor winemaking.

Most appellations include both red and white wines, even if one colour almost invariably predominates. Red Puligny-Montrachet and white Vougeot, for example, do exist.

There are literally thousands of vine-growers on the Côte d'Or, most of whom nowadays sell some wine of their own, even if they hedge their bets by selling off the rest to the négociants. The average grower owns only 5 ha (12.5 acres), but in nine different appellations (which may be only a few hundred yards apart). Each tiny cellar (usually notably low-tech) harbours scores of different combinations of appellation and vintage, each in minuscule quantity. It is particularly difficult therefore in the Côte d'Or to give comprehensive buying advice. Thanks to deaths and marriages, the precise holdings of each vine-grower can seem to be in a state of continual evolution. In the space available all I can offer is as many as possible of the names whose wines have impressed me over the last

few years, but please note that intermarrying is rife in a rural community such as this and many similar but not identical names will be found on bottles from quite distinct domaines. Nothing in Burgundy is simple, and some producers have been known to put slightly different producer names on the same wine for tax reasons.

Some favourite growers:
Reds
Domaine de l'Arlot, Comte Armand, Denis Bachelet, Jean-Marc Boillot, Robert Chevillon, Bruno Clair, various Gros, Henri Jayer, Jayer-Gilles, Hubert Lignier, Domaine Leroy, Méo-Camuzet, Ponsot, Michel Prunier, Domaine de la Romanée-Conti (DRC), Armand Rousseau, Emmanuel Rouget, Tollot-Beaut.

Whites
Jean-Marc Boillot, Louis Carillon, Coche-Dury, Jean-Noël Gagnard, François Jobard, Comtes Lafon, Domaine Leflaive, Bernard Morey, Michel Niellon, Domaine Ramonet.

Some of the most quality-conscious négociants:
Bouchard Père et Fils, Drouhin, Faiveley, Jadot, Louis Latour (whites), Dominique Laurent, Olivier Leflaive, Remoissenet, Verget (whites).

Some appellations generally offering better value than most:
Beaune (has no grands crus but some very good wines), Chorey-lès-Beaune, Monthélie, Pernand-Vergelesses, St-Aubin (especially for whites), St-Romain (whites), Santenay and Savigny-lès-Beaune.

Appellations to be wary of:
Wines carrying these particularly well-known names can be absolutely marvellous but bottlers who care more about money than quality often bottle some of Burgundy's worst bargains under them: Meursault, Montrachet, Pommard, Puligny-Montrachet and (Clos) Vougeot. Beware of suspiciously cheap bottles labelled thus from completely unknown producers.

CHABLIS

Burgundy's white wine outpost is one of France's most northern and it is hardly surprising therefore that these all-Chardonnay wines are naturally relatively sinewy, high in acidity and steely rather than luscious. Rather out of fashion, in fact, and a long way from the obvious, richly alcoholic and oaky style of Chardonnay that in the 1980s became so popular with both consumers and wine producers elsewhere. But this is an archetypally refreshing, long-lived style of white wine which very few wine regions, possibly none other than Chablis, can produce.

We Chablis enthusiasts treasure the purity of flavour, the modest dimensions and the rapier-like effect on the palate of the region's better examples, and cannot understand how the word Chablis ever came to be used, particularly in the United States, for sweetened up blends of the most basic white.

For the consumer, Chablis prices are annoyingly inconsistent. This is partly because Chablis is so well known that it tends to be traded as a commodity and is therefore all too subject to pressures quite unrelated to the wine itself. It is also because the volume of Chablis produced can vary considerably from year to year thanks to spring frosts which annually threaten to freeze off a sizeable proportion of the year's crop. Being so far from the equator, and growing almost exclusively the early-budding Chardonnay vine, Chablis has become famous for its anti-frost measures. Small stoves in the vineyard have largely given way to sprinklers which surround the vines with a protective coating of ice.

Chablis comes in four very distinct quality levels. **Petit Chablis** is the principal, often vapid product of the plantings on the outskirts of Chablis proper, undertaken when the Chablis growers found that they were unable to keep up with international demand. Most of the wine produced around the pretty little village of Chablis qualifies for the straightforward Chablis appellation, which can vary considerably in quality (beware of Chablis bottled outside the region) but should usually be drunk young. The region's particularly well-sited vineyards, comprising about a quarter of total Chablis production, are designated **Chablis Premier Cru** and represent some of the district's most reliable buys. The very best vineyards are on the west-facing hill immediately above the village and qualify as **Chablis Grand Cru**. These are the vineyards, particularly Les Clos, that have made Chablis's reputation as offering a remarkable combination of refreshment and longevity. Other Grands Crus include Blanchots, Bougros, Grenouille, Preuses, Valmur and Vaudésir. Some of the best-known Premiers Crus are Fourchaume, Mont de Milieu, Montmains, Vaillons, and Montée de Tonnerre, which in some particularly successful vintages can develop as appetizingly as a Grand Cru Chablis.

Grand Cru and some of the best Premier Cru Chablis can improve in bottle for more than a decade. Indeed its extra acid can make top quality Chablis a better candidate for ageing than many Côte d'Or whites. But such wines can sometimes smell almost dirty in youth, or if not dirty then at least reminiscent of wet wool or dogs. Wet stones is what I like to smell from young Chablis.

There has been, perhaps inevitably, a trend towards trying to make Chablis in a more luscious, obviously oaky style. This seems a shame to me, but may well be a sign that I and not the Chablis producers am beginning to lose my hold on reality.

Some particularly impressive producers:
La Chablisienne co-operative's top bottlings, Dauvissat, Defaix, Droin, Laroche, Louis Michel, René et Vincent Raveneau.

CÔTE CHALONNAISE

To the immediate south of the grand white wine vineyards of the Côte de Beaune lies the Côte Chalonnaise, named after the town of Châlon-sur-Saône (where in ancient Gaul wine shipped upriver from the south would be offloaded for overland transport northwards). Whereas vines are by far the principal crop of the Côte d'Or, this gentle landscape is much more variably agricultural with the odd vineyard punctuating rolling meadows. The wines, made from Chardonnay or Pinot Noir except for the famous Aligoté of Bouzeron, really do taste like country cousins of those from the Côte d'Or, but their early drinkability makes them extremely useful.

During the 1980s winemaking in the Côte Chalonnaise showed such a high level of consistency that in many cases it made up for the district's lack of top quality sites and its wines offered the best value in greater Burgundy. Inevitably however, the market is fast correcting itself and the price of wines from Côte Chalonnaise's four appellations are about the same as those from the Côte d'Or's less well-known villages.

Givry (which is nothing to do with Gevrey-Chambertin, one of the great villages of the Côte d'Or) produces mainly red wine and is an exremely reliable appellation. The grower Joblot makes wines with far more sophistication than is usual and Domaine Thénard is based here.

Mercurey, also predominantly devoted to Pinot Noir, is the district's most important appellation by far. There are several premiers crus vineyards which are capable of making wines with lovely supple fruit. Although the négociant Faiveley is based well to the north in Nuits-St-Georges, its La Framboisière bottling is a reliable reflection of each vintage. Michel Juillot is one of the district's stars.

Montagny, dedicated to Chardonnay, is a name brought to thousands by négociant Louis Latour's long-standing purchasing arrangement with the Buxy co-operative here, one of the most dedicated and innovative in France. The co-op also makes pretty good sparkling wine in the form of Crémant de Bourgogne.

Rully (easy to confuse with Reuilly near Sancerre) is fairly evenly balanced between growing Pinot Noir and Chardonnay. The large merchant André Delorme's Domaine de la Renarde is one of the more prominent labels, as is Antonin Rodet's Château de Rully. Eric de Suremain of Monthélie's also brings some Côte d'Or class to the appellation.

Typical countryside in southern Burgundy where vines alternate with arable farming and other crops.

MÂCONNAIS AND BEAUJOLAIS

The Mâconnais takes its name from the city of Mâcon and constitutes an intermittent sprawl of vineyards south from the Côte Chalonnaise to the northern limit of Beaujolais. In very broad brushstrokes, its whites, typically sold as **Mâcon Blanc** and all made from Chardonnay grapes which can be attractively round and melon-flavoured, tend to be a much better bet than red wines sold as Mâcon, which are often rather coarse ferments of Gamay grapes (since reds made here from Pinot Noir grapes fetch a higher price if sold as AC Bourgogne). **Mâcon-Supérieur**, **Mâcon-Villages** and Mâcon with the name of a village appended are usually a cut above straight Mâcon Blanc and, from winemakers who are as gifted as André Bonhomme, Olivier Merlin and Jean Thévenet, can be just as thrilling as all but the best whites of the Côte d'Or – at a fraction of the price.

Mâcons-Chardonnay, **-Clessé**, **-Lugny** and **-Viré** are all superior white wines named after their village of origin (Chardonnay is the name of a village in the Mâconnais as well as of the world's most famous grape variety). Lugny has a particularly good co-operative, but the district is a hotbed of ambitious winemaking including botrytized sweet Mâcon-Clessé. They really do have to try harder here in the south.

The top quality Mâconnais white wine vineyards are concentrated in the far south east of the district, right up against the northern frontier of Beaujolais. The most notable appellation of all is **Pouilly-Fuissé** which, despite its mouthful of a name, has become so popular that it frequently sells for more than some humbler Côte d'Or appellations, often without justification. Some of the wine, such as that made by Domaine Corsin, Ferret, Château Fuissé and Guffens-Heynen, is extremely good, substantial, sometimes slightly honeyed stuff, but Pouilly-Fuissé is too fashionable a name to offer consistency. **Pouilly-Loché** and **Pouilly-Vinzelles** can also offer some of Pouilly-Fuissé's extra body and are almost indistinguishable from **St-Véran** and the best examples of **Beaujolais Blanc**, a speciality of the north of the Beaujolais district.

Proper, red Beaujolais can be a quite delicious drink – quite unrelated to red burgundy made further north. The only indisputably successful wine made exclusively from Gamay grapes, it should be fairly light bodied with lots of youthful fruit and relatively high acidity. Most Beaujolais should on no account be kept and is good when served lightly chilled. Unfortunately, it is too often souped up and blurred by heavy-handed chaptalization (see page 72), or hurried through its fermentation and brutally stabilized to yield a **Beaujolais Nouveau** or **Beaujolais Primeur**. Beaujolais is notable for being made in sealed tanks under the influence of carbon dioxide, a method known as carbonic maceration which helps to extract fruit rather than tannin (see page 78). **Beaujolais-Villages** is usually noticeably better than straight Beaujolais, being made from vineyards closer to the gently rolling, heart-breakingly pretty, granitic hills that form the core of the district.

From these hills comes the Beaujolais élite, wines made to lower yields from one of the **Beaujolais crus**, which manage to combine Beaujolais's appetizing character with greater concentration of fruit and some life expectancy (I have tasted a lively one at 40 years old). These wines are confusing because they rarely carry the B-word on the label. They are **Brouilly**, **Chénas**, **Chiroubles**, **Fleurie**, **Juliénas**, **Moulin-à-Vent**, **Morgon**, **Regnié** and **St-Amour**.

The king of Beaujolais, bottling a wide range of reds and whites, some of them from individual estates, is Georges Dubœuf. Other good smaller enterprises include Jean-Marc Aujoux, Château des Jacques, Laurent Daumas, Château de Pizay, Domaine de Poncie, Clos de la Roilette, Michel Tête and Château Thivin.

CHAMPAGNE

Little by little the rest of the world is coming round to the French point of view, that champagne is not just any old fizzy wine, but a place – and a very special place at that. The Champagne region, an hour's drive east of Paris, is one of France's most comfortably confident, devoted to producing one particular luxury product. The Champenois – the inhabitants of Rheims, Épernay and the villages which dot the rolling countryside that looks like, and once was, a continuation of the English South Downs – know that only they can, and sometimes do, produce the world's pre-eminent sparkling wine. It is the combination of being as far north as vines can be grown commercially in France; a high proportion of chalky soils which encourage the roots to burrow as far as a regular but by no means generous supply of water; no shortage of cool, dark, humid cellars; and a head start in the public relations game of establishing champagne as *the* wine of celebration and glamour that makes Champagne unique. This uniqueness has fuelled the Champenois' energetic vendetta against those who use their precious C-word to describe products other than their own. American producers may still call any wine that fizzes 'champagne', but most of the rest of the wine-producing world has been brought to heel by the Champagne lawyers.

VINES AND VINEYARDS

Unexpectedly for a wine that is quintessentially light and white, champagne is made from predominantly black grapes. Less than 30 per cent of Champagne's 30 000 ha (74 000 acres) of neat, low rows of densely planted vines are light-skinned Chardonnay, the white burgundy grape. The red burgundy grape Pinot Noir is planted on about a third of Champagne's infertile vineyard soils, but the most common champagne grape is Pinot Meunier, a fruitier,

earlier maturing relative of Pinot Noir. Only Pinot Meunier will ripen reliably throughout the region, which is why it is by far the most commonly planted variety in the cooler vineyards of the Marne valley and the outlying Aisne vineyards to the north. Pinot Noir and Chardonnay need particularly well-favoured sites and in general the Chardonnay vine thrives best on the south and east facing chalky slopes of the Côte des Blancs south of Épernay, while Pinot Noir grows mainly on the lower slopes of the wooded Montagne de Reims between Rheims and Épernay, as well as being a speciality of the slightly warmer Aube vineyards in the far south of Champagne.

All of the 300 Champagne villages are graded for their grape-growing potential between 80 and 100 per cent, with those 17 earning 100 per cent qualifying as Grands Crus. Of these, Ay, Bouzy and Sillery are some of the best known for black grapes and Avize, Cramant and Le Mesnil for Chardonnay.

White wine can be made from dark-skinned grapes only if they are pressed very gently indeed, and the best juice is generally that which flows first from Champagne's superdelicate wine presses. There are strict limits on how much juice can be squeezed out of a given weight of grapes, but the cheapest champagnes are usually made from the hardest pressed grapes so that they can taste astringent (and, especially when made from grapes grown in the more marginal areas and given a minimum of bottle age, horribly acid).

GROWERS V. HOUSES

Although most non-French champagne drinkers associate champagne with a handful of what are essentially brand names – Bollinger, various Heidsiecks, Moët & Chandon, Mumm, Perrier Jouët, Pol Roger, Veuve Clicquot and so on – in fact 90 per cent of all the raw material for champagne, the grapes themselves, is grown by 15 000 smallholders, whose average vineyard is just 2 ha or 5 acres. Grape prices are higher in Champagne than anywhere else in the world, with a kilo selling in some vintages for more than a greengrocer might charge for hothouse grapes.

This far from the equator, spring frosts and poor weather at flowering threaten each year's crop, with no regard for the state of the champagne market. The fact that Champagne's total harvest can be sufficient to fill nearly 300 million bottles, or may be less than a third of this, adds considerable spice to the relationship between the vine-growers and the wine producers, the houses or 'maisons' of Champagne, including all the well-known names.

Although most growers sell their fruit directly either to a co-operative or to one of the big houses, some of them do produce their own champagne, which is particularly popular on the French market. It varies enormously in quality, some demonstrating cottage industry at its very worst, others representing fine examples of their particular local conditions.

The big houses argue that only by using a wide variety of different base wines, often bought in from all over the region, can a good champagne be produced year in and year out,

DIFFERENT STYLES OF CHAMPAGNE

Non-vintage: The basic emissary of every champagne producer, representing more than 80 per cent of the region's output, based substantially on a single vintage, typically about three years old. Wildly variable in quality.

Vintage: A more expensive blend made exclusively from grapes grown in one specified year, typically released at about six years old but usually reliably superior and capable of ageing for more than a decade.

Prestige, de luxe, or luxury cuvée: The top of the range, often packaged in a fancy bottle, usually vintage dated, almost always exorbitantly priced. The best, such as Bollinger Tradition, Dom Pérignon, Krug and Roederer Cristal, are almost worth it.

Blanc de Blancs: Made exclusively from Chardonnay grapes; good examples can age very well.

Rosé: Variable in both colour and quality and usually made by blending still red and still white wines before the fermentation in bottle. Often fruitier and slightly sweeter than average.

Demi-sec or Rich: Champagnes sweeter than the normal Brut or (slightly less dry) Sec.

and it is certainly true that grower champagnes tend to vary far more from year to year than those of the houses, whose function is to maintain a house style whatever the individual year's conditions. See page 30 for some suggested specific producers.

As well as the famous houses, some extremely successful champagne producers specialize in making 'buyer's own brand', or BOB, champagnes to the individual specifications (and price) of, for example, a supermarket or a hotel chain.

THE ART OF BLENDING

Champagne is quite unlike any other fine wine, apart from sherry and port, in that its existence depends on blending. This is mainly because this far from the equator, the character of each vintage can vary so much, from the lean, hardly ripe grapes of years such as 1987 to years such as 1989, in which hot weather produced particularly ripe base wines unsuitably low in acid.

With the exceptions of Blanc de Blancs and Blanc de Noirs, all champagnes are more or less judicious blends of all three grape varieties, in which Meunier gives youthful exuberance, Pinot Noir gives body, and Chardonnay gives a backbone. Growers' champagnes may not embody geographical blending, but the houses' champagnes (about three in every four bottles) are made from blends, or **cuvées**, painstakingly assembled from scores and sometimes hundreds of different vineyards. (One or two single vineyard champagnes such as Krug's Clos de Mesnil are aberrant exceptions to the Champenois' dedication to blending.)

This process of blending the base wines into a well-balanced cuvée that will be bottled and encouraged to re-ferment, producing carbon dioxide (see sparkling winemaking on pages

One of the bleakest jobs in the world of wine is pruning during Champagne's harsh winter months. The dead cuttings are traditionally burnt in mobile bonfires.

Veuve Clicquot was such a successful champagne saleswoman that she was able to build a grand, new Château de Boursault for her family in the mid-nineteenth century.

84–6), takes place every winter after the harvest. The tasters' most important job is to assemble the all-important non-vintage blend which must represent the house style and replicate as closely as possible its predecessors (although over the years houses sometimes allow their style to evolve with fashion or availability of grapes). To even out the differences in both quality and quantity between the years, the young wine is typically rounded out with up to 20 per cent of 'reserve wines', still wines kept in store from previous vintages.

There is a school of thought in Champagne that **vintage** champagne (champagne carrying a vintage year and made exclusively from grapes grown in that year) is rather poor form, an ambitious style that tends to cream off the best grapes and diminish the quality of the non-vintage, 'proper' champagne. And the proliferation of luxury, prestige, or de luxe cuvées since Moët's hugely successful Dom Pérignon was launched in 1937, has tended to cream off the finest produce of the top rated villages in the best years.

By spring, all of these blends have been assembled and bottled, along with some yeast and sugar, and stacked horizontally by the thousand in the famous cellars of Champagne.

THE CHARACTER OF CHAMPAGNE

Anyone who has tasted the relatively rare still wines of the Champagne region, sold under the name Coteaux Champenois, will understand the extent to which the champagne-making process can transform the thin, acid, lightweight wines which the region's vineyards produce into noble, creamy, deep-flavoured essences of sophistication. Like base wines for distillation into cognac, the best sorts of base wine for sparkling wine are those that are high in acidity and relatively neutral. Champagne may get its defining bubbles as a by-product of a second fermentation in sealed bottles, and its useful extra degree or two of alcohol as a direct result of the same process, but it, possibly more than any other sparkling wine, owes its nuances of flavour, its savoury definition, to the time the bottles spend simply lying quietly in the dank cellars of Champagne, many of them ancient limestone quarries known as *crayères* (from the same root as 'crayon'). The longer the wine remains in contact with the unappetizing-looking sediment of dead yeast lees which gathers on the underbelly of the bottle, the more character will be imparted to the final wine, and the fuller and richer it tastes. Research shows that this process has a perceptible effect on the wine after about 18 months' contact, and then an even greater one after about five years. It is a shame therefore that the current legal minimum for ageing non-vintage and vintage champagne on the lees is 12 months and three years respectively, so that the cheapest champagne will hardly have benefited from any flavour development as a result of lees contact. Serious champagne producers, however, allow their non-vintage blends at least two years on lees, and vintage champagnes are generally released after at least six years.

In terms of rounding out champagne's leaner characteristics, bottle ageing is a great substitute for some of the sugar traditionally added just before final bottling (see page 85), called the 'dosage', although champagne's naturally high acidity can bear a great deal of added sugar before any real sweetness can be tasted.

HOW TO DECIPHER A CHAMPAGNE LABEL

1 Look for vintage year. If there is none, the champagne is a non-vintage blend.
2 'Blanc de Blancs' or 'Chardonnay' on the label indicates that only Chardonnay and no black grapes have been used and the wine may be slightly austere. ('Blanc de Noirs' means that only black grapes have been used and the wine may be quite full bodied.)
3 Look at the two-letter code which accompanies the code number of the producer:
NM négociant-manipulant, one of the big houses/maisons/négociants (see page 30).
RM récoltant-manipulant, a grower who makes his own wine (see page 30).
CM co-opérative de manipulation, one of the co-operatives.
RC récoltant-co-opérateur, grower selling wine made by a co-op.
MA marque d'acheteur, buyer's own brand, usually a made-up label.

ALSACE

In a nutshell: *Terribly useful, often overlooked, soft, smokey, varietal whites.*

Grapes: *Riesling, Gewürztraminer, Pinot Blanc, Pinot Gris, Sylvaner, Muscat*

Alsace is one of the great, underappreciated treasures of the wine world. This pretty enclave of fairy-tale villages in the lee of the forested Vosges mountains offers a wide range of varietally labelled wines, of which the aromatic whites are much more successful than the light reds. For much of its history Alsace was Elsass and part of Germany. The local surnames and tall green tapered bottles reflect this, along with the dominance of Riesling and the fragrant nature of many of the wines. But unlike in Germany, winemaking philosophy in Alsace is to ferment all of the grape sugar into alcohol, resulting in dry, full bodied wines (quite different in structure from Germany's lighter, sweeter counterparts). Both deliberately avoid new wood and the second, softening, malolactic fermentation, however, preferring to preserve the direct, fruity aromas of each grape variety.

Alsace is unusual within France in that it has just two appellations, one simply **Alsace** for any wine produced within the region and the other **Alsace Grand Cru** (see page 179), both of which may be followed by the name of a grape variety. The following are the most important wine names, the first four of them being designated 'noble' grape varieties.

Riesling is the most respected grape variety in Alsace, and quite rightly. Alsace Riesling is steely, sometimes tough in youth, and perhaps a little austere for newcomers. It handsomely repays ageing in bottle, however, for up to 10 years in the case of top bottlings such as Trimbach's Clos Ste Hune (although most examples are fine after three or four years). Like all but the very richest Alsace wines (VT and SGN), these wines can make great aperitifs. The late-ripening Riesling vine has to be planted in one of Alsace's most favoured sites, typically in a well-exposed situation in the hillier southern half of the region.

Gewürztraminer – often spelt Gewurztraminer here in France – is the easiest Alsace wine for beginners to enjoy. In fact for many of us, 'Gewürz' (probably the most frequently misspelt wine name of all) is one of the first wine tastes we ever latch on to. It is full bodied, almost fat, and tastes pleasantly off dry and generally stuns the taste buds into admiring submission – although in very hot years it can topple over into oily flab. The most lightweight, cheapest examples smell gently flowery (often very similar to Muscat) but a really rich, concentrated version can smell of bacon fat, on top of the vaguely lychee-like smell of any Gewürztraminer. This is the white wine to drink with 'red wine food' or, many argue, spicy food.

Pinot Gris, known as Tokay d'Alsace until the Hungarians started to make a fuss about confusion with their sweet white Tokay, can make wonderfully full bodied-yet-dry wines that go quite happily with such strongly flavoured dishes as venison. These wines are not particularly aromatic, but they taste delightfully smokey and exotic. Pinot Gris makes particularly good late picked (VT) wines (see page 179).

Muscat, or Muscat d'Alsace, is one of the region's most distinctive styles. Usually a blend of Muscat Ottonel and Muscat Blanc à Petits Grains, this unusual wine is delicate, dry, yet smells often overpoweringly grapey and therefore almost sweet. It is not made in huge quantities, and rarely ages particularly well, but can make a delightful aperitif.

Pinot Blanc is Alsace's bread-and-butter variety, and very useful too. Known sometimes as Klevner, the wine is broad and smokey with the distinctive perfume of any Alsace white, but with less definition than a Riesling and much

less body than a Gewürz-
traminer or Pinot Gris. A
similar but distinct variety
called Auxerrois is often
blended with it to be sold
as Pinot Blanc. A Pinot
Blanc from a good pro-
ducer is one of the wine world's bargains.

Riquewihr (seen here from the Grand Cru
Schoenenberg vineyard) is not only
Alsace's picture postcard village, it also
houses the important firms of Hugel,
Dopff au Moulin and Dopff & Irion.

producing steely Rieslings
(such as Trimbach) can
taste really quite distinguished.

Edelzwicker means
'noble mixture' but is in
fact a blend of any old
varieties, in practice usually the lowly Chasselas

Sylvaner is much more difficult to appreciate. It can taste quite lean and needs a good site
to ripen fully, even though it does not fetch
particularly high prices, which is why its fortunes are declining in Alsace. Nevertheless, a
Sylvaner from a producer particularly good at

variety, Sylvaner and Pinot Blanc. This easy,
soft blend is also sometimes sold as Gentil.

Pinot Noir is Alsace's contribution to the
world of red wine, except that in all but the
hottest years it is some shade of pink and tastes
very lightweight too. A few producers are trying

map), is the region's eaux-de-vie, potent colourless spirits distilled from the fruits that grow there. These can smell like essence of raspberry (Framboise) or pear (Poire Williams) and probably need never actually be sipped.

Favourite producers include Beyer, Hugel and Trimbach among the bigger merchants (who buy in substantial quantities of grapes) and Blanck, Marcel Deiss, Kientzler, Kreydenweiss, Muré, Ostertag, Rolly Gassmann, Schlumberger, Schoffitt, the Fallers at Domaine Weinbach and Zind-Humbrecht.

ALSACE LABEL LANGUAGE

(These terms may be applied to wines only from one of the four noble varieties.)

Grand Cru – one of more than 50 individual vineyards granted superior status, amid some controversy, relatively recently. The words Grand Cru are no guarantee of quality as some producers have seen Grand Cru simply as an excuse to charge more rather than an opportunity to make seriously fine wine – although admittedly the maximum permitted yields are lower than the Alsace norm. Many of Alsace's best wines are Grands Crus, however.

Vendange Tardive (VT) – translates directly as Late Harvest, which is indeed what these wines are. Certain minimum ripeness levels have to be met (the best producers generously exceed them) and the grapes may be picked only when official authorization is given. The trouble with Vendange Tardive wines is that they can vary from almost dry (but quite concentrated) to really quite sweet, yet no hint of sweetness level is given on labels. The best of these wines can be aged for many years.

Sélection des Grains Nobles (SGN) signifies a wine made from even riper grapes, often at least partly concentrated by the botrytis fungus (see page 88). These relative rarities are easiest to make in the region's sunniest years, from the obliging Gewürztraminer grape. Their sweetness level can also vary quite considerably, although individual producers will generally ensure that their SGNs are definitely sweeter than their VTs.

to make more full bodied Pinot Noir but most are consoled by the fact that the hordes of German tourists seem quite happy to buy even the palest French 'red' wine.

Crémant d'Alsace is the region's dry sparkling white wine, made like champagne. It can be very refreshing and can age for a few years, but is more notable for its youthful crispness than for great substance.

One of Alsace's great attractions for the gastronomically inclined, other than the wines and the enormous number of Michelin-starred restaurants (so great that Alsace warrants its own specially enlarged box on the Michelin star

LOIRE

In a nutshell: *France's most varied,
and neglected, wine region. Most wines
noticeably crisp.*
Grapes *(going downriver): Sauvignon Blanc,
Cabernet Franc, Gamay, Chenin Blanc,
Melon de Bourgogne.*

Outside northern France, the wines of the Loire, with the exception of Sancerre and Pouilly-Fumé, have been consistently over-looked by modern wine enthusiasts, perhaps because at this northerly limit of commercially viable viticulture the grapes have to struggle to ripen, so the wines' unfashionable hallmark is relatively high acidity. Because long, hot summers are the exception, relatively few of the reds conform to the current expectation of high density, alcohol, tannin and obvious oak ageing, and most of the whites here are also made to the old-fashioned recipe of trapping the fruit in the bottle as early as possible, without exposing them to new wood. It may perhaps seem strange that the wine regions with easiest access to the

best oak in France (the forests of the Nevers, Allier and Tronçais are all in the upper Loire) are not great users of it, but grapes have to be really quite ripe before their fermented juice can take the weight of an oak barrel (see pages 91–3).

Another factor may be the relative complication of wine names and identities here. The same name, Saumur or Anjou for example, may be applied to a range of wines that includes all three colours and a confusing range of grape variety possibilities and sweetness levels.

France's longest, laziest river joins not only some of the most beautiful châteaux and what was once the playground of the French court and is now that of well-heeled Parisians, but also scores of wine districts which can, very roughly, be divided into three zones: the Sauvignon-dominated vineyards of the Upper Loire; the Muscadet region at the mouth of the river (more than 300 miles downstream from Pouilly-sur-Loire and Sancerre); and the vast and varied vineyards in between which produce some great sweet and some useful sparkling white wines as well as a host of still reds, whites and rosés from a host of grape varieties of which Chenin Blanc, Cabernet Franc, Gamay and Sauvignon Blanc are the most important.

UPPER LOIRE

Sancerre and **Pouilly-Fumé** (sometimes called Blanc Fumé de Pouilly) are the Upper Loire's, indeed the Loire's, most famous ambassadors. The two wine districts are separated only by the river, and the hilltop town of Sancerre is just 10 miles north west of the decidedly unspectacular town of Pouilly-sur-Loire. Both of these much-exported wines are made exclusively from Sauvignon Blanc grapes into lean, green, sappy, aromatic palate-sharpeners. Such has been demand for them in the world's restaurants that most of the wines made under either appellation are remarkably similar.

Neatly hedged rows of Sauvignon vines traverse the gentle slopes above the river, vineyards being interspersed with cereal crops and sunflowers, for this is an area of mixed farming. Mechanical harvesting has been the norm for some time and the combination of a damp

climate and generous yields can result in almost aggressively aromatic, light bodied, relatively tart wines, reeking of nettles and cats' pee.

Only at the highest quality level is the particular nature of the various terrains in the appellations apparent. Serious restaurants in Sancerre, for example, list their local wines under the names of the appellation's best-favoured communes such as Bué, Ménétréol and Chavignol, where some of France's best *crottins*, or miniature drums of goat's cheese are made.

The region's *enfant terrible* is Didier Dageneau, a gifted and energetic producer of Pouilly-Fumé based in a modest cottage in St-Andelain just north of its grandest building, the Château du Nozet, home farm of the Upper Loire's best-known wine producer, Baron de Ladoucette. Dageneau believes passionately in reducing average yields, in restoring soil texture and quality through an extreme form of organic viticulture, 'biodynamism' (see page 65). He has been in the vanguard of a move towards making local wines concentrated enough to benefit from fermentation and ageing in new oak.

However similar the wines may be, locals argue that the inhabitants of Pouilly and Sancerre are creatures from two different planets, or at least from two different French regions, which amounts to much the same thing: greater Burgundy and Berry respectively. In wine terms the two districts differ because Sancerre produces some light red and rosé appellation contrôlée wine from Pinot Noir grapes, while Pouilly-sur-Loire is the name of a distinctly inferior VDQS wine made from Chasselas, which is a white table grape. Other superior producers include Henri Bourgeois, Lucien Crochet, Gitton, Joseph Mellot, Henry Pellé and Vacheron.

Reuilly, Quincy and **Menetou-Salon** are wine districts to the west of Sancerre producing wines of a very similar style to Sancerre and Pouilly-Fumé but sometimes with more appealing craftsmanship. Their names are so much less well known that the wines have to find a market purely on the basis of their inherent

MIDDLE LOIRE

Wine geography is at its most complicated along the central, westbound stretch of the Loire. Travelling upriver from the Muscadet region, the wine enthusiast is first bamboozled by **Anjou**, the name of the region around the city of Angers, and associated with the often grimly commercial Rosé d'Anjou; the extraordinarily long-lived fine pink Cabernet d'Anjou; the distinctly variable, medium dry, Chenin Blanc-dominated Anjou Blanc; crisp, light reds under the names Anjou Rouge and Anjou-Gamay; and, finest of all when the region is blessed with a hot summer, smooth, silky Cabernet-moulded red wines under the **Anjou-Villages** appellation.

The grape that reaches its highpoint in the Middle Loire is the oft-maligned Chenin Blanc. In cool years it may simply produce a tart and relatively aromatic medium dry white (historically with too much sulphur), but when nature co-operates in producing thoroughly ripe grapes and, ideally, the magic mould noble rot, such appellations as **Coteaux de l'Aubance**, **Coteaux du Layon** and, especially, the particularly well-favoured enclaves, **Chaume**, **Quarts de Chaume** and **Bonnezeaux** within it, can produce great, honeyed, long-living sweet white wines to rival some of the best in the world. Some ultra-sweet

Sélection de Grains Nobles wines have been made in recent years.

Savennières is Anjou's minuscule but world-famous dry white Chenin Blanc appellation. Nicolas Joly at Coulée de Serrant keeps the famous flame alight and is one of France's most vociferous proponents of biodynamism. The wines are hard to appreciate when young, and the combination of high demand and low production neatly restricts the wines to their greatest enthusiasts.

Current overperformers in Anjou and environs include Domaine de Bablut, Pascal Cailleau, Château de Chamboureau, Châteaux de Fesles, Christian Papin at Domaine de Haute Perche, Claude Papin at Château Pierre-Bise and Vincent Ogereau.

Saumur is the next region upstream and the eponymous town is best known for its usually dry and racy sparkling wines, whose tiny, often persistent bubbles can demonstrate real winemaking skill. All that prevents these wines from finding a wider market is the decidedly un-champagne-like flavours of the Chenin Blanc grape which dominate Saumur Mousseux and the more rigorously made Crémant de Loire, although increasing amounts of Chardonnay used in these traditional-method wines are beginning to 'internationalize' them. Three outposts of Champagne houses perform particularly well here: Bouvet-Ladubay (Taittinger), Gratien & Meyer (Alfred Gratien) and Langlois-Château (Bollinger).

The Château du Nozet, the Ladoucette family's country cottage, is the Loire's most famous wine property, just up the road from the humbler abode of Didier Dageneau, Pouilly-Fumé's wild man.

quality. Claude Lafond, Jean-Michel Sorbe and Pierre Clement make reliably good wines.

Typical middle Loire valley gable in St-Nicolas de Bourgueil – Cabernet Franc territory par excellence.

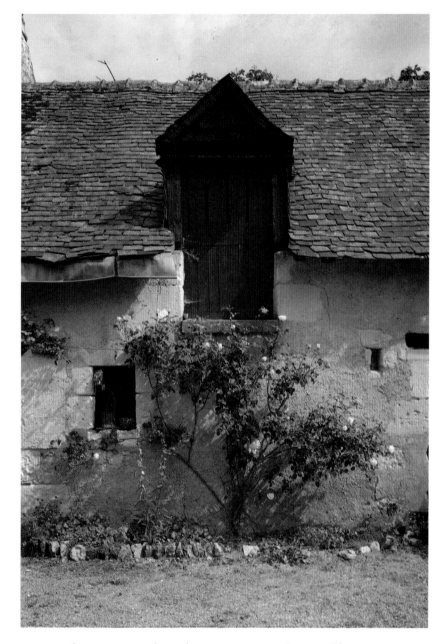

Saumur's other claim to wine fame is Saumur-Champigny, the Loire's most fashionable, and therefore often overpriced, Cabernet Franc-based red. In particularly ripe years these fragrant, silky-textured, gulpable liquids can benefit from careful maturation in small oak barrels. Filliatreau and Foucault are two of the better producers, and superior bottlings were launched with the 1993 vintage.

The Loire's most famous reds, Chinon, Bourgueil, and St-Nicolas de Bourgueil, are made to the same recipe as Saumur-Champigny, indeed Chinon is virtually an eastern extension of it. Bourgueil can be the beefiest, longest-living Loire red of all, while the lighter St-Nicolas de Bourgueil is even more rarely seen outside its own parish. All three appellations fall within the wine region around the city of Tours, **Touraine**, where the landscape is dotted with wine cellars and even houses carved out of the soft, well-drained limestone known as tuf-feau, to which the region's châteaux owe much.

Gifted producers in these appellations include Daniel Chauveau, Pierre-Jacques Druet, Charles Joguet and Olga and Jean-Marie Raffault.

Touraine is one of France's most confusing wine names. White versions can be made from any or all of four grape varieties – although Sauvignon is the most common and the best examples can rival wines of the Upper Loire. Reds and rosés may be a blend of Gamay (the most common), Cabernet Franc, Cabernet Sauvignon, Cot (Malbec), Pinot Noir, Pinot Meunier, Pinot Gris and two local vine varieties Pineau d'Aunis and Grolleau. An early-bottled Touraine Primeur version rivalling Beaujolais Nouveau is a further confusion. The districts of Amboise, Azay-le-Rideau and Mesland append their name to the Touraine appellation but offer no guarantee of superior quality.

Cheverny and Valençay are two small Touraine satellites which have avoided being subsumed into the appellation Touraine.

Touraine's arguably most distinctive wines are Vouvray and its reflection across the river Montlouis. Like the great sweet wines of Anjou they are made from Chenin Blanc grapes, and vary considerably in quality and even style according to the year's grape sugar level. In great years such as 1947 and 1989, the combination of noble rot, sky-high sugar levels and the naturally high acidity levels of Chenin grown this far from the equator ensure that the deep green-gold versions labelled Moelleux or Liquoreux will last virtually forever. In cool years, however, the grapes may well be better suited to making a crisp base for sparkling wine. And between these two extremes a host of wines labelled Sec (dry) and Demi Sec (medium dry) are made. These can also develop for decades in bottle, and even the Demi Sec versions have enough tang to make them delicious partners for many fish dishes, notably those involving a creamy sauce. Quality-conscious producers include Courtemanche, Domaine Delétang, Foreau of Clos Naudin, Fouquet of Domaine des Aubuisières, Gaston Huet, Prince Poniatowski and Jacky Supligeau.

Parisians should not be allowed a monopoly on all the best wines of the Loire: the stylish sparkling wines and, in riper vintages, the sweeter Chenins and keenly-priced Cabernet-based reds.

MUSCADET REGION

Like Brittany to the immediate north, the Muscadet region at the mouth of the Loire, is quintessentially oceanic. Clouds and sea spray blow in off the Atlantic, untainted by any contact with land for thousands of miles. The relatively light, neutral wine was the creation of the energetic Dutch in the seventeenth century (they encouraged locals to plant the Muscadet grape, the slightly vapid Melon grape of Burgundy) and, as it happens, the terrain round Nantes looks perfectly suited to windmills and tulips.

Muscadet de Sèvre-et-Maine, named after two small rivers which flow to the south and east of Nantes, is by far the most common form of Muscadet. Because the Melon grape is not exactly flavour-packed, many local winemakers leave the fermented wine on the lees, *sur lie*, for several months in order to leech a bit more character (and often an appetizingly light tingle) into the wine (see page 82). When Muscadet was popular as France's white answer to Beaujolais, the term 'sur lie' was far too generously applied and the regulations were, not before time, tightened in 1993. Some ambitious producers – notably Bosset, Guindon, Landron, Marquis de Goulaine, Master de Donatien, Louis Metaireau, and Sauvion – are trying to turn their Muscadets into wines of the 1990s by using oak and dramatically reducing yields, but 99 bottles of Muscadet out of 100 should be drunk as young and casually as possible. Muscadet Côtes de Grandlieu is theoretically a more floral style of wine from the west of the region.

Gros Plant (Nantais) is the region's light, tart white varietal for masochists.

See also page 205 for details of the Loire valley's numerous winemaking outposts. The Loire has attracted more than its fair share of VDQSs.

RHÔNE

In a nutshell: Concentrated, beefy red
wines designed for ageing.
Grapes: Syrah, Grenache (RED), Marsanne,
Roussanne, Viognier (WHITE)

The wide, lazy Rhône links two important
French wine regions (and, in narrower,
swifter form, the vineyards of Savoie, and some
of Switzerland's best). The Northern Rhône
produces small quantities of some very fine wine
indeed, while the much more extensive vineyards of the Southern Rhône produce one of
France's 'commodity' wines, Côtes-du-Rhône,
as well as a host of other wines based on the
Grenache grape.

NORTHERN RHÔNE

It's not difficult to see why vine-growing is relatively uncommon on the steep, wooded banks
of the Rhône south of Lyons. These vineyards,
probably the oldest in France, have had to be
etched into the mountainside on narrow terraces (not unlike port country in the Douro)
and some are so steep that pulley systems have
to be used for grapes and equipment as in
Switzerland. This, furthermore, is countryside
that has now been fully invaded by industry and
is well adapted to other, easier crops such as
fruit trees on the plateaux above the river. To
grow vines in the Northern Rhône's only commercially viable sites, the ones that catch the
sun for long enough to ripen grapes fully, you
have either to inherit an established vineyard
(usually on the right bank) or to be sure of
fetching a high price for the resulting wine.

The great majority of wine made here is
made from the Syrah grape, and the region's
most famous wines are the deep-flavoured, long-
lived reds Hermitage and Côte-Rôtie.

The Northern Rhône is also notable
because it is still in the hands of family enter-

prises. The three biggest are Marcel Guigal of
Côte-Rôtie, who has been described as the
planet's finest winemaker; Chapoutier where a
new generation is endeavouring to restore ultra-
traditional techniques such as encouraging the
extraction of colour from grape skins by foot
(*pigeage*); and, another Hermitage specialist,
Paul Jaboulet Aîné. They each have their own
vineyards but buy in extensively from the hundreds of smallholders who still cultivate these
physically demanding vineyards. As elsewhere,

an increasing number of these smallholders are now bottling their own wine and their challenge, along with that of a few ambitious newcomers to the region, has done nothing but good for the overall quality of Rhône wine.

Côte-Rôtie is in fact not just one but a series of 'roasted slopes' folded above the little town of Ampuis. Only those facing south or south east on the schists of this right bank of the river are worth the extreme discomfort of cultivating them and, especially, picking their produce. Those to the south are collectively known as the Côte Blonde and the wines they produce supposedly mature rather earlier than those produced on the Côte Brune just to the north, although traditionally the wines from these areas have been blended. (There are vineyards on the flatter land above these slopes but they are entitled only to the generic Côtes-du-Rhône appellation which very much more commonly applies to wines made in the Southern Rhône.)

One man has made a name for himself, and indeed the whole appellation, by flying in the face of Côte-Rôtie convention. Marcel Guigal's special bottlings of single-vineyard Côte-Rôtie wines La Mouline, La Landonne and La Turque have become the most sought-after bottles in the world, thanks to low yields and their uniquely long maturation in new oak, which makes them massively appealing in youth as well as promising an exciting old age.

Côte-Rôtie is stereotypically distinguished from Hermitage by its perfume, which is supposedly due to the possible inclusion of white Viognier grapes (the same as those grown in the neighbouring appellation of Condrieu), but in practice most Côte-Rôtie is 100 per cent Syrah. The appellation's vines are trained to help withstand the twin local dangers of wind damage and soil erosion, with pairs of vines staked to meet in a point, making the roasted slopes look as though they are covered in Christmas trees. Some other reliable producers of Côte-Rôtie are Barge, Clusel-Roch, Rostaing and Vidal-Fleury (the merchant house for which Marcel Guigal's father once worked as cellarmaster but which now belongs to Guigal).

The amount of Viognier grown in the Northern Rhône is relatively tiny,

Marcel Guigal's pickers (left) are fed in shifts by his wife Bernadette and given much rougher wine than his famous Côte-Rôtie to drink. Thirty miles downriver, above the small town of Tain, are the famous Hermitage vineyards (right), overlooking the Rhône river. Perhaps the most famous wine made here, by the large family firm of Paul Jaboulet Aîné, is Hermitage La Chapelle, a reference to the chapel which dominates this vine-covered hill.

and the peachy, full bodied **Condrieu** it produces could generally be sold three times over by growers such as Cuilleron and Vernay, so fashionable has this wine style become. The merchants try to buy as many Condrieu grapes as possible. Guigal's single-vineyard Doriane is setting a new standard, while Delas has a long history of getting Condrieu right. **Château-Grillet** is a 3 ha (5 acre) single-property appellation slightly downriver of Condrieu whose wines are even more dramatically priced.

Hermitage is produced 30 miles downriver on a bald suntrap of a hill on the left bank above the narrow town of Tain, or rather Tain l'Hermitage as it has become known thanks to the fame of Hermitage's densely strapping wines. There was a period in French wine trade history when it was common practice to order red wines that had been *hermitagé*, or had had Hermitage added to them for colour and strength. White Hermitage is also made, from Marsanne and Roussanne grapes. It is unusually full bodied and can be difficult to appreciate until its bouquet has developed after many years in bottle. Sweet *vin de paille* is a speciality.

In and around Tain and its sister town of Tournon, just across a rickety footbridge over the Rhône, are a bevy of gifted and determined winemakers, not just the large merchant houses of Chapoutier, Paul Jaboulet and Delas but much smaller family domaines such as superstar J. L. Chave. The co-operative Cave de Tain l'Hermitage is also admirably aware of quality.

Most of these producers also make **Crozes-Hermitage**, the area's much, much bigger, less demanding red and white wine appellation on the flatter land around the hill of Hermitage. Red Crozes from one of the area's best merchants or one of the more gifted producers such as Belle, Graillot or Pochon are the Northern Rhône's great wine bargains.

While Crozes Hermitage regularly represents more than half of all the wine produced in the Northern Rhône, **St-Joseph** (another red and white appellation made from Syrah, Marsanne and Roussanne) can often represent almost one

bottle in four. The appellation was, often unwisely, expanded dramatically in the 1970s and 1980s and straggles down the right bank of the river from Condrieu almost as far south as St-Péray. There can be a dramatic difference in concentration and quality between the wines made on difficult terraces just above Tournon and those which gush forth from the much flatter land. It is worth paying St-Joseph's price premium above Crozes only for the likes of Chave, Cuilleron, Émile Florentin, Gripa, Grippat, Jean Marsanne and André Perret.

Even though the Northern Rhône has benefited from an enormous amount of attention in recent years, **Cornas** is still an underappreciated appellation producing very worthy and, after eight years in bottle, exciting Syrah reds. Clape is the local hero, with Robert Michel fast building a reputation too.

The curiosity of the Northern Rhône is **St-Péray**, a heavy, usually sparkling white made from Marsanne and Roussanne grapes which has yet to dazzle outsiders.

SOUTHERN RHÔNE

In a nutshell: *Warm, rich reds.*
Grapes: *Grenache*

This is the region of France's most user-friendly wines, and its important source of appellation contrôlée wine after Bordeaux. Côtes-du-Rhône is south east France's warmer, richer, spicier answer to the dry austerity of AC Bordeaux. The wines of the Southern Rhône are France's most alcoholic, with 12.5 per cent being a minimum and 14 per cent by no means uncommon for its most famous appellation, Châteauneuf-du-Pape (and no chaptalization, or extra alcohol from added sugar, is allowed this far south).

Perhaps it is the alcohol that makes these Southern Rhône reds so easy to appreciate. Perhaps it is the openly fruity character of the Grenache grape which dominates here, concentrated by the relatively low yields forced upon it by the stony soils and low rainfall. Perhaps it's because the Southern Rhône is the gateway to Provence, a land of olive trees, cicadas, sunshine and Impressionist summer landscapes.

The wines made in this seductive countryside are, contrarily, best drunk in much cooler climates. They can seem head-thumpingly inappropriate when drunk in the place and season that produces them (although the small proportion of roses and dry whites made in the Southern Rhône solve this problem – see below).

The Southern Rhône is an important hunting ground for the merchants of the Northern Rhône, and a significant proportion of the wines made here are shipped north in bulk to be sold with a Tain or Tournon address on the label. Co-operative wineries are also extremely important here.

While **Côtes-du-Rhône** can come from a vast area of almost 40 000 ha (100 000 acres) around the southern end of the French Rhône Valley, **Côtes-du-Rhône-Villages** comes from a tightly defined area barely an eighth as big on particularly suitable land north and west of Châteauneuf-du-Pape. Most Côtes-du-Rhône is vinified using the Beaujolais carbonic maceration technique (see page 78) to yield juicy, fruity wines for which life is short. Among the hundreds of Côtes-du-Rhône-Villages producers, however, are many with greater ambitions for their wines, which are made to develop for five and sometimes more years in bottle. With maximum permitted yields a good sixth lower than those allowed for Côtes-du-Rhône, Côtes-du-Rhône-Villages is one of France's best-value appellations, perhaps because promotion prospects are so obvious. Since the appellation was formed in 1966, two of the nearly 20 villages have been granted their own appellations – Gigondas and Vacqueyras – and Cairanne is on the brink of this commercial breakthrough. Some other village names encountered on labels are also marked on the map.

Châteauneuf-du-Pape is the region's most famous and best wine, and all other reds and whites made here seem to use it as their model. Châteauneuf is most famous in wine books as

the appellation in which 13 different grape varieties are permitted. In practice, however, the reds are made predominantly from Grenache, supplemented by Syrah, Mourvèdre and, to a decreasing extent, Cinsaut, while the relatively rare whites are made from a more variable recipe that includes Grenache Blanc, Clairette, Bourboulenc and Roussanne.

Red Châteauneuf is a big, beefy wine with lots of alcohol and extract, with a come-hither, if slightly bludgeoning, approach to the wine drinker. I find this one of France's most reliable appellations, and have had remarkably few disappointments among wines bottled in the signature-embossed, heavy bottle. (In fact if there is a regional fault it is that in some very hot years the wines can be just too alcoholic, and in particularly dry years they can be too tannic – but these faults are so rare among French wines that they are almost refreshing.) The fact that so much Châteauneuf meets a certain minimum standard probably reflects the fact that yields must be kept remarkably low as well as the mandatory selection of only healthy, ripe grapes.

There is considerable variation in how the wines are made, but high-tech methods are rare

Two faces of the Southern
Rhône: (above) the setting
summer sun, responsible for
so much alcohol, above
Châteauneuf-du-Pape; and
(right) the dreamy vineyards
of Gigondas, whose wines can
provide much the same
pleasure, often more cheaply.

here among the pines. The stereotypical Châteauneuf vineyard has low bush vines struggling up for sunlight between large boulders (*galets*), illustrated on page 139, whose effect is to continue the warming process well into the night, but in fact many of the best vineyards are on much more conventional ground.

White Châteauneuf obeys far fewer rules. Some of them are still very flabby and unappetizing, while an increasing proportion have enough fruit and acidity (with, always, lots of alcohol) to make truly interesting bottles of wine. Roussanne can be a particularly interesting ingredient.

Châteauneuf has a multitude of good to very good producers, but Beaucastel, Rayas, Vieux Télégraphe, Bosquet des Papes, Clos des Papes and Réserve des Célestins are almost always excellent (and Rayas's second label Pignan and even its Côtes-du-Rhône label Château de Fonsalette are well above average).

Gigondas is another relatively reliable wine made, as a red and full rosé, in the image of Châteauneuf. It costs less and usually tastes rather more rustic, a characteristic which has its own charm these days. Reliable names include Domaine Les Goubert, Domaine St-Gayan and Château du Trignon.

Vacqueyras, the other upgraded Côtes-du-Rhône-Village, is not usually quite so dense, but can be very good value.

With the exception of Châteauneuf, whose regulations are stricter than almost any other's in France, wherever red wine is made in southern France, rosé is too, most of it being drunk locally during the hot summer months. The Grenache and Cinsaut of the Southern Rhône, with their relatively thin skins and open, fruity flavour are particularly suitable for making pink wine. The Southern Rhône's most famous rosé by far is **Tavel**, made on the right bank of the Rhône and a serious, historic wine in its own right. Just as Châteauneuf is France's most positive red, Tavel across the river is its most powerful pink. This is a wine not for gulping in the garden but as a substantial red wine substitute in hot weather. Chilling is essential. Château d'Aqueria is one of the best-known estates.

Just north of Tavel, **Lirac** produces considerable quantities of rosé very similar to Tavel and full blooded red wine, as well as some full bodied dry white. Domaine de la Mordorée is one of the best producers.

The Southern Rhône also produces some sweet, relatively alcoholic vin doux naturel (see page 89), most famously **Muscat de Beaumes-de-Venise**. This golden, grapey mix of the juice of the best Muscat vine with alcohol is made in the village of Beaumes-de-Venise, which is one of the designated villages whose red wines are sold as Côtes-du-Rhône-Villages. Another of these villages, **Rasteau**, has its own special appellation for red and oak-aged tawny vin doux naturel which has a much less cosmopolitan taste than Muscat de Beaumes-de-Venise. (Regular red Rasteau is interesting for the amount of Mourvèdre grown there.)

Almost a bridge between the Rhône and Provence is **Côtes du Ventoux**, whose vineyards lie on the slopes of Mont Ventoux, one of the few peaks ever to be covered in snow for the winter in this region. The Grenache-based reds and rosés are considerably lighter than most Côtes-du-Rhônes but can be all the more refreshing for it. La Vieille Ferme is a very successful brand built on this appellation by the Perrin family of Château de Beaucastel.

Coteaux du Tricastin tastes like a half-way house between Côtes-du-Rhône and Côtes du Ventoux, even though it is in fact effectively a northern enclave within the Côtes-du-Rhône-Villages. Across the Rhône is the rather similar VDQS **Côtes du Vivarais** where Domaine du Belvezet outperforms its neighbours.

And finally, the greater Rhône Valley has its curious eastern outpost, around **Die** on the river Drôme. Hannibal and his alpinist elephants are invoked in the names of the local wines, of which the most famous are sparkling: either dry Crémant de Die made in the image of champagne or the grapier, fuller Clairette de Die. The co-operative is in charge here.

PROVENCE AND CORSICA

In a nutshell: *Dry rosés and some firm, spicy reds.*
Grapes: Grenache, Cinsaut, Syrah,
Cabernet Sauvignon (RED), Rolle (WHITE)

Although most people firmly associate Provence with holidays rather than with wine, this disparate region's wines are getting better and better. What seems to work particularly well is a conscientiously made, often oak-aged blend of the Cabernet Sauvignon grapes of Bordeaux with the Syrah of the Northern Rhône. What is most obviously made in enormous quantity, however, is light, dry rosé which, if drunk young and well chilled, can seem justification for wine's very existence when sipped on a vine-shaded terrace to the sound of cicadas. (Too much of it, however, seems to be made on the assumption that tourists don't notice what they're drinking.)

The most common appellation of all is the catch-all **Côtes de Provence** stretching right across most of the region. More than six bottles in every 10 carrying the name contain rosé of some sort. Grape varieties also include Carignan, Cinsaut and, a local rarity which can add spice to rosé, Tibouren. Rolle is the region's most distinctive white grape. In this, mainland France's driest, sunniest climate, fungal diseases are not the perennial threat they are elsewhere and the region is particularly well suited to organic viticulture. The area seethes with experimentation but little evidence escapes France.

Coteaux Varois is a new appellation on cooler territory within Côtes de Provence, named after the Var *département*, and harbours some ambitious incomers at estates such as Domaine du Deffends and Château Routas. The other significant appellation is **Coteaux d'Aix-en-Provence**, which is not quite so rosé-dependent. At the western end of this appellation is the very particular **Les Baux de Provence**, vineyards around the haunting rocks which gave

their name to bauxite. Domaine de Trevallon is the real star here, producing seriously deep red wines for ageing, although good bottles can also be found chez Mas de Gourgonnier, Château Revelette as well as the organic Domaine des Terres Blanches.

Provence also has a number of more specific appellations of which the most important is **Bandol**, known principally for its characterful, warmly spicy reds and rosés made predominantly from Mourvèdre. So warm is the climate here right on terraces immediately above the coast, sheltered from the piercing local wind, the *mistral*, that this late-ripening variety can, unusually in France, be relied upon to ripen every year. Domaine Tempier is the best-known producer but there is a remarkably high general standard among Bandol producers.

To France's wine authorities the rapidly improving appellation **Côtes du Lubéron** is part of the greater Rhône Valley, but to estate agents and the millions who have read Peter Mayle the Lubéron *is* Provence – and in viticultural terms it is certainly cooler than either the Southern Rhône or most Provençal vineyards. **Coteaux de Pierrevert** to the immediate north east is even cooler, and sleepier.

In wine books Corsica is traditionally hitched to Provence's wagon, and they share some vine varieties just as they once shared rulers. Few bottles are exported while the island sorts itself out from the wild and usually unwise vineyard expansion of the 1980s. The Corsican variety Sciacarello is increasingly appreciated, and Sangiovese is grown, as Nielluccio. Vermentino (Rolle) is regarded as the island's own white grape. Most of the island's production is sold as France's most cleverly named Vin de Pays de l'Île de Beauté (Island of Beauty) but its most interesting wines are probably its rare, sweet, strong vins doux naturels, notable among them Muscat du Cap Corse.

SOUTH WEST FRANCE

*In a nutshell: Mostly bordeaux-like,
plus some Basque influence.*
*Grapes: Cabernet, Merlot, Malbec,
Tannat, Negrette, Fer (RED), Sauvignon,
Sémillon, Mauzac, Gros and
Petit Manseng (WHITE)*

South west France really means all the wine regions in the south western quarter of the country, with the major exception of the most important one, Bordeaux, and the Cognac region to the immediate north of it, which enjoy separate status. This ragbag of a collection can be roughly divided into those which are effectively continuations of Bordeaux, its vine varieties and its wine styles upriver of the Bordeaux region itself, and those further south and east which have their own distinctive identity. All of them, however, are influenced by the Atlantic rather than the Mediterranean, and tend to have the same sort of build (light to medium bodied) as bordeaux.

Into the first, Bordeaux Fringes, category fall Bergerac (and its sub-appellations Montravel, Rosette, Saussignac, Pécharmant and Monbazillac), Buzet, Cahors, Côtes de Duras and Côtes du Marmandais.

Bergerac will continue to have its work cut out to establish a truly independent identity from its big, commercially acute brother just down the Dordogne river. (The town of Bergerac is hardly 30 miles east of Bordeaux's St-Émilion.) Although those sold as Côtes de Bergerac are usually more concentrated, its wines are basically just what the map suggests, country cousins of red and dry white bordeaux, with the sub-appellations rarely seen outside France except for **Monbazillac**. In very sunny years such as 1976 and 1990, Monbazillac can provide some truly great value sweet whites

LEFT *A wine bar in
Toulouse. The local herby
red and rosé wine is made
around the town of Fronton
to the immediate north.*
RIGHT *The rolling
countryside of the Tarn-et-
Garonne département.
Any further north is too
cool for widespread
viticulture, although a
small quantity of
Lavilledieu, like light
red bordeaux, is made here.*

made in the image of Sauternes but veering towards the slightly more obvious flavours of barley sugar rather than crème brûlée. An increasing number of Monbazillac producers are prepared to wait for botrytis (noble rot – see page 88) to develop in exceptional years, and some of the resulting wines can be bargains. Châteaux La Jaubertie, de Panisseau and du Priorat have all made distinctive wines.

Immediately south of Bergerac is **Côtes de Duras** which, with **Côtes du Marmandais** centred on the town of Marmande, continues to skirt Bordeaux in a clockwise direction. It is history more than geography that excludes these vineyards from the cosy umbrella of the Bordeaux appellation and I would take my hat off to any blind taster who could unerringly distinguish between the Bordeaux, Bergerac, Côtes de Duras and Côtes du Marmandais appellations.

Buzet produces similar wines, but with a little more stuffing and cohesive direction since the region is largely governed by a particularly ambitious local co-operative – one of the French coopers' better customers for many years.

Cahors is quite another matter. In fact many producers of Cahors on the river Lot would be insulted to be categorized as a shadow of Bordeaux since the wines have etched their own very distinct personality – chiefly because the devastating winter frosts of 1956 hit Cahors's vines particularly badly and a dramatic replanting programme was undertaken virtually from scratch. Rather than relying on the standard Bordeaux recipe of varying the proportions of Merlot with the two Cabernets, Cahors depends principally on a variety considered relatively minor in Bordeaux, Malbec (called Auxerrois in Cahors), typically bolstered with more or less Merlot and/or Tannat. (Cabernet Sauvignon would not ripen reliably this far inland.) The result is a plump, full bodied but often rather coarse country red, although those made from grapes grown on the less fertile plateau land last notably longer than the produce of lower land. Cahors has attracted a number of well-heeled outsiders, whether from Paris or New York, and is in the throes of redesigning itself as a thoroughly modern wine in its historic image as deep, dark, colouring wine for blending with the vapid stuff produced downriver in Bordeaux. Châteaux de Haute-Serre, Lagrezette, Pech de Jammes, St-Didier-Parnac and Triguedina are trying harder than most.

Almost due east of the city of Bordeaux and yet way up on France's flat, wild interior, the Massif Central, the **Marcillac**, **Entraygues** and **Estaing** appellations cling to existence with scented, peppery distinctive wines which owe much to the local Fer Servadou vine, the sort to send a shiver down the spine of vine-variety sleuths like me.

Gaillac has an identity and history that is indisputably quite distinct from Bordeaux. Vines were almost certainly planted on the rolling farmland around the historic city of Albi long before they were known in the Bordeaux region, and they were long used for strengthening the light reds made downriver. All of which gives the locals a certain inherent superiority, but the truth is that in the modern marketplace, Gaillac has yet to make much of a stir. Such a wide range of grape varieties are planted here, and such a broad variety of wine styles, that Gaillac tends to be a local hero rather than international superstar. The most exciting local red varieties are Duras (no relation to Côtes de Duras) and the Fer of Marcillac, but they are usually blended with Gamay and Syrah (imports from Beaujolais and the Rhône respectively) and sometimes the Cabernets and Merlot of Bordeaux. Mauzac is Gaillac's signature white variety and adds a certain twist of apple peel to its whites which come in all degrees of sweetness and fizziness. The Bordeaux white varieties of Sauvignon, Sémillon and Muscadelle are also widely grown together with local specialities Len de l'El and Ondenc. Is it any wonder that Gaillac's image is confused? The appellation is dominated by two co-operatives, Labastide de Levis and the Cave de Tecou, whose wines are tasting more and more sophisticated, but

Robert Plageoloes is the media star of the appellation and makes, among other things, local answers to sauternes, champagne and sherry.

Côtes du Frontonnais is a small but interesting red and rosé appellation just north of Toulouse where the grainy local variety Négrette is preserved, and producers such as Châteaux Bellevue-La-Forêt and Montauriol make thoroughly modern, almost 'international' wines. But the really characterful wines of the south west come from Gascony (Armagnac country) and Basque country in the far south of the Atlantic hinterland.

Madiran is that region's most substantial wine, a deep-coloured, barrel-aged masculine red made to last and last, chiefly because of the local Tannat variety (whose name, it is assumed, derives from its mouth-puckering tannin content). There are some exciting winemakers here such as Alain Brumont of Châteaux Bouscassé and Montus, who seem to have mastered getting subtlety and smoothness out of the variety, which is usually blended with Cabernets and a little Fer. Other notable producers include Château d'Aydie and Domaine Laffitte-Teston. Anyone with a serious interest in wine should keep a keen eye on developments in this often underrated, proud Gascon winemaking outpost.

The group of local co-operatives, known collectively as Plaimont, has played an important part in reviving the area's viticultural traditions and is the most important producer of the keenly priced wine **Côtes de St-Mont** as well as of Gascony's real bargain, fruity dry white Vin de Pays made from grapes surplus to the requirements of the Armagnac distillers. A counterpart from Cognac country to the north is also now available (see page 204).

The white wine made, in relatively small quantity, in the Madiran district is **Pacherenc du Vic-Bilh**, which itself is an often slightly paler shadow of the great white of this corner of France,

Jurançon, made in the green foothills of the western Pyrenees around the town of Pau, not far from Lourdes. A palette of local grape varieties is responsible for Pacherenc but green-gold tangy Jurançon depends on its own vine specialities, Gros and Petit Manseng. The small-berried Petit Manseng is the key to making Jurançon Moelleux, which owes its sweetness not to noble rot but to shrivelling, or raisining, on the vine. Jurançon comes dry (Sec) or sweet (Moelleux). Domaine Cauhapé makes some of the best wine (the dry can make a great aperitif) but great bottles have also come from Château Jolys and Charles Hours at Clos Uroulat.

The small appellation of **Tursan** is being revived, with sophisticated oak-aged white wines, and the light wines of **Béarn** (of Béarnaise sauce fame) are also produced in several different parts of this area.

But the real curiosity comes from Basque country, where almost dangerously steep, high vineyards right up in the Pyrenees produce white, pink and light red **Irouléguy**, chiefly from Cabernets and Mansengs. The co-operative makes interesting light but firm wines and Brana is the most dedicated individual producer.

LANGUEDOC

In a nutshell: France's New World wine region, with some improving appellations too.
Grapes: Carignan, Syrah, Grenache, Mourvèdre, Cinsaut (RED), Maccabéo, Grenache Blanc, Bourboulenc, Picpoul, Clairette (WHITE)

The Languedoc is my adoptive French home. I see it as Provence without the tourists, without too many incomers like me pushing up prices and without, regrettably, the ubiquitous smell of lavender, thyme and pines. It is, however, archetypal mediterranean wine country, with wild landscapes, Spain just over the Pyrenees, and vines stretching in every direction. Those which stretch on the flattest land, notably the vast, arid plains between Narbonne and Montpellier, are chiefly responsible for France's still significant production of basic light red Vin de Table (see page 48) and therefore for much of the European wine lake.

Although the Languedoc was the first French region to be introduced to vine-growing and winemaking by the Romans, its modern reputation as a wine producer has been for quantity at the expense of quality. Once the railways had reached this reliably sunny southern part of France, it was developed as an outdoor factory producing vast quantities of light red to be shipped to the recently industrialized north of the country. The hillside vineyards established by the Romans were rapidly swamped by the sea of much less demanding vineyards established on the wide coastal plain.

So high were yields – often far more than 200 hl/ha (11 ton/acre) – and so ignoble the grape varieties that France came to be dependent on importing robust, deep-coloured red wine from Algeria and then Italy and Spain in order to bolster the produce of the Languedoc. Co-operatives dominate, and still the great majority of growers, peasant smallholders in the main, have no experience at all of winemaking.

By the 1980s the Languedoc was regularly producing 10 per cent of the entire planet's wine output, but as the decade progressed, and French consumption of basic Vin de Table plummeted, it became clear that there was no long-term future for the sort of wine on which the Languedoc rural economy was based.

Today one of Europe's most pressing problems is how to transform the Languedoc from a region of thousands of vignerons producing wine no one wants to drink into a much smaller one in which perhaps hundreds of producers concentrate on the medium- to high-quality wine of which the region is capable.

The hills of the Fitou, Corbières, Minervois and Coteaux du Languedoc appellations are home to some of France's oldest vines, often gnarled stumps of Carignan, which ooze super-concentrated, often super-tannic deep red, suitable for blending with more recent plantings of fashionably Rhônish varieties.

In the 1990s the Languedoc is producing two types of wine, among which are some of the best value bottles in the world: not just these appellation wines but members of the rank below, Vin de Pays d'Oc, which has become the region's most important product, and a host of other, more geographically specific Vins de Pays (see pages 202–4), many sold as varietals.

This is red wine country, although small proportions of rosé (particularly from Cinsaut, Syrah and Grenache) and increasingly interesting whites are made (from a cocktail of varieties including Grenache Blanc, Bourboulenc, Maccabéo, Rolle, and Viognier, Marsanne and Roussanne of the Rhône, and the local varieties Picpoul, Terret and Clairette). Tough old Carignan still makes up the backbone of most Languedoc reds, but the proportion of improving varieties' is increasing all the time. These include Grenache, Mourvèdre and, particularly, Syrah. Thanks to the influence of the Southern

Rhône to the east of this enormous sweep of vineyards, Grenache predominates in the east of the Languedoc while Syrah is more important in the west. Mourvèdre is restricted to the warmest sites.

Selling prices have been very low, which has put a natural brake on modernization of the Languedoc's often primitive wineries. Destemmers and oak barrels are still widely seen as luxuries, and the prevailing habit has been to vinify whole bunches of Carignan in a version of Beaujolais's carbonic maceration (see page 78) so as to soften its often rasping tannins. Things are fast becoming more sophisticated, however, and the best wines offer a bordeaux-like structure (rarely more than 12.5 per cent alcohol) to support much wilder, more mediterranean flavours – at prices rarely more than AC Bordeaux.

Fitou, unusually for the Languedoc an all-red appellation, is its most southerly, in the arid foothills of the Pyrenees in the south of the Corbières region. Its enormous potential is as yet unrealized, perhaps because the dominant co-operatives, with the exception of the Cave de Mont-Tauch, have been slow to realize that quality is the key to survival. Château de Nouvelles is one of the few individual producers of any distinction.

Corbières just to the north is, for the moment, a much more exciting appellation, with scores of ambitious, dedicated smallholders determined to persuade the varied, dry, hillsides of the appellation to yield herby, slightly wild red wines of real quality and integrity. The Val d'Orbieu association of co-operatives does a good job and individual properties of note include Châteaux La Baronne, Caraguilhes (organic), Cascadais, Étang de Colombes, Hélène, Lastours, Les Ollieux, Les Palais-Rondolin, Pensées Sauvages, St-Auriol, La Voulte-Gasparets, and Domaines Fontsainte, du Grand Crès and du Révérend. Some of the cheapest bottlings of Corbières (and Minervois), however, taste little better than basic Vin de Table.

Immediately inland of Corbières are the gentler hills which are responsible for Blan-

Vines can seem to stretch forever in the Languedoc.

quette de Limoux and Crémant de Limoux, the Languedoc's very serviceable traditional method sparkling wines. The former is made chiefly from the region's Blanquette grape (the Mauzac of Gaillac), the latter includes substantially more Chardonnay and is a less distinctive but probably more sophisticated product. **Limoux** is a promising new appellation for barrel-fermented, still Chardonnays – very cosmopolitan!

Côtes de Malepère and **Cabardès** are twin wine zones south and north of the walled city of Carcassonne which can produce some excellent value, relatively simple reds in which the grapes of south west France (Cabernet, Merlot and Fer) are blended with those of the Languedoc.

Minervois in the north west corner of the Languedoc produces slightly smoother, more refined wines than Corbières, but is otherwise quite similar (and equally dominated by co-operatives with extremely varied degrees of skill). The hills are gentler here but some of the most characterful wines are made high up in the foothills of the Cévennes, notably above the ancient wine village of La Livinière, such as Château de Centeilles and Domaines La Combe Blanche and Piccinini. Other producers who have produced exceptional wines include Châteaux Fabas, de Gourgazaud, La Grave, Laville-Bertrou, d'Oupia, La Tour Boisé, Viller-ambert-Julien and Violet and Domaines Maris and Ste-Eulalie. A small amount of dry rosé and increasingly sophisticated white is also made.

St-Chinian is right up in the dramatically craggy Cévennes foothills and it benefits from the dynamism of the dominant co-operative, whose wines are sold under the Berloup label (whites can also be good). Sandwiched between eastern Minervois and Faugères, it can produce characterful reds which represent a half-way house between Syrah and Grenache influences on the ubiquitous Carignan. Other good pro-ducers include Château Coujan and Domaines du Fraisse and des Jougla, although many of the most interesting wines are Vins de Pays.

Faugères has a similar profile, with over-performers including Gilbert Alquier and Château de la Liquière. Both St-Chinian and Faugères are effectively regarded as special 'crus' or growths within the wide-ranging **Coteaux du Languedoc** appellation. The region stretches from the strange seaside hill of La Clape on the coast south of Narbonne (particularly good for marine-scented, dry whites based on Bour-boulenc) to the mountainous vineyards of Pic-St-Loup. This terrain yields hundreds of interesting Vins de Pays made from a wide range of vine varieties, but properties such as Abbaye de Valmagne, Domaines d'Aupilhac and de l'Hortus, Châteaux de Flaugergues, Pech-Redon, Pech Céleyran and Rouquette-sur-Mer, and Mas Jullien also make AC reds, whites and rosés to show they have not given up France's beloved appellation precepts altogether. Picpoul de Pinet is a special full bodied white.

Costières de Nîmes is really part of the Southern Rhône, and its wines tend to taste like a blend between a Languedoc and Rhône wine, as one would expect from looking at a map. I have enjoyed wines from Domaine de L'Escattes, Grand Plagnol and Paul Blanc.

One reason why I like the Languedoc so much is that it produces the full gamut of wine styles: not just reds, whites and rosés well man-nered enough to drink on a hot summer's day, and the fizz of Limoux, but also not a few sweet wines, vins doux naturels made from the Muscat grape. **Muscats** de Frontignan, Lunel, Mireval and, most delicate and tender of all, St-Jean-de-Minervois. These golden syrups tend to be about 16 per cent alcohol, should be served well chilled, but once opened keep for a week in the refrigerator. As in Roussillon, an increasing pro-portion of the region's pale grapes are made into scented, dry full bodied white table wines.

ROUSSILLON

In a nutshell: A tradition of rich dessert wines.
Grapes: Grenache (RED), Muscat,
Grenache Blanc, Maccabéo (WHITE)

Roussillon is often appended to the Languedoc, as in Languedoc-Roussillon, but has a quite distinct character of its own, in landscape, in ethnic roots (Roussillon still regards itself as part of Catalonia across the border in Spain), and in wine styles. Whereas the Languedoc is almost entirely dependent on vine-growing, the farmers in Roussillon's fertile valleys, overlooked by the brooding Pyrenees, can choose between all sorts of fruit. The climate here is almost Spanish, and is particularly suitable for growing cherries, plums, peaches, apricots and nectarines.

Roussillon's wine speciality is a wide variety of vins doux naturels, France's answer to port in which barely fermented sweet grape juice is stabilized by a good dollop of neutral grape spirit (a technique discovered long before the distillation of stronger stuff). See page 89.

Banyuls is the most revered of these, made mainly from almost-raisined dark Grenache grapes grown on rocky, terraced vineyards that tumble into the sea just north of the Spanish border. The vin doux naturel producers employ all sorts of methods to trap their region's sunshine in their wines. Some put the young wine in large glass jars or barrels and leave them out in the hot sunshine to bake (as shown on pages 58-9). Others employ a complicated regime of moving it between barrels of different sizes and ages. Most leave the wine for some time to bake under the rafters during at least one summer. The result is wines which can vary from light red to deep brown, often tasting quite raisiny, sometimes having acquired a nutty, almost rancid taste called 'rancio' by exposure to air and heat. Banyuls Grand Cru wines have to be aged in wood for more than two and a half

years, but producers such as Domaines du Mas Blanc and de la Rectorie may prolong the ageing for many years to produce treacly yet balanced wines which are recommended by many fastidious palates as good partners for chocolate.

Maury is Banyuls's inland cousin and wines made by the likes of Mas Amiel can be almost as fine. Between Banyuls and Maury is a vast area allowed to produce both **Rivesaltes** and **Muscat de Rivesaltes**, which are generally very much less distinguished products, better suited for pouring into halves of melon than for sipping with attention. Muscat de Rivesaltes is produced in enormous quantity, mainly from the less distinguished Muscat of Alexandria vine (unlike Languedoc and Beaumes-de-Venise Muscats). Quality is gradually improving however. A really well-made Rivesaltes could be very fine but most are vague blends of Grenache of various depths of colour aged, not necessarily in very demanding circumstances, for the statutory minimum of just over a year.

The unfortified wines of Roussillon are generally less remarkable but there are more and more exceptions such as those made by Casenove, Gauby, Piquemal, Mas Crémat, Mas Segala and the top bottlings of larger merchants Sarda-Malet and Cazes. The **Côtes du Roussillon-Villages** appellations are still struggling to establish their identity and many of the region's most interesting wines are Vins de Pays (see overleaf) or even, in the case of Fernand Vaquer, Vin de Table. Some of the most interesting wines are full bodied, often oaked whites flavoured with such varieties as Roussanne, Rolle (Vermentino) and Marsanne with Grenache Blanc providing body and Maccabéo providing acidity. Muscat is increasingly made into a grapey, dry, sometimes lightly fizzy white. **Collioure** is the heady, almost fiery red wine made from well ripened Grenache vines in the Banyuls zone. It speaks Spanish rather than French...

VINS DE PAYS

In a nutshell: Some fine value underappreciated by the French. **Grapes:** *Practically anything but especially the international varieties*

Vin de Pays means 'country wine' to the French, but can mean New World with a French accent to outsiders. These are the wines which the French authorities unreservedly allow to be labelled with the grape variety from which they were made.

It is difficult to overestimate the importance of this large and growing category of wines for the future of the French wine trade. The French themselves tend to see any Vin de Pays as distinctly inferior to any AC wine (see page 48) whereas many of their customers abroad see the better Vins de Pays as good-value, user-friendly emissaries from the world's most revered wine producer.

The Vin de Pays category, a product only of the 1970s, is designed to allow greater flexibility, and higher yields, than the AC rules. A much wider range of grape varieties (including the 'international' ones Chardonnay, Cabernet Sauvignon, Sauvignon Blanc, Merlot etc.) is allowed for Vins de Pays, and some producers bottle the produce of vines too young for AC wines as Vins de Pays. The normal maximum permitted yield for a Vin de Pays is 90 hl/ha (5 ton/acre) whereas most ACs are limited to about 50 or 60 hl/ha (3 or 3.5 ton/acre), although the smaller the area designated by the Vin de Pays, the more demanding the rules.

The two systems overlap geographically so that most wine producers have a choice between making an AC wine or Vin de Pays, but the choice tends to be dictated by economics. Few Burgundian producers choose to abandon their valuable appellation wines in favour of making a Vin de Pays de la Côte d'Or. But scores of producers in the Languedoc, for exam-ple, find it commercially more rewarding to pro-duce a Vin de Pays d'Oc which can also be labelled varietally with a magic name such as Chardonnay or Merlot, or a more geographically specific Vin de Pays, than to make an AC Coteaux du Languedoc.

Partly because the appellations of the Languedoc-Roussillon don't command a particularly high price, and partly because so many vineyards lie outside these appellations (having been planted to produce Vin de Table), the great majority of Vins de Pays come from this vast vineyard area. The Languedoc's regional Vin de Pays, called 'd'Oc' after the defining local word for 'Yes', is the single most important Vin de Pays produced, and certainly France's principal varietally labelled wine.

Because the area is so large, individual Vins de Pays d'Oc vary considerably but Chardonnay and Merlot seem to have adapted particularly well to the mediterranean climate here (even though they are relatively recent arrivals). Sauvignon Blanc, Cabernet Sauvignon and Syrah are more variable but can shine, while plantings of Viognier continue to multiply as this variety's fame spreads. Vins de Pays are also a good vehicle for such local vine specialities as Terret, Rolle and Clairette. Oak ageing and rarity (in the case of early Viognier plantings) pushed the price of some Vins de Pays above that of appellation wines.

The most striking example of high-priced Vin de Pays is the Languedoc's Mas de Daumas Gassac, whose concentrated wines are sold simply as Vins de Pays de l'Hérault but at classed growth bordeaux prices.

This illustrates one of the most common sorts of Vin de Pays, one named after the local *département*, or county. The Aude and Gard are the other two Languedoc départements, while the most common Vins de Pays of Roussillon are 'Catalans' and 'des Côtes Catalans'.

The French authorities have always been most keen to avoid any possibility of confusion between Vins de Pays and any of their precious appellations, so the names of Vins de Pays can sometimes be very difficult for those of us with a less-than-complete grasp of French history and geography.

The table shows some more common Vins de Pays with some geographical guidance as to where they are located (often with reference to the nearest AC) and the likely style of wine.

Vineyards near Cucugnan, ideally suited to producing dense red wine within the Corbières appellation in the Languedoc, but with its very own Vin de Pays which allows more prolific yields.

VIN DE PAYS DU/DE LA DE L'/DES	LOCATION	MOST COMMON WINES
Aude	W. Languedoc inc. Minervois, Corbières	Wide range of international and experimental wines
Bouches-du-Rhône	Around Aix-en Provence	Useful varietals
Catalans	Flatter Roussillon	International varieties
Charentais	Cognac country	Very light dry white, surplus to the distillers' needs
Cîté de Carcassonne	Between Cabardès and Côtes de la Malepère	Light reds
Collines Rhodaniennes	Northern Rhône	Lightish Syrah, Marsanne, Viognier
Comtés Rhodaniens	Anywhere in N. Rhône, Beaujolais or Savoie	Light reds
Comté Tolosan	All south west	Bordeaux-like reds
Coteaux de l'Ardèche	Plateau on right bank of the Rhône S. of St Péray	Some interesting Chardonnay and Viognier
Coteaux de Murviel	S. of St-Chinian	Some very good varietals
Coteaux du Quercy	SW of Cahors	Good value country Cahors
Côtes Catalanes	Hillier Roussillon	Deep flavoured reds, dry Muscat
Côtes de Gascogne	Armagnac country	Fresh, fruity dry whites made from Colombard and other brandy grapes
Côtes de Thongue	NE of Béziers	Some fine varietals, esp. Syrah and Chardonnay
Gard	Costières de Nîmes	Country versions of Côtes du Rhône
Gers	Armagnac country	Very similar to Côtes de Gascogne
Hérault	Central Languedoc	Very wide variety
Île de Beauté	Corsica	Light reds, some rosés
Haute-Garonne	Around Toulouse	Some very serious international varietals
Jardin de la France	Loire Valley	Crisp, 'northern' wines of all three colours
Loire-Atlantique	Muscadet country	Occasional Chardonnays of interest
Oc	The whole Languedoc	Very wide variety of grapes and wine-making skill, some excellent value
Principauté d'Orange	N. end of S. Rhône	Some fine varietals
Sables du Golfe du Lion	Sand spit near Sète	Light whites and rosés, from Listel

REST OF FRANCE

Any voyage round France via the main wine regions tends to overlook the eastern ones that are extremely important locally but whose wines rarely make much export impact.

The wines of Savoie tend to taste of the French alps in whose foothills they are made – all crunchy crispness and herby, sappy flavours. My favourite is the curious deep-coloured, racy, slightly bitter red Mondeuse, but there is a wide range of light but fruity, crystal clear whites, of which Roussette is potentially the finest, and some increasingly interesting Pinot Noir. The local fizz, Seyssel, can be a bargain and other names occasionally seen outside France include Crépy, Apremont and Chignin-Bergeron (Bergeron is the Rhône's Roussanne). Superior wines come from Michel Grisard, Château Ripaille and a clutch of producers called Quénard. Even less Bugey escapes its base around Bourg-en-Bresse (the Bresse of chicken fame) but some wines do manage to spread knowledge of the Jura's very particular styles. The seclusion of the Jura in the hills due east of Burgundy has perhaps preserved its traditions of making a sort of sherry, called *vin jaune* (matured under a film of yeast just like sherry; see pages 23–5) and, even rarer, the ultra-sweet *vin de paille* made from grapes dried on straw (see page 89), which is also made in Hermitage. The key names of the appellations here are the extremely varied Arbois and Côtes du Jura together with L'Étoile and Château-Chalon, the latter for *vin jaune* only. Some sparkling wine is also made here.

Even further north in eastern France are the very light, often tart whites and rosés of the Côtes de Toul and Vins de Moselle, the latter being effectively a continuation of the wines produced on the river Moselle in Luxembourg.

The Champagne region produces markedly acid, dry still wines too, mostly in the Coteaux Champenois appellation, which may be white or, in very ripe vintages, lightish red such as the unforgettably named Bouzy Rouge. A local still pink speciality is Rosé des Riceys.

There are also various obscure appellations in the south west such as Côtes du Brulhois, which are very Bordeaux-like, and the weirdly named Vins d'Entraygues et du Fel and Vins d'Estaing, which share characteristics with neighbour Marcillac. The rest of France's AC and VDQS wines mostly fall within the greater Loire basin (which is very great indeed). Sauvignon de St Bris is regarded administratively as part of greater Chablis but the razor-sharp style of this Sauvignon Blanc is pure Loire in taste.

Travelling upstream from the mouth of the Loire, the extremely light whites of the Fief-Vendéens are like Muscadet shadows, while Coteaux d'Ancenis and Vins du Thouarsais are on the fringes of Anjou-Saumur. Haut Poitou is far from the river itself, well south of the Touraine, and produces a wide range of well-made modern wines almost exclusively from a single co-operative. Coteaux du Loir is the confusingly named northern outpost of Touraine with some very fine dry and sweet Jasnières being made from Chenin Blanc grapes – most successfully by Joël Gigou and Aubert de Rycke. Coteaux du Vendômois makes light wines around the town of Vendôme, while Orléans and Gien give their names to the local Vins de l'Orléanais and Coteaux du Giennois on the most significant bend in the river Loire.

Well inside that bend are the Gamay-dominated Châteaumeillant and St-Pourçain-sur-Sioule which make wines from a wide range of grape varieties, with the Loire's hallmark of high acidity and relatively light body. Between St-Pourçain and Lyons are the very similar, gutsy Beaujolais-like wines of Côtes du Forez and Côte Roannaise, as well as the varied but rarely exported wines of the Côtes d'Auvergne.

Coteaux du Lyonnais are Beaujolais-like wines made in the outer reaches of Lyons.

ITALY

A h, Italy – what a beautiful, hedonistic, disorganized, frustrating country! Italy can provide wine lovers with so many distinctive, unique flavours and styles, bottles full of Italian verve and creativity. It also sluices forth rivers of disgracefully thin, characterless stuff to be sold under its most commercially useful names: Soave, Valpolicella, Lambrusco, Frascati and the like.

Although the key to understanding Italy is to understand that it is a group of regions rather than a single homogeneous country – from the heady, often sweet, ferments of the deep south to the delicate subalpine essences of the north – it is possible to generalize about Italian wine styles to a certain extent. Reds have a certain bitterness that is by no means unpleasant. In fact it is so addictive that I find Italy is the one country I come home from positively determined to continue to drink its wines (rather than, as usual, desperate for a complete change). Italian white wines have in the past been distinguished by their lack of aroma and lack of obvious fruitiness (very unmodern), but this is changing – not least as a result of incoming 'flying winemakers' (see page 68).

*For many of us, this is Italy. A simple shop in Chianti country where no one needs
a special licence to sell something as life-enhancing as wine.*

UNDERSTANDING LABELS

cantina means literally cellar or winery.

A **Cantina Sociale** is a co-operative winery.

Classico, usually original heartland of a wine zone.

cru is, especially in Piedmont, a specially designated vineyard.

DOC, Denominazione di Origine Controllata, Italy's failed attempt at a system of distinguishing its superior wines fashioned in the image of France's Appellation Contrôlée. Some argue it was imposed too early and too strictly, others that it was too late and not strict enough. The truth is probably that the Italians do not willingly submit to regulation. For the consumer, DOC means precious little, for in many DOCs the allowed yields are often far too high to concentrate quality in the resulting wines.

DOCG, Denominazione di Origine Controllata e Garantita, the super-DOC category introduced for the 1982 vintage to which DOCs have since been promoted. DOCG wines are reliably among Italy's better bottles.

frizzante, lightly sparkling.

Riserva generally denotes prolonged ageing under carefully prescribed conditions.

spumante, sparkling.

Superiore, usually a little higher in alcohol.

tenuta, wine estate or smallholding.

vendemmia, vintage.

Vino da Tavola, Italy's supposedly basic table wine category, designed to be on a par with France's Vin de Table, now also includes a significant proportion of Italy's best wines, which don't happen to conform to any DOC regulations, especially but by no means exclusively in Tuscany (the so-called Supertuscans).

NORTH WEST ITALY

PIEDMONT

In a nutshell: *Italy's most* terroiriste *area,
with strong similarities to Burgundy.*
Grapes: *Nebbiolo, Barbera, Dolcetto* (RED)*,
Moscato, Cortese, Arneis* (WHITE)

Of all the places I visited in the preparation for
this book, Piedmont won my heart for its sheer
joie de vivre. And the use of French is not too
undiplomatically inappropriate here, for this
region is only just over the alps from France and
the local dialect is perfectly comprehensible to a
French speaker. I have to admit that Piedmont
also stole my stomach. I know of no other part
of the world where every café and restaurant in
the smallest village, no matter how unprepos-
sessing, seems able and willing to serve course
after course of stunningly fresh, stylishly but
minimally prepared food – the raw meat-based
antipasti, the risotti, the tartufi. Tartufi are
knobbly white potato-like truffles which are
hunted by carefully trained, zealously guarded
and occasionally sabotaged dogs – ideally white
so that the hunting can take place in the dead
of night and everyone can keep their favourite
spots a secret ... but I must stop. This is a book
about wine.

The scenery is stunning too, however, especially in autumn at the height of the white
truffle season when each patch of vines turns a
different shade of pink, orange, brown, purple
and green. Whenever the fog, or *nebbia*, clears,
the tightly folded Langhe hills which expose the
Barolo and Barbaresco vineyards (Piedmont's
most famous) are dwarfed by the snow-covered
alps to the north and west. Most of Piedmont's
excitingly varied wine is produced in conditions
of enviable beauty and gastronomic luxury. Do
these people pay tax?

Unusually for Italy, Piedmont is a wine region
to which grape varieties are the key. Its great,

dark, intense, subtly perfumed, alcoholic, long-
lived, occasionally unbearably tannic red wines
owe everything to Nebbiolo (supposedly named
after the fog), but enormous quantities of much
lighter, lively Barbera and softly mouth-filling
Dolcetto are also grown as well as some local
rarities such as strawberry-flavoured Brachetto,
curiously sweet and sparkling Freisa, light and
tangy Grignolino and unusual Ruchè or Rouchet.
(See Section Three for details of how these and
other varieties taste.)

Piedmont is also home to a variety of local
white grape specialities which to my palate share
delicacy, dryness and an aroma that often
reminds me of ripe pears. Cortese is the grape of
the most respected white, Gavi; the perfumed
Arneis has been very fashionable; and Favorita
is also grown in the Roero just north of Barolo
and Barbaresco country. Erbaluce makes small
quantities of sweet white wine but the most
prolific white grape of Piedmont is Muscat,
which is responsible for oceans of Asti and various other featherlight, grapey Moscatos, many of
which are sparkling, or spumante.

Many of these wines are labelled varietally,
as in Nebbiolo delle Langhe, Barbera d'Asti and
Dolcetto d'Alba. Monferrato, Diano, Ovada and
Acqui are other geographical zones. One of these
wines labelled Nebbiolo can offer some of
Piedmont's dark, satanic majesty in a bottle at
a fraction of the cost of a great Barolo or
Barbaresco, although so can some of the best
Barbera. Barbera is grown in great quantity all
over the region and is generally regarded as the
light, tart, quaffing wine to be drunk as young as
possible. The produce of low-yielding Barbera
vines matured in small French oak barrels, or
barriques, can be a revelation however, and is
also definitively Piedmontese in character.

Wines here have traditionally, as throughout Italy, been matured in large, old Slovenian
oak oval casks, but the importation of French

barriques has recently caused a stir and some revision of wine styles, making some of them more open and less distinctive (or, to put it another way, earlier maturing and less cussed). Much has been made in the last two decades of the modernists v. traditionalists debate in the Langhe, but in truth the wines have in general gently evolved so that none of Nebbiolo's extraordinarily haunting resonances, reminiscent of violets, tar, truffles and sometimes roses are lost, but these relatively expensive wines are approachable after a decade or so in bottle.

Piedmont's most friendly wine is Dolcetto which should burst with fruit while being impressively deep-coloured and, often, quite alcoholic. Dolcetto is particularly useful for growers because, unlike ultra-fussy, late ripening Nebbiolo, it will ripen on less favoured sites, even north-facing ones.

More and more producers are beginning to look at the wider world of wine (for reasons I don't entirely understand; if I made wine here I'd be an incorrigible introspect). The result is that many of them are beginning to plant little plots of 'international' varieties: Cabernet Sauvignon; some Chardonnay which can be transformed into very elegant wine, thanks to barrel fermentation; some Sauvignon Blanc; and even some Riesling and Viognier. If the Piedmontese are importing grape invaders, it's no wonder the rest of the world is.

It is beyond question, however, that the greatest wines of Piedmont are Barolo and, very slightly lighter and earlier maturing, Barbaresco. These are two of the wine world's pinnacles but, as Aldo Conterno placidly observes, they are not easy to understand and, since they are made in small quantity, that matters little. The Langhe hills around the town of Alba, with their different altitudes and expositions, are Italy's answer to Burgundy's Côte d'Or, and different vineyards can, similarly, produce quite different wines, which is why there has been an increase in single-vineyard bottlings such as Gaja's Barbaresco Sori Tildin. Other particularly notable producers abound and include Elio Altare,

Giacomo Bologna, Ceretto, Clerico, Giacomo Conterno, Bruno Giacosa, Elio Grasso, Marchesi di Gresy, Mascarello, Prunotto, Ratti, Vajra and Voerzio.

Another group of slightly earthier, lighter bodied Nebbiolo wines is made in communities around the town of Gattinara in subalpine hills almost due north of Alba where Nebbiolo is known as Spanna: **Gattinara**, **Ghemme**, **Boca**, **Lessona**, **Bramaterra**, **Sizzano**, **Fara** and, right on the border with the Valle d'Aosta, **Carema**.

VALLE D'AOSTA

Very little wine leaves this alpine region on the French border but it is fertile hunting ground for lovers of ancient grape varieties. Chambave, Morgex, Nus and La Salle are all names found on the labels of these wines, which can often taste, not surprisingly, Swiss.

LOMBARDY

Some of the best-known wines produced on the plains and hills closest to Milan are the slightly tough Nebbiolo-based reds of **Valtellina** on south-facing slopes just south of the Swiss border, the innocuous dry white **Lugana** made on the shores of Lake Garda, and **Franciacorta**, an extremely varied but interesting area for serious red, dry white and sparkling wines. The region also produces most of the raw material for Italy's most skilled sparkling winemakers such as Ca'del Bosca. This is most certainly an area under-represented on export markets.

LIGURIA

The dramatic vineyards of the coast around Genoa produce hardly enough wine for the region's tourists. Cinqueterre and Dolceacqua are the place names most commonly encountered outside the region. Local grape varieties are Ormeasco (the Dolcetto of Piedmont), dry white Pigato, light red Rossesse, and crisp white Vermentino.

NORTH EAST ITALY

This is the land of the Tre Venezie: Veneto, Friuli and Trentino.

VENETO

In a nutshell: Lots of commercial Soave and Valpolicella, centre of dried grape wine production. Grapes: Corvina, Molinara, Rondinella (RED), Garganega, Trebbiano di Soave, Chardonnay (WHITE)

The Veneto, centred on Verona in the hinterland of Venice, is Italy's wine factory. Here lakes of pale red Valpolicella and Bardolino and watery Soave are drained into bottles by the million for shipment to Italian and Italianate restaurants all around the globe where, one must assume, they are gulped by a thoroughly undiscriminating public. Vineyards that are typically flat and fertile have been allowed to spew forth overgenerous yields of characterless wine which still qualifies as DOC. Soave, Valpolicella and, to a certain extent, Bardolino have been reduced to the same status as Liebfraumilch – wine as a commodity.

The Veneto is the world's capital of grape-drying, a process which concentrates the natural grape sugar and results in alcoholic, concentrated wines.

The difference, however, is that whereas no one would even try to make truly serious Liebfraumilch, many ambitious winemakers within these three wine zones are making extremely good wines. As their influence, fortunately, increases, the real challenge for the consumer (and the wine retailer) is to distinguish the goodies from the baddies.

One easy (although not infallible – this is Italy, after all) starting-point is to look for wines described as Classico, which are pro-

The handsome Villa Allegri near Grez-zana north of Verona, surrounded by vines in the Valpaltena zone of Valpolicella.

duced within the original central zone rather than the current much larger regions cynically expanded to make the most of the names' currency on international markets. Valpolicella described as Superiore must be at least 12 per cent alcohol and aged at least a year before bottling (whereas basic Valpolicella may be just 11 per cent alcohol and as much of a rush job as Beaujolais Nouveau). Another indi-cator of quality, it must be said, is a premium price. Valpolicella that is lively crimson rather than sludge pink, and tastes of bitter, juicy cherries rather than just tasting bitter cannot be produced cheaply. Yields must neces-sarily be much lower than on flatter, more easily mechanized vineyards. Reliably superior Valpoli-cella producers include Allegrini, Boscaini, Dal Forno, Masi, Quintarelli, Santi and Tedeschi.

Something has gone wrong with the Valpolicella recipe too. Corvina is by far the most characterful of the three grape varieties from which it may be made, but all-Corvina wines are outlawed by the Valpolicella regulations so that they, like so many good Italian wines, must be sold simply as a Vino da Tavola. The Molinara vine tends to produce thin, acidic wine, while it can be difficult to squeeze much flavour out of Rondinella.

The classic way of adding depth and bite to Valpolicella (which should be a refreshing, tangy wine rather than one to age years and years) is to add additional grape skins, ideally those whose sugar content has been concentrated by drying, a technique known as *ripasso* or 'repassed', which increases the final alcohol and phenolic content in wines described as *passito*.

The Veneto's true distinction in the world of wine is that it is the only region where any serious quantity of wine is still made using grapes dried to concentrate their sugar content. This was the only way the Greeks and Romans had of increasing the resulting wines' alcohol content, because distillation and therefore alcoholic spirit was still unknown. Such wines are described as **Recioto**, and may be red or white, dry or sweet. If all the grape sugar is fermented out to alcohol such wines are also described as **Amarone**, or bitter, for Valpolicella grapes dried to yield a wine of perhaps 16 per cent alcohol can certainly taste extremely intense (and should be sipped with care, ideally after a meal like port rather than swigged throughout a meal).

The white wine version, a refreshingly sweet Recioto di Soave, is much less common but it too concentrates the inherent qualities of the local grapes, in this case the appley Garganega. Soave, the Veneto's most famous white wine ambassador, is every bit as unpredictable in quality as Valpolicella, with the added variable that a wider range of grape varieties may be used: not just the local Garganega and Trebbiano di Soave (Trebbianos of various sorts

abound in Italy) but also Chardonnay, Pinot Bianco (Pinot Blanc) and the neutral Trebbiano Toscano. Good Soave is straw coloured and has a distinctive flavour reminiscent of almonds and apples.

Anselmi and Pieropan have for years shown that Soave can be so much more than a vapid, aroma-free mouthwash, but other producers now giving them a run for their money include Bertani and Prá.

Bardolino made on the shores of Lake Garda is basically a lightweight Valpolicella and good examples from producers of the calibre of Corte Gardoni, Guerrieri Rizzardi and San Pietro can make delicious summer drinking. The rosé version is called Chiaretto and local, pretty Soave-like whites include Lugana (just over the border in Lombardy) and Bianco di Custoza. Prosecco is the region's sparkling wine, generally more treasured by locals than abroad.

As almost everywhere in Italy, some of the finest wines are sold as Vino da Tavola under what are effectively miniature brand names. One of the most distinguished Veneto producers outside the DOCs cited above is Maculan of Breganze who makes some of Italy's finest sweet white wines.

FRIULI

In a nutshell: Pure, aromatic varietals.
Grapes: All the universals plus Refosco (RED),
Tocai Friulano, Picolit, Ribolla, Verduzzo (WHITE)

Friuli, or Friuli-Venezia Giulia to give this curious north east corner of Italy its full name, is worshipped by many Italian wine lovers. Its popularity illustrates nicely that the 'grass is always greener' rule holds as firmly in the world of wine as elsewhere. Basically, every nation of wine consumers treasures most what it finds most difficult to produce. In Germany, for example, the homeland of light, aromatic whites, it is full bodied, deep-coloured reds that are in greatest demand. But because Friuli is the only part of Italy in which light, aromatic whites have been produced with ease (thanks largely to the early introduction of refrigerated ways of getting pure, fresh, varietal fruit into a bottle), Italian connoisseurs have been prepared to pay well over the odds for them.

In a way Friuli wines are foreign to Italians. They are a product instead of a hilly no man's land between the Veneto, Slovenia and southern Austria – and they taste like it. This is the land of the varietal, wine made principally to express the fruit of the grape variety specified on the label. All of 17 different varietals are allowed within the scope of Friuli's two most respected DOCs, **Collio** and **Colli Orientali** (which means Eastern Hills). Of these the most common are Tocai Friulano, Pinot Grigio (Pinot Gris), Sauvignon Blanc, Pinot Bianco (Pinot Blanc), Merlot, Chardonnay and Cabernet Franc/Frank, but local specialities include Ribolla, Verduzzo and the always expensive Picolit for white wines and the tangy Refosco and rare Schioppettino and promising Pignolo for the red wines of Colli Orientali.

Now that Italian winemakers south and west of Friuli have also mastered the art of making fresh, fruity white wines, however, their counterparts in Collio and Colli Orientali are having to try harder to justify their price premium, typically but not necessarily with greater use of small oak barrels. The standard of winemaking here is generally very high, and yields relatively low, even if the price for this is that the wines can taste remarkably similar.

Some of the producers most revered within Italy are Abbazio di Rosazzo, Borgo Conventi, Girolamo Dorigo, Felluga, Gravner, Jermann, Marin, Puiatti, Radikon, Ronco del Gnemiz, Schiopetto and Villa Russiz, whose wines can continue to develop in bottle for two or three years.

Other important DOC zones such as **Isonzo** and, especially, the prolific **Grave del Friuli** are on flatter land and tend to produce much less impressively rapier-like flavours. Other DOCs produced here include **Lison-Pramaggiore, Aquileia, Latisana** and **Carso.**

TRENTINO-ALTO ADIGE

In a nutshell: Alpine vineyards producing usually lightish varietals.
Grapes: All the universals plus Teroldego, Schiava, Lagrein (RED), Traminer, local Muskatellers (WHITE)

The two neighbouring wine regions of Trentino (the lower, more southerly part of the Adige valley around the town of Trento) and the upper Adige valley produce Italy's most alpine wines in a region dominated by co-operatives. **Trentino** is the catch-all DOC for a wide range of varietal wines, from smudgy, light, sweetish red Schiava (Vernatsch in German) to some fine high-altitude, barrel-fermented Chardonnays. Marzemino and the toothsome Teroldego Rotaliano are local red wine grape varieties but the full range of international varietals is produced, generally in rather pale versions. The likes of Pojer & Sandri (who make one of the world's few sought-after Müller-Thurgaus) and the research institute at San Michele all'Adige prove just what can be achieved in this lower zone due north of the commercial battleground of Verona. The region's potential for top quality sparkling wines has long been demonstrated by Ferrari.

Alto Adige, however, is a more distinctive environment – not just because it is known as the South Tyrol (German is spoken by many of the older inhabitants here) but also because of the contrast between the warm summers and cold winters of vineyards grafted on to the Dolomite foothills. The region undoubtedly has enormous, but often unrealized potential (although some of its wines might well impress more widely if chaptalization were allowed as in Switzerland to the north). Schiava is quantitatively important but Alto Adige can rival Friuli for pure, varietal, more internationally familiar flavours from producers such as Castel Schwanburg, Franz Haas, Hofstätter, Alois Lageder and Tieffenbrunner, notably Gewürztraminer which may have its origins in this alpine valley.

TUSCANY

In a nutshell: *Italy's dynamic wine powerhouse.*
Grapes: *Sangiovese, Cabernet Sauvignon* (RED)*,
Trebbiano, Malvasia, Vernaccia* (WHITE)

It may seem logically and geographically absurd to single out Tuscany from the rest of central Italy (see page 218) but it makes perfect sense for wine lovers. The Veneto may be the Italian wine industry's commercial centre, Piedmont may be the source of the country's greatest gastronomic thrills, but in the forever medieval

*Some rather upmarket grape pickers
having lunch on the terrace at Riecine,
one of the most admired estates in
Chianti Classico (below). In most years it
would be unthinkable to remain exposed
to the sunshine for longer than absolutely
necessary, but as the autumn deepens,
mists can often invade Tuscany's valleys
below the many-towered
San Gimignano (opposite), famous for its
full, dry white Vernaccia.*

hills of Tuscany is Italy's greatest concentration of ambitious, dedicated winemakers. Toscana, as it is known in Italian, is the land of the small-holder rather than the co-operative, many of these smallholders having earned their not inconsiderable fortunes elsewhere (as in California's Napa Valley). Since the 1970s they have invaded this beautiful countryside dedicated to olives, pines and vines, which was once dominated by aristocratic, Florentine wine-merchant houses such as Antinori, Frescobaldi and Ricasoli.

The relentlessly undulating landscape and its temperate climate make it ideal for producing red wines with the same sort of digestible weight (about 12 to 13 per cent alcohol) and ageing potential as red bordeaux. But the wines' flavours are very different from their French counterparts. The Sangiovese vine is king here and the quality of wine it yields depends heavily on the exposure and altitude at which it is planted. (As anyone who has visited Tuscany in the winter knows, it can be inhospitably bleak.)

Greater Chianti is Tuscany's, indeed Italy's, most important, if much-divided wine zone. Chianti is in principle made from Sangiovese lightened to a greater or lesser extent with the unexceptional white Trebbiano grape and occasionally with white Malvasia and red Canaiolo. Not surprisingly, it comes in all quality levels, from dire to sublime (the sublime not necessarily costing all that many times more than the dire). A wine labelled simply Chianti is likely to be a very basic red sold to meet a price. To discover what the Tuscan hills really have to offer the taste buds it has usually been necessary to seek out a wine labelled with the name of one of the seven superior subzones.

Named respectively after the hills surrounding Arezzo, Florence, Pisa and Siena, **Chianti Colli Aretini**, **Chianti Colli Fiorentini**, **Chianti Colline Pisane** and **Chianti Colli Senesi** are not widely exported. **Chianti Montalbano** is generally a lightish wine made west of Florence while **Chianti Rufina**, from east of the city, can be both one of the finest and longest lasting.

Undoubtedly the most important Chianti zone in terms of quality and durability, however, is **Chianti Classico**, which is the hilly heart of the Chianti zone.

It is fair to say (and this is a generalization which can rarely be made of any other wine zone anywhere) that Chianti Classico is one of the most consistently well-made wines in the world. You may not like the defiantly rural, almost farmyard-like flavours of Sangiovese but an admirably low proportion of all Chianti Classico is carelessly made.

Regulations introduced in 1984 (and with almost farcical disregard for the fact that this was Tuscany's most disastrous vintage in living memory) elevated Chianti Classico to DOCG status (straight Chianti is just a DOC) and insisted on suitably low yields, sensible minimum ageing periods and disqualification of the produce of vines younger than five years old. The rules also formalize what had in reality been happening for some time in recognition of the shortcomings of the Chianti grape variety recipe. Although Sangiovese continues to provide the backbone of Chianti Classico (and the better clones, carefully transformed into wine, can display lovely ripe, pruney nuances), producers may all but ignore the white grape varieties specified in the basic Chianti recipe and may add up to 10 per cent of such immigrants as Merlot, Syrah and Cabernet Sauvignon, all of which have produced some stunning wine in Tuscany. (Some argue that Syrah may in fact be the most successful of the three.) If French grape varieties have been the most notable recent import to Tuscany's vineyards, then small French barrels have had the same dramatic effect in its cellars. Wines were traditionally aged in large old Slovenian oak ovals, but the effect of widespread use of newish, small, French oak barriques has been to concentrate and smooth the flavours of wines matured in them.

The typical Chianti Classico estate produces much more, however, than a straight Chianti Classico red. Most of them also make a Chianti Classico Riserva, aged for longer before bottling, a basic white wine sometimes called Galestro, into which their portion of Tuscany's Trebbiano surplus goes, perhaps a barrel-aged Chardonnay or Sauvignon Blanc, usually some olive oil produced from the estate's olive trees (still recovering from the frosts of 1984), often some sweet, strong, barrel-aged Vin Santo (a Tuscan speciality), and almost invariably a serious, premium red wine based on Cabernet, Merlot or Syrah vines, often blended with each other or with varying proportions of Sangiovese. These so-called **Supertuscans** qualify only as Vino da Tavola, so their producers have dreamt up a plethora of special names for them – just as the house of Antinori did with its prototype Supertuscan Tignanello (a barrique-aged blend of Sangiovese and Cabernet Sauvignon) in the early 1970s. To work out which Supertuscan belongs to which Chianti Classico estate can require considerable sleuthing at the bottom of the wine label. Some of the better estates include Badia di Coltibuono, Castello di Ama, Castell'in Villa, Fattoria di Felsina, Fonterutoli, Fontodi, Isola e Olena, Fattoria di Montevertine, Il Poggio, Castello di Querceto, Querciabella, Castello di Rampolla, Riecine, San Giusto a Rentennano, San Polo in Rosso, Selvapiana, Vicchiomaggio and Castello di Volpaia. The larger merchants Antinori, Frescobaldi and Ruffino all produce some very fine wines, many of them single vineyard bottlings and, in the case of Antinori, produced from all over central Italy.

Essence of Sangiovese is captured in the southern **Brunello di Montalcino** zone around the town of Montalcino near Siena, Brunello being a super-concentrated local strain of Sangiovese that is solely responsible for this, potentially one of Italy's greatest wines. If Chianti Classico is generally best at between four and eight years, Brunello can evolve for a decade or sometimes two. The lighter (and in many ways more useful) wines of the zone are sold as Rosso di Montalcino and, from one of the best producers such as Altesino, Biondi-Santi, Caparzo, Case Basse, Col d'Orcia, Costanti, Poggio Antico,

Il Poggione and Talenti, can be an especially good buy and are drinkable at three to seven years.

Vino Nobile di Montepulciano was elevated to DOCG status at the same time as Brunello but, with the exception of local hero Avignonesi, is yet to show quite the form and concentration of Brunello – perhaps because of its slightly warmer climate or because the overall standard of winemaking is lower. It, too, produces a slightly lighter and earlier maturing wine sold as Rosso di Montepulciano. The local strain of Sangiovese is called Prugnolo Gentile.

Tuscany's fourth DOCG is **Carmignano**, a small but interesting zone near Pisa which has embraced Cabernet Sauvignon for years and has therefore been a particularly easy wine for non-Italians to understand. The Capezzana estate dominates production.

The most interesting Tuscan dry white wine is Vernaccia di San Gimignano, made from the powerfully flavoured Vernaccia grape around the wonderful, be-towered hilltop village of San Gimignano (pictured on page 215).

All over Tuscany are various small wine zones but the area that seems to have the most serious potential for great winemaking is the Maremma on the western coast south of Livorno around the little village of Bolgheri. A member of the extended Antinori family first showed at the Tenuta San Guido that the area could produce world class Cabernet in the form of Supertuscan Sassicaia. More recently, a younger Antinori has made his name with Ornellaia (mainly Cabernet) and Masseto (mainly Merlot), produced almost next door, and there are now ambitious plantings aplenty along the old Appian Way. These are mostly the hobby wineries of rich men, built with every modern appliance that money can buy and designed to produce wines of the stature and, for better or worse, style of the great wines of Bordeaux.

It is heartening for thirsty observers such as me to see that even one of the world's oldest wine producers can discover, or perhaps rediscover, new wine regions.

REST OF CENTRAL ITALY

EMILIA-ROMAGNA

The wide plains south of the river Po are the source of a great deal of relatively dreary light red Sangiovese di Romagna (bearing no relation whatever to top quality Chianti Classico) and neutral dry white Trebbiano di Romagna. This large region is also home to Lambrusco, which in the 1980s was to Italy what Liebfraumilch was to Germany. The larger companies, supplied mainly by a handful of giant co-operatives, have turned Lambrusco into a sweet, low-alcohol, fizzy drink in virtually any colour, which bears little resemblance to wine. Good Lambrusco exists, however, in the form of deep cherry red, lightly fizzy dry wine that can taste perfect with the porcine dishes of Bologna, but is rarely exported.

MARCHE

The most famous wine product of the central eastern coast is Verdicchio, a dry white which can please but rarely excites – although the large producers Umani Ronchi have worked wonders with some special red and white bottlings. Rosso Conero and Rosso Piceno can, thanks to Montepulciano grapes, be juicy reds.

UMBRIA

Umbria, effectively a south eastern extension of Tuscany, is potentially the most interesting region of this varied collection. Lungarotti was for long the dominant producer, with a creditable track record of long-lasting Torgiano wines showing fruit to the end. Antinori also have some highly successful vineyard holdings in Umbria, most notably at Castello della Sala.

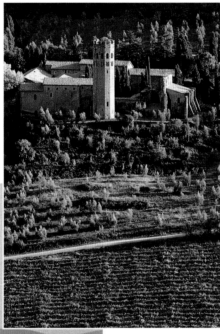

Some interesting Pinot Noir is being produced as well as barrel-aged, full bodied dry whites (and nobly rotten *muffato* sweet wine) from such local grape varieties as Grechetto, sometimes blended with Chardonnay and/or Sauvignon Blanc. But the region's most famous wine by far is Orvieto, a full bodied Trebbiano-based white which is usually dry but may be slightly sweet or *amabile*. Bigi's is better than most. The somewhat obscure and usually extremely tannic red wine Sagrantino di Montefalco was, for no particularly obvious reason, elevated to DOCG status in the early 1990s.

LATIUM

Frascati is to the vineyards that surround Rome in Latium (called Lazio in Italian) what Orvieto is to Umbria. It can sometimes be difficult to distinguish between these two full bodied dry white wines – which can too often lack discernible characteristics. Fontana Candida and Villa Simone are trying particularly hard.

ABRUZZI AND MOLISE

These wild eastern regions of central Italy produce little in the way of international wine stars, although Valentini makes some almost literally incredibly dense, long-lasting red Montepulciano d'Abruzzo and a very special, age-worthy Trebbiano d'Abruzzo. Montepulciano d'Abruzzo is usually keenly priced relative to its warmth and flavour. In Molise, Di Majo Morante makes some fine organically produced wines of both colours.

Late autumn mists over vines stripped of their foliage in Umbria (left), whose most famous wine is Orvieto (above) where more and more vineyards are now producing some seriously good stuff.

SOUTHERN ITALY AND ISLANDS

APULIA

In a nutshell: *Cheap blending wine*
but improving fast.
Grapes: *Negroamaro, Montepulciano* (RED),
Bombino Bianco (WHITE)

Apulia (Puglia in Italian), on the heel of Italy's boot, is, with Sicily, Europe's chief source of cheap blending wine, red and white, for producers of everything from basic German sparkling wine to vermouth. In this hot climate it is not too difficult to ripen grapes that will produce deep-coloured, fairly alcoholic reds that marry conveniently well with the much thinner produce of southern France's least distinguished vineyards. Negroamaro is the region's hallmark, deep, rich grape variety which, if well vinified, can produce seriously good value substantial red wines. Some of the finest examples come from the heel itself, sold under such DOCs as Copertino, Squinzano, Salice Salento, Alezio, Brindisi, Leverano, Matino and Nardó. Imported winemaking expertise in the form of the odd 'flying winemaker' has added real polish to some wines. The Montepulciano d'Abruzzo grape is grown to sometimes useful effect in the north of Apulia (just south of Abruzzi itself), while the Primitivo grape, California's Zinfandel, makes often absurdly alcoholic wines in the south.

CAMPANIA

The wines produced in the hinterland of Naples were famously fine in Ancient Roman eyes, but today the dry white Fiano di Avellino is more of a curiosity, as is its equally powerful neighbour Greco di Tufo (whose name echoes Greek origins). Taurasi is the concentrated, long-lived red of Campania and Mastroberardino is the most energetic producer of a wide range of wines from the Aglianico grapes.

BASILICATA

Aglianico del Vulture, another Greek grape variety, is this small, deep southern region's claim to wine fame. Its depth of colour and impressive tannin level certainly distinguish it in youth, although it needs many years in bottle to show its best. Leading producers Fratelli D'Angelo show some real mastery of local conditions in their special Canneto bottling.

CALABRIA

The vineyards on the toe of Italy are as wild as every other aspect of life there with few exported, or even exportable wines being produced. The curious exception is the extraordinary, classical-tasting, sweet white Greco di Bianco (Bianco being the name of the main town in the production zone; see pages 110–11). The obvious exception is Ciró, which desultorily produces a deep, intense red.

SARDINIA

In a nutshell: *Developing.*
Grapes: *Cannonau, Carignano* (RED),
Vermentino, Nuragus, Torbato (WHITE)

Sardinia is more than an island, it is only just part of Italy. For much of its modern winemaking history it was governed from Spain, and many of its distinctive local grape varieties such as Carignano, Cannonau, Vermentino and possibly Torbato are Spanish in origin. (This is just one of scores of examples of social history being reflected in a country's vineyards.)

The island lies somewhere between Corsica and Sicily, both in terms of geography and wine. Like Corsica (see page 193) it experienced a recent boom and bust in heavily subsidized new vine plantings. Like Sicily it shows signs of real potential and determination to make the most of its own raw ingredients (the Centro Enological Sardo is an active wine research station).

Most of its produce is varietally labelled, some of it is aggressively modern and characterless (the co-operatives ruled without vision until recently). Vermentino is often a creditably light, appetizing white, nowadays made particularly in the north of the island. Nuragus di Cagliari can occasionally be a worthy modern dry white example of one of the island's oldest grape varieties. Carignano di Sulcis from the south shows just how juicy the tough red Carignan can be if exposed to enough warmth, while Cannonau is the local strain of Grenache, or rather Spanish Garnacha. Vernaccia di Oristano is western Sardinia's answer to sherry – interesting but unlikely to be a big commercial hit. Sella & Mosca is one of the few notable producers independent of the co-operatives.

SICILY

In a nutshell: Dessert wine tradition but in complete transformation.
Grapes: *Catarratto, Inzolia* (WHITE), *Nero d'Avola, Nerello Mascalese* (RED)

Sicily is as fascinating to students of the modern wine world as it is to those of ancient civilizations. This large island, not far from the African coast, regularly produces as much wine as Australia, Chile and Bulgaria put together – yet exports remarkably little under its own flag. Like Apulia, it is a key supplier to northern blenders and, less usefully, a key contributor to the European wine lake. Surprisingly, it grows far more white grapes than red, the local Catarratto being so widely planted that it is second only to Sangiovese in Italy's league table of grape varieties.

Yet there are more signs of dynamic indigenous winemaking here than in any of the southern mainland regions. The island's chief viticultural research station just outside Palermo is hard at work harnessing the potential of local varieties such as the white Inzolia and red Nero d'Avola and Nerello Mascalese. There has also been considerable progress with cooler and more sophisticated fermentations and, inevitably, the use of small oak barrels.

Particularly quality-conscious producers of unfortified wines from both local and imported grape varieties include Castiglione, Donnafugata, Duca di Salaparuta, Regaleali and Terre di Ginestra. Regaleali's heady yet structured red Rosso del Conte, made from Perricone and Nero d'Avola, provided the first signs of Sicily's modern revival as a producer of table wines, thanks to vineyards at an altitude of more than 500 m (1600 ft) – generally the key to producing high-quality table wines on the island.

For years the island's most famous wine was Marsala, made in Sicily's wild west. Made from very ripe white grapes to which heated, or cooked (*cotto*) musts and grape spirit are added before ageing in the hot warehouses of the port of Marsala, the wine is not unlike madeira but tends to be darker brown, sweeter, much less acid and, in most cases, much less admired. Until recently Marsala producers were allowed to reduce the wine to something simply cheap, strong and sickly. The rules have recently been tightened up, however, so that although basic cooking Marsala and the odd eggy syrup designed to put a *zabaglione* taste in a bottle exist, there are some truly fine wines produced here – notably by De Bartoli who offers a range of different strengths and sweetness levels.

Sicily's temperatures make it ideal for dessert wine production and the island has a long history of making noble, rich Muscat. Moscato di Pantelleria is still made on an island just off the Tunisian coast but a more subtle, still orange-tinted, powerful sweet wine made off Sicily is Malvasia delle Lipari. Carlo Hauner was single-handedly responsible for the survival of this curious wine, a direct link with ancient civilizations and winemaking techniques on the almost black, volcanic island of Lipari off the north east coast. There are also some admirable attempts to revive serious mainland Moscato.

SPAIN

In a nutshell: *Land of American oak, sherry,*
and low-yielding bush vines.
Grapes: *Tempranillo, Garnacha (Grenache)*
(RED), Airén, Viura (Maccabéo),
Verdejo, Albariño (WHITE)

Spain is a viticultural miracle waiting to happen, and has been in this pregnant state for longer than seems decent. Proud possessor of more land devoted to vines than any other, Spain is only just beginning to capitalize on this resource in any consistent or cohesive way – which is perhaps not surprising. If it had Germany's love of efficiency, or France's respect for bureaucracy, Spain might be sending us oceans of judiciously priced wine made expressly for the international market. But Spain is an anarchic jumble of districts and regions, just as its landscape is an anarchic jumble of staggeringly raw scenery and heartbreakingly awful human constructions, and has to be treated as such by the wine enthusiast. There is real treasure to be found by those prepared to dig, however and, as a connoisseur class develops in Spain itself, all manner of ambitious investors are planning to change the image of Spanish wine.

A look at the map suggests just how much climatic diversity there is likely to be between Spain's many wine regions, from the soggy vineyards of Galicia on the north Atlantic coast to the baked Mediterranean south east. Spain's saving grace, viticulturally, is the altitude of her vineyards, many over 650 m (2000 ft). A high proportion of Spanish vineyards therefore manage to produce grapes with good levels of colour and acidity simply because night-time temperatures are relatively low, and grapes do not ripen until the end of a usefully prolonged growing season. And because irrigation is not officially allowed in Spain (although this rule seems to be bent by most of those who can afford to), vines are typically planted as widely spaced bushes so that yields tend to be very low, ideally resulting in grapes packed full of flavour. Lower altitude vineyards, notably those of the Levante area on the southern Mediterranean coast, tend to produce wines whose main problem is an excess of alcohol and a lack of acidity. The standard Spanish recipe for correcting this imbalance is to add white grapes or white wine. Spain's wine surplus makes an ideal complement to the vapid sort of red that makes up France's wine lake.

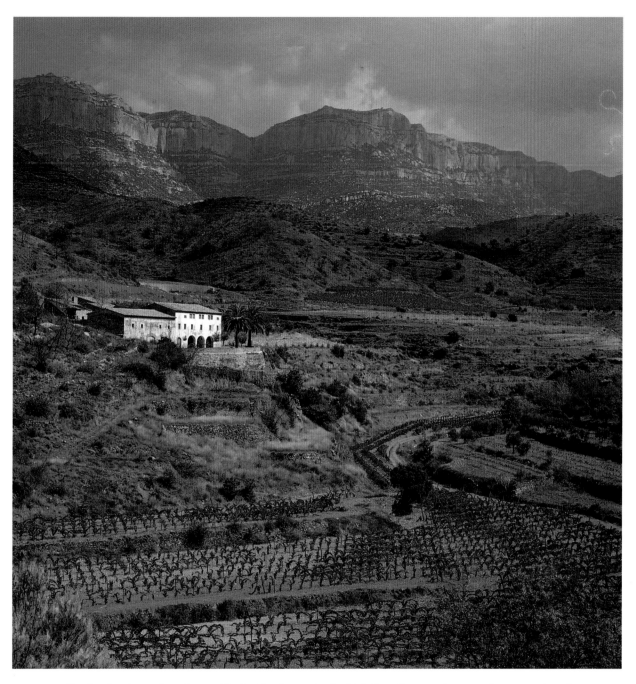

Spain also has a handsome array of indigenous grape varieties. Tempranillo produces some of the country's most admired red wines and is planted widely under several aliases. France's Grenache was probably imported as Garnacha, one of Spain's most planted varieties. The Monastrell vine so common in the

Typical landscape in the high Penedès. Vines trained on wires, rather than growing unsupported, are still the exception.

Levante is none other than the fashionable Mourvèdre. Two white grape varieties of undisputable class are Rueda's Verdejo and Galicia's Albariño , the former having been rescued quite recently from obscurity. There are many other possible candidates, with Rioja's Graciano and Galician Godello being obvious examples.

223

Spain's main wine problems lie not in the vineyard but in the cellar, or rather the cellars of many of the co-operatives that vinify so much of the country's wine and the blending halls of the big bottlers which have dominated the country's wine trade. Only since the early 1980s has a significant number of quality-conscious individual producers emerged, and even today it is extremely rare for wine producers to grow all their own grapes. Almost all of the top names in the top regions depend on local farmers to a greater or lesser degree.

Another common national characteristic is Spain's traditional fondness for American oak. Ever since the colonization of the Americas there has been a lively import trade in American oak, which has been used extensively in Spanish wine cellars for extended maturation of both reds and whites. This often resulted in red wines that were relatively light in colour and marked by a vanillin-sweet overlay, but more recently Spaniards have come to worship more deeply coloured, tannic reds (which has encouraged the spread of Cabernet Sauvignon vines imported from France).

THE SMARTEST REGIONS

Wine names likely to be encountered on labels outside Spain are listed here in my own highly subjective and debatable descending order of current prestige. The map on page 222 shows how they relate to each other geographically.

Red wines	White wines
Ribera del Duero	Galicia
Priorato	Rueda
Rioja	Somontano
Penedès	Conca de Barberá
Navarre	
Somontano	
Conca de Barberá	
Costers del Segre	
La Mancha	
Valdepeñas	
Jumilla	

But in one sense Spain's great gift to the world of wine is not a table wine at all but its incomparable late-fortified wine, a sure-fire appetite-whetter that has been much copied elsewhere, and often downgraded even in its homeland Jerez: sherry (see pages 233–5).

The Spaniards are also extremely enthusiastic consumers of sparkling wine, mostly their own answer to champagne, Cava, almost all of which is made in Penedès in north east Spain. For more details see page 228.

UNDERSTANDING LABELS

blanco, white.

bodega, wine cellar or winery.

clarete, unique light red somewhere between pink and full tinto, now outlawed by EU.

Crianza, the most basic level of wine that has been deliberately aged, usually for at least a year, in small oak barrels. Intermediate quality level between Joven (Sin, or without, Crianza) and a Reserva.

DO, Denominación de Origen, Spain's answer to France's AC. Most of Spain's best wines qualify for their local DO; Spain is not as anarchic as Italy.

DOCa (Denominación de Origen Calificada) is a theoretically superior category, to which Rioja was elevated in 1991.

espumoso, sparkling.

Gran Reserva, top of the range wines, aged for longer than a Reserva.

Joven, literally young, a wine that has not been aged like a Crianza or Reserva.

Reserva, special bottling aged for longer than a Crianza.

rosado, pink wine – quite popular in Spain.

seco, dry.

tinto, deep red (cf. clarete)

vendimia, vintage.

viña, vineyard.

vino, wine.

Vino de la Tierra, Spain's answer to France's Vin de Pays.

Vino de Mesa, table wine (as opposed to DO or Vino de la Tierra).

RIOJA

Rioja, in north east Spain, was for long Spain's only high-profile wine region, but in the 1980s it lost many friends by overpricing and underperforming (a pattern which shows signs of recurring in Ribera del Duero now that it has taken over the mantle of Spain's most revered red wine region).

Rioja has traditionally been American oak's most expressive ambassador. The wine is made from a blend of Tempranillo and Garnacha (Grenache) grapes aged for a considerable number of years in the sweet, vanilla-scented warmth of small American oak barrels. The result of this prolonged ageing was to allow a high proportion of phenolics (see page 73) to be left behind in the bottom of the barrel, making bottled Rioja a relatively pale, gentle, soft wine reminiscent of strawberries and stewed fruit. It was this flattering, easily appreciated character, and the fact that fully mature examples did not cost very much, that made Rioja the first non-French wine to woo British wine drinkers in the late 1970s.

Rioja producers have since been confused by the canny fickleness of modern wine consumers. Unimpressed by a succession of younger and younger, duller and duller, yet dearer and dearer wines, Rioja's old customers became disaffected. Seeing the recent success of Ribera del Duero's much deeper-coloured, more tannic and, often alcoholic, wines, many producers are trying to ape this style. A number of technically well-made red wines which have no American oak characteristics whatsoever are now made.

Some producers are deliberately leaning more heavily on the fuller bodied wines produced in Rioja Baja, the region's lower, Mediterranean-influenced vineyards, when constructing their blends. (Very, very few Riojas are estate bottlings, although Contino and Granja Remelluri provide notable exceptions.) Rioja Alta is in the mountainous far west of the region, so high and Atlantic-dominated that grapes are regularly picked in late October. That part of the region which falls within the province of Alava to the north is known as Rioja Alavesa and can produce some very fine wines on soils that are not too fertile.

Although Tempranillo and Garnacha dominate the vineyards of Rioja, Mazuelo (local name for Carignan) and the much more exciting but rare Graciano are also allowed for red Rioja. Viura, the rather tart Maccabéo of southern France, is the staple ingredient for white Rioja but white Grenache, Garnacha Blanca, sometimes adds ballast, and the small amounts of Malvasia still grown can add real character. Most white Rioja is either a squeaky-clean, cool-fermented thirst-quencher as pioneered by Marqués de Caceres or a very oaky, often heavy wine such as Viña Tondonia. There has been a limited amount of Cabernet Sauvignon grown in the region for more than a century, however, and the area devoted to international imported grape varieties, both red and white, is increasing every year, whether officially sanctioned or not.

Rioja's fortune was made in the late nineteenth century when Bordeaux wine producers, devastated by the twin scourges of mildew and phylloxera, brought their techniques over the Pyrenees. The oldest bodegas therefore tend to be centred on the small town of Haro in Rioja Alta which had good rail links, although Logroño in the centre of the region is its administrative capital. Firms such as La Rioja Alta, CVNE, Lopéz de Heredia, Muga, Marqués de Murrieta and Marqués de Riscal belong to what might be called the Rioja aristocracy, all with long-standing reputations – even if Marqués de Riscal's dipped in the 1980s. Other, newer, reputable producers include Martinez Bujanda, Bodegas Bretón and Bodegas Palacio, which has benefited from advice from international consultant winemaker Michel Rolland of Pomerol.

RIBERA DEL DUERO

This barren plateau between Valladolid and Aranda, self-styled roast lamb capital of the world, is currently producing Spain's most admired red wines, much to the amazement of the peasant farmers who have lived on the banks of the Duero river for generations. Downstream and over the Portuguese border their counterparts farm port grapes in what is known as the Douro valley. But whereas port has been famous for three centuries, the wines of the Ribera del Duero region are a relatively recent phenomenon.

Only at the end of the last century did one producer, now called Vega Sicilia, gain some sort of recognition for the intensity of its wines. And it was not until the mid-1980s that another, an agricultural machinist Alejandro Fernandez of Bodegas Pesquera, managed to establish the region as a viable source of high-quality, long-lived, concentrated, deep-coloured wines with relatively high acidity.

It is the altitude, about 650m (2000 ft), which keeps nights cool and extends the grape-ripening process until well into October, sometimes November in a particularly cool year. This means that the grapes are harvested with very high levels of colour and flavour.

Most of the vines grown are Tempranillo – which is so common here it is often called simply Tinto (red) Fino or Tinto del Pais – but Cabernet Sauvignon is encroaching and was indeed imported in 1864 at Vega Sicilia so is hardly an upstart. Rot rarely threatens in the crisp dry air of this tableland with its little plateaux and clumps of umbrella pines. Spring frosts, on the other hand, are a perennial danger. This is sweater country; it has nothing whatever in common with Spain's popular mediterranean image. Flocks of long-haired sheep are still driven along the main roads.

A high proportion of the locals have always made some wine for their own consumption. Almost all of those with some to spare used to sell it to the co-operative in Peñafiel in the centre of the region. But since Pesquera became a cult wine in Madrid and the United States, all manner of bodegas have sprouted up, some of them showing the same sort of vibrant potential as Pesquera but many of them clearly staffed by opportunists rather than skilled winemakers.

There is little correlation between price and quality within this DO but Dehesa de los Canónigos, Ismael Arroyo, Pago de Carraovejas, Ribeño and Viña Pedrosa are generally reliable. Watch out for Altair.

Thanks to a policy of maturing wine in small barrels for years longer than any other producer I know, Vega Sicilia produces a very individual and necessarily expensive style of Ribera del Duero (now supplemented by the faster maturing Alión wines). In 1995, for example, Vega Sicilia launched its finest bottling, Unico, from the 1970 vintage (as well as magnums of its legendary 1968). Even the lesser Valbuena bottlings were matured in wood for up to five years. Vega Sicilia clearly has impeccable cellar techniques in both the original winery and its newer Alión bodega.

Pesquera's modern style of bottling the wine after just three or four years in cask is more commonly adopted by the newcomers – for obvious financial reasons, but also probably because the livelier style of the wine finds more favour with modern drinkers. In 1995 Alejandro released his first bottlings from the high-altitude Roa de Duero vineyards, hewn out of rocky land east of Pesquera under the name Condado de Haza.

A young vineyard (of which there are many) in Ribera del Duero on high-altitude tableland with a high chalk content, which is good for drainage and therefore wine quality.

NORTH EAST SPAIN

NAVARRE

Navarre is effectively a north eastern extension of Rioja, and is centred on the great bullfighting town of Pamplona. Like Rioja it benefited from Bordeaux's misfortunes in the late nineteenth century. Like Rioja its vines tend to be grown by smallholders, many of whom sell their grapes to co-operatives (more dominant in Navarre than in Rioja), while its wines are bottled by one of the larger merchants.

For many years Garnacha was by far the most planted grape variety in the vineyards interspersed with the fruit and vegetable farms for which Navarre is so famous. Once temperature control systems were introduced into Navarre's wineries, Navarre was able to churn out vast quantities of clean, fruity, dry rosado so beloved by the Spaniards, thanks to the light-coloured Grenache's suitability for pink wine production. Chivite's Gran Fuedo is Spain's pink answer to Marqués de Caceres' white Rioja and is available in any self-respecting Spanish restaurant.

The Navarrans realize, however, that it would be unwise to base their future on demand for simple pink wine and, considerably aided by a local government research programme, they have been evaluating grape varieties such as Cabernet Sauvignon, Merlot, Chardonnay and, especially, Tempranillo, which is already making some fine, concentrated wines, typically aged in American oak. Palacio de la Vega and Ochoa can offer good value bottlings for early consumption while Chivite and Guelbenzu have some more ambitiously styled reds.

SOMONTANO

This small region right up in the southern foothills of the Pyrenees is one of Spain's most exciting, even if much of its produce tends to be fashioned in the image of international classics (including red and white burgundy) rather than demonstrating more inherently Spanish qualities. The innovative producer Viñas del Vero nevertheless has a fine, juicily vinified Tempranillo and a bottling which contains a good dollop of the local speciality, the bitter cherry-flavoured Moristel. This is another Spanish wine region worthy of international attention.

COSTERS DEL SEGRE

Costers del Segre, in the arid, harsh hinterland around the Catalonian city of Lerida, is almost a one-winery DO. Raimat is an extensive property converted to wine production over several decades by the owner of Codorníu, the giant Cava producer. Tempranillo and the usual gamut of international grape varieties are planted and the wines have so far been workmanlike rather than inspiring. The region does serve to illustrate, however, that you can irrigate in Spain, whatever European rules say, provided you have the right connections.

PENEDÈS

Penedès is the most important and most dynamic wine region in Catalonia, the proudly self-conscious, hard-working region in the north east of Spain. Its most obvious product is sparkling Cava (see opposite) but the region also produces a wide range of still wines of many colours and styles. Although Tempranillo is widely grown here, as throughout northern Spain (and called Ull de Llebre in Catalan), Miguel Torres was responsible for importing French (and German) varieties and techniques in the 1970s and has for long been the region's most famous producer, turning out an increasingly confident array of bottlings of imported and local varieties, typically blended together.

Jean León has also pioneered sophisticated Chardonnay and Cabernet Sauvignon, which have found a ready market in Spanish restaurants. Other producers who are more ambitious than most include Can Feixes, Cavas Hill, Molí Coloma, Mont Marçal, Puig & Roca and Ràfols dels Caus, but it is hard to describe a specifically Penedès style, so determinedly cosmopolitan is this corner of Spain.

CAVA

Cava is not the name of a Spanish wine region but of a type of wine, Spain's much-loved answer to champagne, a dry white wine made sparkling by the traditional method.

The great majority of Cava is made from grapes grown in Penedès, in one of a handful of giant bodegas based in and around the town of San Sadurni de Noya. Grapes used traditionally were extremely local: Macabeo (the Viura of Rioja), Parellada and the somewhat earthy-tasting Xarel-lo. The result of these varieties and the local relatively warm environment is that Cava, although usually technically very well made with a steady stream of tiny bubbles, often tends to seem aggressively frothy, and to taste oddly rustic and sometimes rather sweet, to those brought up on Chardonnay/Pinot fizz such as champagne (although Chardonnay plantings have been increasing steadily since being officially allowed in 1986).

This may well simply be a question of conditioning and certainly one of the top bottlings from the likes of Codorníu, Freixenet, Juvé y Camps, Marqués de Monistrol, Mestres, Nadal and, especially, Moët & Chandon's Torre del Gall should do what all the best sparkling wines do: refresh and stimulate.

The Spaniards buy so much Cava that the larger Cava houses Codorníu and Freixenet have managed to finance their own sparkling wineries in California (see page 273).

Although the Cava business was established on a commercial scale in Penedès as recently as the 1880s, by José Raventos, founder of the Codorníu dynasty, after a trip to France, it now produces about 130 million bottles of traditional method sparkling wine a year, roughly half as much as France's Champagne district.

CONCA DE BARBERÁ

Conca de Barberá is effectively a western extension of Penedès in which the winter temperatures fall even lower. The area grows many of the grapes used for Cava and is most famous as the home to the Chardonnay responsible for Miguel Torres's highly acclaimed rich, oak-aged Milmanda.

PRIORATO

If potential were measured in financial and human investment, then Priorato (Priorat in Catalan) is Spain's most exciting wine region. On dramatically steep slate terraces like those of Banyuls just over the French border, low-yielding Garnacha and Cariñena vines ooze tiny quantities of super-concentrated, tannic, occasionally over-alcoholic wine, sometimes well over 16 per cent.

Until recently Priorato was a relatively unsophisticated product but a recent influx of capital and enthusiasm, spearheaded by René Barbier, originally of the eponymous Penedès winery, has resulted in several estates, or 'clos' run by ambitious newcomers such as Alvaro Palacios. When these wines mature (in the next millenium) they may prove to be Spain's most thrilling wine sensations. Most of these new producers are adding some Cabernet, Merlot and/or Syrah to provoke yet more layers of flavour in these inky wines.

OTHER REGIONS

Other DO regions include Alella (for white wine), Ampurdán-Costa Brava, Campo de Borja, Calatayud, Cariñena, Terra Alta and Tarragona, historically famous for strong, sweet sacramental wine.

NORTH WEST SPAIN

In a nutshell: Spain's centre of fine
white wine production.
Grapes: Tempranillo (aka Tinto Fino
or Tinta de Toro) (RED),
many local specialities (WHITE)

The most important wine region of north west
Spain is Ribera del Duero – see page 226.

GALICIA

First-time visitors to Galicia in far north west
Spain are almost invariably amazed to find quite
how un-'Spanish' it is. The countryside is green,
lush and gentle, sometimes oddly reminiscent of
Ireland. Rain-bearing clouds speed in off the
Atlantic, which forces its way into the mainland along many-fingered estuaries called *rías*,
bringing an enviably rich variety of fish to an
originally Celtic population.

For years Galicia made slightly fizzy, bone
dry, light dry whites and reds rather similar to
the Vinho Verde made over the border in Portugal (see pages 236–7), which rarely escaped the
fish restaurants of the region itself. But since the
early 1980s Galicia has been increasingly valued
by Spaniards as their one source of fine, often
exotically scented, crisp white wines and the
top white Galician wines, usually made from
the Albariño grape, are some of the most sought
after in Spain.

Rias Baixas, right on the coast to which
Christopher Columbus returned with the news
that it did not represent the end of the world, is
the most famous region in which Albariño
seems to thrive and the locals swear it must be
related to Riesling, so pure is its aroma and surprising its ability to age in bottle. Morgadio,
Quinta de Couselo, Pazo de Barrantes and
Granxa Fillaboa are some of the most admired
producers, and Adegas das Eiras and Agro de
Bazán have pioneered barrel fermentation,

which may not be ideal for these delicate wines.

Ribeiro is slightly further inland and is most
like Portugal's Vinho Verde in that it is
upstream along the same river (the Miño in
Spanish), depends heavily on Treixadura vines,
but also makes substantial quantities of light,
tart, deep-coloured reds made from a special
red-fleshed strain of Garnacha, Garnacha Tintorera, for strictly local consumption – often,
curiously, in white porcelain bowls. Emilio Rojo
and Vilerma make some fine wines here.

Even further inland is **Valdeorras**, whose
best, light dry whites are flavoured by the local
Godello grape, most successfully by the likes
of Senén Guitián, Godeval and Joaquin
Rebolledo. The steep, inhospitable vineyards of
Valdeorras can also produce some quite juicy
light reds, mainly from Mencía, which may be a
fruity relative of Cabernet Franc.

RUEDA

Rueda is Spain's most promising and most versatile white wine region, its produce having rather
more body and international appeal than that
of Galicia. On the same high plateau as Ribera
del Duero, Rueda has its own highly successful
grape variety, Verdejo, whose crisp nuttiness
hints at its previous existence in a sherry-like
wine. It now makes very modern, aromatic
unfortied table wines and the region's success
in this field was much helped by the importation of Sauvignon Blanc vines by Marqués de
Riscal of Rioja in the 1970s. Other individual
producers experimenting with serious techniques such as barrel fermentation include
Angel Lorenzo Cachazo, Marqués de Griñon
(whose red wines are produced round Toledo
south of Madrid, in Rioja and also in Ribera del
Duero in a joint venture with Berberana) and
Palacio de Bornos. The region, with its cool climate and good acreage of fashionable Sauvignon

vines has also attracted flying winemakers such as the Lurton brothers of Bordeaux.

Typical vineyards in the Rias Baixas district of Galicia, in the rain-washed far north of Spain, with vines raised high off the ground on pergolas made of the local granite to keep rot at bay.

with this DO, whose wines, mostly red, are like slightly coarser versions of Ribero del Duero. In **El Bierzo**, just east of Valdeorras, José Luis Prada is reviving the local Mencía,

OTHER REGIONS

The vineyards of **Toro** lie just west of Rueda and are planted mostly with the local variant on Tempranillo, Tinta de Toro. Few producers other than Bodegas Fariña make much effort

while to the south some fine red is made from the local Prieto Picudo. The rosés of **Cigales** are particularly valued, while relatively tough non-DO reds are produced in the province of León.

CENTRAL AND SOUTHERN SPAIN

This vast and important wine production centre is a sleeping giant in the process of being awoken by all sorts of outside winemaking influences and preferences. It makes some crisp cheap whites and some heady reds.

LA MANCHA, VALDEPEÑAS AND ENVIRONS

The majority of Spain's vineyards lie on the tableland around the capital Madrid, particularly on the plains of La Mancha, which provide much of the country's basic Vino da Mesa and raw ingredients for the Brandy de Jerez drunk in such quantities by the Spaniards. Much of this is relatively characterless dry white made from the Airén grape, so common here – and planted at such a low vine density in these extremely arid, non-irrigated vineyards – that its total acreage is greater than that of any other single grape variety in the world. La Mancha itself is Europe's largest single demarcated 'quality' region (i.e. DO), encompassing 160 000 ha (400 000 acres), although little of its wine is seriously superior.

This is inhospitable country, whose name is derived from Manxa or 'parched earth', as it was known by the Moors. In summer it is boiling hot and there is hardly enough rain to sustain a crop. In winter it can be freezing cold for weeks at a time, with frequent frosts. The one advantage of this dry climate is that vine diseases are practically unknown, so no expensive spraying is required. Most of the vines are grown as low bushes. This is minimalist vine-growing.

Since the mid-1980s modern winemaking has gradually invaded La Mancha, and in particular temperature controls for fermentations, which have resulted in fresh, crisp, inexpensive, if fairly characterless dry whites.

Such vineyards not planted to Airén tend to be planted with Cencibel, the local name for the ubiquitous Spanish red Tempranillo. This is a speciality of Valdepeñas, a southern enclave within La Mancha which is a source of some delightfully keenly priced, juicy, sometimes carefully aged reds. So dense is the colour of much of the Tempranillo harvested from the low-yielding vines of La Mancha and Valdepeñas that the wines have traditionally been lightened by adding surplus white grapes.

As evidence that even the most workaday wine region can today attract ambitious outside investment, La Mancha now has at least two top quality estates, both of them at altitudes of almost 1000 m (3000 ft). Baronia and Manuel Manzaneque are, perhaps inevitably, introducing international grape varieties and being rewarded with rapturous acclaim in Madrid.

Outside the denominated zone of Mentridá, famous only for the strength of its mainly co-operative-made reds, is the dynamic red wine-making estate of Marqués de Griñon, which is making some of Spain's most respectable Cabernet Sauvignon and promising Syrah.

THE MEDITERRANEAN COAST

The Levante has traditionally produced wine too sweet, sickly and strong to appeal to the serious wine drinker but all this is changing as the Monastrell is re-evaluated (largely in the light of its French counterpart Mourvèdre's international stardom). Salvador Poveda in Alicante, Bodegas Piqueras in Almansa and Agapito Rico in non-denominated Murcia (who blends in a little Merlot to add breeding) have pioneered these rich but well-balanced, inexpensive Spanish reds. Dry Muscats are made although sweet Moscatel is still popular. Names of the local DOs are **Alicante**, **Almansa**, **Jumilla**, **Utiel Requena** and **Valencia**, named after the port on which the wine industry is centred.

SHERRY

In a nutshell: The world's most neglected wine treasure.
Grape: Palomino

Many modern wine drinkers will look at this section and wonder why on earth I think it worthwhile devoting three whole pages to such a dinosaur of a wine as sherry. The answer is plain to anyone who has tried a good quality version. The trouble is that most people have not. They tend to have been put off by the tired, very undistinguished syrupy stuff that lurks in the bottom of sherry bottles and decanters all over the world.

So fine, varied and noble a wine is sherry – and so intriguingly complicated is it to make – that replicating sherry, just like imitating a top quality champagne, is a common daydream for many of the more talented winemakers in the world.

There are two basic styles of proper sherry, neither of which bear any relation to the sweetened-up popular brands. **Fino** sherry and the similar **Manzanilla** are very pale, delicate, prancing, palate-reviving thoroughbreds that are only about 15.5 per cent alcohol, bone dry and tingling with life and zest. These sorts of sherry are as fragile as an unfortified table wine and rapidly lose their appeal if kept in an opened bottle for longer than a few days. They should be drunk well chilled, and their life can be prolonged by keep-ing them in ever smaller bottles in the refrigerator.

The other major style of sherry is dark, nutty and can thrill the palate with its subtle shadings of mahogany and nuances that are the direct and delicious results of extended ageing in oak. Dry **Amontillado** and, even deeper, Dry **Oloroso** seem tailor-made for staving off winter chills. These names are also given to sweetened, darkened commercial blends of young wines, but the best owe their character more nobly to time, and top quality base wines. Sweet sherry can also delight, but also has to be much older than the heavily advertised **Cream** sherries usually are. (**Pale Cream** is just Cream with the colour taken out.)

The sherry region, the only one that is allowed to use the word sherry in Europe, is one of the hottest fine wine regions in the world, just a short distance from the coast of North Africa in the south of Spain's most southern province, Andalucía. It takes its name from the principal sherry town Jerez (pronounced 'Hereth'), characterized by its brilliant white bodegas, dusty jacaranda-lined avenues and *mañana* culture.

It is just as well that the Jerezanos are not impatient people because the sherry-making process is prolonged. Ordinary sherry-like wine can be made by blending relatively young ingredients, but true, intense, subtle sherry demands decades (and yet, thanks to its current unfashionable status, its price rarely reflects its age).

SHERRY-STYLE WINES OUTSIDE SPAIN

Flor-influenced wines are made in the Jura as vin jaune, and to an even more limited extent in Gaillac. Most countries sell fortified local wines in various styles labelled as though they were sherry but they can be rather stale, raisiny, distinctly inferior products. Both Australia and South Africa, however, have a sound tradition of producing the full range of sherry styles with some competence. Cyprus has been making cheap sherryish wines for decades, as well as supplying much of the dubious base grape concentrate for UK-reconstituted stuff called British sherry (see page 305), but the winemaking culture is not nearly so demanding here.

The vineyards are on dazzling, white undulating countryside between Jerez and the two sherry ports of Sanlucar de Barrameda and Puerto de Santa Maria, with the most valued being predominantly chalky and able to dripfeed the vines with what little rain falls each year. Palomino is the light-skinned sherry grape and a certain amount of slightly flabby, full bodied, dry white table wine is made from it but, as still Coteaux Champenois demonstrates champagne's worth (see page 172), it serves mainly to demonstrate that the Jerez vineyards are designed to produce sherry.

These are some of the world's hottest vineyards and so pressing stations tend to be close by (yet another parallel with Champagne), with base wines transported to the major wineries for transformation into the final product, the first stage of which is to fortify, or add neutral grape spirit to, freshly fermented, clarified wine.

But the making of Fino sherry requires more than the chalky albariza soils of Jerez and the Palomino grape. Fino owes its special tangy character to a strange sort of yeast called *flor*, indigenous to the Jerez region, which grows a bread-like film on the surface of the wine. To give it surface to work on, and to sustain its effect and its protection against oxidation, winemakers fill the barrels, or butts, in which sherry has always been matured only about five-sixths full, and add younger wine at regular intervals so as to give the yeast something new to feed on. Fino style wines matured in the bodegas of Sanlucar rather than in the warmer, drier climate of inland Jerez are called Manzanilla and can taste even tangier. It is easy

SOUTHERN SPAIN'S OTHER SPECIALITIES

*The **Montilla-Moriles** region east of Jerez doesn't benefit from Atlantic cooling and therefore has a less satisfactory relationship with the flor yeast. The result is that Montilla wines are very similar to sherry (in fact Amontillado means 'in the style of Montilla') but lack some of the finesse. Some even looser imitations of sherry are made to the west of Jerez in the region of **Condado de Huelva**. For wine lovers, the busy Costa del Sol town of **Málaga** is associated with a delicious, dark, raisiny, treacly fortified wine of the same name, of which Scholtz Hermanos produce the lion's share.*

to persuade oneself that there is a whiff of ozone and salt in these lovely wines, so light they are drunk with the tapas and seafood of the region as though they were table wines.

Flor is very particular, however, and grows only on wines with an alcohol content of around 15.5 per cent. The finest, most elegant base wines are therefore fortified to exactly that strength, whereas more alcohol is added to the rather more full bodied, perhaps slightly coarser wines that are destined to become darker, nuttier sherries, sometimes sweetened with specially concentrated Pedro Ximénez (PX) grapes.

The constant replenishment of Fino and Manzanilla barrels has led to another unique feature of sherry production that is known rather technically as fractional blending or, in Spanish, the *solera* system. This is the sherry producers' clever way of maintaining a consistent blend year in, year out. With very few exceptions, sherry is not a vintage-dated wine but the blended product of a system whereby a certain proportion of old wine is taken out of a blending stage and replaced by the same amount of younger wine. The more blending stages there are to a system, and the older the system, the more subtle the wine, and in theory at least, every bottle of sherry should contain some fraction, however tiny, of wine as old as the blending system itself – which may in some cases be more than a century. Sherry is surely one of the most undervalued wines made today.

Most of the large sherry producers make small quantities of top quality wines, but the following rules should help pick out the real

Jerez: sherry sales would revive if more people visited this beautiful bit of Andalucía.

sherries from the more commercially expedient, sweetened-up blends.

• Most bottles labelled Dry Amontillado and Dry Oloroso are trustworthy.

• Look for Fino and Manzanilla at alcoholic strengths as low as possible. Those at 15.5 per cent will be as the Spaniards drink them, more like table wines than fortified wines.

• Quiz your retailer or waiter about the date of shipment of any Fino or Manzanilla, and avoid any bottle that has obviously been open for more than a few days. These wines do not improve in bottle.

• Sherries labelled Almacenista are from special private stockholders and are usually well worth the price premium for their extra character.

PORTUGAL

In a nutshell: The home of port,
madeira and a host of increasingly modern,
often bargain, table wines.
Grapes: Rich variety of local specialities
still being researched

Portugal's advantage in wine terms, its isolation which has kept its inheritance of indigenous vine varieties intact and virtually unaffected by Chardonnay- and Cabernet-mania, is also its disadvantage. The Portuguese have had this strange habit of making wines to suit the palates of other Portuguese rather than making the sort of fruity, juicy-yet-structured wines that appeal to the majority of the world's wine consumers. The wines that are most respected within Portugal are incredibly tough reds that have typically spent rather too long in storage before being bottled, and some slightly tired whites whose unfamiliar flavours may strike some outsiders as slightly rank.

In fact Portugal has some first-class raw materials and is gradually amassing the will and skill with which to transform them into exportable wines. There seems to me to be little correlation, however, between the country's denominated regions (DOCs) and inherent wine quality. Dão is one of the traditionally most respected wine regions, for example, but I have found infinitely more pleasure in bottles from much more obscure corners of this essentially Atlantic-influenced country (where vines are grown almost everywhere).

Rainfall varies enormously according to proximity to the coast. The Vinho Verde region in the far north west, famous for light, dry whites, for example, is one of the wine world's wettest, while the Douro valley to its immediate south east is one of the driest during the crucial growing season. This extraordinarily arid, harsh valley is responsible for Portugal's second greatest gift to the wine world, port, the sweetest, strongest, darkest wine known to man and his cranium (see page 240). Its most significant contribution of course is cork, of which it is by far the world's most important source.

Wine production has been largely in the grip of co-operatives which have only slowly been rejuvenating their ideas and techniques. The picture is further confused by the fact that some of the DOCs – Carcavelos for example – reflect Portugal's rich wine exporting history more than modern reality.

The main wine regions follow, roughly from north west to south east.

VINHO VERDE

The verde or 'green' in Vinho Verde (pronounced something like 'Vino verge') refers not to the colour of the wine but to its youth. The red and white Vinho Verde wines produced in this rainwashed region just south of the Minho river which forms the border with Spain are all designed to be drunk when still young and fresh. High acidity and more than a trace of post-fermentation fizz are their hallmark. They bear a very strong resemblance to the Rias Baixas

---

UNDERSTANDING LABELS

adega, winery or cellar.
branco, white.
colheita, vintage.
DOC, Denominação de Origem Controlada, Portugal's equivalent of France's Appellation Contrôlée system, but a less sure guide to the country's most user-friendly wines.
garrafeira, supposedly superior, well-aged wines.
IPR, Indicação de Proveniencia Regulamentada, Portugal's answer to France's VDQS.
quinta, farm or wine estate.
Vinho Regional, like Vin de Pays.

wines made just over the river in Spain's Galicia – indeed the same aristocratic white grape variety, here spelt Alvarinho, is the most admired. Some of the more commercial bottlings are deliberately sweetened and slightly carbonated, but the likes of Palacio de Brejoeira bottle a wine that a local would recognize. (The locals drink twice as much red as white but hardly any is exported, with good reason.)

DOURO

The dramatic Douro valley, for long dedicated almost entirely to port production, is beginning to be a significant producer of robust, characterful red table wines with some of the tannins which distinguish vintage port. To some port producers such wines are heresy but to quality-conscious wine drinkers they are intriguingly satisfying, with a concentration of flavour many winemakers elsewhere would kill for. Port producer Ferreira's Barca Velha was the prototype and still commands very high prices, but an exciting range of much cheaper dense crimson table wines is now available from the likes of Duas Quintas, Quinta do Cotto Grande Escolha, Quinta da Gaivosa, Quinta de la Rosa, Redoma and Sogrape (see Bairrada below).

DÃO

This large red and white wine region south of the Douro valley has been well and truly strangled by old-fashioned winemaking methods, particularly long maceration with bitter stalks and unwisely prolonged ageing before bottling so that most wines taste hard rather than fruity. The finest port grape, Touriga Nacional, should be a significant ingredient in any red and Tempranillo, known as Tinta Roriz or Aragonez elsewhere, is also grown – although a host of other, less inspired varieties are allowed. White Dão has tended to be an even more anachronistic product, even if the Encruzado grape used in most blends can be quite crisp and fragrant. Dão will surely realize its potential before too long.

BAIRRADA

Unusually for a Portuguese wine zone, this mixed farming region between Dão and the coast is dominated by a single grape, the small, thick-skinned Baga, which would result in relatively tannic wines even if all Bairrada wineries were equipped with destemmers. As it is, many of the all-important co-operatives still make tougher wines than necessary, although it is (just) thinkable that one day the concentrated reds of Bairrada might be as popular outside Portugal as they were in early seventeenth-century London. Luis Pato makes better wines than most and the region is in the process of revitalization. Some interesting dry whites and sparkling wines are also being made in Bairrada.

The famous Palace Hotel on the edge of Bairrada bottles its own blends of wines bought in Bairrada and Dão which are renowned as some of Portugal's best, but perhaps the region's most famous wine is Sogrape's blended Mateus Rosé which is produced at a giant winery within Bairrada. Mateus's mid-twentieth-century success supposedly owed much to the fact that it was neither sweet nor dry, white nor red, still nor sparkling. The Guedes family who developed Mateus have sensibly been branching out into more distinctive wines designed to introduce wine drinkers all over the world to some of the flavours and styles Portugal has to offer.

COLARES

This tiny DOC is more famous for its exceptional situation, a narrow strip of sand on the windy Atlantic coast not far from Lisbon, than for the quality of its wines. Since phylloxera (see page 96) cannot live in sand, the Ramisco vine responsible for red Colares (yet another tannic, tart Portuguese red) is possibly the only vine variety never to have been grafted on to phylloxera-resistant American vine roots. Here the modern wine drinker's interest in Colares may end. Some full bodied white Colares is made from Malvasia grapes.

BUCELAS

Bucelas or Bucellas is a name often found on nineteenth-century decanter and bin labels in Britain, showing just how popular this 'Portuguese hock' was then. The wine is a potentially scented dry white based on Arinto grapes. It is made in relatively small quantity but some newish producers are trying hard, perhaps encouraged by the proximity of the capital Lisbon, and its thirsty populace.

RIBATEJO

This large fruit- and vegetable-growing region upstream of Lisbon, whose name means 'the banks of the river Tagus', is Portugal's most important source of basic blending wine (together with the Oeste or Estremadura region between it and the Atlantic). Much of the wine produced here is relatively light, but that can be a blessing relative to some of Portugal's more austere wine styles. Co-operatives rule the roost, but sometimes benevolently, as witness keenly priced reds carrying names such as Arruda, Almeirim, Cartuxo and Santarém.

SETÚBAL/PALMELA/ARRÁBIDA

The Setúbal peninsula south of Lisbon and the two wine zones that flank it, Palmela and Arrábida, are the sources of some of Portugal's

LEFT *Grapes for Tinta da Anfora being picked in the useful Alentejo region.* OPPOSITE *Typical Portuguese tiles on a house near the Setúbal peninsula.*

most exportable and exported table wines. Setúbal or Moscatel de Setúbal (pronounced 'Shtooble') is a noble, historic copper-coloured Muscat to which grape spirit is added before ageing so that it tastes like a cross between a southern French Muscat de Beaumes-de-Venise and a tawny port. Of more general interest, though, is the wide range of dry red and white wines made in Azeitão in Arrábida. José Maria da Fonseca Successores is a family firm which bottles blended table wines such as Periquita and Quinta de Camarate while J. M. da Fonseca Internacional is most famous as the bottler of Lancers, Mateus's big pink rival. Australian Peter Bright has done much to put this wine-making base on the map, notably with the full, dry Muscat João Pires from J. P. Vinhos.

ALENTEJO

The warm, dry Alentejo region in the south east is probably the country's most promising source of full bodied, deep-coloured, accessible table wine. Another Australian, David Baverstock, who tired of making nothing but port in the Douro, is exporting increasingly interesting wines from the large Esporão property. Co-operatives such as Borba, Granja, Redondo, Reguengos de Monsaraz and Vidigueira are some of Portugal's most energetic. But there are many exciting individual estates such as Mouchão and Quinta do Carmo (part-owned by the Rothschilds of Château Lafite), and special bottlings such as Peter Bright's Tinta da Anfora. Prices here are still reasonable and this is certainly one of the most promising wine regions in the world. Even whites can be interesting.

REST OF PORTUGAL

Many other parts of the country apparently have the ability to produce sound wine at a good price – Tras-os-Montes and Beiras to name just two. It is worth noting that retailer reputation can often be a sounder clue to quality than producer geography.

PORT

In a nutshell: Deep, sweet, strong wine, mostly very consistently made in many different styles.

Grapes: *Touriga Nacional and many others* (RED)

Although there are wines made outside Portugal to taste like port (see below), there is nowhere in the wine world at all like the Douro valley in northern Portugal, the home of port. The peasant farmers who inhabit this wild, silent valley in which only the vine will grow, rely for their livelihood almost entirely on the port shippers, the un-Portuguese likes of Cockburn, Croft, Dow, Graham, Sandeman, Taylor and Warre, based half a day's drive downstream in Oporto – or rather in lodges on the quayside of Vila Nova de Gaia across the river from it. Ever since the late seventeenth century when British merchants scoured friendly Portugal for goods that would replace heavily taxed items from France, the commercial end of the port wine trade has been in predominantly British hands, which has made for an even more delicate relationship between growers and bottlers than in most wine regions.

The steep, rocky, necessarily terraced vineyards of the Douro were long since mapped according to the concentration of the wine they are able to produce, and grape payments decided accordingly. The best port country is about 75 miles upstream of Oporto, well away from the rainy coast. Some very promising vineyards are not that far downstream of the point at which the Duero of Spain (see page 226) becomes the Douro of Portugal. The land is so inhospitable here, with only a dusting of topsoil, that many a vine sends it roots yards down into deep fissures in the schist, apparently the only possible route to the water necessary for growth.

It has taken the port producers much longer than most to understand, or even just identify the 80-plus vine varieties responsible for their amazingly concentrated, deep-coloured product. But then port, like sherry, champagne and madeira, is essentially a blended wine and many of the greatest ports I have ever tasted were made decades before the term 'varietal' was even coined. Touriga Nacional is generally regarded as the top quality port vine, supplemented with Tinta Barroca, Touriga Francesa, Tinta Cão and Tinta Roriz.

The aim of the port producer is to make a wine that is as deeply coloured and sweet as possible. To preserve the grapes' natural sweetness, spirit is added at quite an early point in the fermentation process to stun the yeasts, which means that colour and tannin must be extracted as fast as possible. The Douro valley is one of the very few wine regions where foot treading is still practised, to the delight of photographers and visitors from tamer wine regions, but machinery usually does the job.

The most ordinary port goes into the shippers' basic blends, sometimes called wood ports

NON-PORTUGUESE PORT-STYLE WINES

Many winemakers in climates as hot at the Douro valley try their hand at making dark, sweet fortified wines in the image of port – notably in Australia, but also in South Africa and California.

Very few producers have any substantial plantings of the port vine varieties however (although this is slowly changing). Any wine labelled Tawny is likely to be the product of long ageing in cask while a Ruby is likely to have been bottled relatively young. Perhaps the wines most like port are Banyuls and Maury made in Roussillon, southern France (see page 201).

as they are not expected to age in bottle (although many of them nowadays are aged in cement or stainless steel rather than barrels). A **ruby** port is a young port bottled after two or three years in bulk. The great majority of port sold today, and certainly all the advertised brands, is this vigorous, juicy stuff. (If it carries the words **late bottled vintage** or **LBV** it will be a ruby from a single year bottled after four to six years' ageing.)

A cheap **tawny** port is ruby's commercial cousin, from lesser vineyards or made lighter and browner by blending in some **white** port, the result of applying port production techniques to the Douro's minority of white grapes. Real **aged tawny** owes its alluring light, shaded, jewel-like tawny colour to extended ageing in wood, for 10, 20, 30 or over 40 years, according to the label. Some of my most hedonistic port-drinking experiences have been with 20-year-old ports, which taste as good served chilled in the heat of a Douro summer as they do next to the fireside in a British winter. This is the style drunk most regularly by the port shippers. Some

---

MADEIRA

In a nutshell: *Exceptionally long-lived, tangy, fortified wines.*
Grapes: *A sorry tale*

Madeira is a volcanic island in the middle of the Atlantic, a wine, and a miracle. Good quality madeira (which, alas, can cost at least as much as classed growth bordeaux) is the world's longest-living wine. Its high alcohol and natural acidity and the fact that it has been virtually baked during the production process mean that it is indestructible, whether in a wooden cask or glass demijohn, maturing under the rafters of a lodge in Funchal or in a bottle at home, however long ago it was opened. Madeira is the only wine that can be kept in a decanter on a sideboard for months without deteriorating. I also reckon that this unique fortified wine also has the strange property of protecting the drinker, well this drinker anyway, from a hangover (cf. port).

The trouble is that most of the madeira produced today is rather ordinary – very good for cooking and adding richness to meat reductions, but hardly fine enough to savour by the thimbleful. This is partly because so many of the noble grape varieties Sercial, Verdelho, Bual and Malvasia (for Malmsey) were replaced by the easier to grow, much more prolific but coarser Tinta Negra Mole. A shortcut to good quality madeira is to look for one of the four noble varieties on the label.

Sweeter madeira is made very much like port in that it is fortified half-way through fermentation while drier styles, like sherry, are fermented fully to dryness before grape spirit is added. But madeira's real distinction is that the young wine is subjected to extreme heat, which is where its deep caramel colour comes from.

UNDERSTANDING MADEIRA LABELS

Bual / Boal, rich, dark, sweet madeira that ages well but can be drunk younger than Verdelho and, especially, Sercial. Drink with or after cheese. Lesser imitations made from Tinta Negra Mole are labelled Medium Sweet.
Malmsey, the sweetest, darkest madeira, for drinking after a meal. Lesser versions are labelled Sweet or Rich.
Sercial, the driest style of madeira which can make an extremely fine aperitif but demands many decades of ageing before it reaches its full potential. Lesser versions are labelled Dry.
Solera, madeira that is the produce of gradual, fractional blending like sherry (see page 233) in an ageing system that began in the year specified. (A madeira labelled Solera 1870 comes from an ageing system established in 1870.)
Verdelho, the second lightest, driest madeira with a delicious tangy nuttiness. Lesser versions are labelled Medium Dry.
Vintage madeira. A madeira labelled, say, 1944 without any mention of the word Solera should contain nothing but wine harvested in 1944.

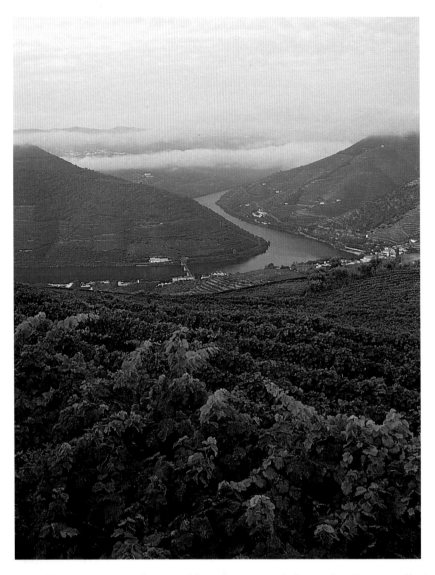

The Douro valley above Pinhão in summer (left), and in autumn (opposite). Only recently has there been systematic research into the best way to design vineyards in this wild, underpopulated region, which comes alive only during the grape harvest in September.

Such wines, the produce of a single, superior year, generally about every third year, depending on the quality of the wine and state of the market, have to be made from the Douro valley's finest, most concentrated, most tannic produce, to benefit from all those years in bottle (during which they develop a monstrous sediment, known as 'throwing a crust'). Such wines have to be decanted. These wines, called simply by the shipper's name and year, as in Fonseca 1992, represent only about one per cent of the Douro valley's output. Poor man's vintage port is **single quinta vintage** port which is the produce of a single wine farm, typically but not exclusively one owned by a shipper, such as Graham's Quinta dos Malvedos, from a year not 'declared' as a vintage by that shipper. It offers a way of experiencing the style of vintage port without having to pay quite so much or wait quite so long.

Then there are some intermediate styles. **Crusted** port is a blend of different years bottled early in a specified year without filtration so that, like vintage port, it matures in bottle and has a heavy sediment from which it should be decanted (see page 25).

Portuguese port shippers (they do exist and the likes of Ferreira, Nieeport [Dutch in origin] and Quinta do Noval make some superb wines) age a blend of tawny ports from a single vintage for many years in wood to produce **colheita** ports.

All these ports are matured in bulk before bottling rather than being expected to mature, like fine table wine, in the bottle in which you buy them.

The style of port traded in the auction room, however, and talked about most, is **vintage**, a long-lived wine that is relatively easy to produce because it is bottled after two or three years in cask and then left to mature in consumers' own cellars for decade after decade.

GERMANY

In a nutshell: Some of the world's finest,
lightest, longest-living whites.
Grapes: Riesling, Riesling-like crossings,
Pinots and their derivatives.

The German wine business is in turmoil, thank goodness. Throughout the 1970s and 1980s it prided itself on its equipment and administration – a combination unrivalled else-where in the world – but somewhere along the line lost sight of the taste of the wine itself. Today it is, somewhat painfully, rediscovering what makes it so special.

The well-intentioned German Wine Law of 1971 neatly assigned a number to every batch of wine, and allowed all but a tiny minority of them to call themselves 'quality wine', or Qual-itätswein, the same rank as France's Appellation

UNDERSTANDING LABELS

German labels are some of the world's most confusing. Quite apart from the usual advice that producer is crucial and vintage year (see page 309) can affect quality, look for (1) quality level, (2) grape variety and (3) region.
1 In ascending order of natural grape ripeness: Tafelwein, Landwein, QbA, Kabinett, Spätlese, Auslese, BA and TBA (see below).
2 Most German wines are made from single grape varieties, specified on the label. For more details see, in declining order of importance within Germany's vineyards overall, Müller-Thurgau, Riesling, Silvaner, Kerner, Spätburgunder (Pinot Noir), Portugieser, Scheurebe, Bacchus, Faberrebe, Morio-Muskat and so on. Riesling, Scheurebe and Silvaner in Franken tend to be the best bets, although some fine dryish Grauburgunder (Pinot Gris) and Weissburgunder (Pinot Blanc) is also produced.
3 Labels on all but the most basic German wines should carry the name of one of the wine regions (listed on the following pages), which may be a lot more helpful than the often very complicated name of the wine itself. Like burgundies, German wines tend to be named with a combination of village and vineyard name, although in the case of German a possessive 'er' is usually added to the village name, as in Bernkasteler Schlossberg for the Schlossberg vineyard in the Bernkastel

district. The Germans have made life even more difficult for consumers than it was already by giving vast zones called a Grosslage a familiar name so that it is extremely difficult even for a professional like me to remember whether, for example, Badstube is a Grosslage zone or a small, single vineyard or Einzellage. Some of the most famous Grosslagen are Zeller Schwarze Katz, Kröver Nacktarsch, Bernkasteler Badstube, Bernkasteler Kurfürstlay, Piesporter Michelsberg, Klüsserather St Michael, Wiltinger Scharzberg, Niersteiner Gutes Domtal and Oppenheimer Krötenbrunnen – how on earth is the poor wine drinker to distinguish these from the genuine produce of a single site?

Auslese, naturally fully ripe grapes produce what is usually a long-living medium sweet wine, although dry, very alcoholic Auslesen are sometimes made.
Beerenauslese (BA), very sweet rarities usually sold at a very high price.
Deutschertafelwein, the most basic sort of German wine constituting less than five per cent of an average crop. Although see also Tafelwein.
Eiswein, Ice wine, which often fetches more than Beerenauslese. See page 89 for details of how it is made.
Gutsabfüllung, estate bottled.
halbtrocken, half dry, wines which taste medium dry.

Contrôlée élite. More disastrously, it ordained that wine quality could be measured with one simple device, the refractometer with which vine-growers check the sugar content of their grapes. To qualify as a higher grade, or Prädikat, of wine (see panel), the grape juice simply had to be sweeter. The result was a steady invasion of German vineyards by vine varieties specially bred to provide super-ripe grapes (which tend to produce wines which taste as bland as giant, prize-winning vegetables). The major casualty was the difficult-to-ripen Riesling vine, Germany's greatest asset.

Yields, for long unregulated (in sharp contrast to France and Italy), grew so that such flavour as grapes could be persuaded to develop in a climate as cool as Germany's was all too often virtually undetectable in a sea of inexpensive, low-alcohol, medium dry white shipped abroad at ludicrous prices and sold as innocuous, but hardly vinous, blends labelled Liebfraumilch, Niersteiner Gutes Domtal, Piesporter Michelsberg, and so on.

Meanwhile, a small band of obstinately quality-minded estates continued to provide evidence of the miracles that can be achieved

---

Kabinett, the least ripe of the QmP categories. Such wines can make lovely light bodied dryish aperitifs.

Landwein, Germany's answer to France's Vins de Pays. Still embryonic as a serious category but arguably the entire QbA category should be demoted to Landwein status.

Liebfraumilch, strictly a creation for export markets. In practice almost any medium dry, vaguely aromatic blend can qualify as Liebfraumilch, which is traded savagely as a commodity.

Qualitätswein is sometimes used as an abbreviation for QbA.

Qualitätswein bestimmter Anbaugebiet (QbA), Germany's shame. By far the dominant quality (*sic*) category, this includes all Liebfraumilch and the basic Grosslage blends sweetened up with added grape concentrate (Süssreserve). The category also includes, however, some perfectly creditable wines from top producers who decided they needed chaptalization (which is outlawed for QmP wines) to make them balanced.

Qualitätswein mit Prädikat (QmP), the best of Germany, truly its higher-quality wines which qualify for one of the following 'predicates', in ascending order of natural grape ripeness: Kabinett, Spätlese, Auslese, BA and TBA. Much of the meat of German Wine Law is laying down minimum grape ripeness levels (measured by a system called degrees Oechsle) for each combination of predicate, vine variety and region.

Sekt, sparkling wine, usually made from imported (often Italian) wine rather than the products of German vineyards.

Spätlese means literally 'late harvest'. This category includes many fine, concentrated wines from bone dry (trocken) to medium dry.

Tafelwein, basic table wine which may not even be made entirely from German wine – in fact these 'European blends' are often made up of cheap dry white from Spain or Italy, 'Germanized' by a dollop of a particularly aromatic German wine and sweetened by added grape concentrate.

trocken means 'dry' and any wine so labelled is designed to be drunk with food. It is also likely to be more alcoholic than wine not labelled trocken because the grape sugar has been fermented into alcohol. These wines are particularly popular in Germany and increasingly so abroad.

Trockenbeerenauslese (TBA) (literally 'dried grapes that were late-picked', a reference to the shrivelling effect of botrytis or extreme heat), the sweetest, richest most luscious sort of QmP wine, produced in tiny quantities and usually sold for fabulous prices. Noble rot (Edelfäule) is usually needed to concentrate grape sugars sufficiently to meet the required ripeness levels – although some grape varieties (such as Ortega and Optima) have been specifically bred to ripen spectacularly, if not always sumptuously.

Winzergenossenschaft, Winzerverein, two common names for co-operatives.

in German vineyards, where the relatively cool climate generally provides summers which result in high levels of natural acidity, and cold winters which favour ultra-natural winemaking, relying on long, cool fermentations and minimal wine treatments. The classic wines of Germany may be high in extract (see page 16), thanks to the soils, but relatively low in alcohol. Riesling grown on the steep, slaty banks of the river Mosel is the epitome of traditional German wine: aromatic, delicate, racy, long-lived, and unlike any wine made anywhere else in the world, which is more than can be said for most of the wine made over the border in France.

But since the mid-1980s a healthy air of self-doubt has refreshed the almost infinitely fragmented German winescape (the average vineyard is an acre or two farmed as a weekend income supplement), so that at long last a new generation of wine producers has emerged to join the standard-bearers of the old brigade. Aware of the great progress made in the rest of the world since the inception of the somewhat stultifying German Wine Law, they have been experimenting, even occasionally using new oak barriques when the traditional German wine container was either a neutral large oval barrel or more commonly a stainless steel tank. The best of them know that limiting yields is the first essential step towards producing wines of real interest and flavour.

There has also been a trend towards making much drier wines in Germany than was the norm, so that the average alcoholic strength of German wine has risen (as more of the natural sugar has been fermented into alcohol instead of remaining as sweetness in the wine). This means that those of us who used to regard German wine as incapable of producing a hangover have had a few nasty shocks, but it has resulted in a new palette of wine styles from Germany which are much more at home on the dinner table than their predecessors: relatively full bodied, positively flavoured racy whites, but always with a backbone of fine acidity which can make them much more refreshing than most Chardonnays, for example.

If Germany's wine drinkers have developed a taste for drier wines, they have nurtured a passion for red wine, encouraging a dramatic increase in plantings of red wine vines, specifically early ripening varieties such as Pinot Noir, known here as Spätburgunder.

The vineyards are green, the river is green and the wines somehow even taste green, here at Cochem in the lower reaches of the Mosel valley.

MOSEL-SAAR-RUWER

The vines which grow on the banks of the Mosel (Moselle in French) and its tributaries Saar and Ruwer constitute Germany's third biggest wine region in terms of area, but its most important in terms of international prestige and dependence on viticulture. No other crop could economically be grown on the land dedicated to the steepest, finest vineyards, and many of the thousands of small-scale vine growers in the region complain that vines are hardly economic at today's low prices.

The large modern bottling plants which have sprouted in this extraordinary, green, essentially rural landscape process so much wine that the Mosel has become Germany's most important source of wine, even if by no means all of it was grown in the Mosel, or even in Germany. The tourist village of Bernkastel is well used to having supertankers thundering through it.

The Upper Mosel valley is uncannily like the English Lake District, with its late Victorian mansions, slate and water everywhere, its permanent residents mainly long-established farmers or caterers to the needs, real and confected, of the region's swarms of tourists.

This picture-postcard, steep-sided valley follows the meandering Mosel river, folding the land into such an irregular concertina that without the sun, visitors can be completely disorientated. Local vine-growers, on the other hand, know that the great Riesling grape can be ripened only on the sunniest south and south west facing sites, steep enough and close enough to the river to benefit from its function as mirror, on porous slate soils which not only drain away the region's frequent surplus rainfall, but also retain daytime heat to act as night storage heaters.

These are the most labour-intensive vineyards in the world, requiring about seven times as many man-hours as, for example, the flat vineyards of the Médoc. In the Mosel it is said that each stake, up which individual vines are

trained without restrictive wires in order to allow vineyard workers the flexibility to work the vineyard on the horizontal rather than the more tiring vertical, must be visited at least seven times each year.

Some of the slopes are so steep and so irregular that over the years some vineyard workers have even lost their lives tending these tenacious vines. I know from personal experience that keeping oneself vertical on a slope of even 30 degrees is exhausting, and many vineyards are far steeper than this.

As in Burgundy, where farming inheritance patterns are complicated by the fact that a few metres in one direction can dramatically affect the quality of the wine produced from it, and therefore the land's value, each vine-grower tends to own tiny plots in many different named vineyards. In fact the difference in altitude or exposition can have an even more dramatic effect here in the Mosel than in the Côte d'Or because in some spots the Riesling vine may not stand much chance of ripening at all, and so an earlier ripening but inevitably less glamorous variety may have to be planted instead.

The obliging Müller-Thurgau has been the obvious alternative vine variety here, and has been widely planted on flatter land that never had any hope of matching the Mosel's best sites. In fact its produce is so dull compared with the racy, nervy, tingling, long-lived essence that Mosel Riesling can be, that this inferior Mosel fetches very little money. This, tragically, has had the effect of dampening selling prices for all Mosel wine, even that produced with such care and difficulty from the best sites. Many of the peasant farmers who make up the population of this narrow, isolated valley (regarded as on the fringes of civilization by most Germans) are experiencing real financial hardship as a result of the fragile state of the German wine market.

The silver lining from the consumer's point of view of course is that top quality Mosel is underpriced in terms of the quality on offer for about the same price as a *petit château* bordeaux, for example. In view of the effort that goes into producing wine from the Mosel's steepest, most inaccessible sites, prices are almost ludicrously low – except for the best sweet BA and TBA rarities, which generally sell at highly publicized auctions.

Best value in the Mosel is in Kabinett and Spätlese wines made from the Riesling grape grown in an individual site from the likes of Bischöflichen Weingüter, J. J. Christoffel, Robert Eymael, Friedrich Wilhelm Gymnasium, Fritz Haag, Reinhold Haardt, von Hövel, Karthäuserhof, von Kesselstatt, Dr Loosen, Milz, Egon Müller, J. J. Prüm, Max. Ferd. Richter, Schloss Saarstein, von Schubert (Maximin Grünhäuser), Selbach-Oster, Dr Thanisch, Wegeler-Deinhard, Dr Weins-Prüm and Zilliken.

The Ruwer and particularly Saar valleys high upstream (just east of the Luxembourg border) produce some of the world's finest low-alcohol wines, many of them reaching barely eight or nine per cent alcohol, yet capable of ageing well and being genuinely interesting to drink thanks to their intensely fruity acidity and mineral-layered extract.

The Middle Mosel, the stretch including Klüsserath, Trittenheim, Piesport, Brauneberg, Bernkastel, Graach, Wehlen, Zeltingen, Ürzig and Erden, produce some of the valley's most complete, longest-lasting wines.

AHR

Germans, and practically no one else, associate this very small northerly wine region with light red, often slightly sweet wines made mainly by co-operatives from Spätburgunder (Pinot Noir) vines. Some more notable exceptions exist.

MITTELRHEIN

This small wine region is well known internationally for one producer, Toni Jost of Bacharach, whose concentrated off-dry Rieslings show just what can be achieved in the famous vineyards of the Rhine Gorge.

NAHE

The river Nahe flows into the giant Rhine at the western end of the Rheingau, and the vineyards which flank it are therefore well south of their counterparts in the Mosel, but the best wines often manage to combine the raciness of the best Mosel with the substance of the best Rheingau wine – although they can be easier to appreciate in youth than either. Schloss Böckelheim, Bad Kreuznach, Burg Layen and Niederhausen are all important wine centres of the Nahe, their surrounding vineyards specializing in zesty Rieslings (although Riesling represents only about a quarter of all the region's vines, and will ripen only in the very best sites).

Anheuser, Crusius, Diel, Dönnhoff, Schäfer, Schloss Wallhausen and Staatlisches Weinbaudomänen, the state's own wine estate, are all reliable names to look out for.

RHEINGAU

The Rheingau, a south-facing slab of vineyards on gentle slopes leading down to the Rhine, usefully protected from chill winds by Taunus mountains to the immediate north, was for years regarded as Germany's noblest wine region. This was partly because of its long association with aristocratic estates and the famous abbey Kloster Eberbach, which has been a focus for German wine's promotional activity. Grand and ancient castles such as Schloss Johannisberg, Schloss Schönborn and Schloss Vollrads have winemaking reputations which stretch back almost as many centuries as their cellars. As the 1980s wore on, however, it became clear that winemaking conscious life was much more exciting in some other regions (notably Pfalz) than here and that there was a real danger that the Rheingau was coasting on its past reputation. Fortunately, new life is now being breathed into the region by the likes of August and Johannes Eser and, not least, by the Japanese whisky giant Suntory, which seems determined to extract wines of Yquem's reputation and price from its Robert Weil estate. Key wine villages here, in countryside almost devoted to the vine (separating villages devoted to entertaining the human spillage from Rhine cruise boats) include, moving downstream, Hochheim (inspiration of the word 'hock' which nowadays means just any old Rhine wine), Eltville, Hattenheim, Oestrich-Winkel, Geisenheim (famous for its wine research institute), Rüdesheim and Assmannshausen where red Spätburgunder of varying quality is made.

The best Rheingau wines are almost invariably Rieslings with strongly pronounced mineral qualities and rather more body than most Mosels. A significant proportion of Germany's best sweet BA and TBA wines have been made here (the famously deep golden 1959s, and 1971s which are still in their youth) but the Rheingau is the home of the trend towards making drier German wines. The dynamic Bernhard Breuer founded the Charta (pronounced 'Carter') group of top quality wine estates dedicated to styling Rheingau Riesling into medium bodied, refreshingly crisp, dry wines suitable for the dining table. Twin Romanesque arches embossed on a brown bottle is the Charta group's trademark.

J. B. Becker, Domdechant Werner, the Esers, Knyphausen, Franz Künstler, Langwerth von Simmern and Robert Weil are the region's overachievers, but more should emerge or re-emerge as this somewhat complacent part of winemaking Germany is revitalized. Perhaps it is just too close to the wine-collecting Germans of Frankfurt?

RHEINHESSEN

This varied terrain, much of it rolling farmland across the Rhine from the Rheingau, is Germany's biggest wine region, and one for long used as a source of blending wine (more than half of all Liebfraumilch comes from the Rheinhessen). But it also has its fine wine district, the dramatic Rheinterrasse, vineyards steeply rising from the left bank of the Rhine, of which the Roter Hang strip with its distinctive red soils just north of Nierstein is one of the most characterful. It must be particularly depressing to be an ambitious, dedicated winemaker here, knowing that most of the world's wine drinkers associate your precious Nierstein with the dreariest, cheapest commercial blends sold as Niersteiner Gutes Domtal, made up of over-produced Müller-Thurgau grown miles away on flat, much less promising land.

The Rheinhessen is famous for the variety of grapes it grows and it specializes in the exotic range of new(ish) crossings such as Ortega and Optima which need conveniently few rays of sunshine in order to ripen their grapes to impressive QmP levels. Some of the most conscientious producers include Gunderloch, Guntrum, Heyl zu Herrnsheim and St Antony.

PFALZ

The old Palatinate or Rheinpfalz is, like Rheinhessen, a very varied wine region but one of great current interest to bargain-hunting drinkers. Because of the region's relatively low land prices, increasing numbers of ambitious young wine producers have been able to make their mark here in some of Germany's warmest vineyards, where in many years natural alcohol levels of more than 13 per cent can easily be reached by those prepared to restrict yields. Old estates such as Bassermann-Jordan, Bürklin-Wolf and von Buhl have been joined by some of Germany's winemaking stars such as Josef Biffar, Kurt Darting, Koehler-Ruprecht, Rainer Lingenfelder, Müller-Catoir and Pfeffingen.

Riesling is just one of the varieties capable of producing intensely flavoured, concentrated, full bodied wines, from dry to Trockenbeerenauslese. Others include Scheurebe, Rieslaner and Grauburgunder (Pinot Gris).

BADEN

The most southerly of Germany's wine regions, just across the Rhine from Alsace, has the climate to produce some impressive red wines and some sturdy Grauburgunder and Weissburgunder. By far the most important producer is the Zentralkellerei, or co-op, based in Breisach, which is commendably ambitious. Some very good 'experimental' Pinots, including deep red Spätburgunders, are underappreciated abroad. Dr Heger, Karl Heinz Johner and Wolff-Metternich are notable individual producers.

WÜRTTEMBERG

Most Württemberg wine is consumed locally and is typically slightly rustic, dryish Riesling and light red, sweetish-to-outside-palates wine made from the local Trollinger vine. Fürst zu Hohenlohe-Oehringen makes particularly distinguished wine.

HESSISCHE-BERGSTRASSE

Small and scattered wine region in the state of Hess, producing mainly dry Rieslings, quite like those of Rheingau to the north, for local sale, particularly in Stuttgart.

FRANKEN

Franken is German for Franconia, the most easterly of the many wine regions based on the Rhine or its tributaries, producing earthy, dry white wines that are quite different from the German norm, but which tend to be expensive because of local demand. Because winters can be so severe here, frost is a real danger every year and the size of the harvest varies enormously. For the consumer, Franken wines are distinguished by the flat green flask, or Bocksbeutel, in which they are sold (a shape impossible

to fit into a wine rack). Silvaner is *the* Franken vine but, like Riesling, it needs to be planted in the very best sites to have a chance of ripening fully. Rieslaner, the local crossing of Silvaner with Riesling, can produce some impressive late harvest wines too. Würzburg is the capital of the region and Würzburger Stein is one of the most famous vineyards. Bürgerspital, Castell, Juliusspital and Wirsching are some of the top producers.

EASTERN GERMANY

East Germany's two main centres of wine production Saale-Unstrut and Sachsen (Saxony), almost on the Polish border, are still in the process of being reconstructed. It is likely to be many years yet before their light, dry produce is widely exported.

Assmannshausen, a red wine enclave at the western end of the Rheingau.

AUSTRIA

In a nutshell: Great dry Rieslings and
reliably botrytized sweet wines.
Grapes: Grüner Veltliner, Welschriesling,
Riesling, Müller-Thurgau (WHITE), Zweigelt,
Portugieser, Blaufränkisch (RED)

Austrian wine is possibly the best kept secret
in the wine world – partly because the Austrians themselves are such dedicated, and well-
heeled, wine enthusiasts that they are not keen
to let the rest of the world know just what
exceptional liquids lurk behind their easily misunderstood wine labels.

It will be many decades before Austrian
winemakers are allowed to forget that in 1985
some Austrian wine merchants tried to give
extra body to certain wines by adding a harmless but illegal substance, most unfortunately
also an ingredient in antifreeze. As a result of
this national disgrace, Austria now probably has
the world's strictest wine regulations, and its
wine producers (most of whom were entirely
unimplicated in the scandal) are making some
of the world's purest, highest-quality white
wines, which range from dry and piercing to
sweet and racy.

LOWER AUSTRIA

The north eastern corner of the country (which
is known in German as Niederösterriech) is
where most Austrian wine is produced. The
Wachau is a beautiful stretch of crags above the
Danube, upstream of Vienna, and is probably
the Riesling grape's most consistent showcase.
(The Mosel and Rheingau in Germany have
similar potential, but much of it is unrealized at
the moment.) On terraced vineyards Riesling
and Austria's own signature grape variety, the
crackling white Grüner Veltliner, provide long-
ripened grapes which small, family concerns
(such as Alzinger, F. X. Pichler, Prager, Knoll,

Jamek, and Hirtzberger) transform by punctilious winemaking into powerful yet fragrant,
fine, dry whites that are all too rarely seen outside Austria. Its most concentrated wines are
called Smaragd. Federspiel is one category
lower. There is also some experimentation with
producing BA and TBA wines, but dry Rieslings
are the Wachau's strength.

Kremstal, centred on the ancient town of
Krems and **Kamptal**, whose chief wine town is
Langenlois, are to the Wachau's immediate east
and produce wines of almost as much finesse but
which tend to cost rather less. Bründlmayer is
one the best producers.

Donauland and **Carnuntum** encompass a
great sweep of varied vineyards round the east
of Vienna, and are home to the most famous of
Austria's many wine abbeys, including the
research institute and winery Klosterneuburg.

Thermenregion is the new, post-1985 name
for the district responsible for the plump, fiery
whites of Gumpoldskirchen.

The **Weinviertel**, or 'wine quarter', is the
extensive, fertile, Danube plain stretching
north from Vienna to the Czech border, which
produces most of Austria's everyday wine, its
sparkling Sekt and some interesting red wine
too. Müller-Thurgau and Welschriesling are the
common grapes here.

VIENNA

Austria has the only capital city in the world in
which wine-growing, as well as wine drinking, is
seriously important. Vienna has some fine vineyards in its suburbs, as well as the unique
Heurige tradition, whereby the city's vintners
are allowed to sell their wine straight from the
fermentation vat, in their own taverns, most
famously in the suburb of Grinzing. Franz Mayer
(whose son-in-law is an ebullient Australian)
and Wieninger are two of the best producers.

BURGENLAND

This flat, quintessentially Middle European region is almost as Hungarian in spirit and landscape as it is Austrian, and produces almost all of Austria's great sweet white wines and most of the best red.

Neusiedlersee is the most important sweet white wine district, named after the large, shallow lake that dominates it (although so flat is the landscape that visitors have to climb towers to see the lake beyond the reeds). This large body of water is partly responsible for reliable, annual 'noble rot' infections (see page 88) that shrivel the grapes, concentrating the sweetness, and making wines rich enough to qualify as Beerenauslesen and Trockenbeerenauslesen, rivals to great Sauternes. The fact that many of the best vineyards are surrounded by land designated as a bird sanctuary makes life particularly difficult for growers such as Alois Kracher, Nittnaus, Stiegelmar, Umathum and Willi Opitz, who grow an unusually wide variety of grapes that includes Weissburgunder (Pinot Blanc), Traminer, Scheurebe, Chardonnay and Welschriesling, which performs particularly well here.

Neusiedlersee-Hügelland is on the western lakeshore and produces wines that are similar to Neusiedlersee. The historic local speciality is Ausbruch wines made in the postcard-pretty village of Rust. Ernst Triebaumer is widely admired.

Mittelburgenland is celebrated as Austria's red wine district, where hot summers help to ripen such grapes as the lively central European Blaufränkisch, Pinot Noir, Cabernet Sauvignon and Austrian specialities Zweigelt and the Pinot-like St Laurent. Producers such as Gesellmann and Igler have shown that, now that they have mastered malolactic fermentation, Austrian winemakers are capable of producing ambitious, deep-coloured, well-structured red wines too.

Südburgenland is best known for lightish red Blaufränkisch.

STYRIA

Styria, or Steiermark in German, is the mountainous south east of the country, producing relatively little but often extremely exciting varietals – notably aromatic Sauvignon Blanc and some variable Chardonnay often labelled Morillon. The wines are less characteristically Austrian than close relatives of those piercing grape essences made in neighbouring Slovenia, or even Friuli in north east Italy. It is officially divided into south, south east, and west (Süd-, Süd-Ost-, and Weststeiermark respectively). The most important of these in terms of quantity is Südsteiermark (southern Styria) where on relatively high-altitude vineyards round Liebnitz, producers such as Alois Gross, Reinhold Polz, Sattlerhof and, particularly, Tement make pure, mainly white varietals.

UNDERSTANDING LABELS

Ausbruch, traditional sweet wine speciality of Rust, usually deeply coloured and with more than a hint of Tokay character (see page 257).
Auslese, late picked, lightly sweet wines.
Beerenauslese (BA), very sweet wines, often with noble rot, with more weight and usually less acid than their German counterparts and should therefore be drunk sooner.
extratrocken, bone dry.
halbtrocken, medium dry.
Kabinett, light, dryish crisp wines with real character.
Landwein, superior to Tafelwein.
lieblich, medium sweet.
Qualitätswein, quality wine.
Spätlese, between Kabinett and Auslese in quality and character.
süss, sweet.
Tafelwein, basic table wine, rarely exported and sold only in larger bottle sizes.
trocken, dry.
Trockenbeerenauslese (TBA) – nobly rotten grapes produce some truly fine wines almost every year in Burgenland. Austrian TBA is less expensive than German.

SWITZERLAND

In a nutshell: *Fragrant whites and some surprisingly concentrated reds from three very different cultures.*
Grapes: *Chasselas, Sylvaner (WHITE), Gamay, Blauburgunder (Pinot Noir), Merlot (RED)*

M ost non-Swiss people dismiss Swiss wine as slightly heavy, nondescript liquids called Fendant and Dôle, sold far too expensively in mountain restaurants. It is true that Swiss wine, like Swiss anything, is expensive. It is a direct reflection of the Swiss cost of living, and its reputation has not been helped by the fact that the bigger Swiss wine merchants have been allowed too free a hand with blending imported wines. (Because Switzerland is not a member of the European Union, it is not answerable to European wine law, although it is in the process of developing its own appellation contrôlée system.)

But all over Switzerland are passionately obsessive winemakers who each year are making better and better wines, many of them red, in such small quantities that they go straight into the cellars of the connoisseurs of Geneva, Zurich and Vaduz (Liechtenstein is close to one of the best wine regions) and are rarely mentioned in the international wine press.

The Swiss have been careful to preserve their agricultural heritage, which means not only the preservation of the clanking cowbell, Heidi tradition, but the preservation of some of the world's prettiest and most inconvenient vineyards – the great majority of which are in the western, French-speaking part of the country.

Swiss wines taste quite unlike those of Germany and Austria, for example, because Swiss winemakers routinely encourage the second, softening malolactic fermentation (see page 72) so the wines seem much less obviously acid. They also increase most of their wines' final alcohol content quite considerably by adding

sugar to the fermentation vat (a practice that is familiar to any Frenchman as chaptalization) and so most Swiss wines are much less tart and thin than the country's high altitude and relatively continental climate might suggest.

FRENCH SWITZERLAND

The main grape variety here by far is Chasselas, which is also sometimes sold as a table grape. The sunny, south-facing slopes of the **Valais** in the upper Rhône valley south east of Lake Geneva produce more Swiss wine than any other region. So dry and warm are summers here that some vineyards, many of them so steep they need to be worked with pulleys, may need irrigation from time to time. Local vine variety specialities in some of the highest vineyards include Petit Arvine, Humagne and Amigne and some serious late harvest sweet wines are made, sometimes from raisined, or *flétri*, grapes. Further down the valley some concentrated whites from Fendant (Chasselas), Johannisberg (Sylvaner), Ermitage (Marsanne), Malvoisie (Pinot Gris) are made, as well as some deep, red Syrahs which would impress many winemakers in Tain l'Hermitage, miles further down the river Rhône in France. Much of the Pinot Noir and Gamay grown in Valais is blended to be sold as Dôle, Switzerland's answer to Burgundy's Bourgogne-Passe-tout-grains (see page 166). The best producers include Josef-Marie Chanton, Marie-Thérèse Chappaz, Urbain Germanier, Didier Joris and Simon Maye.

The canton of **Vaud**, on the northern shore of Lake Geneva is also an important Swiss wine region, and houses many of the larger merchants. Aigle, La Côte, Lavaux, Dézaley, Chablais and Yvorne are the main Vaud wine regions and are dominated by Chasselas, sometimes labelled Dorin. Salvagnin is Vaud's version of Dôle, although it usually displays even

Densely planted vines, almost certainly Chasselas, in vineyards above Sion in French-speaking Switzerland, where every square metre is made to pay its way.

less Pinot Noir influence. Some Chardonnay and Pinot Gris is also grown here on vineyards which slope gently towards the lake, benefiting from its reflected, grape-ripening light. Some of the most respected winemakers are Jean-Michel-Conne and Henri Cruchon.

There is also a wide range of vine varieties grown around the city of **Geneva** itself. Gamay is particularly easy to sell. In **Neuchâtel**, pale pink Œil de Perdrix (partridge's eye) is a popular local invention.

GERMAN SWITZERLAND

The wines of eastern Switzerland are quite different. Pinot Noir, or Blauburgunder, is particularly popular and is made in a wide range of styles from slightly sweet and juicy through seriously Burgundian to a strong, sweet version made from dried grapes in the **Graubünden** region, a hotbed of experimentation. Müller-Thurgau dominates white wine production, and

indeed the largest wine region **Schaffhausen** is effectively a southern extension of Germany's Baden region. Baumann, Gantenbein, Kesselring and Schwarzenach are some of the most promising performers.

ITALIAN SWITZERLAND

The **Ticino** is yet another quite distinct winemaking zone in Switzerland (with an unusal tradition of still cultivating hybrids – see page 97). Much of its produce is light Merlot designed to satisfy the Swiss thirst for wine of any quality so long as it's red.

Some top quality, oak-aged Merlot del Ticino and other international reds are made, however, from low-yielding vines grown in particularly well-favoured sites – even if few of them escape the clutches of the Swiss themselves. Daniel Huber, Adriano Kaufmann and Werner Stucky are some of the most cosmopolitan winemakers.

CENTRAL &
EASTERN EUROPE

HUNGARY

*In a nutshell: Some fiery whites and some
good value, plus a historic sweet relic.*
*Grapes: Furmint, Hárslevelű, Leányka and
many more (WHITE), Kadarka plus the
usual international mix (RED)*

Like all wine-producing countries in eastern
Europe (and there are many), Hungary is busy
trying to restructure its wine business in the
wake of the collapse of the Soviet bloc. Until
1989 wine was viewed as simply a commodity
like grain or potatoes to be supplied, according
to long-term economic plans, to Hungarians
and, particularly, Russians. The state monopoly
handled all wine sales and distribution and,
although much of the vineyard land remained
in private hands, many vines were planted in
unsuitable areas. Quantity was the priority.
Quality was regarded as subversive.

Today, Hungary's vine-growers and winemakers are trying to grapple with a completely
new system which offers them no security and
no very obvious market. The Russian one has
evaporated, the domestic market is shrinking,
and export markets have never been so competitive. All things considered, Hungarian wine is
doing quite well, in the British market at least.

Of all the eastern European wine producers,
Hungary has been most comprehensively
invaded by the so-called 'flying winemakers',
technically clued-up wine producers who spend
just enough time in the wine region to make the
cleanest, fruitiest, most 'international' wine out
of that harvest's grapes. This has resulted in a
bevy of inexpensive, well-made, if not breath-
stoppingly characterful varietals from Hungary
– notably Chardonnay, Sauvignon Blanc, Pinot
Noir, Cabernet and Merlot, which are increas-

ingly joined by the likes of Hárslevelű, Irsai
Oliver, Furmint and Leányka among whites and
Kadarka, Kékfrankos and Kékoporto among
reds.

If Hungarian whites can be said to share a
characteristic it is that the whites are relatively
full bodied and have a certain Magyar fire or
spice. Reds are less distinctive. The best
exported tend to be merely clean, frank and
fruity, although locals swear by the more characterful offerings of the likes of Josef Bach.
Young Kékfrankos can be particularly juicy and
appetizing, while some vintages (Hungary's
weather can vary considerably from year to
year) yield some fine Pinot Noir fruit.

If many Hungarian vineyards are under-
achievers, many Hungarian wineries are severely
underfunded, as the production system moves
into private hands. Most of the newer equipment has been provided by western investment,
often with only one intermediary between a
British supermarket shelf and the imported tank
press.

The country's legacy of native vine varieties
is distinctive, rich and diverse, encompassing
light-skinned grapes such as Furmint, Hárslevelű,
Irsai Oliver, Juhfark, Kéknyelű, various Muscats,
Sárfehér and the rarities Ezerjó and Juhfark.
Olaszrizling is the Welschriesling of Austria,
Szürkebarát is the Hungarian name for France's
Pinot Gris, Tramini is Traminer, Leányka is
Romania's grapey Feteasca, while Királeányka is
Fetească Regală.

Kadarka is Hungary's signature red grape
variety, although it has been a casualty as growers have increasingly planted the internationally better-known varieties Cabernet, Merlot
and Pinot Noir. Some of the best Kadarka is
grown in Szekszárd, although it is also cultivated in Kiskun, Hajos-Vaskút, Csongrád and

Villány-Siklos. Kékfrankos (sometimes called Nagyburgundi) is Austria's Blaufränkisch and Kékoporto is Germany's Portugieser. All of these are found on labels of wines exported from Hungary, some in considerable quantity.

Quite apart from the difficulty of pronouncing and spelling most of them, it will surely be some time before wine drinkers outside Hungary come to demand Hungarian wine by the names of the regions. It is also far too early in Hungary's reconstruction to make long-term generalizations about the aptitude of various regions for different varieties and wine styles. The country is still being plundered by outside investors and the success of the resulting wines can often reflect the level of investment more than the natural potential.

It seems unlikely, for instance, that **Sopron**, which is effectively a continuation of Austria's Neusiedlersee sweet wine region, will be producing wines to match Austria's most sought-after half-bottles in the foreseeable future. It is best known for dry reds today. **Somló's** wines tend to aromatic whites, while the town of Mór and nearby **Etyek** are establishing a reputation for exportable varietals of both colours.

On the shores of **Lake Balaton** are many important and increasingly modernized vineyards, with **Badacsony** on the westernmost part of the northern shore and **Balatonfüred-Csopak** at the north eastern end.

Three wine regions on the right bank of the Danube (Duna) in the south of the country are **Szekszárd**, **Villány-Siklós** and the **Mecsek** hills centred on the town of Pécs, once famous for its Olaszrizling. Many fine, concentrated red wines are made here and the historic Italian firm of Antinori conferred international respectability on Szekszárd by launching a joint venture with its co-operative to produce wines under the Bátaapáti Estate label.

Just across the Danube from here is Hungary's famous **Great Plain**, or **Alfold**, a flat, sandy expanse populated largely by gypsies and horses. Vines joined them in quantity soon after phylloxera invaded the country (phylloxera

cannot thrive in sand). This is the source of Hungary's bulk of basic blending wine, although it has three designated areas which can produce some good value international varietals, **Hajós**, **Kiskun** and **Csongrád**.

The rest of Hungary's vineyards are in the north west of the country. In the **Mátra Foothills (Mátraalja)**, vines are protected from cold winds by the Northern Massif, and the Chardonnay and Sauvignon Blanc of Gyöngyös Estate were some of the first 'new wave' Hungarian wines to be exported.

To the east is the historic town of **Eger** whose most famous wine, Egri Bikavér was sold for years on export markets as red, sometimes powerful but often not, Bull's Blood. Today the Egervin Vineyard Company, the old monopoly revitalized by a $10 million injection of capital, is trying to forge a new, controlled, recognizable identity for Bull's Blood.

But Hungary's most famous wine by far is made in the north east corner of the country in a strange region known as **Tokaj-Hegyalja** (which historically extended over the border into Slovakia – except that the Czechs exchanged the right to use the name Tokay for a large beer contract). Tokaji, the wine named after the town of Tokaj (and often called Tokay outside Hungary), was in its time the world's greatest sweet white wine, made from nobly rotten grapes as early as 1650, according to local history – long before botrytized wines were recorded in Sauternes and the Rheingau, the birthplace of such wines in Germany. The main ingredients are Hárslevelü and, especially, Furmint, with some Muscat grapes. The local conditions around the 28 Tokaj-Hegyalja villages in this very protected corner of middle Europe are such that in a good year the best are affected by noble rot, here called *aszú*, and can reach exceptional sugar levels. (As in Sauternes, a confluence of rivers encourages morning mists.) They range from dry to quite extraordinarily sweet, with the following descriptions: Szamorodni (in which there is no selective picking of grapes affected by noble rot), dry or sweetened; then Aszú 3, 4, 5 or 6 puttonyos, a puttonyo being the traditional hod of sweet grape paste (made from pulverized botrytized grapes) added per barrel (big enough to hold 7 puttonyos) of wine made from unaffected grapes before a slow second fermentation. Aszú Essencia is made only from the produce of the best years and the best vineyards, while Essence or Tokaji Nectar is very rare grape sugar essence made from the tiny amount of free-run juice from the botrytized grapes that are used to make Aszú paste. Because its sugar content is so high, yeasts can work only at a snail's pace and these wines continue to ferment in cask for many a year. These were the sorts of wine which made Tokay's reputation as elixir of life and love. The final ingredient in Tokay's extraordinary character is that it is aged rather like sherry, under a film of local yeast, in barrels partly filled, in strange underground caverns lined with mould like black felt and signalled only by the low doorways hollowed out of the region's small hills. Of all Hungarian wine regions this one has attracted most attention from outside investors who include no fewer than three French insurance companies (AXA own Disznókó), and a consortium, the Royal Tokay Wine Company, involving the British wine writer Hugh Johnson. Many wines made since 1992 have much less characterful, 'cleaner', more Sauternes-like and less Hungarian flavours than their predecessors, which were effectively thrown into a communal blending vat by the state monopoly. All of them are bottled in a distinctive half-litre clear glass flask.

BULGARIA

In a nutshell: *Cheap international varietals.*
Grapes: *Cabernet Sauvignon, Mavrud, Melnik* (RED), *Rkatsiteli, Aligoté, Chardonnay* (WHITE)

With much less promising raw materials than Hungary, but a similar commercial climate, Bulgaria managed a minor economic miracle in the 1970s and 1980s. Lacking a domestic wine market

of any size, and an exciting range of indigenous varieties, what was then the Bulgarian state wine monopoly successfully sold most of its basic wine to the Soviet Union and systematically planted the varieties it somehow knew it could sell, in vast quantities, to the British market: Cabernet Sauvignon, Merlot, Pinot Noir, Chardonnay, Sauvignon Blanc, Traminer and Riesling.

Of these, the full-throttle, somewhat rustic but recognizable blackcurrant-flavoured Bulgarian Cabernet Sauvignon has been by far the most successful, to such an extent that Bulgaria became the UK's fifth most important supplier of wine (after France, Germany, Italy and Spain) in 1988. California winemaking expertise was extended to Bulgaria, provided the country granted the cola market to PepsiCo. In the mid-1980s the state-controlled Bulgarian wine industry, bolstered by huge and regular orders from the Soviet Union, seemed in good shape.

But by 1989, even before the collapse of the Soviet bloc and with it Bulgarian wine's most important market, Bulgaria's vineyards were in considerable disarray. Gorbachev's anti-alcohol measures were immediately reflected in neglected vineyards left to grow wild, or at most to produce poor quality wine. Total wine production in 1990 was only a quarter as much as in 1985, despite buoyant sales in Britain.

The Bulgarian wine industry is slowly trying to reconstruct itself in the entirely new economic climate into which it has been propelled so rapidly. Winemaking discipline, hygiene and equipment are still more important factors in determining whether a Bulgarian wine is likely

Racking wine in the strange, mould-lined cellars responsible for the rich, golden, but extremely variable wines of the Tokaj region in Hungary. Winemaking standards slipped considerably towards the end of the Soviet regime, but are currently being revived by a host of outside investors.

to suit a western palate than the natural conditions of where the grapes were grown. Many of the older wineries such as Assenovgrad in the south were built, Soviet style, effectively as bottling and distribution centres close to cities rather than vineyards (although Assenovgrad has produced a run of excitingly rich, age-worthy Mavrud). Wineries such as Russe and Suhindol close to the Romanian border to the north, Preslav and Burgas in the Black Sea hinterland in the east and Sliven in the Balkan foothills have been relatively successfully modernized. Other wineries which regularly supply western markets include Suhindol and Svischtov in the north, Khan Krum and Varna in the east, and Stambovolo in the south.

I have yet to taste a white Bulgarian wine that I would buy – most are very pale renditions of the variety specified, both 'international' and the local grapey Misket, Aligoté and Rkatsiteli imported from Russia, and Fetiaska (*sic*) imported from Romania. As I write, however, there is doubtless a stunning barrel-fermented Chardonnay just waiting to be bottled... Bulgarian reds, on the other hand can be great value. I have detected a certain inadvisable love affair with oak chips and am not entirely convinced by some Bulgarian wineries' determination to make soft, plummy, light, fruity blends of such varieties as Merlot and Pinot Noir, Merlot and Gamza (the Bulgarian name for Hungary's Kadarka), and Merlot and Pamid (Bulgaria's least exciting native red grape), but there is undoubtedly some well-made, absurdly inexpensive Cabernet Sauvignon, Mavrud and Melnik, the impressive speciality of the eponymous town near the Greek border.

ROMANIA

In a nutshell: Seriously underdeveloped.
Grapes: Feteascas, Welschriesling, Tămâîioasă
(WHITE), Cabernet Sauvignon (RED)

Romania has great potential for varied and high-quality wine production, but it is unlikely to be fully realized for many years. The country has a greater area of vineyard than any other in eastern Europe (other than the ex-Soviet Union), and the sweet white wines of Cotnari in the north east were as famous as Tokaj and Constantia in their day.

Romania is also, unlike Hungary and Bulgaria, a wine-drinking country. It lies on the same latitude as France, even if its climate is more dramatically continental (although winters tend to be much less harsh on the Black Sea coast in the east).

Romania boasts that it has considerably more Cabernet Sauvignon planted than Bulgaria (which has had such success with exporting the variety) but the chief grape varieties are the indigenous white Feteasca and a twentieth-century crossing Fetească Regală. They yield aromatic wines which vary enormously in sweetness level and quality. Welschriesling (the variety behind Banat Riesling from the far west of the country), Aligoté and Merlot are other important varieties, although there are also considerable acreages of Sauvignon Blanc, Pinot Gris, Rkatsiteli, Muscat Ottonel, Traminer and the native Romanian Grasă and Tămâîioasă which were responsible for Cotnari.

The atmospheric, wooded hills of Transylvania in the middle of the country are the source of many, potentially haunting white wines, notably in the **Tîrnave** (or **Tarnave**) region. Other geographical names to have escaped the country on the mere 15 per cent of wine production that is exported include **Murfatlar** on the coast, which has a certain reputation for sweet wines (a Romanian speciality) and **Dealul Mare** on the Carpathian foothills north of Bucharest, which can turn out some superior red wines, including some rather soupy but very inexpensive Pinot Noir.

For the moment, however, Romania's wine producers suffer like all Romanians from the chronic shortages of materials and equipment that are considered commonplace in the west, notably bottling equipment and refrigeration to control fermentation temperatures.

MOLDOVA

In a nutshell: *Right climate, lots of vines.*
Grapes: *International mix*

The independent state of Moldova is so far the only member of the CIS to have established any sort of reputation as a wine producer abroad. Sandwiched between Romania and the Ukraine, both geographically and ethnically, it has its own very strong, if troubled, wine identity. An extraordinary 10 per cent of this gently rolling country, with ideal natural conditions for wine production, is taken up with vineyard – much of it planted with export-friendly varieties such as Cabernet Sauvignon, Chardonnay, Sauvignon Blanc and Pinot Noir. Immediately after independence in 1989 the country's wine industry attracted considerable interest from outside investors. Even Penfolds, the giant Australian wine producers, not to mention a fleet of flying winemakers, got in on the act.

There is nothing wrong with Moldova's natural gifts as a wine producer, but those involved with trying to export bottled wine from the country still bear scars marked 'no decent corks', 'transport strike' and the like. This is an area to watch.

CONFEDERATION OF INDEPENDENT STATES

Within the old Soviet Union (now known as the Confederation of Independent States), the states surrounding the Caspian Sea all produce considerable quantities of wine, notably Georgia, Azerbaijan, Kazakhstan and Uzbekistan, although much of it would seem raisiny, unsophisticated stuff if it were ever exposed to western palates.

The Ukraine, and in particular the Crimean peninsula, has clearly excellent potential – as witness the Massandra central winery bottlings of rich dessert wines sold by Sotheby's in the late 1980s. Russian winters are so cold that most vines have to be carefully banked up or trained to avoid them freezing to death. Rkatsiteli and Saperavi are two fine indigenous white and red varieties respectively.

CZECH REPUBLIC AND SLOVAKIA

Wines here tend to be white, light and crackling, often lacking the dead hand of co-operative wineries and post-fermentation sweetening that blurs much of the eastern European wine picture. Some exciting and inexpensive Grüner Veltliner and Pinot Blanc has escaped. Slovakia is the major producer, with the **Nitra** region in the south exporting with particular enthusiasm.

SLOVENIA

This is the most westernized wine producer of all, making some extremely fine, pure, lively, mostly white varietals in two zones, respectively in the extreme west and east of the country. The western wines are made in the image of the best of Friuli just over the border in north east Italy, while there are some similarities between the eastern wines and their near neighbours in Austria's Styria. Welschriesling, often called Laskirizling here, was a staple for many years, exported in often murkily sweetened-up form under the Lutomer label in the days before the Germans managed to ban calling this unrelated central European vine variety 'Riesling'.

EX-YUGOSLAVIA

Some hints of the potential here escape this troubled region which has traditionally supplied Germany with vast quantities of cheap, slightly sweet red wine. Croatia may eventually yield up some secrets about its vine varieties and their relation to various Italian and Greek names. Fruska Gora in Vojvodina can produce some very pretty white varietals with a middle European accent. Vranac is a deep and respectable red from Montenegro in the south with real potential for ageing.

MEDITERRANEAN COUNTRIES

In very general terms, the wines produced close to the eastern and southern shores of the Mediterrean tend to be full bodied, relatively alcoholic, and most successful when either red and concentrated or sweet but, as ever, there are exceptions.

GREECE

Largely unobserved by the rest of the world, Greece has been modernizing her wine industry rapidly. There is no shortage of the sorts of ambitious, pig-headed wine producers with international tasting experience who is keen to prove that Greece, too, belongs to the dynamic greater world of wine.

This is particularly thrilling in view of the fact that the Greek wine industry is so ancient and seems determined to avoid the Chardonnay-and-Cabernet-only trap in its modern incarnation. It is quite possible that some of the vine varieties grown today are the same as those experienced by participants in classical symposia (much more hedonistic gatherings than their modern namesakes) and Dionysian revels. (One common and widely spread vine at least owes its name to its Greek origins: Malvasia is a corruption of the name of the Greek port of Monemvasia, through which many ancient sweet Malvasias passed in the Middle Ages.)

Many Greek varieties are extinct or nearly so but the aromatic white Malagousia has been rescued, as has Lagorthi, and Crete's Vilana. Assyrtiko, Roditis and Savatiano are widely planted varieties for white wines and Limnio, Mavrodaphne, Xynomavro and Agiorgitiko are some of the better-known dark-skinned grapes.

Modern Greek wine is very much more than retsina, the aggressively pine resin-flavoured full bodied white of blessed taverna memory. North-facing slopes are increasingly valued for their moderating effect on the high summer temperatures in Greece just as, for the same reason, high-altitude vineyard sites are being replanted. Wineries such as Tsantalis' new extension at Aghios Pavlos, Kourtakis at Ritsona and Boutari's outpost on Santorini are some of the world's most modern and best equipped. Greece now has small, well-funded, quality-at-all-costs winemaking establishments such as Gentilini on the almost Adriatic island of Cephalonia, Ktima Mercouri near Olympia, Ktima Hatzimichalis near Parnassus, and Strofilia not far from Athens (with a useful, eponymous high-quality wine bar in the city itself). The country's first modern, family-owned winery was Domaine Carras, established in Chaldiki in the late 1960s by shipowner John Carras.

The vinescape is changing rapidly, but some of the most interesting wines to reach export markets are the scented dry whites made from Robola grapes on Cephalonia and Roditis of Patras, firm and oak-aged Naoussa made from Xynomavro in the far north, intensely perfumed Agiorgitiko grown at Nemea on the east coast of the Peloponnese and a host of sweet wines such as Muscats of Samos, Lemnos and Patras, which also produces some gloriously mellow wood-aged Mavrodaphne. There is undoubtedly, however, more to come – especially as this renaissance in winemaking coincides with a dramatic fall in wine consumption in Greece.

TURKEY

Turkey's vineyards are most famous for producing dried fruit but some modern (that is to say,

Greek café culture prefers spirits to wine.

cool-fermented) wine is also made. For the time being this is largely being consumed by tourists, but the rest of us can expect a sustained export drive any day now.

CYPRUS

The island's most exciting vine product is Commandaria, a historic dark, raisiny dessert wine which could be very good indeed. Cyprus has otherwise concentrated too heavily on very ordinary bulk wine, grape concentrate and pretend sherries to have a particularly bright medium-term future. See also page 305.

LEBANON

The latitudes of the Lebanon on the eastern Mediterranean coast may seem too low for high-quality wine production, but the Bekaa Valley on an inland plateau as high as England's highest mountains eases the temperatures considerably and can yield some very exciting red wines. Château Musar is the label best known outside the Lebanon and its bordeaux-like structure (filled out with much headier Cabernet Sauvignon and Cinsaut fruit than the Médoc is ever likely to produce) was inspired by a visit to the Bartons of St-Julien. Whites tend to flab (although Musar's Serge Hochar is working on his) but some respectable dry rosés are also made by producers such as Kefraya and Ksara.

ISRAEL

Some fine modern varietals have been produced on the Golan Heights, although most of the rest of the country's produce, all of it kosher, tends to the sweet and sickly.

MOROCCO

In the 1950s North Africa was one of the most important sources of wine for European consumption, when French blending vats depended heavily on the deep, heady reds produced in colonial Algeria. Today, wine production along the North African coast is plummeting as the influence of Islam increases, but Morocco still makes some interesting wines and has the potential to produce more. The state still has a heavy hand in wine production, which is geared to tourists and export to couscous cafés all over France. Some characterful dry pink wines sold as Vin Gris and some rich, strong Muscat dessert wines are made.

USA

It is not generally appreciated that the USA regularly makes more wine than any country other than France, Italy or Spain. Its annual output is, for example, well over three times as much as Australia's. All but the Midwestern states produce some wine, but the output of each of this diverse collection of wine regions (most of them young) varies enormously in both quantity and style – as one might expect of such a vast country.

California, with its ideal mediterranean climate, produces nine out of every 10 bottles of American wine. Washington and New York state are the only other two states to produce wine in any significant quantity (although rainy Oregon has earned quite a reputation for quality).

When Europeans colonized the North American continent one of their first botanical discoveries was its rich diversity of indigenous vines. Botanists have identified more than 20 different species of vine native to north eastern America. At the time the early settlers hardly appreciated just how different these American vines are to the European vine species *Vitis vinifera* (see pages 96–9). They soon tried to make wine from native American grapes but found their flavours and textures off-puttingly unfamiliar. As early as 1619 they were trying out imported cuttings of European vines in eastern states, and for nearly three centuries were to be mystified at how poorly these vines adapted to life on the other side of the Atlantic. (What ungrafted European vines lacked of course was the native American vines' resistance to native American vine pests and diseases such as mildew and phylloxera.)

To this day north eastern states in general and upper New York state (like Ontario in Canada) in particular continue the tradition of making wine from the native *Vitis labrusca* species, hybrids of native American vines (American hybrids) and hybrids of American and European vines (French hybrids). The most popular variety is Concord but others include Baco, Catawba, Maréchal Foch, Seyval Blanc and Vidal. In the south east of the United States musky wine is still made from the slithery juice of the Scuppernong vine.

Improved communications have brought increasing internationalization, however, and the proportion of American wine made from well-known, easy-to-sell vinifera varieties such as Cabernet and Sauvignon Blanc continues to increase, even in areas which were traditionally the stronghold of all-American wine made from all-American vines and hybrids that are particularly suited to the local conditions.

Many of the smaller, so-called 'boutique' wineries which have sprouted in new wine colonies such as Connecticut, Pennsylvania and New Mexico have been founded with tourist visitors and owner life-style considerations in mind rather than to grasp an unmissable viticultural opportunity.

So varied is the terrain, the climate and the varietal heritage of the United States that few generalizations can be made. But one national wine phenomenon is the AVA, or American Viticultural Area, an embryonic American answer to the controlled appellations of Europe which concerns only the specified area's geographical, and sometimes distinctly questionable, boundaries.

The great majority of American wines are named after the grape variety from which they are principally made. A 'fighting varietal' is one which commands less than a premium price. 'Jug wines' are the American equivalent of European 'table wines' (and are generally better made, if rather sweeter). Blush wines (rosés by another name) have been particularly popular, often called by a dark-skinned grape variety prefixed by the word White (as in the hugely popular White Zinfandel).

CALIFORNIA

In a nutshell: Some very fine wine indeed,
but relatively few bargains.
Grapes: Colombard, Chardonnay (WHITE),
Zinfandel, Cabernet Sauvignon and some
surprisingly successful Pinot Noir (RED)

Of all the wine regions in the world, California is the most fun to visit. The climate is
benign. The people could not be more welcoming
(in stark contrast to Bordeaux and Burgundy,
the wineries of Northern California seem to
operate for, rather than despite, tourists). The
food is fantastic; you can eat superbly, and be
served wine knowledgeably (by the glass or
bottle), in hundreds of sensibly priced restaurants. In most California wine regions the gentle,

golden landscape is well protected against the
construction industry's baser instincts. Life is
easy; man has devised ways of overcoming all
natural discomforts. To a California wine producer, life-style can be what it is all about.

The California wine business is easily misunderstood from the outside, however. It seems
blindingly obvious in the most famous wine
regions of Napa and Sonoma that winery proprietors here live a charmed life, enjoying a
standard of living unknown among wine producers since the Golden Age of the Médoc
estates in Bordeaux. They live in lovingly
restored Victorian mansions or villas specially

265

The Napa Valley, with its wealth of local talent, perhaps the most photographed wine region in the world. The milk cartons used to protect the young vines are clearly visible, and can be seen all over the valley as it struggles to reconstitute itself in the face of the damage caused by phylloxera (see page 269).

commissioned from famous architects. They have not only swimming pools and poolhouses, but also their own stables, art galleries and concert halls. They play croquet at the country club and dance to jazz at the regular charity auctions.

This glossy façade is often coupled with the fact that hardly any California wine bargains are seen outside the USA, and interpreted as gross overcharging or misplaced priorities in the California world of wine – especially as virtually every other wine-producing nation seems desperate to export at whatever price. What such criticisms overlook, however, is the size of the American population. California does not need to export in the way that Australia, Chile and many Europeans do. And as the effects of the phylloxera invasion (see opposite) are reflected in declining volumes of premium grapes, the state will probably have even less to spare non-Americans.

Which is a great shame as, at the top end of the quality scale, California is all but unbeatable. Because Californians have not carved out a solid base of non-American consumers introduced via less expensive bottles, many of the world's wine drinkers are unaware of the sheer exciting glamour of the state's finest wines which, thanks to local demand, are in short supply and are often overpriced. Indeed, even those of us who are already convinced of California's achievements can find it difficult to keep up with the latest developments unless we live in the state itself – so small are some of the quantities involved, and so fast-changing the roster of winery and winemaking names.

This lack of permanence is one of California wine's distinguishing marks. Even if few New World wine regions experienced such a dramatic boom as California did in the 1880s (when wine from what was by then established as America's 'wine state' was admired around the world), almost all of them have at least experienced fairly constant evolution. California's wine history is a series of jerky stops and starts, with phylloxera pulling the plug on the performance of the nineteenth century, and total

national Prohibition stopping play altogether between 1918 and 1933.

It was not until the late 1960s that a serious, ambitious, premium California wine industry began to emerge (the construction of the Robert Mondavi winery in Oakville, Napa, still one of the most recognizable landmarks of California wine, is generally agreed to have marked the start of this new era). Throughout the 1970s and 1980s California wine country, particularly the Napa Valley and to a lesser extent Sonoma, was invaded by those who had made a fortune in a more conventional business but were determined to exchange it for the good life.

With one or two notable exceptions, the California wine industry is the friendliest, least competitive, most open in the world. Which means that when a new idea or scheme appeals to one of these new wine producers, it tends to spread like wildfire throughout the industry. Trends have, furthermore, been accentuated by a very concentrated, critical national wine press (famous for awarding points out of 100 to individual bottles) and conservative wholesaling and retailing systems.

The result of this is that a wine-producing development, which in any other part of the world might be a just-perceptible eddy, can in California easily become a tidal wave. The enormity of the phylloxera problem is one example of this, but so is the dominance of Chardonnay and Cabernet Sauvignon, and the strong similarities in the style of many of them.

One obvious brake on progress in California, although this began to change in the 1990s, has been the emphasis on winemaker at the expense of vine-grower. As in most New World regions, the functions of grape-growing and winemaking are generally quite distinct, with cash-conscious farmers supplying more urbane characters, who tend to have cleaner hands, with the necessary raw material. The heat of a California summer has also helped to keep the state's vineyards the domain of the Mexican work-force rather than its new generation of wine producers. At long last, however, the California wine industry acknowledges that the best winemakers are those who know their product from the roots up.

Although midsummer afternoon temperatures in most California vineyards are blistering, in the best sites they are mitigated by a unique climatological phenomenon which delays ripening so that interesting flavours and structure can develop, and this is the main reason why California can produce any serious wine at all. The **Central Valley**, the baking hot, flat sprawl of vineyards between Sacramento in the north and Bakersfield in the south, is indirectly responsible for this phenomenon, and for an amazing three-quarters of all the wine produced in the state (as well as providing the world's biggest supply of raisins).

If Napa and Sonoma are the Bordeaux and Burgundy of California in terms of attracting all the attention and high prices, then the Central Valley is its Languedoc-Roussillon which really does the work – except that while the Languedoc is now almost fashionable, there seems to be no such danger for the Central Valley.

The far northern end of the Valley around the state capital is, strictly speaking, the Sacramento Valley where Lodi and Clarksburg, not far from the Sacramento Delta, can produce some much more distinctive Zinfandel and Chenin Blanc respectively than further south. But most of the vineyards are well south of here in the San Joaquin Valley, with a third of the annual crush being supplied by the vineyards of Madera and, to a lesser extent, Fresno counties. High-yielding French Colombard (the local name for Colombard) and Chenin Blanc produce vast quantities of medium dry white for jug wine, but Zinfandel is an important red wine grape and Quady has shown that there is potential for quite serious dessert wine and port and madeira styles, next time they swing into fashion.

The unremittingly high temperatures in the Central Valley encourage the cold wall of fog that hangs over the Pacific for much of July and August to be sucked into the narrower valleys between the coast and the Central Valley, depending on how much land mass is in the way. The marine expanse of the San Pablo Bay north of San Francisco in particular encourages morning fog to cool down the Carneros region on its northern rim, and the southern ends of the Napa Valley and Sonoma's wine districts too. In fact in Northern California it is an almost invariable rule that the further north you travel, the warmer it gets.

In the state's wine showcase the **Napa Valley**, for instance, the land round the Trefethen winery in the far south is quite significantly cooler than Calistoga at the northern end of the valley. 'The Valley', as it is known by its residents, is fiercely protected by ordinances designed to keep its agricultural base. As recently as the early 1970s this narrow 20-mile

THE PHYLLOXERA SAGA

Never has California wine optimism been so tested as in the late 1980s when it was found that the rootstock onto which practically all Napa and Sonoma vines had been grafted, AXR-1, was not in fact phylloxera-resistant after all (see page 97). This means that, at a cost of billions of dollars, the great majority of California's most celebrated vineyards have had to be replanted, to be converted from luxuriant fields of dollar-generating vines to bare land punctuated only by old milk cartons protecting the tiny young vines inside them. The University of California at Davis, supposedly the fount of all wine industry knowledge, had counselled AXR-1, admitting its phylloxera resistance was low but condoning the popular wisdom that this was more than outweighed by the high yields it generated. Privately there has been much recrimination. Publicly, California wine industry enthuses about this great opportunity to plant the right varieties in the right place according to the right training method with less embarrassingly luxuriant leaf and riper fruit than of old.

ABOVE *Mustard in flower in the spring near Rutherford in the Napa Valley. Such cover crops
are increasingly planted to improve the texture of the soil and cut down on excess leafiness in the vines.*
OPPOSITE *Cabernet Sauvignon vines in Knights Valley show the summer face of
northern California – luxuriant, irrigated vines beneath the parched hillsides.*

stretch of valley floor was planted with crops as unglamorous as walnut and plum trees. Today, Highway 29, which bisects the valley, is lined with spruce, folksy, kitsch and slick wineries, each apparently frantic to attract any visitor to its tasting room and winery tour. The middle reaches of the valley floor, around Oakville and Rutherford, have established an entirely justified reputation for their intensely coloured and flavoured Cabernet Sauvignon which, now that winemakers have been weaned off the habit of adding acid automatically (the 'tannin is good so lots of tannin is very good' theory fell out of favour earlier), regularly exhibit a layer of richness most Bordeaux wine producers only dream of. Many of the most consistent vineyards lie on higher ground at the foot of the low mountains which flank the valley floor.

All over the state hillside sites, with their excellent drainage and low fertility, are being cleared and planted by those who can afford it and may well prove even more exciting sources of wine quality.

Most wineries buy in grapes from such a wide variety of sources, many of them outside the valley (although any wine labelled Napa Valley must contain 85 per cent of grapes grown in it), that there is little correlation between winery location and the style of wine it produces. The Napa Valley has, however, proved a source of great Cabernet Sauvignon, extremely good Chardonnay and Zinfandel, and some ground-breaking, full bodied Sauvignon Blanc (labelled Fumé Blanc by Robert Mondavi in the early 1970s). Such has been the reliance of winemakers on new oak for fermenting white wines and maturing wines of both colours that the Valley houses several highly successful cooperages. There is such a concentration of ambition and high achievement in the Valley that it seems invidious to name names, but labels with an established track record for top quality include Beringer's top bottlings, Caymus Special Selection, Chateau Montelena, Cuvaison, Dalla Valle, Dunn, Grace Family, Heitz Martha's Vineyard, Hess Collection, Robert Mondavi

Reserve, Newton, Niebaum Coppola, Joseph Phelps' Mistral, Stag's Leap Wine Cellars, Shafer, Silver Oak, Stony Hill, and two joint ventures with Bordeaux luminaries Dominus and the luxuriously priced Opus One.

Prices of just about everything in Napa and Sonoma are high and wines have been robustly priced to reflect this, but the new economic realism of the 1990s has spawned a new generation of second labels, some of which, such as Caymus' Liberty School, can offer excellent value, for winemaking standards are almost uniformly high.

For years **Sonoma** could not help nursing a grudge about the publicity attracted by Napa Valley, its neighbour just over the Mayacamas mountains to the east, but the stunning quality of so many of its wines, exhibiting the sort of district/varietal patterns that comfort wine classicists, has given Sonoma new pride and status. The easiest generalization was that Napa made the Cabernet and Sonoma the Chardonnay, but there is much more to the varied wine districts of Sonoma than this. Simi has done much to raise the profile of the Alexander Valley around Geyserville in the north, which seems to be able to produce a well-balanced example of virtually every varietal. Chalk Hill to the immediate south makes fine Chardonnay while Dry Creek Valley to the west enjoys a well-deserved reputation for sleek Zinfandel and aromatic Sauvignon Blanc. Dry Creek Vineyards is the Sauvignon Blanc specialist while Lytton Springs, Nalle, Ravenswood and several Ridge bottlings have established Dry Creek's reputation for Zinfandel. Thanks to a gap in the coastal range, the Russian River Valley south of this is even foggier and can therefore produce wonderful examples from such delicate varieties as Gewürztraminer and Pinot Noir (as Williams Selyem and Rochioli have proved and Marimar Torres may be about to). Producers such as Ferrari-Carano, Chalk Hill, De Loach, Kistler, Matanzas Creek, Marcassin, Peter Michael and Sonoma-Cutrer show just what can be done with Sonoma Chardonnay – depth as well as gloss. Top quality sparkling wine is also made here by Iron Horse and Piper Sonoma. Sonoma has also been chosen by Gallo as the focus of its range of finer Estate wines.

South of Sonoma and Napa, and straddling both counties, is **Los Carneros**, whose reliable fog quotient keeps it cool enough to be the most important source of sparkling wine grapes in the state (even if most of them are trucked out to be vinified further north). Taittinger have built a replica of a champagne manor house in Domaine Carneros, while the Spanish colossi of sparkling wine have established Codorníu and Freixenet's Gloria Ferrer. Saintsbury and Acacia make extremely thoroughbred still Pinot Noir and Chardonnay and Fred Cline is busy making a little enclave of Rhône varieties at the south western end of Carneros.

California's 'Rhône Rangers' (those, led by Randall Grahm of Bonny Doon who have fallen in love with the likes of Syrah, Mourvèdre and Grenache) scour the state looking for low-yielding old plantings of these last two varieties, spurned for many years. Cline's grandfather's plantings in **Contra Costa** county just east of San Francisco have been an important source while newer plantings of Syrah, Viognier, Roussanne and Marsanne, such as those of Jade Mountain and McDowell Vineyards, mature.

To the north of Napa and Sonoma are **Mendocino** and **Lake** counties, rather hotter and much less sophisticated. Fetzer are busy extending their empire of organically farmed vineyards – and indeed California's extremely low rainfall means that much of the state could be farmed without recourse to chemical sprays. Even Gallo, the California wine giant based at the world's largest winery in Modesto in the Central Valley, have adopted 'organic' techniques (at the same time as zooming upmarket, notably on their Sonoma Estate). Roederer Estate and Scharffenberger make some fine sparkling wines in the cooler reaches of Anderson Valley, which fall in Mendocino county, while Navarro make some of California's most consistent late harvest Riesling and Gewürztraminer.

In the **Sierra Foothills**, the old gold mining counties El Dorado, Amador and Calaveras still have thick-stemmed vines, mainly Zinfandel, which date from the last century. Since being rediscovered these far eastern vineyards have produced Zinfandel in all forms, from porty to pink (White) as well as a wider range of varietals than is common in Napa and Sonoma.

High on a ridge above Silicon Valley, south of San Francisco in the **Santa Cruz Mountains**, is Ridge Vineyards, established as a weekend hobby as long ago as 1962 and one of the state's standard-bearers for Zinfandel and Cabernet quality for decades.

A little further south is **Monterey** county, where valley floor vineyards have struggled to eliminate grassy and vegetal flavours from their wines but there are exciting, idiosyncratic outposts in the mountains to the east, such as Chalone and, on a limestone outcrop technically in San Benito county, Calera. Both of these make some exciting Pinot Noir.

Some of the most exciting new developments in California wine have occurred much further south of San Francisco, as northern wineries such as Mondavi and Beringer search for a reliable source of grapes from vines unaffected by phylloxera. In **Paso Robles** and **Santa Maria** fog again plays a vital part in making vineyards here very much cooler than the latitude suggests. Meridian is the much-extended Estrella River winery by another name and has played an important part in Beringer's bargain second label Napa Ridge. Byron has been supplying Mondavi with Italian varietals, among others. This foggy hinterland of Santa Barbara is a great area for Pinot Noir, as eloquently demonstrated by wines from Au Bon Climat, Sandford and Wild Horse. Edna Valley has a fine track record of bargain, rich but well-balanced Chardonnays. There are many more wineries in the **Santa Ynez Valley** immediately south of Santa Maria and in the environs of Los Angeles, but they tend to be gobbled up by that city's restaurants – even more fashion-conscious than their northern counterparts.

WASHINGTON

In a nutshell: Reasonable prices and pure,
crisp well-made varietals.
Grapes: Merlot, Cabernet (RED), Riesling,
Semillon, Chardonnay (WHITE)

Washington state, in the far Pacific Northwest, is the USA's second most important producer of wine made from European vinifera vines (New York is still primarily a producer of wines with less mainstream names and flavours).

Most of the vineyards are far from the capital Seattle in the underpopulated Columbia Valley in the west of the state, in the rain shadow of the Cascade Mountains and in severe need of irrigation. Plantings therefore tend to be limited to the reach of river water and to slopes which protect vines from the area's harsh winters. The Yakima Valley is the chief, very dry wine zone, but the Walla Walla Valley south east on the Oregon border has slightly higher rainfall and looks promising.

Some vines have also been planted in the completely different, relatively wet, mild climate of western Washington, however, with the result that some very Oregonian Pinot Noir has emerged from just north of Portland as well as some interesting Müller-Thurgau and other aromatic whites from Bainbridge Island in the Puget Sound off Seattle.

A high but decreasing proportion of eastern Washington wine is vinified or at least aged in the Seattle area, miles from the Columbia Valley vineyards. The Washington wine business is dominated by one large company Stimson Lane, whose labels such as Chateau Ste Michelle, Domaine Ste Michelle, Columbia Crest and Snoqualmie are to be found on half of all Washington wine produced and an even higher proportion of the wine that leaves the state. This is not boutique life-style winery country but there are several extremely dedicated individual producers, notably Leonetti

(amazing reds) and Woodward Canyon, who have established international reputations. Single vineyard bottlings of the Columbia Winery and some Hogue Cellars whites also deserve to. Winemakers here tend to use American oak as well as French, and there are many refugees from more precious California wineries to the south – though little close contact with the neighbouring Oregon wine industry.

Merlot has shown itself much more at home in the hot, dry summers of western Washington than Cabernet Sauvignon, which is often stringy and austere thanks to its late ripening and the Washington winter's early arrival. In fact Washington had demonstrable success with this variety long before it became fashionable in California (it is a natural habit to compare everything in Pacific Northwest wine with the dominant state to the south). The wines are generally supple, attractively fruity but with good, crisp natural grape acidity, often preserved by cool September nights.

But Washington is probably more distinguished from its competitors as a producer of fine white wines, of all degrees of sweetness. Chardonnay is now, perhaps inevitably, the most planted variety and winemakers generally show good craftsmanship with it, but the aromatic varieties Riesling and, to a lesser extent, Gewürztraminer can also be deliciously pure here. Washington appears to be one of the few wine regions of the world to take Riesling relatively seriously, and even styled itself a Riesling specialist – before Chardonnay-mania overtook the local population. Semillon can also be distinctively attractive, with some plumpness but Sauvignon-like aromas.

---

*Cabernet Sauvignon vines on Mercer Ranch in
eastern Washington. The circles in the background
are made by revolving sprinklers.*

OREGON

In a nutshell: Pinot Noir.
Grapes: Pinot Noir and Pinot Gris

Oregon produces quite a small amount of wine but an awful lot of noise. Which is not at all to say that the state's wine industry is overrun by brash publicists – rather the reverse. The typical Oregon wine operation consists of relatively neat, high-trained vines round a few old wooden shacks manned by a highly educated loner who revels in the contrasts between his wine region and California.

The most obvious difference is the climate, which in most of Oregon is distinctly cool and cloudy, especially in the Willamette (pronounced with the emphasis on the 'a') Valley just south of Portland where most of the wineries are clustered. Much is made locally of the fact that Oregon shares the 45th parallel with Bordeaux – although Burgundy would have been more convenient, given the determination with which Oregon wine producers have pursued the Holy Grail of Pinot Noir. This supposedly fickle grape is the state's most planted by far, representing more than a third of all vines. Chardonnay, Riesling and Pinot Gris follow. Oregon has no such thing as cheap, bulk wine of indeterminate pedigree.

The other wine areas include the drier Umpqua Valley and the much hotter Rogue Valley almost on the California border (though many miles from any California vineyards), as well as a few vineyards which are effectively extensions of Washington state wine regions.

The perennial challenge for most Oregon wine producers is to persuade their grapes to ripen fully on the vine before the autumn rains arrive, bringing rot and spoiling the colour and flavours of the delicate Pinot Noir grape especially. So variable are the vintages here that the grape harvest may take place at any time from early September to November.

Wineries tend to be small family affairs (although Montinore Vineyards, and the even newer King Estate in the south of the Willamette Valley, are exceptions). Winemaking equipment has therefore tended to be fairly homespun, with steel-lined open fruit boxes commonly used as fermentation vats for example. Perhaps the most carefully designed winery, however, is Domaine Drouhin, the first American outpost of a Burgundian merchant and, quite rightly, a source of great local pride.

There is more evidence of Oregon's appeal to outsiders in Argyle, a sparkling winemaking venture spearheaded by Brian Croser of Petaluma, arguably Australia's most influential winemaker, and Beaux Frères, a small but successful Pinot Noir producer owned by American wine critic Robert Parker and his brother-in-law.

Long-serving members of the Oregon wine community (and it is very much a community rather than an industry) include Adelsheim, Bethel Heights, The Eyrie Vineyards, Knudsen Erath, Ponzi, Sokol Blosser and Tualatin. Christom is a noteworthy newcomer. All these and more are involved in a uniquely friendly annual winefest known as the International Pinot Noir Celebration at McMinnville in Yamhill county, just south of the Red Hills of Dundee, Oregon's most famous wine terroir.

Success tends to be measured in terms of Pinot Noir, and Oregon Pinot tends to be delightfully true, not too heavy and convincingly variable in character according to the autumn weather. But Oregon Pinot Gris shows real distinction (which is more than can be said for most Oregon Chardonnay), as do some Rieslings and Gewürztraminers.

There have been experiments with using Oregon oak for wine maturation and it seems unlikely that the idiosyncratic inhabitants of this characterful wine region will stop their quest for ever greater wine quality.

REST OF NORTH AMERICA

NEW YORK

New York state is an important wine producer with four quite different wine regions. Most important in terms of quantity of wine produced (as opposed to grape juice or table grapes) is the **Finger Lakes** region in the west of the state. The slopes of these deep lakes are sufficiently steep to keep cold air moving in winter while vines bud too late in spring for frost to be a serious threat. The Cayuga Lake is warm enough to ripen European vinifera vines, but most of the wine is produced from earlier ripening hybrid or American vines of which red Concord is the most common example. The vineyards surrounding **Lake Erie** produce mainly grape juice, Concord jelly and table grapes while those of the **Hudson River** due north of Manhattan are notable for their continuous existence over 300 years. Most of the wine, made from European, American and hybrid vines, is sold locally.

The most exciting wine region is only just in New York state, the easternmost tip of **Long Island** where the climate, thanks to the ocean which surrounds it, is mild enough to allow vinifera vines to flourish in all vineyards. Cabernet Franc, Chardonnay and Merlot do particularly well here and have a finesse, natural acidity and delicacy that distinguishes them from most other American wines. The North Fork of the island, potato country, is the predominant wine region and high achievers include Bedell, Gristina, Hargrave and Palmer.

OTHER AMERICAN STATES

Although wineries have sprouted all over the United States (even in Hawaii), one of the states which has taken a predictably large-scale stake in the burgeoning American wine industry is **Texas**, where wine styles are still emerging but are sufficiently encouraging for Bordeaux wine merchants of substance, Cordier, to have invested heavily in the high plains of **Trans Pecos** in the west of the state.

CANADA

Canadians are extremely proud of their wine industry (or rather their wine industries – 2500 miles divide those of **Ontario** in the east and **British Columbia** in the west), and quite rightly. Surely the most delicious products of Canada's icy winters are her Ice wines, refreshing yet sweet liquids made from lightly pressed frozen grapes (see page 89). Unlike the Germans, Canadians can be sure of making these every year, usually from Riesling or the hybrid Vidal (which has no 'foxy' characteristics and can taste very pure and refreshing). Many of Canada's vineyards are still planted with Concord and American and French hybrids to maximize the chances of ripening grapes before winter sets in, but the proportion of European varieties has been increasing considerably and Canada can make some fine Chardonnay and Pinot Noir – as well as many a respectable Baco and Maréchal Foch. Ontario's grape-growing environment is not unlike that of New York's Finger Lakes, while British Columbia's is more like Washington state. A little wine is also produced in **Quebec** and **Nova Scotia**.

MEXICO

Unlike Canada, Mexico's problem is a surfeit of heat, which can hustle grapes to ripeness before they have developed much flavour. For this reason, top quality vineyards tend to be in the far north of the country, in **Baja California**, or at high altitudes further south. Some distinguished full bodied wines, most of them red, are made by the likes of L. A. Cetto, Domecq, Monte Xanic, San Antonio, Santo Tomas and Valmar.

CHILE

In a nutshell: Historic wine industry
in the process of dramatic modernization.
Grapes: *Cabernet Sauvignon* (RED)

The Old World envies Chile for its low costs, lack of vine pests and diseases and its dependably dry, warm summers. Much of the New World, and Australia in particular, envies its plentiful and regular supply of water from the melted snows of the Andes. Few winemakers, however, would envy the wine cultural vacuum in which their Chilean counterparts work.

Chile's golden age was the end of the nineteenth century, when the rest of the wine world had been crippled by downy mildew and phylloxera (see page 96) but this isolated wine producer could supply almost limitless quantities of healthy, deep-coloured wine, made from familiar vinifera vines that had been imported into Chile earlier in the nineteenth century. The world's most prosperous wine industry was then owned by just 10 Chilean families, many of them still in control today. For the next 100 years there were very few changes in the vineyards and cellars of Chile but the return of democracy fuelled extraordinary economic growth throughout Chile in the early 1990s, including a real determination to drag the Chilean wine industry into the modern world.

The vast old *rauli* (evergreen beech) vats are being replaced by oak barriques imported from the US and France. Refrigeration is being installed both for fermentation and maturation. The lazy, hazardous technique of irrigation by

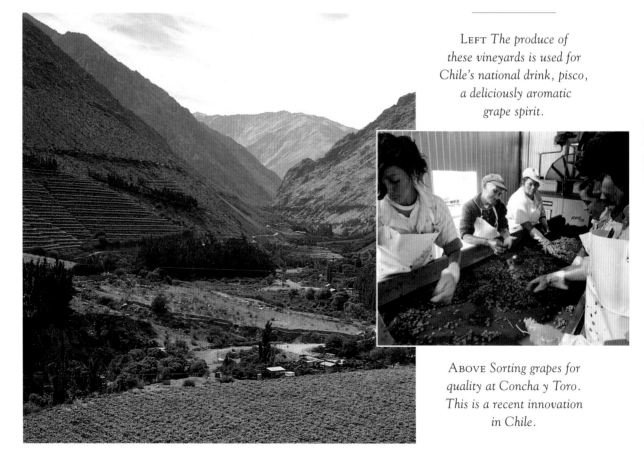

LEFT *The produce of
these vineyards is used for
Chile's national drink, pisco,
a deliciously aromatic
grape spirit.*

ABOVE *Sorting grapes for
quality at Concha y Toro.
This is a recent innovation
in Chile.*

simply flooding a vineyard and hoping the water will drain down specially dug channels and water each vine equally is gradually being replaced by the use of drip irrigation systems which administer set amounts of water to individual plants. New wine regions are being sought out which may be more difficult to work than the traditional areas in the hot Central Valley but should yield more interesting wine.

Thousands of acres of vines in the hotter regions to the north of Santiago are dedicated

When Santa Rita, one of Chile's largest producers, bought 7000 new barrels to replace their rauli *vats in 1988, it was seen as a milestone not just for the company but for the Chilean wine industry in general.*

to Chile's thriving fruit industry and, in the case of some specific aromatic varieties, to the local spirit pisco. Pisco sours are the great revelation for most wine professionals visiting Chile, who soon become frustrated at the oxidized styles of wine bottled for the local market (often under the same names as fruitier, more modern blends designed for export). Few urban Chileans are interested in wine.

This may be frustrating for Chile's small élite of dedicated native viticulturists and winemakers, but it has done nothing to stop an influx of foreigners attracted by Chile's growing reputation for making good to very good wine. A number of prominent Frenchmen have invested in the Chilean wine business, not least the Rothschilds of Château Lafite (Los Vascos), the owner of Cos of St-Estèphe and the winemaker at Château Margaux (Aquitania) – as well as Miguel Torres of Catalonia who was, famously, the first to import small oak barrels into Chile.

Chile's brake on progress, apart from a historic lack of investment, has been the gap between grape-growers and wine producers. Until very recently almost all grapes were grown on large ranches by gentlemen farmers who knew very little about wine and cared even less. By not having to use phylloxera-resistant rootstocks, Chileans were denied this tool for controlling excessively vigorous vines and some soil pests. By the mid-1990s, however, most exporting wineries (of which there were still only about 35) were planting heavily in order to be more self-sufficient in terms of fruit supply. Grape-growers, who benefited considerably during the Chilean wine boom of the very early 1990s, are expected to switch to other fruit crops, although some are building their own wineries.

This new extended control of production should curtail excessive yields, achieved by over-enthusiastic irrigation, should introduce trellis systems designed to maximize quality, and should result in a wider spread of vine varieties matched more carefully to the sites on which they are grown. However, detailed mapping of viticultural potential is still in short supply in Chile.

Apart from the very basic local variety Pais, grown mainly in the unirrigated south for cheap wine sold predominantly in cartons to Chileans, Chile's most important red wine variety by far is Cabernet Sauvignon, which produces particularly exuberant, lush wines here, even if most of them in the pre-barrique age have lacked the structure to develop in bottle. Merlot looks promising, however, and Carmen winery are proud of what has been identified as Carmenère. Young plantings of Pinot Noir have resulted in some surprisingly juicy, pure flavours from the likes of Cono Sur and Valdivieso, while Canepa has been trying its hand with Zinfandel. Meanwhile some wine producers dream of Syrah and Sangiovese.

Most of Chile's 'Sauvignon' is in fact Sauvignon Vert or Tocai Friulano, which can produce crisp, aromatic wines but newer plantings are exclusively Sauvignon Blanc and can be very lively if the site is cool enough. Semillon is extremely widespread (often mixed in the vineyard with Sauvignon) and therefore thoroughly scorned – although there have been some experiments with sweet wines and barrel-aged examples. Chardonnay was planted at a lick and for the moment the style is simply a reflection of winemaker and New World fashion (barrel ferments, malolactic fermentation and so on), although prices are low enough to make this lack of distinction perfectly acceptable. Gewürztraminer can work in cooler, newer areas and the range of white wine varieties will doubtless widen.

The vineyards dedicated to wine production stretch down the Central Valley south from the Aconcagua Valley (where Errazuriz has its base) and its fashionable new subregion Casablanca, sufficiently cooled by the Pacific that it can be seriously prone to spring frosts. Casablanca's piercing (real) Sauvignon Blanc is particularly distinctive – although the Chardonnay mania which prevailed when most of the new plantings went in, at the end of the 1980s, ensured domination of this particular variety. The western end is cooler than the inland section.

The Chilean wine industry has been keen to promote its own embryonic controlled appellation system, and its chosen geographical areas are the valleys which run from east to west, following rivers from the Andes to the sea. It is particularly difficult to generalize about the three main wine valleys Maipo, Rapel and Maule, however, partly because until a formal control system was instituted for the 1995 vintage, companies were none too strict about correlating where the fruit came from with what was put on the label.

Maipo is the most famous Chilean wine region, at least partly because it is so close to Santiago, Chile's capital and centre of wealth. Some famous vineyards such as those of Cousiño Macul are right up against the Andes just south of the city itself. Here wines tend to be fragrant and more elegant than those from central Maipo around Pirque and Buin, where the industry giants Concha y Toro and Santa Rita have their respective main wineries (though each follow the Chilean pattern of buying grapes from all over the Central Valley). Both companies have been developing separate subsidiaries, but such is the extent of their vineyard holdings that Concha y Toro can, for example, claim to be the world's most important grower of Cabernet Sauvignon. There has been some experimentation with growing vines on the west side of the Coastal Range, but it is much more expensive to ensure water supplies here (boreholes have to be drilled instead of just opening sluice gates). Canepa, an own-label specialist, is based in the south of Maule.

For all the focus of the appellation system, the differences between the east and west of the Central Valley are every bit as telling as those between the north and south. On the eastern edge of the valley, the nights are much cooler than on the valley floor thanks to cold air from the Andes, so that mornings are coolest and acid and colour in the grapes grown here are particularly marked, but frost can be a very real problem. The western edge, on the other hand, is cooled in the afternoon by regular sea breezes whose extent varies with the precise shape of the Coastal Range nearby. A vineyard's distance from the rivers can also affect how usefully cool and damp the soil is.

The wider, wetter **Rapel** Valley south of Maipo has an even less distinct viticultural identity, although Colchagua, which can also boast a great concentration of premium, mainly Cabernet, grapes, is more marked by the ocean's influence. Soils here tend to be fertile alluvial deposits and vines can sprout leaves rather than ripe fruit to a worrying degree. Fog-cooled Chimbarongo in the Colchagua Valley and Cachapoal to its immediate north are addresses occasionally found on wine labels.

The new appellation system separates **Curicó** (including Lontué) from **Maule**, although few wine professionals could describe the difference in the wines. Curicó has vast tracts of land planted with high-yielding vines and yet there are individual mesoclimates (see page 62) obviously capable of producing distinctly superior wine. San Pedro is one of the biggest wineries to be based near Curicó and has hired Jacques Lurton to squeeze maximum fruit character out of its vines. The large California outfit Kendall Jackson has been experimenting in Talca in the south of Maule (which, despite the latitude, is generally hotter than Rapel). Parts of Maule with clay soils can be good for fruity Merlot, even at high yields.

Itata and **Bío-bío** comprise the southern region south of Maule and are generally regarded as fit only to produce Pais for boxes, but Concha y Toro is experimenting on a family ranch in Mulchén and there has been French interest in this cooler southern region too. Frost can wipe out crops here, as can fungal vine diseases which are a threat in such a relatively humid climate.

Most wineries are careful to bottle their best produce as Reserve wines. Of the big four companies Concha y Toro, Santa Rita, San Pedro and Santa Carolina, most own several wineries and many different vineyards, although it is also the norm to buy in grapes from a wide range of growers. The estate wineries such as the historic Cousiño Macul, Los Vascos, Montes, Portal del Alto, Viña Porta, Santa Monica (whose Riesling can be fine), and Santa Inés are unusual in today's Chilean vinescape, though the signs are that more and more individuals will be tempted to try to fashion greatness out of the great raw materials that Chile has to offer.

REST OF SOUTH AMERICA

South America was the first continent to be systematically colonized by the European vine, taken there by the Spanish conquistadores in the sixteenth century. (Winemaking was introduced first to Mexico, but Peru, then Chile and Argentina followed soon afterwards.) The following are South America's wine-producing countries other than Chile (see pages 278–81), in decreasing order of importance.

ARGENTINA

Chile dominates South American wine exports but Argentina makes almost five times as much wine, and (like the USA) regularly produces more wine than any country other than France, Italy, Spain and the ex-Soviet Union.

Only in the 1990s, however, was business confidence in Argentina sufficient to justify the investment needed to drag its wineries into the twentieth century, and exports on a serious scale are only just beginning. The distinguishing feature of Argentine wine has been the extraordinarily high yields, with reliably sun-ripened grapes literally pumped full of melted Andean snow via irrigation channels constructed in the nineteenth century. Since the late 1980s vines have begun to be planted in cooler areas deliberately to prolong the ripening process, and trained carefully on wires for maximum quality of the resulting fruit.

The main Argentine wine region, **Mendoza**, is less than an hour's spectacular flight over the Andes from Santiago, the capital of Chile and its wine industry, but Mendoza is much hotter. Its most promising zone is **Luján de Cuyo** where vines are planted as high as 1100 m (3600 ft) above sea level – although **Tupungato**, a new area currently being developed by the giant wine company Peñaflor (whose premium label is Trapiche), is at 1200 m.

Malbec was for years Argentina's most planted red wine grape and is therefore regarded by Argentines as distinctly infra dig (especially in relation to Cabernet Sauvignon), but to many outsiders it seems the perfect grape for

Luján de Cuyo, producing rich, intensely fruity yet ageworthy wines which can be far more impressive than any Malbec-based Cahors from south west France. Some of the best well-established producers are Luigi Bosca, Navarro Correas, Norton, Senetiner of Vistalba, Trapiche and Weinert, but Chandon and Catena are developing newer, more 'international' varietals.

Chandon is a subsidiary of the champagne giant and makes enormous quantities of cuve close sparkling wine (see pages 85–6) from Chenin Blanc and other early-picked white grapes for the Argentine market (which has been so effectively trained to worship all things French that domestic wine brand names include Pont l'Éveque and Carcassonne).

The second most important wine region in terms of quantity is **San Juan** immediately north of Mendoza, but it is even hotter and is generally best suited to Argentina's rather coarse vine specialities Criolla and Cereza. These pink-skinned grapes are used for grape concentrate and the deep-coloured, often slightly sweet white that is sold at rock bottom prices, often in cardboard cartons, within Argentina.

The only other area of obvious interest to export markets is the high-altitude vineyards around Cafayate in the province of **Salta** in the far north of the country. The local vine speciality here is a form of Torrontes which can yield crisp, flavourful, very aromatic dry whites – absolutely the last thing most wine drinkers would expect from Argentina. Michel Rolland of Pomerol has been a consultant to Etchart here for some years and is establishing his own El Recreo label there.

BRAZIL

Brazil makes more wine than Chile from some vintages. Its wine industry is concentrated in the south on the high **Sierra Gaucha** in the Rio Grande do Sul state, although some vines are grown in the **Frontera** region on the border with Uruguay. Small amounts of wine are also made, from more than one crop a year, in the tropical **San Francisco Valley**. The high rainfall in the Sierra Gaucha has encouraged many to plant hybrid vines, although European varieties are on the increase.

Chandon again are important players in the domestic wine market, and have even begun to export a crisp sparkling wine, Diamantina.

URUGUAY

Uruguay is South America's fourth most important wine producer and, thanks to a substantial immigration from the Basque country in south west France in the nineteenth century, is one of the world's centres of Tannat vine-growing. Blends of this with other French varieties (and a Semillon-Chardonnay white blend) were first exported to British supermarkets in 1994. The wines are full bodied and promising.

Peru and **Bolivia** also make small quantities of wine, but hardly any is exported – so far.

Argentina's largest producer Peñaflor is particularly proud of these high-altitude vineyards at Tupungato, overlooked by the snowy Andes.

AUSTRALIA

In a nutshell: Export-driven industry making waves and fruit-driven wines, all over the world.
Grapes: *Shiraz, Cabernet Sauvignon* (RED), *Riesling, Chardonnay, Semillon* (WHITE)

For some years now Australians have seen themselves as at the cutting edge of the New World of wine, and now more and more non-Australians do too as the country has dramatically increased the extent to which it exports both its wines and winemakers (see page 68).

Their wine industry is not fundamentally distinguished by history (Australia was one of the vine's later conquests), and certainly not by geography (Australian wine producers are congenital truckers of grapes and blenders of wines), but by its philosophy. 'Can do' perhaps best sums up the Australian attitude to wine production.

The wine regions of Australia constitute different departments in one huge wine factory, any one of which may be called upon to deliver a spare part as and when required. Part of the explanation for this lies in the division between wine-making and grape-growing as commercial activities – a division even more marked than in California. The typical Australian wine producer buys in most of his grapes and, thanks to the refrigerated transport systems needed in a country as big and as hot as this, may well buy them from several hundred, or even thousand, miles away.

This pragmatism continues through the business of grape processing, as an Australian would call what the French might call vinification. If the winery hasn't enough fermentation tanks, the fruit or juice will simply be stored at low temperatures until there is enough space for the winemaker's carefully controlled fermentation. If the typical French winemaker sees nature as the driving force and the typical American sees it as a demon to be tamed, their Australian counterparts see themselves as simple processors of farm output.

This is underlined by the status of the formal wine training the vast majority of them undergo, at centres variously called Roseworthy, Wagga Wagga and Adelaide, which have enjoyed the status of agricultural colleges. The Australian Wine Research Institute of Adelaide is one of the most admired centres of wine academe in the world and the graduates who use the results of its intensely industry-linked work are taught a healthy respect for science, technology and for what man can achieve when given a free hand.

Australians revel in their lack of the sort of restrictions which dictate what and how a traditional European vine-grower must grow. They can establish a vineyard anywhere they like (although the availability of water is usually an important determining factor) and indeed the current distribution of vineyards old and new suggests there are undiscovered pockets of suitable vineyard land all over the southern quarter of this vast country.

A few higher tracts of Queensland such as the Granite Belt notwithstanding, viticulture is a southern Australian phenomenon. Most of Australia's vines grow where summers are cool enough to allow some flavour to build up in the grapes before they are so embarrassingly high in sugar that they must be picked lest acids plummet to uncorrectable levels. (Most Australian wines will have some acidification, acid deliberately added – see page 72.)

Nearly half of all vines grow in the state of South Australia, a third in the state of Victoria and most of the rest in New South Wales. Australian wine is conventionally divided by these state boundaries (across which strict quarantines may apply such as those designed to keep the phylloxera louse crossing from Victoria into South Australia) but there is a more fundamental divide than this.

A high proportion of Australia's vines are farmed, intensively, on the green oases of the heavily irrigated vineyards of the parched, dusty interior. These districts, known variously as Riverina, the Riverlands, the Murray River, the M.I.A. (Murrumbidgee Irrigation Area), Sunraysia, Mildura, Griffith and Renmark, straddle the boundaries between the three most important wine-producing states. Here Australia's two most common vine varieties Sultana and Muscat Gordo Blanco (the less fine Muscat, of Alexandria, known sometimes as Lexia here) are cultivated in profusion and used alternately by the wine and dried fruit industries according to the vagaries of supply and demand. These less distinguished grapes can make useful bulk filler for the wine boxes, or 'casks' as they are known, that have made up the bottom end of the Australian wine market since the 1970s, but considerable acreages of the irrigated areas are also devoted to so-called premium varieties, Chardonnay particularly but by no means exclusively. Australians are adept at transforming this fairly humdrum raw material into a palatable and completely dependable drink, often with the help of oak chips.

But the reputation of Australian wine depends on much more exciting fruit produced in one of the country's more distinguished wine regions (even if that fruit is often blended between regions so that its provenance can often be difficult to determine from the wine label). Britons, who fell so deeply in love with Australian wine in the early 1990s that exports tripled between 1989 and 1994, became used to seeing on labels the catch-all appellation 'South Eastern Australia' (which conveniently encompasses all wine regions except the relatively limited ones of Western Australia, including the irrigated areas).

These regions are examined in detail below, but the importance of trucking should not be underestimated. The typical large winery is probably based in South Australia, often in the Barossa, but will buy in grapes from as far afield as Coonawarra or the irrigated interior and possibly even the Hunter Valley in New South Wales. (Conversely, it has been a source of persistent irritation to South Australians that they have long provided so much fruit to bolster the reputations of wineries based in New South Wales.) The Australian wine industry is dominated by three companies, of which the giant is Southcorp Wines, owning not just Penfolds, but Lindemans, Seppelts, Seaview, Wynns, Tulloch, Tollana and a host of others. Their greatest rival is the French-owned Orlando-Wyndham, whose brand Jacob's Creek has been Australia's most marked export success. The third biggest company is BRL-Hardy, a curious amalgam of an old, family-owned company with a co-operative group based in the irrigated interior.

Australians are not short of energy or sunshine but they are short of water and, in most wine regions, labour. California can at least rely on a substantial Mexican work-force, but the Australian wine industry is thoroughly mechanized, and hand-picking is now relatively rare. Many vineyards are deliberately picked by machine at night in the relentless battle against heat at harvest time. The campaign tends to continue with deliberate chilling of grapes and must. (Water consumption can be as high in the cellar as in the vineyard.) Oxygen is seen as the other great enemy and protective winemaking has been the norm.

Australians have been avid users of American oak, for ageing whites as well as reds, and the wines' flavours can be so full and exuberant that they stand up well. South Australia has some fine coopers of American and French oak. One technique developed in Australian wineries is to move red wines off the grape skins into small barrels before fermentation is complete. It would be impossible in most of France, where a post-fermentation maceration is often needed to extract enough colour from the skins, but many Australian reds from warmer areas are softened and bolstered by this technique. The aim of most Australian winemakers is to exhibit the flavour of the fruit from which the wine was made rather than the characteristics of the place (usually places) where it was grown. Hence the phrase 'fruit-driven' for such wines.

One final particularly Australian phenomenon is the wine show, effectively an agricultural exhibition held annually in the state capitals, in which panels of carefully chosen, extremely professional judges award medals and trophies to wines entered from all over the country. It is all taken extremely seriously.

Ultra-ripe grapes being harvested (left) in the Hunter Valley in New South Wales (right), which has historically benefited from its proximity to Sydney.

SOUTH AUSTRALIA

South Australia produces well over half of the raw material for Australia's wine industry, and most of the large wine companies, many of the small, and all of the official wine trade organizations have their headquarters in the Wine State, whose capital is Adelaide, a city founded on wine. Wine areas are spread over a wide climatic range and are listed here in very approximately descending order of average temperature.

RIVERLAND

This is Australia's most quantitatively important wine region by far, the efficiently irrigated, high-yielding vineyards way up the Murray River towards Victoria's own irrigated wineland. Around townships such as Waikerie, Loxton, Berri and Renmark grape-growing to keep pace with the growth of Australian wine exports is in full swing, thanks to government encouragement. Vineyards here can easily supply drinkable Chardonnay at rock bottom prices, ideally suited to oak chips if not to prolonged contemplation and discussion of its nuances.

ADELAIDE PLAINS

Two or three wineries persist on the hot flats north of the city of which Primo Estate can produce some hand-crafted specialities, some of them from local fruit.

BAROSSA

After a long period in the wilderness, the Barossa Valley is now recognized as Australia's quintessential wine region. There are many obvious physical similarities with California's Napa Valley – heavily laden vines growing on a fertile valley floor bounded by hills that are brown throughout the summer, an hour's drive north of a major city, desperately trying to stave off urban development and retain the valley's viticultural character. There is even an old railway running parallel to the valley's major north–south highway in both Napa and the Barossa. But whereas the Napa Valley's wine industry, with its art galleries and music festivals, is substantially founded on well-heeled emigrés from the professions or big business, the Barossa Valley is founded on an extraordinary social group, about 500 families of Prussian descent who emigrated here in the 1840s to escape discrimination and establish a modest, hard-working, Lutheran farming community. They continue these traditions to this day. Tanunda has its Wursthaus and its Kegelbahn. Maranenga has its own brass band, headquartered a conveniently short march from the Gnadenfrei church. The settlers tried all manner of crops but vines were a particular success here and, thanks to the dogged work ethic of the 'Barossa Deutsch', a high proportion of the valley is still devoted to vines, some of them exceptionally old. Many of these grape-growers (most of whom sell grapes rather than vinify) still speak German among themselves. The dusty, unpaved roads that criss-cross the valley are hung with grape-growers' signs, with hardly a non-German name among them.

In the 1970s and early 1980s the Barossa Valley was regarded as distinctly inferior to the new 'cool climate' regions which the Australian wine industry was developing. Thus, the giant wineries of Tanunda, Nuriootpa and Rowland Flat (many by now owned by multinational corporations) were proud to sell bottles with the words Coonawarra or Padthaway on the label, but tended to keep quiet about the fruit they bought on their own doorstep in the Barossa.

A new wave of smaller, local wineries, typically started up in the 1980s by escapees from the big companies (Peter Lehmann, St Hallett's,

Rockford, Charles Melton and others), signalled a resurgence of pride in the Barossa Valley, particularly in the big, bold style of Shiraz that is the valley's signature.

Dry-farmed (non-irrigated) old vineyards on the cooler west side of the valley are the most treasured and provide fruit for Australia's most famous wine, Penfolds Grange, as well as for an increasing range of top quality concentrated bottlings such as Peter Lehmann's Stonewell, Rockford Basket Press and St Hallett's Old Block.

There is now increasing interest, as elsewhere, in the other Rhône varieties Grenache and Mourvèdre (which for years, as Mataro, was scorned). Barossa Chardonnay is another big, bold statement and can respond well, like Barossa reds, to American oak. Some of Australia's finest coopers are long-established family companies based in the Barossa.

SOUTHERN VALES

The growing suburbs of Adelaide are stretching remorselessly further south into what was once wine country so that only the most financially secure vineyards, or those too far from the city centre to be of current interest to the developers, survive. Yet (or perhaps therefore) the winemakers of **McLaren Vale**, south of the city, are a determined, friendly lot who realize that they have much to offer the Australian wine industry.

The local mesoclimates vary enormously according to altitude and exposure to cooling sea breezes. Some of the most promising wineries and vineyards occupy ridges with quite amazing views of the blue Gulf St Vincent, which is the starting-point for most of Australia's wine exports. Notable achievers among wineries in this tight-knit community include Chapel Hill, Coriole, Geoff Merrill, Wirra Wirra and the much bigger Thomas Hardy, whose traditional Tintara winery can turn out some bargain masterpieces. Chardonnays, Cabernets and Shiraz can all dazzle.

Langhorne Creek is a separate and slightly cooler wine region on Lake Alexandrina to the south east, supplying considerable and useful blending material to the bigger companies.

CLARE VALLEY

This is effectively a northern but considerably cooler extension of Barossa and one of the few wine regions of the world in which the great German grape Riesling comes into its own. Australian Rieslings are – not surprisingly in view of the climate – not at all like the German archetypes. Usually called Rhine Rieslings, or just 'Rhine', they have much more body, a bit less acid (although winemakers tend to compensate for nature's deficiencies in this respect), and a host of different flavours (see Section Three) but are none the worse for that. Like all Rieslings, they age well. Clare Rieslings tend to reach 12 to 13 per cent alcohol and to show strong lime or some form of citrus flavours. With five or 10 years in bottle they can become distinctly toasty and some can even survive 20 or more years in bottle. Leo Buring was the great label here. Today much of the fruit is bottled south of the region itself – indeed it is not too great an exaggeration to say that most serious South Australian wine producers bottle an Eden Valley Riesling or Clare Rhine Riesling (so called because Clare Riesling was once a synonym for the undistinguished Crouchen vine) but dependable producers include Jeffrey Grosset, Mitchell, Petaluma, Pikes Polish Hill and Tim Knappstein, some of whom occasionally manage to make sweet botrytized examples.

This relatively warm region, including **Watervale** in the south, also makes some fine Cabernet and Chardonnay.

COONAWARRA, PADTHAWAY AND BEYOND

Coonawarra was Australia's first widely recognized top quality wine region – and it even had its very own grape variety, Cabernet Sauvignon, to prove it. Coonawarra Cabernet can be a glorious thing, with all the structure, intensity and mineral overtones of a classed growth red bordeaux. The key to this flat, visually completely undistinguished mile-wide stretch of vineyards in the far south eastern corner of South Australia is its famous terra rossa, red loam or clay over a limestone base to ensure that quality precursor, good drainage. When the terra rossa peters out, so do the vines, and the wine industry is still doing its best to convert all available land to vines. Razing houses means the elimination of what was already a sparse work-force, and Coonawarra is probably the most mechanized fine wine region in the world. Some commentators argue that yields are too high, and certainly in cooler vintages some wines can lack sufficient concentration for their austere frame, but there are always wines such as Bowen, Hollick, Parker Estate, Penfolds, Penley Estate, Petaluma's red and Wynns to renew wine lovers' faith in Coonawarra Cabernet. Shiraz and Chardonnay can also prove their worth.

Padthaway made its name soon after Coonawarra but was such a one-company (Seppelt) wonder that too few operators have had a vested interest in putting the name on the label. Slightly warmer and even more remote than Coonawarra, Padthaway's strong point is white wine, especially Chardonnay, with a fine streak of natural acidity and good, round fruit. Lindemans is now the prime producer, but much of the fruit is vinified outside the region.

Other suitable land in this cool corner of the Wine State is being prospected at a rapid rate while there is a shortage of premium grapes, including an area near Robe on the coast and Bordertown near the border with Victoria.

EDEN VALLEY

Higher and cooler than Clare, the more disparate Eden Valley to the east of Barossa is Australia's other Riesling region. Narrow roads curve through the gum trees, past old homesteads on the way to vineyards as high as Adam Wynn's Mountadam (which makes excellent Chardonnay and Pinot Noir) and the neighbouring Penfolds' Riesling plantations. Road signs warn motorists of kangaroos, and parrots skitter through the trees. Rieslings here tend to be slightly lower alcohol, less obviously fruity and exhibit more floral than citrus characters – although they do become toasty with age. Winemakers many miles away, such as the talented Pam Dunsford of Chapel Hill, regularly plunder Eden Valley vineyards for their Riesling bottlings.

The Henschke family are the wine aristocrats of the Eden Valley and have red wine vineyards of such distinction (such as the famous ancient Hill of Grace planting of Shiraz) that they regularly make some of Australia's finest red wines from their base near Keyneton high above the Barossa Valley.

ADELAIDE HILLS

The Eden Valley shades south into the Adelaide Hills, where a handful of ambitious pioneer wine producers punctuate the leafy suburbs in the hills to the east of the city with expensive but promising vineyards. Almost all the vineyards were planted in the 1980s or 1990s, in some of Australia's coolest wine country. Acid is rarely added here, and malolactic fermentation is encouraged in most wines to soften the naturally high grape acids. This makes it an unusually good producer, especially by Australian standards, of sparkling wines (Croser at Piccadilly) and Sauvignon Blanc (particularly round Lenswood). Chardonnays can have exceptional depth and ageing ability and Merlots have already proved themselves. Brian Croser of Petaluma has been the most influential winemaker by far (and this region is about craft rather than industry), but fine wines are to be had under the Henschke, Tim Knappstein, Shaw & Smith and Stafford Ridge labels.

Cloud over McLaren Vale in South Australia,
which is more often swathed in sunshine.

VICTORIA

Wine was once extremely important to the state of Victoria, but phylloxera struck in the late nineteenth century and many of its scattered vineyards were abandoned. Even today, the Victorian wine map is more disjointed than that of any other Australian state, although the great bulk of its production comes from the **Mildura/Sunraysia** vineyards irrigated by the Murray River – not that far upriver of South Australia's Riverland (which produces twice as much wine). Victoria can boast Australia's biggest winery, however, Lindeman's base at Karadoc in Mildura, which manages to produce its Bin 65 branded Chardonnay to an admirably high standard for such enormous volumes.

The real interest of Victoria to the fine wine drinker, however, are the vineyards in the southern half of the state, which is the coolest part of mainland Australia. The cloudy **Yarra Valley** just north east of Melbourne has been making top quality wine for a century and has earned itself a reputation for delicate Pinot Noir such as Coldstream Hills, Mount Mary and Tarrawarra. Excellent sparkling wine is made at Domaine Chandon (Green Point is the export label) and the historic Yeringberg estate makes a thoroughly complex Cabernet.

On the other side of Melbourne and not much further away and cooled by Port Philip Bay, is **Geelong**, which has also shown an aptitude for Pinot Noir in various Bannockburn bottlings. And Melbourne can boast a third wine region within easy striking distance, on the **Mornington Pensinsula** due south across the Port Philip Bay from Geelong. A tight-knit group of small estates such as Dromana Estate, Main Ridge and Stoniers are working hard here to promote the reputation of this promising cool-climate wine region, which has managed to demonstrate a real affinity with Pinot Noir and Chardonnay.

Much of the rest of the Victorian wine map is dotted with isolated single wineries such as Seppelts' at Drumborg on the far western coast and loners such as Virgin Hills and Craiglee of **Macedon**, Balgownie and Jasper Hill of **Bendigo**, Delatite and Tisdall, all of which produce fine, concentrated, characterful wine in cooler conditions than most other Australians.

In this state, even the smallest cluster of wineries constitutes a wine region. **Great Western** was made famous by Seppelts, who have a Champagne-like honeycomb of sparkling wine cellars there, but Best's and, especially, Mount Langhi Giran make great still wines (notably peppery Shiraz and taut Riesling) nearby. The high **Pyrenees** to the north east can boast Taltarni and Dalwhinnie's best bottles as evidence of their potential.

The **Goulburn Valley** is rather warmer and houses two of Victoria's most commercially notable wineries, Mitchelton (so cosmopolitan it lends winemaking expertise to one of the largest wine producers in Spain) and the historic Chateau Tahbilk. Both make a wide range of varietals but Marsanne is a local speciality.

But Victoria's glory – indeed one of Australia's great gifts to the wine world – is **North East Victoria**, on the border with New South Wales, source of a unique style of rich fortified wines, Liqueur Muscat (from a dark-skinned version of the best Muscat vine) and Liqueur Tokay (in fact Muscadelle). Ultra-ripe grapes are picked, part fermented, the wine is fortified (as in port production) and the result is matured for decades in small oak barrels in baking hot sheds so that the wines are like ultra-syrupy, grapey Banyuls with a touch of madeira. Bailey's of Glenrowan-Milawa (also the base of Brown Brothers, who are doing a great deal to vary Australia's varietal mix) are prime producers, although they are rivalled by Morris, Chambers and Stanton & Killeen of Rutherglen.

NEW SOUTH WALES

The New South Wales wine map has been substantially redrawn since the good old days when the Australian wine industry was ruled from the Hunter Valley conveniently close to Sydney – and when the average Australian was introduced to wine via Lindemans Chablis (in fact Semillon) and McWilliam's Hermitage (Shiraz).

Today that cloudy, humid and often swelteringly hot area is known as the **Lower Hunter** and is as much about tourism as about vine-growing. As well as myriad restaurants, motels and hotels, it houses the headquarters of the influential Rothbury Estate, Len Evans's baby, and his own Evans Family vineyards, and such high achievers as Broke Estate, Brokenwood, Lake's Folly, McWilliam's, Petersons and Tyrrells (who have the distinction of having produced Australia's first commercial Chardonnay – as recently as 1971). Notwithstanding that, the Hunter's best, certainly most original, wine is its full bodied dry Semillon which, after many years in bottle, can become a most extraordinarily entrancing liquid, smelling of burnt toast and tasting of limes. It has also shown that it can produce great, luscious, long-living Shiraz, once famous for smelling of sweaty saddles.

A good hour's drive to the north from the Lower Hunter is the newer **Upper Hunter**, where the vine already occupies half as much land as in the historic Lower Hunter. The Upper Hunter's great advantage is markedly lower rainfall and therefore less risk of vine disease, although both areas can be dogged by rain in the crucial pre-harvest weeks.

Rosemount is the dominant producer here, and although it buys in fruit from all over the country, its most revered wine continues to be the increasingly sophisticated Chardonnay from the nearby Roxburgh vineyard.

It is significant, however, that Rosemount's winemaker has planted his own vines in a much cooler area than the Upper Hunter, south west of Mudgee in Orange, where lower temperatures are beginning to result in some much finer Chardonnays – albeit on a very small scale.

Much longer established is **Cowra**, even further south (due west of Sydney in fact), which has for years been growing thoroughly hedonistic, golden Chardonnay surprisingly capable of ageing. There are isolated vineyards and wineries all over Australia's most populated state, none more isolated, indeed idiosyncratic, than Cassegrain way up the coast at Port Macquarie which has been experimenting with hybrids in this damp region.

The source of the cuttings for Tyrrell's Chardonnay was **Mudgee**, one of Australia's most self-sufficient and well-established wine regions on the dry (but still hot) side of the Great Dividing Range. Mudgee has had its very own controlled appellation system for some time and boasts wineries as successful as Huntington Estate, Montrose and, Australia's first organic wine estate, Botobolar. Wines here tend to full-blooded Chardonnays and Cabernets.

But, like South Australia and Victoria, New South Wales has its giant wine factory, this one dependent not on the Murray river but on the Murrumbidgee, hence called the Murrumbidgee Irrigation Area (M.I.A.), although the area's chief towns **Riverina** and **Griffith** tend to be names used more often than Murrumbidgee. This is Australia's second most important region and has a distinctly more glamorous profile of vine varieties. Semillon is Murrumbidgee's most important variety by far, although Shiraz is still important. Griffith is distinguished by its small production of often stunningly good botrytized sweet Semillons. De Bortoli and McWilliam's are notable producers but the area is well and truly cherry picked by out-of-state wineries, too.

All in all, a wine labelled New South Wales is a pretty safe bet.

WESTERN AUSTRALIA

'WA', as this state is invariably known, may grow less than two per cent of the country's grapes, but it produces a very significant proportion of the country's best wine. Although all of the state's vines are grown in the south westernmost corner of this vast state, the most promising wine regions are those on the far south western tip, which are so new that there is still some disagreement about exactly what some of them should be called.

The most established wine region in south western WA is **Margaret River** (whose history dates all the way back to the 1960s), which is as close to paradise as I have been on my wine travels. Three hours' drive south of Perth is a virtually unpopulated surfer's paradise on a coast lined with gentle eucalyptus forests full of wild parrots and the odd kangaroo. Around the small settlement of Margaret River is a cluster of more than 30 wine estates making some of Australia's best-built Cabernets, some exceptionally long-living Chardonnay and the odd successful Pinot Noir and even Zinfandel. Cape Mentelle (birthplace of New Zealand's Cloudy Bay), Cullens, Leeuwin Estate, Moss Wood and Vasse Felix make an indecent proportion of Australia's most refined wines.

To the south, in regions known variously as Mount Barker, Frankland River and Manjimup and sometimes collectively as **Lower Great Southern**, there may be even more potential to be realized, certainly for cooler climate grape varieties such as Riesling and Pinot Noir. The cool flavours and nat-

ural acids are vaguely reminiscent of New Zealand. Goundrey have been producing some great bargains from here, but the higher prices of Alkoomi, Howard Park, Plantagenet and Wignalls are well justified.

The greater volume of Western Australian wine is made to the north, however, in generally hotter vineyards close to Perth. The **Swan Valley**, conveniently close to the state's only population centre, was the traditional source of supply, with Houghton (a subsidiary of South Australia's Hardys) being the dominant producer. Australians buy more of the full bodied aromatic, tangy dry white they call Houghton's White Burgundy (sold more discreetly in Europe as HWB) than any other white. Moondah Brook also demonstrates the quality of varieties such as Chenin Blanc and Verdelho in WA's older vineyards.

Today, vineyards are being planted intermittently all down the long coastal stretch south from Perth almost to Margaret River and there is much to look forward to.

Heemskerk winery in Tasmania, much of whose produce has been used to make the sparkling Jansz for Roederer of Champagne.

TASMANIA

Wine production on Tasmania has always been small, but its potential may be on the point of being realized. The proudly self-conscious island of Tasmania south of the state of Victoria is Australia's coolest, most distinctive wine region with a varied climate and terrain quite unlike anywhere on the mainland. A spate of new plantings in the early 1990s brought the total number of vine-growers to 90, of whom hardly more than 20 make wine, and each of them only on a small scale.

Tasmanians are particularly fond of their own edible and drinkable produce and only about a quarter of the wine produced from their vineyards escapes from the island itself.

The oldest wine producer of note is Moorilla Estate in the south (established in 1958), but among the continually changing roster of hopeful vine-growers who have followed them there is still considerable disagreement about exactly which one of the island's varied wine districts, which tend to be clustered around Launceston in the north and Hobart in the south, is most suitable for viticulture.

Vineyards here benefit from many hours of summer sunlight, but average temperatures tend to be much lower than mainland Australia and in some years flowering and the harvest itself can be prejudiced by bad weather. Some Tasmanian winemakers argue that they should be excluded from the Australian national constraints on chaptalization, adding sugar during fermentation to make up for a lack of natural, sun-ripened grape sugar, so cool are some summers this far south.

Most of the wines are obviously the produce of a cool climate, with their naturally high acidity, relatively subtle flavours and, often, good balance of clean fruit flavour – a build more German than New Zealand. The chief grape varieties planted have been Riesling, Chardonnay, Pinot Noir and Cabernet Sauvignon, and the well-made examples, which constitute by far the majority, tend to age particularly gracefully.

Aromatic, dry whites predominate but many producers, among them Piper's Brook in the wet and windy north east of the island, Freycinet on the east coast and Domaine A Stoney Vineyard in the warmish Coal River Valley north of Hobart, are making ambitiously styled, relatively concentrated reds. Tasmania is yet another place where Pinot Noir may flourish (see New Zealand, Oregon, California, Chile).

Over the years there has been considerable input from foreign, notably Swiss, investors but the island's Chardonnay and Pinot Noir fruit has attracted attention from champagne producers. Louis Roederer was for long in partnership with Heemskirk, one of the island's bigger producers, struggling to establish commercially viable north coast vineyards for Jansz, their lean, traditional method fizz. Moët's Domaine Chandon ships grapes from the island to its Yarra Valley winery on the mainland and others are expected to follow suit.

The small, isolated nature of the Tasmanian wine industry has enabled it to set up its own controlled appellation system for 100 per cent Tasmanian wines, of which it is especially proud.

OTHER WINE REGIONS

Queensland has more land devoted to vines than Tasmania but usually produces considerably less wine, thanks largely to its low annual rainfall. Almost all vineyards are on the Granite Belt where high altitude compensates to a certain extent for low latitude. There is also a cluster of small winemaking concerns around the capital **Canberra**, effectively an extension of New South Wales viticulture. Even the arid interior of the **Northern Territory** can boast one winery, at Alice Springs, of interest chiefly to visitors to Ayers Rock.

NEW ZEALAND

In a nutshell: New World wines with crisp fruity acids.

Grapes: Chardonnay but most famously Sauvignon Blanc (WHITE)

The New Zealand wine industry, which produces a small fraction of one per cent of the world's wine, has a real problem. Like the country itself, it is so small and vulnerable that navigating a safe course across the treacherous waters of the international wine market can be extremely difficult. One strong economic wind and a pronounced list to starboard can threaten to capsize the craft altogether.

In 1986, fearing over-production, the government encouraged growers to pull out a quarter of the country's vines. Just seven years later (thanks to short vintages, and damage done by the phylloxera louse) there was such a desperate shortage of grapes that there simply wasn't enough wine to mount a serious export effort.

The results of fast and furious plantings in the mid-1990s should help to introduce more and more wine drinkers to the unique character of wines from these Pacific islands three hours' flying time south east of Australia.

New Zealand wines combine the well-preserved pure fruit flavours of New World winemaking with the natural grape acidity associated with northern Europe. This crispness, sometimes piercing and a characteristic of New Zealand reds as well as whites, is a feature markedly lacking in the great majority of New World wines, including most of those still made in Australia, which is why a number of Australian producers buy wine and even grapes from New Zealand (especially Sauvignon Blanc and ingredients for sparkling wine blends). Vines in Europe tend to be planted on poor soils, so yields are low and the grapes can ripen fairly well despite the high acidity, but New Zealand's soils can be very fertile so New Zealanders have

had to devise ways of manipulating their vines, stripping leaves, and making every ray of sunshine contribute towards the ripening process. (New Zealand is the home of 'canopy management' – see page 64.) New Zealand wine producers are allowed to make an unusually wide range of adjustments to the basic wine recipe: irrigation, chaptalization, acidification and deacidification (see How Wine is Made, in Section Two) are all sanctioned in recognition of the country's extremely varied climate.

Those few wine drinkers outside New Zealand who have experienced New Zealand wines (most of them British) tend to regard the country's distinctively fruity way with the razor-sharp Sauvignon Blanc as the country's hallmark wine, but in fact this aromatic variety is less widely planted than either Müller-Thurgau, which used to dominate the country's wine production, or Chardonnay which does so today. Whatever the vicissitudes of fashion, it is clear that New Zealand is likely to remain a predominantly white wine producer. Some particularly well-favoured vineyard sites can yield seriously concentrated Cabernet/Merlot blends but the outside world is likely to be more interested in New Zealand's most successful, impressively authentic Pinot Noirs.

The country's three biggest wine regions by far are Marlborough, Gisborne and Hawkes Bay. Here hundreds of farmers produce grapes, typically just one of several agricultural activities, for one of the country's big three bottlers: Montana (which produces one bottle of New Zealand wine in every two), Corbans/Cooks and the Villa Maria/Vidal/Esk Valley group which consistently produces more fine red wine than any other operation in New Zealand. Montana's strength is in white wines, especially those of the Marlborough region which it pioneered, while Corbans manages to combine both North and South Island expertise. Trucking grapes from a grower in one wine region to a wine-maker in another, many hours' drive (and sometimes voyage) away, is becoming a thing of the past, as are the rather astringent wines that sometimes resulted from the obligatory pre-fermentation maceration involved.

MARLBOROUGH

The wide, flat, vine-covered expanse of the Wairau Valley and the mountains around it are now New Zealand's most photographed wine region (see over), but in 1973 the entire South Island was *terra incognita* to the country's wine industry. The Marlborough region at the island's north eastern tip was created by the Montana winery, which bought up sheep farming land almost by stealth, gambling on its assessment of the region's potential to produce wines that would be as attractive to consumers as to accountants.

Marlborough Sauvignon Blanc seduced the imagination and palates of thousands of wine drinkers outside New Zealand in the mid-1980s when the first releases of Cloudy Bay trickled on to the British, American and Australian markets. At that stage Cloudy Bay was just a clever name, label and concept dreamt up by Western Australian winemaker David Hohnen of Cape Mentelle, but the distinctively lush tropical flavours he and winemaker Kevin Judd coaxed from this sometimes austere variety were sufficient to put Marlborough Sauvignon on the international wine map. Other winemakers such as Hunter's established an early reputation for their Sauvignon and Chardonnay too, while the recent increases in grape prices have encouraged all manner of investors, gamblers and local farmers to chance their arm at vine-growing. Although most of them sell their grapes to the bigger companies many of them also sell some wine under their own label made at Vintech, the contract winery established by Hunter's ex-winemaker John Belsham, which has transformed the country's wine industry by processing Marl-borough grapes for the large companies based in the North Island (or Australia).

Marlborough Chardonnays can be attrac-tively lean and refreshing – the ripest of them benefiting imperceptibly from some barrel fermentation and maturation, the lightest making an increasing contribution to some fine traditional method sparkling wines. There is also talk here, as elsewhere in the world, of a Riesling renaissance, although the most exciting examples to date have been intensely refreshing sweet wines made in years when the botrytis mould (see page 88) develops. Red wines are steadily gaining more flesh with some of the most convincing examples coming from the new Swiss-owned Fromm winery and Vava-sour (second label Dashwood) which has colo-nized the warmer Awatere Valley to the south.

GISBORNE/POVERTY BAY

The North Island's self-styled Chardonnay garden was ravaged by phylloxera in the late 1980s but is now on course to provide creamy, rather tropical fruit-flavoured grapes, mainly as raw material for the larger producers. It has also produced the country's best Gewürztraminer (notably from the idiosyncratic Matawhero), which can be very good indeed in some years. The estate bottler of most note is The Millton Estate which preached the gospel of biody-namism (see page 65) years before Burgundy's top producers had even heard of it.

HAWKES BAY

South of Gisborne on the east coast of the North Island, Hawkes Bay is New Zealand's most varied and possibly most promising wine region. Parts of it are quite warm and well drained enough to produce fine, concentrated Cabernet/Merlot red wines following on the coat tails of the region's standard-bearer Te Mata estate, established by John Buck, right-hand man to the head of an important British brewery-owned wine merchant in the mid-1960s. C. J. Pask's and Ngatarawa's reputations were built on rather later vintages.

The vast Brancott estate in Marlborough, which is owned by New Zealand's largest wine company, Montana. Their size keeps their Sauvignon Blanc inexpensive.

OTHER REGIONS

At one time most of the country's wine producers were based in the suburbs, particularly Henderson, of its largest city, **Auckland**. Today vine-growing is focused on cooler areas but worthwhile producers such as Collards, Delegat's, Matua Valley and Selaks still have their headquarters in Auckland, and the family operation Kumeu River continues to pursue French-inspired techniques with grapes ripened in the Auckland suburb of Kumeu. St Nesbit makes tiny quantities of fine red wines. A short ferry ride from the city, **Waiheke Island** is the local centre of the 'boutique' or 'life-style' winery phenomenon, with Stonyridge's Cabernets setting a standard.

Between Auckland and Gisborne the dual-named **Waikato/Bay of Plenty** region houses several successful wineries of which Morton

Estate is the best known. The **Wellington/ Wairarapa/Martinborough** region in the south east of the North Island has produced some stunning Pinot Noir and Chardonnay from wineries such as Ata Rangi, Martinborough and Palliser Estate.

In the South Island Neudorf and Seifried are the stars of **Nelson**, for rich Chardonnay and sweet Riesling respectively, while further south the climate can be so variable that few wineries can promise top quality year in and year out. In the **Canterbury** region round Christchurch some inspiring wines have been made by Waipara Springs and St Helena, and Pinot Noir and Chardonnay were the first varieties to show promise. Even further south in **Central Otago**, the world's most southerly wine region, viticulture is a truly marginal activity, but one being pursued with vigour by the likes of Rippon and Gibbston Valley.

SOUTH AFRICA

In a nutshell: *Mainly whites, some bargains and increasingly convincing answers to international styles.*
Grapes: *Chenin Blanc* (WHITE), *Pinotage* (RED) *and the usual international mix*

One of the exciting things about the wine business is the reliable way in which it mirrors social and political change. The mixed races of the South African population patiently lining up in the hot sun to vote together for the very first time may well be the most moving image we ever see in our lifetimes. As soon as Nelson Mandela was voted in to power and apartheid reliably a thing of the past, wine lovers the world over had to revise the habits of a lifetime and begin to take a positive interest in once-reviled exports from South Africa, of which wine, with its labelling for all to see, is the most obvious.

For South African wine producers the transformations of 1993 and 1994 heralded an era of potential prosperity, with previously forbidden export markets opened up almost overnight, but also the new challenge of seeing their wines exposed to international competition. One result of South Africa's prolonged and only recently ended isolation is that wine consumers, commentators and producers there seem, doubtless only temporarily and perhaps inevitably, almost unhealthily obsessed by the detailed results of comparative tastings.

Thanks to the country's surplus of clean, well-made, bargain basement dry white (and to systematic export subsidies), South Africa saw her wine exports to the UK grow so rapidly in 1994 that they overtook those of Chile and New Zealand. By 1995 the US was beginning to take a serious interest in wines from an exporter which had previously been scorned. In the mid-1990s South African wines were enjoying the indulgent and optimistic aura which made all things South African glow. And the fact that South Africa's wine country is the most dramatically beautiful in the world has surely done little to harm the fortunes of its produce abroad.

Within South Africa's vineyards and cellars themselves, producers have shown how rapidly they can absorb and adapt new techniques and fashions in wine styles. They have progressed as far in the 1990s alone as many others have in the 1980s and 1990s combined. The current objectives are to continue to maximize the quality of their raw material – most obviously systematically replacing the vines whose output has been seriously affected by viruses, but also continuing to understand better which clones are best suited to local conditions (and getting them through national plant quarantines).

Wine has been made on the Cape of Good Hope since the mid-seventeenth century, which means that South Africa has a much longer, unbroken history of winemaking than either Australia or California. Even today the influence of the Cape Dutch, the original settlers, is strong, as witness the scalloped white gables of many a winery and Afrikaans names whose pronunciation many potential wine importers find quite unfathomable.

Only this southern limit of the country (and continent), lapped by the Indian Ocean but cooled to a varied extent by winds off the Atlantic and currents from the Antarctic, is suitable for vine-growing. The climate of the wine regions is in very general terms slightly hotter than California's best known (few coastal fogs here) but ever cooler areas are being sought, found and planted.

Most table wines are labelled varietally (not so the Cape's sizeable production of dessert wines, made in the image of European classics such as rather raisiny 'port' and some often oily 'sherry'). The chief grape variety (almost invariably called 'cultivar' in South Africa) by far is

Chenin Blanc, which is yet to produce anything as sweet and sour as a luscious Vouvray on the Cape, but which can easily be persuaded to produce large volumes of clean, refreshing dry and medium dry white, often called Steen. Other important white wine varieties include Colombar(d) (a significant ingredient in South Africa's cheap dry whites), 'Cape Riesling' (Crouchen), Clairette, Semillon, Ugni Blanc, Riesling, various Muscats and, of course, Chardonnay and Sauvignon Blanc. It has taken South African nurseries time to offer any seriously good Chardonnay cuttings, which may help to explain South Africa's unusual fondness for Chardonnay blends (notably but not exclusively with Sauvignon Blanc). Sauvignon Blanc, on the other hand, has been planted here for a century and can make some wonderfully self-confident, fruity wines – as well as some very inexpensive, less concentrated ones.

Only about 15 per cent of the country's vineyard is planted with red wine grapes, of which the national speciality is a 1920s Cape crossing of Pinot Noir and Cinsaut called Pinotage. As national pride was regained, so was local pride in this lively, aromatic red varietal, South Africa's answer to California's Zinfandel and Australia's Shiraz.

Cabernet Sauvignon is regarded as the aristocrat of the Cape's vineyards, but it needs careful treatment in the cellar in order to yield a deep-coloured, well-balanced, seriously long-lived wine. Tannins can be obtrusive. Merlot is increasingly made as a varietal as well as being used to blend with Cabernet. Some increasingly interesting Shiraz and even Zinfandel is made. Pinot Noir is grown only in the coolest spots with any success and even here growers have been hampered by a lack of Burgundian (as opposed to Swiss) clones. The Cape's portmaking heritage has also resulted in significant plantings of port vines such as Tinta Barroca which are often made into substantial dry reds.

It would be a shame if, in their rush to prove that they too can produce answers to Bordeaux and Burgundy, Cape winemakers ignored the country's potential for creating strapping, stable dry reds.

The South African wine business has a curious structure, with the 100-odd quality-minded, usually small-scale wine producers vastly outflanked by producers of bulk wine, wine for distilling, grape concentrate and, especially, grape juice. Co-operatives are very important, processing about 85 per cent of each year's grape harvest (although only about a quarter of those grapes ends up as wine). It is only very recently indeed that the individual wine estates have been even allowed to buy in grapes, although a separate name must be used for the wine they produce – quite a contrast with most New World wine-producing countries!

THE MAIN WINE REGIONS

Constantia, on the southern outskirts of Cape Town, is the Cape's oldest wine region and one of its coolest. Its sweet white wines were once as famous in Europe as those of Hungary's Tokay. The Klein Constantia winery has revived this style with a 'Vin de Constance' Muscat, although it and Buitenverwachting also make a fine range of dry whites and bordeaux-style reds.

The university town of **Stellenbosch** is regarded as the South African wine industry's spiritual home. The natural conditions of the region vary enormously but most vineyards benefit from the cooling influence of the Atlantic in summer. This is where the country's greatest concentration of dedicated individual estates is to be found, with a traditional reputation for reds but some increasingly exciting whites too. Some of the most successful producers have been Blaauwkippen, Delheim, Grangehurst, Kanonkop, Meerlust, Mulderbosch, Neethlingshof, Overgaauw, Rustenberg, Rust-en-Vrede, Thelema, Vriesenhof and Warwick Estate.

Paarl produces even more wine than Stellenbosch and is the headquarters of the powerful KWV organization which for many years controlled the industry's output with stifling regulation and blanket support. Much fortified

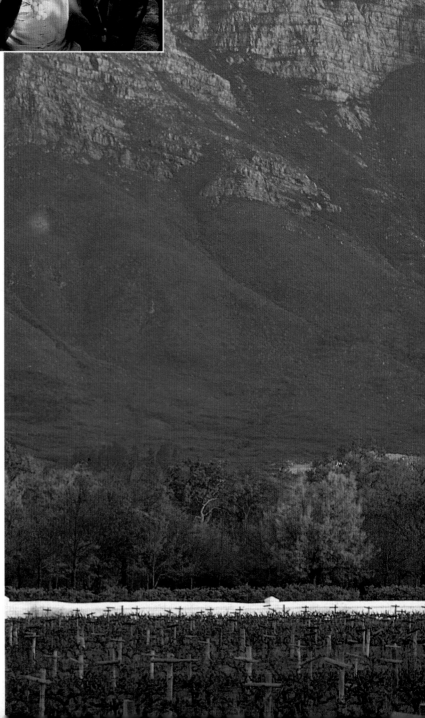

South African vineyard
exuberance (above) over
a grape industry which
can offer the most stunning
landscapes in the world, such
as the Boschendal Cape
Dutch manor house
in Franschoek (right).

wine is made here, including some quite convincing flor sherries (see pages 233–5), and the large producer Nederburg pioneered botrytized Chenin Blanc. Fredericksburg makes good Cabernet. Franschoek (meaning 'French corner', a reference to early Huguenot settlers) is in the east of the region and boasts wineries such as Boschendal, (Clos) Cabrière, Dieu Donné and L'Ormarins/La Motte.

Even further inland than Paarl is **Worcester**, the Cape's answer to California's Central Valley. Hot, dry and fertile, the region's vineyards need extensive irrigation and produce vast quantities of grapes, raw materials for inexpensive dry whites, some rich fortified wines and the full range of 'vine products' other than wine.

South east of Worcester, with a similar dry climate but soils more suited to vine-growing, is **Robertson**, a notable white wine-producing region with some interesting co-operative wines as well as estates such as De Wetshof making waves with Chardonnay.

To the east stretches the increasingly hot and arid **Little Karoo** where vines, mainly for bulk produce, tend to be planted close to rivers for irrigation. There are even hotter, drier conditions in the **Orange River**, many miles north and inland from the main Cape wine regions.

Tulbagh, Piketberg and **Swartland** are adjoining wine regions west and north of Worcester, which are at low latitudes but enjoy some influence from the Atlantic. Swartland was for years associated with heavy reds but all three regions now produce some thoroughly exportable, and exported, crisp dry whites at low prices, chiefly but not exclusively through the co-ops. **Olifants River** is the northern, Atlantic-influenced extension of this part of the Cape, transforming the waters of the Olifants River into bulk and distilling wine and some crisp dry whites such as those exported, with surprising success, under the Goiya Kgeisje and other labels by the Vredendal co-operative, South Africa's largest winery.

On the southern, Indian Ocean coast are a few wine estates chancing their arm in some of the continent's coolest spots. To call Walker Bay, Elgin (in Overberg) and Mossel Bay wine regions is a little premature, but wines from the likes of Bouchard-Finlayson and Hamilton Russell give cause for hope.

WINE STYLES

The great majority of South African wine is white, typically, if not particularly noticeably, based on Chenin Blanc. There are plans afoot on the part of South Africa's wine industry management (who are only too aware that their honeymoon in the international marketplace may be short-lived) to put more flavour and interest into these cheap, dry, relatively tart blends. One day botrytized sweet Chenin Blanc may be less of a rarity.

Other whites include Chardonnay/Sauvignon/Riesling blends and the usual variations on the barrel-fermented Chardonnay and ultra-aromatic Sauvignon Blanc.

Among reds, Cabernet Sauvignon is the most revered variety by far, for the moment, but Merlot is up and coming as both an ingredient and a varietal, and some producers are managing to make some seriously fine, concentrated yet balanced Pinotage.

UNDERSTANDING LABELS

estate – this word usually appears on wines bottled on the farm on which all the grapes were grown, a relative rarity in South Africa.
Méthode Cap Classique, South Africa's own term for the traditional champagne method of making wine sparkle.
Noble Late Harvest, sweet wine made from botrytized grapes.
Premier Grand Cru, dry, light, usually blended white, a misleading term used within South Africa.
Wine of Origin, South Africa's answer to France's AC system, authenticating the grape variety specified on the label, the vintage and the wine's provenance.

OTHER COUNTRIES

CHINA AND JAPAN

China has a burgeoning wine industry, aimed chiefly at its growing tourist trade. A small sector of it in the far west is effectively an extension of Kazakhstan, but most of its vineyards are on the eastern coast, where large foreign companies are planting Western grape varieties as well as local specialities. The great majority of Chinese grape wine is light, white, crisp and just off dry.

The wine industry of Japan is, as one might expect, commercially more sophisticated, with a great variety of companies engaged in both producing and importing wine. Vines have to battle against all sorts of natural hazards in Japan, including very acid soils and, in the far north, perilously cold winters. Thanks to the humid climate, Japanese vines have to be coaxed to produce a reasonable yield of healthy grapes by training them into high trellises and spraying them throughout the growing season. It is difficult to imagine a time when Japan will have such a wine surplus that she exports anything like as enthusiastically as she imports.

INDIA

India on the other hand has been exporting some rather sophisticated wine including some sparkling made to a recipe as close to that of champagne as is practicable in such very different circumstances, often sold under the name Omar Khayyam. Definitely a country to watch.

THE BRITISH ISLES

English wine (the term rather curiously used officially for wine made from grapes grown in both England and Wales) is not a joke, although the average Briton treats it as such. About 2500 acres (1000 ha) of southern England and Wales's best-exposed land (sheltered, south-facing slopes) are planted with vines, which would be a complete waste of time at these latitudes were it not for the moderating influence of the Gulf Stream. Wine has been produced in the British Isles for centuries, but the modern English wine industry dates only from the 1950s when one or two and then dozens of, typically, retired gentlefolk began to plant vines and try their hand at winemaking.

The industry today is much more professional and most wine is made by younger, qualified winemakers who usually have experience of cellars in other countries. Because of England's cool climate, only early ripening vine varieties stand a chance of reliably producing a crop. The most planted varieties are therefore Müller-Thurgau and the hybrid Seyval Blanc. The German crossing Reichensteiner is also quite widely planted but there is an enormous variety of white and some red wine varieties otherwise. (The few red wines made are generally made either from red-fleshed grapes or are ripened in special plastic tunnels.)

Almost all grape musts have to rely on added sugar to produce wines with a decent alcoholic strength (see chaptalization on page 72) and the natural grape acidity is usually notable. Such wines can make excellent bases for sparkling wines and there have been some truly refreshing dry whites which can even stand up to some barrel ageing.

A little wine is also made from vines grown in warmer parts of Ireland.

'British wine' is a very different animal, made from reconstituted grape concentrate imported from whichever region can offer the best price (Cyprus has been a common source). These have tended to be understandably cheap sherry- and port-style wines, strengthened with added alcohol, but the proportion of wine made in the image of table wine has increased.

VINTAGE GUIDE

Italicized type denotes lighter years; normal type means average years; and **bold type** is used for exceptional years.

FRANCE

BORDEAUX
Red

1995 Hot, dry summer resulted in early harvest of healthy Merlot grapes. Relatively tannic Cabernet Sauvignon was picked after a week of mid-September rain. Generous crop levels, best in Pomerol and Pauillac.

1994 The best year since 1990, very ripe but September rains were a problem again.

1993 *Another wet harvest. Picked earlier, the Right Bank (of the Gironde) looks best.*

1992 *Light, fruity, simple wines that need drinking soon.*

1991 *The start of Bordeaux's run of bad luck. Spring frosts decimated Right Bank, top Médocs not bad.*

1990 **A second scorching year in a row. Very ripe, concentrated wines at all levels, many outstanding.**

1989 **A hot summer and huge crop of rich, opulent, expensive wines, drinking astonishingly well young.**

1988 Overshadowed by 1989 and 1990. 'Classic' style i.e. firm and a bit austere.

1987 *A middling year, simple, fruity and pleasant but unexciting. Some attractive Pomerols.*

1986 Dense, brooding and viciously tannic. Some will be legendary but not for 10+ years.

1985 Uniformly lovely, fragrant wines especially from Right Bank, most need drinking soon.

1983 Good but less concentrated than 1982, so need drinking. For once, Margaux excelled.

1982 **Legendary year, horribly expensive but very concentrated and so delicious.**

1981 Patchy quality, but many crisp, appetizing Médocs for current consumption.

1979 Graceful, suave and well-balanced, but drink up.

1978 A perfect autumn saved the crop. The big Left Bank names are strongest.

Dry white

1995 Lots of body and flavour and structure thanks to the warm summer wherever grapes were picked before the mid-September rains.

1994 **Potentially superb as fully ripe grapes were again gathered before the rains.**

1993 Avoided the rains: generally good, soft and full, sometimes outstanding.

1992 Clearly better than the reds, the best are intense and well structured.

1991 *A difficult year, rather light and most are just too dilute to be interesting.*

1990 Mostly richer, fuller and more complex than 1989, but drink now.

Sweet whites

1995 **Best Sauternes vintage since 1990 with rapid development of noble rot. Grapes picked by early October.**

1994 Grey rot in September, so choose the châteaux that could afford to be fussy.

1993 *Another pretty dreadful autumn, hardly anyone made interesting wine.*

1992 *Endless rains ruined the crop. Many estates declassified everything.*

1991 After the April frosts a tiny crop was eventually harvested, of not bad quality.

1990 **Massive rich wines that may be underestimated but presently seem a shade less complex than 1989 and 1988.**

1989 **Huge, almost corpulent wines that are dramatic and exciting.**

1988 **Of the fabulous trio of vintages this shows most botrytis and elegance and may live longest.**

1986 **A very strong year, plenty of botrytis and beautifully balanced.**

1985 Rich and elegant but too little noble rot to add the magic.

1983 **The best since 1976, with similar power and size. Good value too!**

1982 Overlooked as a white vintage. Limited botrytis but Suduiraut and Yquem were successful.

BURGUNDY
Red

1995 Reduced crop of rather austere wines which may take on fat in bottle.

1994 A year to highlight Burgundy's infamy for variability as too many let yields balloon after the rains. Nuits better than Beaune.

1993 Better than average: healthy grapes and well-coloured, fruity, but quite tannic wines.

1992 *Rain at the wrong time again. Soft, tender wines to drink young.*

1991 Grapes had ripened before it rained and some wines from the Côte de Nuits are excellent.

1990 **A great success: rich and fragrant. The top vineyards are majestic.**

1989 **Nearly up to 1990, if not as intense. These are charming now.**

1988 Tough and unusually backward, most are densely concentrated but need time.

1987 Natural ripeness a problem, so many are overchaptalized. Select from reliable growers.

1986 *A very tricky year of rain and rot. Careful growers avoided the dilution. Few worthy.*

1985 **A problem-free year: delicious and fragrant young, but will they age?**

1984 *Poor weather and unripe grapes. Best to avoid.*

1983 A torrid summer and very mixed bag. A handful are brilliant but most are tainted by rot.

1982 *Large yields of soft, pleasant wines, now largely past it.*

1980 Underestimated at first: balanced and scented, the best are still elegant.

White

1995 **Very small crop producing wines with real concentration.**

1994 Generally better than the reds and certainly more consistent, especially the Mâconnais.

1993 A large harvest struck by rain, so concentration is a problem. Quite lean in youth.

1992 Balanced, elegant and refined: best from the Côtes rather than Chablis.

1991 Rain reduced acidity and concentration, some are delightful but many are dilute.

1990 Very ripe but yields were just too high for profound wines. Chablis best.

1989 **A medium-sized crop produced spectacularly rich and horribly expensive wines.**

1988 Lean and austere, they may gain charm with age. Good Chablis vintage.

1986 **Not as consistent as 1985, but great from reliable growers. Drink up.**

1985 **Beautifully balanced, expansive wines which are now gorgeous.**

ALSACE

1995 Varied year in which those who picked low-yielding vineyards well after the rains made great Rieslings, some very ripe. Rot threatened everyday wines. Slightly reduced crop.

1994 September rain, but impressive wines from those brave enough to pick late.

1993 A very good year: ripe wines of weight and intensity.

1992 Better than most French regions: ripe, soft and forward.

1991 *A difficult year, rain hit the harvest and the wines are light and acidic.*

1990 **A third wonderful year of classic, powerful, long-lived wines.**

1989 **Massive sugar levels produced a blockbuster vintage with many thrilling botrytis-affected bottles.**

1988 **Superb and intensely flavoured with the balance to last.**

LANGUEDOC-ROUSSILLON

1995 **Excellent ripeness and concentration in reds, especially in the hills.**

1994 Some real successes among red wines despite occasional rot and raisining.

1993 **After a wonderful summer this is an exciting vintage.**

1992 Irregular quality inevitable after localized autumn downpours. Whites better than reds.

1991 **A really outstanding year of rich, dense and big-structured wines.**

NORTH RHÔNE

1995 Very promising vintage which may eventually deserve being upgraded to bold type.

1994 **All-too familiar autumn rains before some fruit could ripen. A few will surprise.**

1993 *A great summer then rain, hail and mildew, so light, soft wines are the rule, although Chapoutier surprises.*

1992 *Heavy September rains gave a mixed bag of early-drinking wines.*

1991 A good vintage, superb in Côte-Rôtie: fragrant, forward and charming.

1990 **The heatwave slowed ripening. Côte-Rôtie suffered but Hermitage is a star for monster wines.**

1989 A drought year, irregular in Cornas, otherwise rich and opulent.

1988 Unfairly overshadowed by 1989 and 1990, with majestic Côte-Rôties for long ageing.

1986 *Guigal's wines are the exception to a rather lean, charmless year.*

1985 Always opulent and soft, these are delicious to drink now. Good Côte-Rôties.

1983 Outstanding muscular wines for the long term.

SOUTH RHÔNE

1995 Very good colour and really ripe, concentrated reds. Some producers claim it is better than 1990.

1994 Early harvesters were luckier, most picked in rain, so probably only average quality.

1993 An unwelcome repeat of 1992's weather: diluted but easy-drinking wines.

1992 *Torrential harvest rains drowned the vineyards and the results are pretty dilute.*

1991 *The Grenache failed at flowering and harvest time was uninspiring. Not to be pursued.*

1990 Exceptionally sumptuous, powerful and heady wines with low acidity, already at their peak.

1989 Fabulously concentrated with perhaps more backbone than 1990.

1988 Good in all areas: full bodied and with firm tannins, often termed 'classic'.

1987 *Pretty poor generally, cool and wet weather with thin wines the result.*

1986 Mostly picked before the rains, these are firm and tannic with good ageing potential.

ITALY

PIEDMONT

1995 Hail-reduced crop of deep-coloured wines made from grapes which benefitted from a sunny autumn. Probably a notch below 1989 and 1990.

1994 Sugar and acid levels reasonable despite prolonged September rains. Not quite up to Tuscany's 1994s.

1993 Some Nebbiolo and Barbera didn't really ripen before it rained. May outdo 1988.

1992 *A large harvest, generally low on weight and power.*

1991 A smallish crop of light to mid-weight early-drinking wines.

1990 With colossal power and big aromas these are very exciting, but need time.

1989 A superb healthy crop. Top Barolos are thrilling and will need keeping.

1988 Initially overrated, these are attractive, soft, full wines for drinking now.

1985 Many remain impressive, but excessive yields caused some to fade early.

1982 Oddly similar to Bordeaux: gorgeous young, they have the weight and balance to really last.

TUSCANY

1995 Nail-bitingly late harvest saved by an unusually warm, dry October, although acids are still generally high.

1994 At last a dry but cool harvest: rich and structured.

1993 Survived the rains better than Piedmont, concentration held up, but some picked unripe fruit. Very good wines from top estates.

1992 *A big crop of rather light wines to drink young.*

1991 Endless harvest rains so the best are no more than pleasant.

1990 A hot year and low yields, the ingredients for really good wines, especially for Brunello.

1989 *Distinctly inferior to Piedmont. Light if not watery, so best to avoid.*

SPAIN

RIOJA & RIBERA DEL DUERO

1995 Another frost-shrunk crop in Ribera del Duero, although the grapes were riper and probably better balanced than in 1994. Rioja's bodegas, on the other hand, were swollen by an enormous harvest of ripe, healthy grapes.

1994 Quality isn't a problem but quantity is after spring frosts and summer drought. Really promising; best Rioja vintage since 1970.

1993 Heavy harvest rains again. Good but not great seems the rule. Ribera mediocre.

1992 *This looked good until prolonged rains which diluted the grapes and encouraged rot. Some stars.*

1991 An excellent year in Spain, only a small crop but impressive weight and structure.

1990 Another large and fine quality crop in all areas.

1989 Plenty of rich and charming wines from both regions. Ribera exceptional.

1986 Good in Rioja but outshone by fabulous Riberas of complexity and power.

PORTUGAL

PORT

1995 Real potential for vintage port.

1994 Real potential for vintage port.

1992 **Some lovely wines.**

1991 **Great potential, very rich with considerable structure. A long-term vintage.**

1985 **A flattering year: luscious and fragrant for mid-term drinking.**

1983 A shade behind 1985. Good, sometimes exceptional. Maturing relatively fast.

1982 Declared by only a few houses, these are supple and for early drinking.

1980 A medium weight year. Reliable without hitting the heights.

1977 **Destined to be legendary, these have monstrous weight and power and will probably last forever! Similar to 1970.**

1975 *Widely declared but an underperformer.*

1970 **Superb, big, full and deep. Now ready, will last very many years.**

GERMANY

1995 An unusually warm summer was followed by a cold, wet late August and September so that the bulk of wine produced was rather ordinary, but the late, great Riesling showed its stuff in the Mosel after a very warm October.

1994 Horribly variable, but Riesling showed its class with super quality from the good estates.

1993 A nerve racking year. Rain hit the early harvests but patient growers picked grapes with welcome botrytis.

1992 Not bad, particularly in the Rhine. Estates had to control yields to overcome dilution from the rains and maintain balance.

1991 *Ripe, crisp, even slightly austere wines, just the stuff for Kabinetts!*

1990 **Europe's wonder year: a great autumn with plenty of late-picked sweet wines after a botrytis bonanza.**

1989 **A phenomenal harvest. The late-harvested Rieslings show profound complexity. Probably best in Mosel-Saar-Ruwer.**

1988 **Overshadowed by two remarkable years, this is still a superb vintage of elegance and fruit.**

USA

N. CALIFORNIA

1995 Yet another region in which a warm, dry autumn and late harvest saved the day after a difficult growing season. Reds, especially Zinfandels, may be even better than 1991. Small quantities pushed up prices, however.

1994 **Generally compared to 1991, the slow ripening will benefit the reds especially.**

1993 Erratic growing conditions reduced eventual yields. A mixed bag with some excellent wines.

1992 Plenty of good reds and whites, with Merlot a highlight but variable.

1991 **A long growing season reflected in unusually fragrant, complex wines; Pinot Noir strong.**

1990 **A modest-sized crop, the top Cabernets and Chardonnays rival 1985.**

1989 After autumn rains, poorly-drained sites suffered, and many picked too early. Variable, especially the whites. (Central Coast better.)

1988 A cooler summer and light but charming wines to drink up. Good Pinot Noir.

1987 A mixed year, but some marvellous Zinfandels and Cabernets.

1986 Only slightly inferior to 1985 and successful for all varieties.

AUSTRALIA

SOUTH AUSTRALIA

1996 A big vintage at last, with sugars boosted by a late burst of heat.

1995 Inconveniently small crop but some good Shiraz and Rieslings, especially in Clare where quantities were better than elsewhere.

1994 Exceptionally dry but not too hot: the resulting wines are deep and structured, especially from Barossa Valley.

1993 Ripening was slowed by an unusually cool and wet spell. A challenging year, the whites especially, are more variable than usual.

1992 Cool temperatures at harvest ensured balanced wines, exceptional from Clare Valley.

1991 Dry weather restricted yields, but the quality is generally fine for all varieties.

WHERE TO BUY WINE

The United States is not an easy place to sell wine. A sometimes complex web of rules and regulations is designed to squeeze as much tax as possible out of this delicious drink. Complicated, often outdated, and occasionally ignored tax laws can make shipping wine across state lines difficult and occasionally impossible, and there are some constraints on the movement of wine between producers, wholesalers, retailers, and consumers, even via mail and courier services.

But all is not bleak. Parts of the United States are extremely good places to *buy* wine. The competitiveness of the average New York trader makes the city's wine stores some of the greatest sources of bargains (from all over the world) known to wine drinking man and woman. There are similar treasure troves in California, where the state's own wine industry provides the spur to real wine knowledge and enthusiasm in dozens of retail outlets (not to mention hundreds of restaurants).

There are also encouraging signs that a healthy auction business is developing in the United States, offering individual wine enthusiasts the chance to buy and sell fine and rare wines by the case, or occasionally bottle. See auctioneers numbers below.

The following very partial list gives details of some of the most famous American wine retailers.

WINE AUCTIONS

Butterfield & Butterfield, San Francisco (415) 861-7500 Ext 307

Chicago Wine Co, Chicago (847) 647-8789

David & Co, Chicago (312) 587-9500

Morrell & Co, New York (212) 688-9370

Sherry-Lehmann with Sotheby's, New York (212) 838-7500/606-7307

Zachy's-Christie's, New York (212) 546-5930/(914) 723-0241

U.S. RETAIL WINE SHOPS

Wally's Liquor, 2107 Westwood Boulevard, Los Angeles, CA 90025, Ph: (310) 475-0606, Fax: (310) 474-1450

The Wine House, 2311 Cotner Avenue, Los Angeles, CA 90064, Ph: (310) 479-3731, Fax: (310) 478-5609

L.A. Wine Company, 4935 McConnell Avenue #8, Los Angeles, CA 90066, Ph: (310) 306-9463, Fax: (310) 306-0093

The Wine Seller, 9950 Waples Street #115, San Diego, CA 92121, Ph: (619) 450-9557, Fax: (619) 558-0928

The Wine Club, 2110-E East McFadden, Santa Ana, CA 92705, Ph: (714) 835-6485, Fax: (714) 835-5062

The Wine Cask, 813 Anacapa Street, Santa Barbara, CA 93103, Ph: (805) 966-9463, Fax: (805) 568-0664

Beltramo's, 1540 El Camino Real, Menlo Park, CA 94025, Ph: (415) 325-2806, Fax: (415) 323-8450

The Wine House, 535 Bryant Street, San Francisco, CA 94107, Ph: (415) 495-8486, Fax: (415) 495-4720

Prima, 1522 North Main Street, Walnut Creek, CA 94596, Ph: (510) 935-7780, Fax: (510) 935-7955

Kermit Lynch Wines, 1605 San Pablo Avenue, Berkeley, CA 94702, Ph: (510) 524-1524, Fax: (510) 528-7026

Marin Wine Cellar, 2138 4th Street, San Rafael, CA 94901, Ph: (415) 459-3823, Fax: (415) 456-8858

Corti Brothers, 5810 Folsom Boulevard, Sacramento, CA 95819-1358, Ph: (916) 736-3800, Fax: (916) 736-3807

Boulder Wine Merchant, 2690 Broadway, Boulder CO 80304, Ph: (303) 443-6761, Fax: (303) 443-5938

MacArthur Beverage, 4877 MacArthur Boulevard NW, Washington, DC 20007, Ph: (202) 338-1433, Fax: (202) 333-0806

Crown Wine Merchants, 6751 Red Road, Miami, FL 33143, Ph: (365) 689-0225, Fax: (305) 669-9334

Green's Package Store, 2614 Buford Highway NE, Atlanta, GA 30324, Ph: (404) 321-6232, Fax: (404) 633-0232

Schaefer's Wines & Spirits, 9965 Gross Point Road, Skokie, IL 60076, Ph: (708) 673-5711, Fax: (708) 982-9463

Sam's Wine Warehouse, 1000 West North Avenue, Chicago, IL 60610, Ph: (312) 664-4394, Fax: (312) 664-8666

Twenty-First Amendment, 1158 West 86th Street, Indianapolis, IN 46260, Ph: (317) 846-1678, Fax: (317) 846-5687

Party Source, 95 Riviera Drive, Bellevue, KY 41073, Ph: (606) 291-4007, Fax: (606) 291-4147

Martin Wine Cellar, 3827 Baronne Street, New Orleans, LA 70115, Ph: (504) 899-7411, Fax: (504) 899-7577

Geerlings & Wade, 960 Turnpike Street, Canton, MA 02021, Ph: (617) 821-4152, Fax: (617) 821-4153

Brookline Liquor Mart, 1354 Commonwealth Avenue, Boston, MA 02134, Ph: (617) 734-7700, Fax: (617) 232-7525

Winecellar of Silene, 320 Bear Hill Road, Waltham, MA 02154, Ph: (617) 890-2121, Fax: (617) 890-3236

Merchant Of Vino, 254 West Maple Road, Birmingham, MI 48010, Ph: (313) 433-3000, Fax: (313) 433-1214

Village Corner Wines & Spirits, 601 South Forest Avenue, Ann Arbor, MI 48104, Ph: (313) 995-1818, Fax: (313) 995-1826

France 44 Wines & Spirits, 4351 France Avenue South, Minneapolis, MN 55410, Ph: (612) 925-3252, Fax: (612) 925-5870

Sturdyk's Liquor, 303 East Hennepin Avenue, Minneapolis, MN 55414, Ph: (612) 379-3232, Fax: (612) 379-7511

Wine & Spirit World, 626 North Maple Avenue, Hohokus, NJ 07423, Ph: (201) 444-2033, Fax: (201) 592-7829

Welsh's Fine Wines & Spirits, 8 South Union Street, Lambertville, NJ 08530, Ph: (609) 397-0273, Fax: same

Sherry-Lehmann Fine Wine & Spirits, 679 Madison Avenue, New York, NY 10021, Ph: (212) 838-7500, Fax: (212) 838-9285

Morrell & Company, 535 Madison Avenue, New York, NY 10022, Ph: (212) 688-9370, Fax: (212) 223-1846

Zachy's Wine & Liquor, 16 East Parkway, Scarsdale, NY 10583, Ph: (914) 723-0241, Fax: (914) 723-1033

Pop's Wine & Spirits, 256 Long Beach Road, Island Park, NY 11558, Ph: (516) 431-0025, Fax: (516) 432-2648

Premier Liquor, 3445 Delaware Avenue, Buffalo, NY 14217, Ph: (716) 873-6688, Fax: (716) 877-6589

Gentile's Wine Sellers, 1565 King Avenue, Columbus, OH 43212, Ph: (614) 486-3406, Fax: (614) 891-3286

Liner & Elsen, 202 NW 21st Avenue, Portland, OR 97209, Ph: (503) 241-9463, Fax: (503) 243-6706

Town Wine & Spirits, 179 Newport Avenue, Rumford, RI 02916, Ph: (401) 434-4563, Fax: (401) 434-0230

Marty's Wine & Spirits, 3316 Oak Lawn Avenue, Dallas, TX 75219, Ph: (214) 526-7796, Fax: (214) 526-1140

Spec's Liquor Stores, 2410 Smith Street, Houston, TX 77006, Ph: (713) 526-8787, Fax: (713) 526-6129

McCarthy & Schiering, 2209 Queen Anne Avenue North, Seattle, WA 98109, Ph: (206) 282-8500, Fax: (206) 284-2498

HOW TO FIND OUT MORE

VIDEO

Jancis Robinson's Wine Course, Wellspring Media
27 Summit Terrace, Dobbs Ferry, NY 10522,
Fax: (914) 674-6108

WINE COURSES

Bay Area Wine School, 1 Northwood Drive #2,
Orinda, CA 94563

Chicago Wine School, 1633 North Halsted Street,
Chicago, IL 60614

International Wine Center, 231 West 29th Street,
Suite 210, New York, NY 10001

The Wine and Spirits Program, New York City,
Ph: (718) 263-3134

or for a local address contact:
Society of Wine Educators, 132 Shaker Road, Suite 14,
East Longmeadow, MA 01028, Fax: (413) 567-2051

FURTHER READING

MAGAZINES/NEWSLETTERS

Decanter, Priory House, 8 Battersea Park Road, London
SW8 4BG

International Wine Cellar, PO Box 20021, Cherokee
Station, New York, NY 10021

The Wine Advocate, PO Box 311, Monkton, Maryland
21111, Ph: (410) 329 6477

Wine Spectator, 387 Park Avenue South, New York, NY
10016 Ph: (212) 684 4224

GENERAL

Christopher Foulkes (ed), *Larousse Encyclopedia of
Wine*, Larousse Kingfisher Chambers 1994
Hugh Johnson, *World Atlas of Wine* (4th edn),
Simon and Schuster 1994
Jancis Robinson (ed), *The Oxford Companion to Wine*,
Oxford 1994

SPECIFIC FINE AND RARE WINES

Michael Broadbent, *The Great Vintage Wine Book* (2nd
edn), Simon and Schuster 1991

GRAPE VARIETIES

Jancis Robinson, *Vines, Grapes and Wines*, Knopf 1986
Jancis Robinson, *Jancis Robinson's Guide to Wine Grapes*,
Oxford 1996

SPECIFIC REGIONS

France
Elizabeth Berry, *Wines of Languedoc-Roussillon*,
Ebury 1992
Nicholas Faith, *Cognac and Other Brandies*, Simon and
Schuster 1992
Rosemary George, *The Wines of Chablis*, Sotheby's 1984
Anthony Hanson, *Burgundy* (2nd edn), Faber 1995
Matt Kramer, *Making Sense of Burgundy*, William
Morrow, 1990
John Livingstone-Learmonth, *The Wines of the Rhône*
(3rd edn), Faber 1992
Remington Norman, *Great Domaines of Burgundy*,
Henry Holt 1992
Remington Norman, *Rhône Renaissance*, Mitchell
Beazley, London 1996
Robert Parker, *Bordeaux* (2nd edn), Simon and
Schuster 1991
Edmund Penning-Rowsell, *The Wines of Bordeaux* (6th
edn), Penguin 1989
Stuart Pigott and Hugh Johnson, *The Wine Atlas of
Germany*, Mitchell Beazley, London 1995
Tom Stevenson, *Wines of Alsace*, Faber 1993
Tom Stevenson, *Champagne*, Sotheby's 1986
Paul Strang, *The Wines of South West France*, Kyle
Cathie 1994.

Italy
Burton Anderson, *Wine Atlas of Italy*, Simon and
Schuster 1990
David Gleave, *The Wines of Italy*, Price Stern Sloane 1989

Spain and Portugal
Richard Mayson, *Portugal's Wines and Winemakers*,
Ebury 1992
James Suckling, *Vintage Port*, Wine Spectator Press
1990
Kathryn McWhirter and Charles Metcalfe, *The Wines
of Spain and Portugal*, Price Stern Sloane 1988

New World
Oz Clarke, *New Classic Wines*, Simon and Schuster 1993
James Halliday, *Wine Atlas of Australia and New Zealand*,
HarperCollins 1991
James Halliday, *Wine Atlas of California*, Viking Penguin
1993
John Platter, *South African Wine Guide*, Mitchell
Beazley 1995
Bob Thompson, *The Wine Atlas of California*, Simon
and Schuster 1993

A GOOD READ

Gerald Asher, *On Wine*, Random House 1983
Kermit Lynch, *Adventures on the Wine Route*, Farrar
Straus Giroux 1989.
Note: For mail order wine videos and books, especially
those not published in the US, try **The Wine Appreci-
ation Guild,** San Francisco, Ph: (415) 864-1202

PICTURE CREDITS

The publisher thanks the photographers and organizations for their kind permission to reproduce the following photographs in this book.

1 Bilderberg/Klaus Bassemeyer; 2 Cephas/Mick Rock; **6 left** Jerry Alexander; **6 right** Cephas/Mick Rock; 7 Simon McBride; 10–11 Cephas Picture Library/Steven Morris; 14–15 Clay Perry; 19 Cephas Picture Library/Wine Magazine; 21 Paul Bricknell; 22–27 Paul Bricknell; 31 Cephas Picture Library/Mick Rock; 35 Jerry Alexander; 39 Véron/Skinner; 42 Peter Anderson; 43–47 Paul Bricknell; 55 Guy Bouchet; 58–59 Cephas Picture Library/Mick Rock; 63 Anthony Blake Photo Library/Gerrit Buntrock; 66 Scope/Jean–Luc Barde; 70–75 Cephas Picutre Library/Mick Rock; 78 Amphora Design; **79 above** Amphora Design; **79 below** Michael Busselle; **82 above** Cephas Picture Library/Andy Christodolo; **82 below** Amphora Design; **83 above** Jerry Alexander; **83 below** Anthony Blake Photo Library/Gerrit Buntrock; 86 Cephas Picture Library/Mick Rock; 87 Jerry Alexander; **90 above** Cephas Picture Library/Mick Rock; **90 below left** Alastair Miller; **90 below right** Jerry Alexander; 91 Anglea Muir; 94–95 Cephas Picture Library/Mick Rock; 98 Jerry Alexander; 99 Richard McConnell; 102 Robert Harding Picture Library/Explorer; 103 Partick Eagar; 106 Scope/Jean–Luc Barde; 107 Cephas Picture Library/Mick Rock; 110 Scope/Jacques Guillard; 110–111 Cephas Picture Library/Mick Rock; 114–115 Anthony Blake Photo Library/Gerritt Buntrock; 115 Patrcik Eagar; 118 Scope/Jacques Guillard; 119 Partick Eagar; 122 Cephas Picture Library/Mick Rock; 122–123 Cephas Picutre Library/Mick Rock; 126 Jan Traylen/Patrick Eagar; 127 Cephas Picture Library/Mick Rock; 128 Simon McBride; 131 Cephas Picture Library/Mick Rock; **134 above** Explorer/N Thibaut; **134 below** Cephas Picture Library/Ted Stefanski, 134–138 Cephas Picture Library/Mick Rock; 139–142 Patrick Eagar; 143–147 Cephas Picture Library/Mick Rock; **150 above** Cephas Picture Library/Mick Rock; **150 below** Patrick Eagar; 151 Cephas Picture Library/Mick Rock; 154–155 Cephas Picture Library/R&K Muschenetz; 159–163 Véron/Skinner; 167–170 Cephas Picture Library/Mick Rock; **174 above** André Martin; **174 below** Serge Chirol; 175 Alastair Miller; 178 Agence Top/Marie–José Jarry/Jean–François Tripelon; 178–182 Cephas Picture Library/Mick Rock; 183 Richard McConnell; 186 Alastair Miller; 187 Scope/Jean–Daniel Sudres; 190 Scope/Jacques Guillard; 190–191 Images Photoeque/Carcanague; 194 Scope/Jean–Luc Barde; 195 André Martin; 199 Scope/Daniel Faure; 203 Cephas Picture Library/Mick Rock; 207 Agence Top/Pascal Chevallier; 210 Anthony Blake Photo Library/Maureen Ashley; 211 Joe Cornish; 214 Simon McBride; 215 Joe Cornish; 218–219 Simon McBride; 219 Simon McBride; 223–231 Cephas Picture Library/Mick Rock; 235 Agence Top/Robert Tixador; 238 Cephas Picture Library/Mick Rock; 239 Robert O'Dea; 242 Jerome Darblay; 243 Scope/Jacques Guillard; 247 Michael Busselle; 251 Cephas Picture Library/Nigel Blythe; 255–259 Cephas Picture Library/Mick Rock; 263 Bilderberg/Hans Madej; 266–267 Agence Top/G Sioen; 270 Cephas Picture Library/Ted Stefan; 271 Jerry Alexander; 275 Cephas Picture Library/Mick Rock; **278 left** South American Pictures/Sue Mann; **278 right** Marcelo Montacino; 279 Cephas Picture Library/Rick England; 282–283 Cephas Picture Library/Andy Christodolo; 286 Bilderberg/Eberhard Grames; 287 Zefa; 291 Patrick Eagar; 294 Cephas Picture Library/Mick Rock; 298–299 Cephas Picture Library/Rick England; 302 VISA/A Lorgnier; 302–303 Cephas Picture Library/Alain Proust.

INDEX